Child Support Handbook

4th edition

Emma Knights and Simon Cox

Child Poverty Action Group

First edition 1993 by Alison Garnham and Emma Knights
Second edition 1994 by Alison Garnham and Emma Knights
Third edition 1995 by Emma Knights, Alison Garnham and Jacqui McDowell
Fourth edition 1996 by Emma Knights and Simon Cox

Published by CPAG Ltd
1-5 Bath Street, London EC1V 9PY

A CIP record for this book is available from the British Library

ISBN 0 946744 82 3

Cover and design by Devious Designs 0114 2755634
Typeset by Nancy White 0171 607 4510
Printed by Bath Press, Avon

The authors

Emma Knights is a welfare rights worker in CPAG's Citizens' Rights Office and has been the co-author of all four editions of this *Handbook*. She undertakes much of CPAG's work on monitoring, advising, training and lobbying on child support.

Simon Cox is a barrister in a London chambers. He practises in public law, specialising in social security, child support and immigration law. He was previously employed as the Free Representation Unit's social security and immigration caseworker.

Acknowledgements

Tremendous thanks to Jacqui McDowell of Save the Children Fund Scotland who meticulously checked the entire book and always met our tight deadlines. We appreciate Jacqui's patience, thoroughness and good humour displayed throughout the onerous task.

Thanks also to Djuna Thurley for her comments on the new chapter on departures and to David Thomas for making time on demand to discuss legal points and cases. We are also very grateful to staff at the CSA and DSS who answered our queries and provided us with statistics. In particular, we appreciate the CSA's willingness to provide us with information from the new guidance manuals when our production schedule did not fit neatly with theirs.

Thanks are due to Frances Ellery for editing the book and co-ordinating its production and to Nancy White for her excellent typesetting.

As always, we acknowledge the enormous contribution of those who contact CPAG with comments on the book and information about families involved with the CSA.

We also recognise the debt to Alison Garnham, co-author of the first three editions of this *Handbook*. Not only do many of her words remain in Part I, but the evidence of her role in shaping the volume and setting its style and tone will be reflected in many more editions.

Emma would like to apologise for her delays in responding to advice enquiries and to thank Mark for his support. Simon would like to thank his clerks who coped with his long absences, and to thank Polly and Jack and apologise for the many lost weekends.

Emma Knights and Simon Cox
15 March 1996

The law and procedures described in this book were correct at this date.

Contents

Child support rates 1996/97

Children's personal allowances

Under 11	£16.45
Aged 11-15	£24.10
Aged 16-17	£28.85
Aged 18	£37.90

Adult's personal allowance

Single	£47.90
Couple*	£75.20

This is only used in protected income calculation

Premiums

Family	£10.55
Lone parent	£5.20
Disabled child	£20.40
Carer	£13.00
Disability (single)	£20.40
Severe disability (single)	£36.40

The following premiums are only used in the protected income calculation (in addition to those listed above):

Disability (couple)	£29.15
Severe disability	
couple (if one qualifies)	£36.40
couple (if both qualify)	£72.80
Pensioner	
single	£19.15
couple	£28.90
Enhanced pensioner	
single	£21.30
couple	£31.90
Higher pensioner	
single	£25.90
couple	£37.05

Child benefit

For only or eldest child   £10.80
For other children   £8.80

Minimum payment of child maintenance   £4.80

Contribution towards child maintenance
deducted from income support   £4.80

(In some circumstances half this amount can be deducted – see p170)

Benefit penalty

26 weeks   £9.58
Further 52 weeks   £4.79

Income tax

	pa
Personal allowance	£3,765
Married couple's allowance	£1,790
Additional personal allowance for caring for children	£1,790

Lower rate   20% on first £3,900 taxable income
Basic rate   24% on next £21,600 taxable income
Higher rate   40% on taxable income over £25,500

National insurance contributions

Gross weekly earnings
Below £61   Nil
£61–£455   2% on the first £61 and
                     10% on the rest, up to £455

(For full details of means-tested and non-means-tested benefit rates, see CPAG's *National Welfare Benefits Handbook*.)

The terms we use

Use of 'she' and 'he'

As nine-tenths of people with the care of a qualifying child are women, we use 'she' to describe the person with care. We therefore use 'he' to describe the absent parent.

However, the law applies in the same way if the person with care is a man or the absent parent is a woman.

We recognise that in a small minority of cases the absent parent will be the mother and the parent with care the father. But clarity requires that we use 'she' for the person with care and 'he' for the absent parent.

Use of 'absent parent'

We understand that many 'absent parents' find this term offensive, particularly when they are trying to maintain contact with their children. However, we have decided to use the term as it is used in the legislation and in Child Support Agency information.

Use of 'second family'

We use the term 'second family' loosely to describe the situation where a parent of a qualifying child (in our examples, usually the absent parent) also has children with a different partner. This could in fact be a third or fourth family, or even a first family where, for example, a married man remains with his wife despite having a child by another woman.

Use of 'step-child'

We use the term 'step-child' to describe the child of a person's partner, whether or not they are a married couple.

Preface

The Child Support Agency's third year has been another eventful one. While half the changes contained in the White Paper *Improving Child Support* (see p2) were introduced smoothly in April 1995, the other half became the Child Support Act 1995 in July. Although CPAG supported much of the Bill's contents, we were disappointed that the Government did not use this primary legislation to, for example, introduce a guaranteed stability of income for parents with care on family credit, a route for withdrawing applications with a right of appeal, and a child support advisory committee. The Government also failed to tackle remaining shortcomings in the formula and refused to introduce a small maintenance disregard for parents with care on income support to ensure that at least some of the advantage of maintenance went to the poorest children.

Sadly there appears to be little Parliamentary support for abolishing the benefit penalty for those parents with care on benefit who do not want to apply to the CSA. In the first 10 months of 1995/96, 25,572 reduced benefit directions were issued, in addition to the 18,000 since 1993 (see p101), leaving a large number of families with children living below subsistence level. Although there are no forthcoming changes to this part of the law, a lot of time has rightly been spent – both inside and outside the CSA – in monitoring the requirement to co-operate procedures, and we will shortly hear the results of the CSA's own review (see p101). CPAG's evidence to the review detailed the problems reported to us. We very much hope that no more pressure is put on parents with care who, in order to claim exemption from the requirement to co-operate, already have to undergo harrowing enquiries given the very personal nature of the issues involved.

Some of the measures in the new Act came into force in December 1995 and January 1996, while the pilot scheme for the new departure provisions (see Chapter 15) is just beginning. While there is widespread support for the introduction of flexibility to deal with the hard cases, we believe that the CSA will not be able to cope with yet another complex set of rules. The clamour from absent parents about the unfair level of assessments has died down, no doubt in large part due to the changes in the regulations over the past two years. However, clients' dissatisfaction with the CSA – though not universal – appears to be as great as ever. Although some of the remaining objections are to the child support policy itself (see p10), the vast majority of complaints received by CPAG are about poor administration (see p7).

July 1995: The CSA's own 1994/95 Annual Report and Accounts showed that, despite an improved performance, a number of targets had not been met: 568,000 cases had been cleared (see p26) compared with the forecast of 899,000; in April 1995, 70 per cent of uncleared cases were over 26 weeks old and 50 per cent were over a year old, compared with the target of 15 per cent over 26 weeks old and one per cent over 52 weeks. The new cases taken on had been reduced from 718,000 to 398,584 – by deferring the take-on of existing income support claimants (see p32) – in order to be able to transfer staff from assessment work to the maintenance of cases, such as collection and enforcement. Although the benefits savings target has been met, less than half the benefits savings attributed to the CSA resulted from CSA assessments (see p25).

October 1995: The Chief Child Support Officer reported on the adjudication standards for 1994/95 (see p164) and commented that 'The rate of improvement is disappointing.'

November 1995: the House of Commons Public Accounts Committee produced a highly critical report about the difficulties in setting up the CSA and the shortcomings of the first two years. It urged the DSS to learn lessons for future projects.

January 1996: the House of Commons Social Security Committee published its report on the CSA's performance with 20 specific recommendations for operational changes. The Government's response is awaited.

March 1996: the Ombudsman's second report on the CSA was published just days before we went to press. While he had decided in August 1994 that he did not have the resources to investigate all the complaints concerning the CSA (see p29), the number accepted for investigation continues to rise and accounts for one-third of complaints about all government departments: 'Unfortunately they show that the shortcomings in certain aspects of operations of which I was critical in my last report continue to occur.' The Ombudsman identified a number of new problem areas and was concerned about the DSS's aim to cut administration costs: 'I hope that savings will not be required from an organisation which has shown by its past performance how inefficient it can be, if the result is greater inefficiency.'

CPAG agrees with this concern. While the Chief Executive, Ann Chant, has successfully defended the Agency's performance before select committees and in the press, and although this year's – perhaps undemanding – targets may be met, we are very disappointed by the

CSA's standard of administration. The feedback we receive from CSA clients and their advisers shows that all is far from well. The CSA's own monthly statistics show it is still failing properly to administer the scheme:

- only 107,799 maintenance assessments were made in the 10 months up to January 1996 compared with 233,600 in the same period last year;
- the number of applications outstanding at the end of January 1996 has climbed again to 400,000 and is far above what even the CSA regards as appropriate;
- the proportion of applications cleared within 26 weeks has not improved over the year, remaining at just under a half;
- the backlog of second-tier reviews has increased, with 11,077 pending at the end of January 1996 compared with 7,345 at the end of April 1995;
- although the amount of money being collected continues to increase as expected given the increasing caseload, less than one-quarter of accounts are fully paid up and arrears are also increasing: total debt has risen from £525 million at the end of March 1995 to £794 million at the end of November 1995, *and*
- the numbers of complaints continue to rise (see p23).

The longer this state of affairs continues, the more people will ask whether the CSA will ever be able to improve its standards to an acceptable level. Has it been given an impossible task? All this year's reports emphasise the complexity of the system and even the Social Security Select Committee – a staunch supporter of the principle behind the agency – will be looking at ways of simplifying the formula and the implications of transferring the whole operation to the Inland Revenue.

CPAG will be involved in this continuing debate over the next couple of years. In the meantime we are concerned that parents obtain the best possible service from the CSA. Before the child support scheme, access to legal advice on maintenance was comparatively straightforward and legal aid was available for many people. The 1991 Act created a system of unique complexity which has already been substantially amended. Therefore, even with the adoption of appeal tribunals instead of court hearings, it is extremely difficult for the parties to represent themselves. The experience of those who have tried to do so is that expert advice is sorely needed. Surely the government which created such a labyrinthine system should at least ensure that those who need to can find their way round it.

Sadly, advice and representation are very difficult to find. Many providers of social security advice have not extended their services to child support. Absent parents in need of help are often ineligible for legal aid. Those advisers who work in this field are sometimes overwhelmed by the complexity of the legislation or the time needed to see whether there are arguments which can be made for their clients.

We hope this *Handbook* will serve as a guide through the administrative and legal maze of child support. We also hope advisers will continue to ensure that their clients receive the independent advice they are entitled to.

Finally, public and parliamentary interest in the CSA has rarely been concerned with the welfare of the poorest children. Most CSA clients remain on income support. They have not gained and many are worse off. Child maintenance alone can never lift all those families out of poverty. We hope that attention will now turn to further measures for resolving the ever-growing problem of child poverty.

Emma Knights and Simon Cox
March 1996

CHAPTER ONE

Introduction to the child support scheme

This handbook deals only with the child support scheme as it now exists. It covers neither maintenance issues, as these are dealt with through the courts, nor the detail of the social security system. The latter is dealt with in two companion volumes produced by CPAG, the *National Welfare Benefits Handbook* and the *Rights Guide to Non-Means-Tested Benefits*.

This chapter covers:

1. An outline of the scheme (see below)
2. Using the *Child Support Handbook* (p5)
3. Issues for advisers (p7)

I. AN OUTLINE OF THE SCHEME

The child support scheme was created by the Child Support Act 1991 which came into force on 5 April 1993. The main changes were:

- the establishment of the Child Support Agency (CSA) to assess and enforce the payment of child maintenance;
- the use of a rigid formula to set the level of child maintenance, and a complete lack of discretion to vary that amount; *and*
- the requirement for most parents claiming certain benefits and caring for children not living with their other parent to apply for child maintenance or face a reduction in benefit.

This new system deals with applications from both benefit claimants and non-claimants. It replaced both the liable relatives work of the Benefits Agency and the role of the courts in setting child maintenance (although some old court orders continue to exist – see p33 – and in a few specific situations new court orders can be made – see p37). All separating parents who want a legally enforceable child maintenance agreement have to use the CSA.

To overcome some of the many problems that arose with the implementation of the 1991 Act for both parties, there have been a series of changes to the scheme. These began with the first set of changes to the formula used for calculating child maintenance in February 1994[1] and included the White Paper, *Improving Child Support*, in January 1995. About half of the proposals from this White Paper were put into effect on 18 April 1995.[2] These included: further changes to the formula; a change to the date on which liability for child maintenance commences; suspension of CSA fees; abolition of interest charged on arrears; the introduction of two additional types of interim maintenance assessments; and replacing annual reviews with reviews of assessments every two years.

The remainder of the White Paper's package required an Act of Parliament – the Child Support Act 1995. Some of the Act's provisions took effect in late 1995 and 22 January 1996;[3] these include changes to the review procedures, recovery of overpayments, financing of DNA tests, and the indefinite deferral of applications from those not claiming benefits who already have maintenance arrangements. The 1995 Act will also introduce in late 1996 an element of discretion into the setting of child maintenance in the form of departure (see Chapter 15). The child maintenance bonus for claimants leaving income support has yet to come into effect (see p316). Similarly, some form of penalty for late payment of child maintenance will be reintroduced in April 1997.

For information on the background to the 1991 Act and its social policy implications, see *Putting the Treasury First: the truth about child support*, available from CPAG Ltd, Publications Department, 1–5 Bath Street, London EC1V 9PY, for £7.95.

Responsibility for child maintenance

The 1991 Act starts with the principle that both parents of a child have a duty to contribute to the maintenance of that child.[4] This liability is met when an absent parent makes payments of child maintenance assessed under the formula.[5] This duty applies whether or not:

- the child is living with the other parent or someone else;
- the child is living with a lone parent or with a married or unmarried couple; *and*
- the child's parents are on benefit.

However, the liability cannot be put into effect until after an application is made to the CSA (see Chapters 4 and 14).

The 1991 Act introduced new terminology into the language of relationship breakdown and child maintenance.[6] Any parent who does not live with their own child is referred to as an **absent parent**. Where one or both of the parents of a child are absent parents, then the child counts as a **qualifying child** for the purposes of the child support scheme. The person with whom the child is living and who provides them with day-to-day care is known as the **person with care**. If a person with care is also a parent of the qualifying child concerned, then they are termed a **parent with care**. Parents with care have an obligation placed on them to apply for child maintenance if they claim certain benefits (see p4). Other persons with care, or parents not in receipt of a key benefit, have a choice about whether or not to apply for child maintenance. For details of the basic principles and key definitions in the 1991 Act, see Chapter 3.

The Child Support Agency (CSA)

The CSA is the vehicle chosen by the Secretary of State for Social Security to administer the child support scheme. It is a 'Next Steps' agency of the DSS. The CSA is responsible for the assessment of child maintenance payments and their collection where requested. This includes ensuring the co-operation of parents with care who receive a relevant benefit (see below), tracing absent parents, and investigating parents' means. Information can be obtained from a number of sources (see Chapter 6). The powers of the CSA are held by child support officers (CSOs), by child support inspectors and other staff of the Agency acting with the authority of the Secretary of State. The majority of decisions taken by CSOs are non-discretionary, whereas most of those made on behalf of the Secretary of State do involve discretion. Where discretion is available under the Act, a CSA officer must have regard to the welfare of any child likely to be affected (see p52).[7]

Due to the poor standard of service provided in the first two years of operation, the fees usually payable for CSA services have been suspended for two years from April 1995. For more details of the CSA, see Chapter 2.

Take-on of cases

The CSA took over the assessment of all new child maintenance cases from 5 April 1993. The cases of parents already living apart by April 1993 were originally going to be taken on over a four-year period. However, this has had to be extended because the CSA was unable to cope with the number of cases involved. There are still about 300,000 parents with care on income support (IS) who have not yet been contacted by the CSA.

Parents with care who do not receive IS, family credit (FC) or disability working allowance (DWA) cannot apply to the CSA if they have a court order for child maintenance or a pre-April 1993 written agreement (see p55). On the other hand, benefit claimants are required to apply to the CSA even where there is an existing maintenance arrangement and any CSA assessment made overrides any court orders for child maintenance.

The courts retain jurisdiction for all related matters, including orders for contact and residence, spousal maintenance, paternity disputes and property issues (see p32).

The requirement to co-operate with the CSA

Although the duty to maintain qualifying children applies in all cases, the 1991 Act places special obligations on parents with care getting IS, FC, or DWA. Such parents can be required, first, to authorise the Secretary of State to take action to recover maintenance, and secondly to co-operate with the CSA by providing the information needed to pursue the absent parent.[8] Without the parent with care's authorisation, the CSA cannot contact the absent parent or take any other steps to assess maintenance.

Neither requirement applies to any parent who has convinced the Secretary of State or a CSO that she has good cause for withholding permission for them to go ahead. **Good cause** means that there are reasonable grounds for believing that if the parent with care were to give her authorisation or the required information, there would be a risk of her, or any of the children living with her, suffering harm or undue distress.[9]

Non-exempt parents who fail to comply with either requirement can be subject to a reduction in benefit, known as the **benefit penalty**.[10]

For more on the requirement to co-operate, see Chapter 5.

Calculating assessments

Child maintenance is assessed by means of a **formula** set down in the legislation.[11] The formula has five stages or steps and is complex. The CSA uses a computer system to calculate assessments. For an introduction to the formula, see Chapter 7.

The formula is based at all stages on IS benefit levels. It does not take into account the actual expenses of parents and children, other than housing costs, and there has been no discretion to include special items depending on the circumstances of an absent parent – eg, travel costs to visit children. However, a new system to allow departure from the standard formula in certain circumstances begins this year (see Chapter 15).[12]

Penalty assessments

Formula assessments cannot be more than 30 per cent of an absent parent's net income. However where an absent parent has not co-operated in providing the necessary information to the CSA, he can be awarded a penalty assessment – called an interim maintenance assessment (IMA) – which in many cases take no account of his income. The object of IMAs is to convince the absent parent to co-operate but, if he does not, the IMA can be enforced in the same way as any other assessment. For more on IMAs, see p296.

Reviews and appeals

Once an assessment has been made, it is reviewed every two years. Applicants can request further reviews if there has been a change of circumstances or to challenge the CSO's decision – a second-tier review. There is also a right of appeal against CSO decisions on second-tier review to a child support appeal tribunal. For information on reviews and appeals, see Chapter 16.

Collection and enforcement

The CSA has powers to collect and enforce the child maintenance assessed under the formula.[13] For applicants getting IS, FC or DWA, maintenance is usually collected by the CSA. Other applicants can decide whether or not to use the collection service or to make their own arrangements. The collection service is provided at the discretion of the Secretary of State.

If the absent parent falls into arrears the CSA can send an arrears notice to the absent parent and try to negotiate an arrears agreement. If the absent parent is employed, the CSA can issue a deduction from earnings order (DEO). If a DEO is inappropriate, the CSA can take court action and seek a liability order, levy distress, use county court recovery procedures and, ultimately, apply for the absent parent to be committed to prison.

For more details about collection and enforcement, see Chapter 17.

2. USING THE *CHILD SUPPORT HANDBOOK*

This handbook covers the child support scheme as it currently operates in England, Wales and Scotland. Although there are some references to earlier changes, anyone wanting to know exact details of the scheme in previous years must consult earlier editions of the handbook. This edition contains all details known at the beginning of March 1996. Any important developments during the year will be covered in CPAG's *Welfare Rights Bulletin* (see p446) and the next edition of this handbook, which will be published in April 1977. We do not make reference to the corresponding legislation for the scheme in Northern Ireland, although the rules are very similar.[14]

This book is a guide to the scheme for parents and those advising them. It is not intended to be a critique of the child support legislation or of the agency charged with administering it. Instead we attempt to provide a detailed but understandable explanation of the law and an outline of the procedures used by the CSA. We also include, where possible, practical advice and tactics for anyone dealing with the CSA and wishing to challenge decisions.

We usually refer to a person with care as 'she' and an absent parent as 'he', as this reflects the situation in over 90 per cent of cases. We also refer to payments of child support maintenance as **child maintenance**, and to the scheme in general as **child support**. The Child Support Agency is referred to as the **CSA**. In the text we refer to the Child Support Act 1991 as **the 1991 Act** and the Child Support Act 1995 as **the 1995 Act**.

Structure of the book

At the front there is a reference table of the current income support (IS) rates used in the formula and elsewhere, as well as a list of contents.

The first part of the book introduces the reader to the CSA and its service, and explains some of the key principles and terms used in the 1991 Act. It then covers the pre-assessment dealings with the CSA, such as making applications, the requirement to co-operate, and information-provision. The second part explains the calculation used to set assessments once all the information is available. The final part covers the CSA activities which follow the formula calculation – the issuing of the assessment with its start date, any subsequent cancellation, the effect of that assessment on benefits, the new departure scheme, review and appeals, and lastly collection and enforcement.

The appendices contain CSA addresses, information about useful reference materials, an explanation of IS premiums, and calculation sheets. Formula chapters indicate when certain calculation sheets should be used and how they can be used in conjunction with the book.

As with CPAG's other books, the best way to find the information you need is to **use the index** at the back of the book.

Footnotes

Just before the index there is a series of **footnotes** providing the necessary legal or other references required by advisers. These do not necessarily provide additional information to that in the text but give the authority on which the statement is based. Parents and advisers should quote the reference to the CSA if the statement is disputed. Appendix 8 explains what the footnotes mean and how to get hold of the sources.

Reference is made to the *Child Support Adjudication Guide* (CSAG), *Child Support Manual* (CSM) and *Field Officers' Guide* (FOG). However, it should be noted that they are only guidance and *not* law and therefore should not be considered definitive. The CSAG contains an interpretation of the legislation and, if the reader wishes to contest this, s/he will need to consult the relevant part of the law. The CSM and FOG largely contain information on the procedures undertaken by CSA staff.

Although, as yet, there is little case law available, this handbook includes references to relevant child support commissioners' and court decisions (see p385).

3. ISSUES FOR ADVISERS

Although the child support scheme has its origins in the benefits system, there is a significant difference in that the money being paid to the person with care is private and not public money. This means that in all child support cases, other than those in which a parent with care is refusing to authorise the Secretary of State to take action, there are two parties, usually – although not always – with conflicting interests. In particular, representatives at child support appeal tribunals may find themselves in an adversarial situation.

Here we review briefly some of the more frequent problems – caused by the legislation itself and by the CSA's standards of operation – still experienced by persons with care and absent parents in the third year of the scheme, and likely to continue into its fourth.

Operational issues

One major cause for concern for all CSA clients has been the poor standards of administration and adjudication, and the chronic delays. Although there are no easy solutions to these problems for advisers, we suggest various approaches in Chapter 2 (see especially p28).

The protection of personal information (see p156) has resulted in two very different kinds of complaints: first – mainly from persons with care – that they are not informed as to what is happening with the case in relation to the other party; second – mainly from absent parents – that personal information is given to the other party, either contained in the standard notification of an assessment (see p300) or in appeal papers. It is worth warning parents that the application/enquiry forms are routinely included in appeal papers and therefore the other party will gain access to that information if the case goes to appeal. It may help to point out that court proceedings involve all information being made available to both parties; indeed it is difficult to envisage an effective appeal system without access to the relevant information. The information which the CSA can give to the other party has had to be extended (see p157) in order to prevent clients being left in the dark. Where one party is being told too little about the progress of their own case by the CSA, a complaint should be made (see p28).

Persons with care

The problems with the requirement to co-operate largely stem from the policy itself (see below), rather than the way in which the CSA is operating the policy. The problems experienced in the first 18 months – when parents with care were unaware of the exemption and were put under pressure in interviews to give authorisation, often under the impression that the alternative was to lose all their benefit – appear to be largely eliminated. If they do continue to occur, or if new problems arise following the implementation of the CSA's review of procedures (see p101), please keep CPAG informed.

The most common complaint from persons with care during 1995/96 concerned delays in collection and enforcement. This is a particularly acute problem for persons with care on family credit (FC), and we would encourage people to send us examples of the hardship caused in order that we can continue to press for a system of guaranteed maintenance. Tactics for dealing with these delays are discussed on p400. The CSA has been claiming to give collection and enforcement more priority for some time now, and this should begin to have a greater effect during the forthcoming year. Although more money is now passing through the CSA than in the first two years, the majority of accounts still include arrears. Some persons with care complain of the leeway that is given to absent parents when negotiating and re-negotiating the level of arrears agreements; this, as may be expected, is not reflected in the feedback we receive from absent parents on this subject (see below).

Both the assessment and enforcement of child maintenance from self-employed absent parents have caused great problems, with many persons with care still awaiting payments after two years. If the person with care suspects that the absent parent has not declared his full income, she should seek a review; there is a discussion of the options on pp150, 208 and 350. However, departure may become the most effective way of obtaining a more realistic assessment (see p329).

Although the Benefits Agency's policy is not to reduce income support (IS) until child maintenance payments are made, this does not always happen and can result in the person with care being left temporarily without income. Complaints should be made (see p28). Remember that those who request the CSA to take over collection receive the payment regularly along with any remaining IS (see p317). The one disadvantage of this is that IS claimants are not automatically aware of the true state of their child maintenance account, and therefore will need to request updates from the CSA (see p391).

Absent parents

A delay in making an assessment causes a build-up of initial arrears (see p398). Changes made last year – ie, delaying the effective date by eight weeks for absent parents who co-operate and suspending more than six months of arrears where these have been contributed to by the CSA – have partially resolved this problem. However, the latter does not appear to be processed automatically and should be checked. Advisers must warn absent parents of the start date of any assessment and suggest that voluntary payments are made in the meantime; these can be offset against the arrears bill (see p399).

The delay in proceeding with a review can make it very difficult for an absent parent who has to make payment under the assessment in force, which now may be out-of-date, perhaps because of a reduction in wages or the birth of a child in a second family. Overpayments after reviews are of increasing importance (see p393). While a review is pending, negotiations can be undertaken to reduce the payments (see p401) and a request made not to issue a deductions from earnings order (DEO) until the outcome of the review is known.

Many absent parents have complained about the draconian nature of the repayments expected on negotiation or taken by DEOs. For the last year there has been a limit on the amount that can be deducted in total – one third of net income (see p402) – which appears to have alleviated the worst problems. Advisers should check that this limit has been implemented by the CSA. Despite this, absent parents reduced to the protected earnings rate on DEOs (see p409) can suffer hardship. In order to avoid a DEO, absent parents should be encouraged to come to other negotiated agreements (see p401).

Advisers need to be aware of interim maintenance assessments (IMAs) – the penalty assessments designed to encourage absent parents to co-operate. Given that there now exists a limit of 30 per cent of net income on a full assessment, any extortionate assessments are likely to be Category A or D IMAs (see p296). An absent parent may be best advised to provide the required information given that IMAs can be collected by DEOs; even the arrears of the IMA will then be replaced by the lower final assessment.

Policy issues

CSA assessments can override amicable agreements. A parent with care who is concerned about this happening can seek exemption on the grounds of 'risk of harm or undue distress' that would be caused by the upsetting of the existing arrangements; however, it is by no means certain that this will be accepted (see p90). It is important that before a benefit penalty is accepted an adviser calculates the CSA assessment which would apply (this can be done if both parents are working together to supply the information) so that parents have the full information on which to base their decision.

Similarly, there are many examples of contact being disrupted after a CSA assessment is made. With the introduction of departure (see p324) it is hoped that this will happen less often. If undue distress is caused to the children, consideration should be given to withdrawing the application (see p11).

It is important that absent parents are aware that the parent with care on certain benefits is required to apply to the CSA, as she might have done so reluctantly to avoid a benefit penalty.

Although pre-April 1993 property settlements are now acknowledged both in the formula and in departure, new settlements are not. There is concern that absent parents will be less willing to agree to such settlements and children will not have the security of the family home. This feeling of insecurity is added to by the fact that some absent parents used to contribute those parts of the mortgage not covered by IS and have not been able to continue to do that as well as pay the CSA assessment.

Persons with care

Thousands of parents with care continue to withdraw their benefit claim within four weeks of being contacted by the CSA. Some of these parents may have left benefit irrespective of the CSA and some represent reconciliations, but it must be stressed that the CSA cannot take any action to contact the absent parent without the authorisation of the parent with care. Even if the parent with care would be entitled to less than the benefit penalty, she will still gain from the benefit claim as she will be left with the minimal amount of benefit and thus retain entitlement to passported benefits.

There are now tens of thousands of reduced benefit directions in existence, but very few go to appeal. Parents with care should be encouraged to appeal, even if they have to co-operate in the meantime in order to avoid cuts in their benefit (see p123). Advisers must point out that there is no right of appeal until the reduced benefit direction is reached. CPAG needs to receive reports of families subjected to the benefit penalty and the resulting hardship if we are to continue to lobby against the requirement to co-operate effectively. We need to convince parliamentarians that not all parents with care subject to a benefit penalty are receiving undeclared maintenance as is alleged by some. It is likely that the Benefits Agency will step up fraud investigations in this area; it is therefore crucial that parents with care understand that they are within their rights in refusing to co-operate and accepting the benefit penalty. In addition, negotiating a maintenance arrangement with the absent parent is also within the law, but any payments received must be declared to the Benefits Agency.

There are only limited situations in which benefit claimants can withdraw applications or cancel assessments (see p70). A disturbing aspect is the lack of a route for appeal, and we hope to see a test case on this issue. However, one route which has worked in practice is to terminate the claim for benefit and then cancel the assessment, before claiming benefit again and this time withholding authorisation. The existence of the benefit penalty appears, rather surprisingly, to have convinced the Benefits Agency not to use the 'notional income' rule.

Some parents with care end up financially worse off after CSA involvement – sometimes because the CSA assessment is lower than the previous arrangement, sometimes because of the loss of payments in kind which do not affect benefit level, and otherwise because the level of the assessment 'floats' them off IS with the loss of passported benefits.

Lastly, there is a group of parents with care who want access to the CSA but are denied it because they are not benefit claimants and have pre-April 1993 maintenance agreements (see p55). Parents in this situation have the option of returning to court to have the order increased.

Absent parents

During the third year of the scheme CPAG heard far less from second families pushed into hardship as a result of CSA assessments. This may be a result of the changes to the formula in April 1995, in particular the inclusion of housing costs for the whole family, following on from the improvements in protected income level the previous year. Furthermore, many of the remaining problems should be tackled by departure, with the exception of the support of step-children, where help is to be limited to pre-April 1993 step-families (see p325). If there are cases where absent parents are still being brought down to or very near the IS level, please let us know. Although there is still a concern that £30 over the IS level, even when coupled with a 15 per cent taper (see p255), does not provide an adequate work incentive, advisers do have a role in ensuring that absent parents contemplating giving up a job have as much information as possible. As long as reasonable arrears repayments have been negotiated, it is unlikely that he will be better off unemployed.

Those absent parents left worst off are those on IS with deductions of £4.80 a week. The level of this deduction has been doubled from April 1996. This change is in stark contrast to reductions in assessments for absent parents on higher incomes the previous year. In fact, CPAG has received very few complaints from parents in this situation, who number in the tens of thousands; we would ask advisers to bring these cases to our attention.

Despite the reform of the formula, it is still criticised on a number of fronts. The most frequent complaints made are about the inclusion of the 'parent as carer' element (see p175) and the fact that, except at higher incomes, the number of qualifying children has no effect on the level of payments (most absent parents pay at a rate of 50 per cent assessable income irrespective of the number of children – see p226). CPAG has been making these points since the publication of the original White Paper in 1990. [15]

Another common complaint concerns the request to disclose details of a partner's income. There is, in fact, much misunderstanding about the ways in which the income of partners affect the assessment. Some second families gain from the disclosure of this information as it is used to ensure they are not brought below the IS level (see p250). However, if this protection does not apply because the family has an income sufficient to meet at least basic needs, then the absent parent could refuse to disclose the information and take a Category B IMA which would not in fact penalise him (see p297).

Monitoring

Over the last three years, CPAG has been able to lobby the Government for changes to the scheme and the CSA for improvements to its service, because we have been sent summaries of cases and copies of letters from advisers and parents. These have been invaluable in making the case on behalf of parents on low income and their children. The same information has been drawn on in the updating of this handbook. It is important that we keep the scheme under scrutiny. Please continue to send information to the Child Support Monitoring Network at CPAG. Advisers may also want to get involved in local CSA liaison groups (see p27)

Training and support for advisers

Many parents are finding it difficult to obtain free, or even affordable, advice and representation on child support – see Appendix 6 for where to obtain independent advice. Those who do find someone willing to take on their case often complain to us about the standard of advice they are receiving. We would very much encourage advisers to get involved in this area of work, and to contact the Citizens' Rights Office at CPAG for support with difficult cases. Unfortunately we do not have the resources to support individuals.

CPAG also runs training courses on child support.

In conjunction with other groups involved in advising on child support, in particular the National Association of Citizens' Advice Bureaux and the Solicitors' Family Law Association, we are setting up a Child Support Practitioners Group. We hope the group will provide useful information for those involved in child support casework. Do contact us for details.

CPAG's address is 1–5 Bath Street, London EC1V 9PY.

PART ONE

Before the assessment

CHAPTER TWO

The Child Support Agency

This chapter covers:
1. What is the Child Support Agency (see below)
2. Structure of the CSA (p18)
3. CSA standards of service (p23)
4. Take-on of cases by the CSA (p31)
5. Powers retained by the courts (p32)

1. WHAT IS THE CHILD SUPPORT AGENCY

The Child Support Agency (CSA) is a Government 'Next Steps' agency responsible to the DSS along with, for example, the Benefits Agency. It is responsible for collecting information about and tracing absent parents, and assessing, collecting and enforcing child maintenance.

The CSA itself does not appear in the child support legislation. Instead the 1991 Act confers powers on child support officers (CSOs) and inspectors, and on the Secretary of State for Social Security. In practice, the powers of the Secretary of State are exercised by the staff of the CSA. The legislation, and this *Handbook*, specifies whether a task or decision is to be carried out by a CSO or the Secretary of State (see below).

The DSS retains responsibility for child support policy issues, with the CSA being responsible for the administration of the child support scheme. The Chief Executive of the Agency, Ann Chant, is responsible to the Secretary of State for the administration of the Agency.

The 1991 Act provides for the appointment of a chief child support officer (CCSO).[1] The CCSO's role is to advise CSOs on the interpretation of the law and on the discharge of their functions, and to keep the operation of the legislation relating to the making, reviewing and cancelling of maintenance assessments under review. He also has a duty to write an annual report which is published (see p164). The CCSO is currently Ernie Hazlewood who is also the chief adjudication officer and as such plays the same role for the adjudication officers of the Benefits Agency.

There is a separate child support structure for Northern Ireland, accountable to its Department of Health and Social Security. The Chief Executive of this Agency is Pat Devlin and he is based at Stormont. All other functions and roles are broadly the same as for Great Britain. The legislation was framed so as to provide for a single system within the UK.[2] Great Britain and Northern Ireland are each referred to as territories and reciprocal arrangements are in place to deal with the operation of the scheme across territories. Northern Ireland also has its own child support commissioners (see p382) and a chief child support commissioner.[3] There is a child support agency centre (CSAC) based in Belfast which assesses cases for England and Wales; this centre has nothing to do with the Northern Ireland structure.

Child support officers

The CSA employs around 1,500 CSOs, the majority of whom are located in the regional centres (see p19). CSOs are appointed to perform certain specific functions.[4] They are responsible for ensuring that all the relevant facts of a case have been established by the Secretary of State, making or refusing to make the assessment of child maintenance and for the decisions necessary on reviewing or cancelling assessments. CSOs are also involved in the later stages of the refusal to co-operate procedures.

A *Child Support Adjudication Guide* (CSAG) gives advice on the interpretation of the law and adjudication procedures from the CCSO (and can be purchased from HMSO – see p450). Standards of adjudication have been criticised by the CCSO in his Annual Reports (see p164).

Certain CSO decisions are discretionary – eg, when deciding whether or not to apply a reduced benefit direction. In exercising discretion, a CSO has to take account of the welfare of any children likely to be affected (see p52).[5]

If a CSO makes a mistake as to the facts of a case or the interpretation of the law, the decision can be reviewed by a second CSO (see pp360 and 364). There is a right of appeal to a child support appeal tribunal against the decision of a CSO at a second-tier review (see p367).[6] The CSO is a party to the appeal proceedings.

Representatives of the Secretary of State

Employees of the CSA acting on behalf of the Secretary of State for Social Security collect information (see Chapter 6) and make a variety of decisions – for example, decisions concerning the collection and enforcement of assessments (see Chapter 17).

Secretary of State decisions can be taken by staff also appointed as CSOs, although on these occasions they act on behalf of the Secretary of State.[7]

Almost all the decisions made on behalf of the Secretary of State are discretionary ones. CSA officers acting on behalf of the Secretary of State are required to take account of the welfare of any children (see p52) likely to be affected by a decision, when exercising any discretionary powers.[8]

There is generally no right of appeal against decisions of the Secretary of State. The latter can be disputed, even perhaps through an MP, and fresh information put forward, but there is no right of appeal to an independent tribunal, except in the case of decisions about departure from the formula (see p348). However, Secretary of State decisions can be challenged in some instances by judicial review (see p351).

The Acts grant the Secretary of State powers to authorise the right of audience and the right to conduct litigation before a magistrates court or, in Scotland, before a sheriff.[9] This applies only to appeals in connection with deduction from earnings orders, liability orders or committal to prison. (The latter example does not apply to Scotland, where only the Secretary of State can act as the creditor where imprisonment for a civil debt is an issue.[10])

Child support inspectors

Inspectors can be appointed when information is needed by a CSO or the Secretary of State.[11] Inspectors have power to enter premises and make enquiries, to inspect documents and question people. The CSA appoints its own officers in relation to a particular case and for a fixed period. (For details of the role of inspectors, see p153.)

2. STRUCTURE OF THE CSA

The CSA began work with a staff of 3,500, but after three years employs around the equivalent of 6,400 full-time staff.[12] More staff may be needed to deal with the departure provisions (see p334). About two-thirds of staff are located in regional centres (see below). Of the remainder, the vast majority are employed as field officers based at local Benefits Agency offices. Approximately 80 project staff are working at Longbenton, Newcastle, to develop CSA procedures and operational guidance. A Special Payments Unit which considers compensation (see p30) is also sited at Longbenton. There are certain other functions which are attached neither to the regional centres nor to headquarters –

eg, the central appeals unit in Lytham St Anne's (see p372) and the National Enquiry Line based in Liverpool (see p422). By the end of April 1996, CSA headquarters will have moved from London to Dudley on the same site as the regional centre (see Appendix 1 for addresses).

The management structure of the CSA consists of the Chief Executive and a board of directors (see figure 2.1).

Child Support Agency centres (CSACs)

There are six regional CSACs (see figure 2.1); the way in which parts of the country relate to the six centres does not always make geographical sense, with many applications being dealt with at a remote centre. Each of the CSACs houses about 750 staff, approximately half of whom are CSOs (see p70).

Staff at the CSACs are primarily responsible for making child maintenance assessments, collection and enforcement, and carrying out reviews. There are also some sections with specialist functions (see p21).

The CSACs deal with the cases of persons with care from a particular region. Sometimes it is necessary to check which CSAC is dealing with a case – eg, where there is a series of linked cases, the case will be dealt with at the CSAC of the first person with care (PWC) to make an application.[13] She is known as the 'lead PWC'.

Contacting the CSAC

All CSAC contact with clients is through the post or over the telephone. It is advisable to put information in writing to the CSA and to keep copies of correspondence. In case of future appeals or complaints, it may also be helpful to put even routine enquiries into writing. Include the reference number in any letter and mark both the envelope and the letter for the attention of the relevant section (see below). Refer to any previous letters which are unanswered. It is not unknown for post to take some time to reach the relevant member of staff. However, if a response is not received within two weeks (see p27), then this should be followed up by telephone.

Each of the CSACs has a client helpline on which calls are charged at the local rate (see Appendix 1 for the telephone numbers). The member of staff who takes the call has access to the child support computer system and thus should be able to give a general progress report on the case; however, s/he will not have access to the paperwork and therefore may not be able to respond to specific queries. If this occurs, ask to be put through to the relevant section:

• the Business Team if awaiting an assessment – whether on initial

Figure 2.1

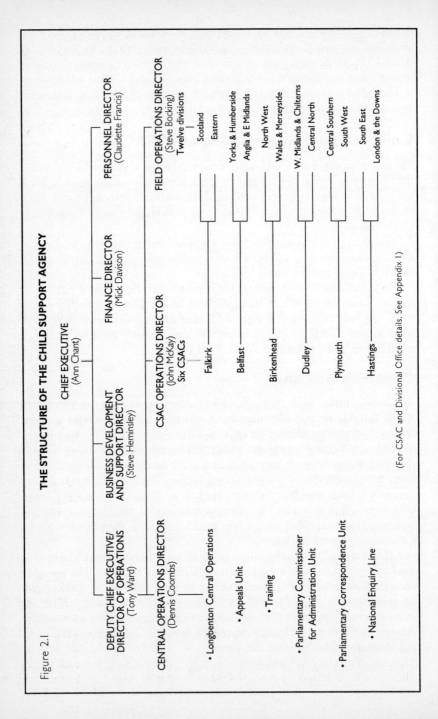

THE STRUCTURE OF THE CHILD SUPPORT AGENCY

CHIEF EXECUTIVE
(Ann Chant)

DEPUTY CHIEF EXECUTIVE/
DIRECTOR OF OPERATIONS
(Tony Ward)

BUSINESS DEVELOPMENT
AND SUPPORT DIRECTOR
(Steve Heminsley)

FINANCE DIRECTOR
(Mick Davison)

PERSONNEL DIRECTOR
(Claudette Francis)

CENTRAL OPERATIONS DIRECTOR
(Dennis Coombs)

- Longbenton Central Operations
  - Appeals Unit
  - Training
- Parliamentary Commissioner
  for Administration Unit
- Parliamentary Correspondence Unit
  - National Enquiry Line

CSAC OPERATIONS DIRECTOR
(John McKay)
Six CSACs

Falkirk

Belfast

Birkenhead

Dudley

Plymouth

Hastings

FIELD OPERATIONS DIRECTOR
(Steve Bocking)
Twelve divisions

Scotland
Eastern

Yorks & Humberside
Anglia & E Midlands

North West
Wales & Merseyside

W. Midlands & Chilterns
Central North

Central Southern
South West

South East
London & the Downs

(For CSAC and Divisional Office details, See Appendix 1)

application, change of circumstances or a periodical review;

- the special cases section – for assessments if one of the parents is self-employed (see p206);
- specialist tracing section – for tracing absent parents (see p133),
- the review section – if a second-tier review is under way (see p358);
- the accounts section – to query the state of the maintenance account (see p387);
- the debt management section – to negotiate an arrears repayments (see p401) or, if a parent with care, to get details of collection action being taken;
- the litigation section – if any court action has been initiated (see p415);
- the customer service section – if help is needed with a problematic case or if a complaint is to be made (see p28); the section includes a welfare oficer who can be contacted if a client is under particular stress.

The client helpline aims to prevent interrupting staff on the sections and therefore may be reticent to put enquiries through to the member of staff dealing with the case. If this happens, a complaint could be made (see p28). Alternatively, correspondence sent by the CSAC may have a direct telephone number, but this will not be at local rate. Staff may be willing to give their extension numbers which again provides a direct line for future use.

Make a brief note of what was said, and with whom, together with the date. If the information is important, follow up the telephone call with a letter confirming the points that have been made so that no misunderstanding can arise. CSA staff are unlikely to write and confirm a telephone conversation. Staff should give at least their first names and their position.

In Hastings CSAC, a complete action service team is being developed where all the staff dealing with a case – from assessment to enforcement – are located in one team. As this is proving successful, the practice will probably be extended.

Field offices

Working with each CSAC is a series of 'field operations' normally based in each of the local Benefits Agency offices. Some field officers, however, are based only in a Benefits Agency district office and not in the smaller offices in the area. Although most CSA staff in the field offices are not CSOs (see p17), the CSA has chosen to call them local child support officers. We prefer not to use this term as it is confusing; instead, we use the term 'field officer'. Each field office has on average four to five field officers, although there are sometimes more in the larger metropolitan areas. Each field officer has an area manager, who in turn reports to the divisional manager (see figure 2.1, and Appendix 1 for addresses). The area manager is also a CSO and has responsibility for issuing any reduced benefit directions (see p110).

The field offices are now responsible for all the work prior to the assessment itself, not only the issuing and checking of application and enquiry forms, but also registering applications onto the child support computer system and ensuring the information provided is complete. Thus, many of the investigations into the parents' circumstances are carried out from the field (see p150). The field office is also responsible for all work on the requirement to co-operate (see Chapter 5) and paternity disputes (see p139). Field officers also carry out the role of presenting officers at child support appeal tribunals (see p378). In addition, during this year, some field staff will be trained to complete assessments locally.

It is the field office in the applicant's area which deals initially with the application; however, the absent parent's field office may have to be involved with the case later on. Some parents find the field officer easier to communicate with than the CSAC, where it can be difficult to get through to the person dealing with the case (see above). However, if the CSAC is already dealing with the case – ie, an assessment has been made – it may be useful to repeat relevant information given by telephone to the field office in a letter to the CSAC.

Requesting a field office interview

A parent may request an interview if s/he has extensive enquiries about the CSA actions in a case or the assessment itself. This face-to-face contact is a service provided by the field office for the whole agency, and therefore, even if the enquiry involves actions taken by the CSAC (for example, concerning reviews or enforcement), any interview would be carried out by field officers. The request for the appointment should include the general area of the problem, so that the interviewing officer can be briefed, if necessary, by the CSAC. It is therefore usually more productive to request an appointment in advance rather than simply turning up at the field office. If no response is received to the request for an interview, the area manager should be approached.

If the interviewing officer is unable to answer the enquiries – for example, how the assessment was calculated – a complaint can be made (see p28). Where the field officer is unable to provide the information requested, check that it is information which can be disclosed (see p157) and then repeat the request in writing. However, where advice has been given by the interviewing officer, written confirmation should be requested straight away if necessary, as the interviewing officer may not keep a full record of the conversation. On the other hand, where the parent has information to give to the CSA – for example, further details to support a review – it is preferable to send these direct to the CSAC rather than rely on the interviewing officer to report the relevant facts.

Summons to attend a local office interview

In some instances, clients will be requested by the CSA to attend an interview at the local office – for example, where a parent with care on benefit has not co-operated with the CSA (see p104 for details of the interviewing procedure) or where there is a paternity dispute (see p143). These are not compulsory, but it may be to the parent's advantage to attend. A client may request a home visit instead if this is preferred. If the parent incurs travelling expenses, these may be refunded by the CSA (see p107).

3. CSA STANDARDS OF SERVICE

As described in the preface, the service provided by the CSA has received much criticism over its first three years. Although the administration has improved to a certain extent recently, there are still major problems (see p7). Indeed, the number of complaints received by the CSA continued to rise, with 2,800 a month received to date in 1995/96 compared with 2,300 per month in 1994/95 (although some of these will contain complaints about the policy, not just the service).[14] Although there are no simple solutions for parents and advisers trying to find their way through the maze of the CSA, this section attempts to provide the ammunition for holding the CSA to account against its own published targets.

Targets

Targets are set for the CSA by the Secretary of State. These are set out each year in the CSA Business Plan, which is publicly available from the CSA. At the time of writing, the targets for 1996/97 had not been published. For performance rates to date, see figure 2.2.

For the CSA's commitment to specific standards of service delivery on individual cases, see the CSA Charter on p27.

Figure 2.2: **CSA PERFORMANCE TARGETS**

Targets for 1995/96 [15]

£300 million of maintenance to be collected either by the CSA or paid direct by absent parents to parents with care (£140 million and £160 million respectively)

90% of parents with care to receive payments within 10 working days of receipt by the CSA from the absent parent

to achieve a continuing improvement in accuracy so that, in at least 75% of cases checked during March 1996, the assessment will be correct

60% of new applications to be cleared within 26 weeks, and no more than 10% of all applications to be over 52 weeks old at 31 March 1996

50% of second-tier reviews to be cleared within 13 weeks, 80% within 26 weeks, and no more than 20% to be taking longer than 26 weeks at 31 March 1996

to achieve a 65% client satisfaction score determined by an independent national survey

to manage resources so as to deliver the business plan within the gross budget allocation of £183 million

Performance to date [16]

£177 million collected in first 9 months of 1995/96 (£87 million via the CSA and £90 million direct between parents)

97% of payments made within 10 working days

72% of assessments checked in November 1995 were correct

39% of applications cleared within 26 weeks and 14% of applications awaiting assessments were over 52 weeks old at the end of November 1995

52% of second-tier reviews cleared within 13 weeks, 68% cleared within 26 weeks, and 23% outstanding for more than 26 weeks at end of November 1995

44% client satisfaction score in 1994/95 (down from 61% in 1993/94)

forecast in line with actual expenditure

Benefit savings

The saving expected in benefit expenditure as a result of CSA activity is no longer included by the Secretary of State as one of the Agency's targets, but is instead described as being one of the key criteria to be used when evaluating the CSA's performance in delivering the overall policy.

The benefits savings target set for the first year of operation was £530m, but only £418m was achieved.[17] The target set for the second year of operation was £460 million and £479 million was achieved.[18] The estimated annual savings in the long term were expected to be £900m;[19] however, for 1995/96 benefit savings of £540m are expected and in the first half year savings of £195 million were reported.[20]

Figure 2.3: **SAVINGS ON BENEFIT EXPENDITURE AS A RESULT OF CSA ACTION**

Category of benefit savings [21]	1994/95 £ million	April–Sept 1995 £ million
Resulting from pre-CSA arrangements		
Paid through CSA to Secretary of State	7.00	1.57
Paid direct between parents	119.52	included below
Resulting from CSA assessments		
Paid direct between parents	13.76	65.69
		(includes pre-CSA)
Paid through CSA to Secretary of State	47.94	30.16
Deductions from absent parents' IS	2.38	4.18
Persons with care ceasing to claim IS		
CSA assessment exceeded benefit	23.83	4.30
IS claim withdrawn within 4 weeks of CSA contact	199.53	80.99
Reductions in other benefits as a result of CSA assessments		
Family credit/disability working allowance savings	12.84	8.14
Housing benefit/council tax benefit savings	52.25	not yet available
TOTAL	479.05	195.03

CSA caseload

It is estimated that in the long term the Agency will have received more than 3 million applications and will be dealing with a caseload of some

2 million families who are affected by an application.[22] At the time of
writing, figures for 1995/96 were available up to December 1995.

Figure 2.4: **FORMS ISSUED AND ASSESSMENTS MADE**[23]			
	1993/94	*1994/95*	*1995/96 to date*
MAFs issued (see p61)	858,000	398,600	233,134
MAFs returned	626,600	260,500	142,873
MEFs issued (see p133)	466,600	276,600	138,143
MEFs returned	296,600	179,400	86,961
Full maintenance assessments	132,100*	187,200	82,766
Interim maintenance assessments	73,300*	63,600	14,291
Total maintenance assessments	205,500	250,800	97,057
Other completed cases	130,800	317,300	145,178
Total completed cases	336,200	568,100	242,235

* Derived from CSA cumulative figures[24]

There were almost 400,000 applications awaiting assessment at the end
of December 1995. Despite the DSS's assurances about improvements
in services, this is no better than the situation a year ago. See p59 for
information on dealing with delayed cases.

Half of the CSA's cases are closed without a maintenance assessment.
Although the CSA is unable to provide a breakdown of these cases, they
include those where:

- the parent with care on benefit does not co-operate with the CSA (see
  p101);
- parents with care withdraw a claim for income support (IS) before an
  assessment is made (there were about 60,000 such withdrawals in
  1994/95;[25] such cases account for a significant proportion of the
  benefit savings made by the CSA – see figure 2.3);
- a reconciliation occurred between the parents;
- parents come to a private arrangement;
- the absent parent could not be identified or traced; *or*
- the CSA did not have jurisdiction (see p295).

Absent parents on IS do not count as cleared without a maintenance
assessment; technically they receive a nil assessment.

CSA fees

In recognition of the poor service being provided by the CSA, the
charging of fees was suspended from 18 April 1995 until 6 April 1997

when they are due to become payable again.[26] Fees charged during 1993/95 which remain unpaid continue to be enforced (see p396). The assessment fee was £44 a year and the collection fee £34, although not all CSA clients were liable to pay fees. See earlier editions of this handbook for the full rules on fees.

The CSA charter

A charter containing the standards for the CSA service was published in April 1993 and is shortly due to be re-published. Commitments were made, among others, to the following standards (which were achieved during 1994/95 to the following extent):[27]

- a letter notifying an assessment will always explain how it is worked out;
- an assessment will be issued within five working days of receiving all the information from both parents (achieved in 15 per cent of cases);
- if there is a delay the CSA will explain how long someone has to wait and, as a matter of course, will let a person know if there is an undue delay;
- when an assessment is issued a person will be told of their rights to review and appeal, and how long a review will take;
- the CSA aims to respond to 80 per cent of calls to the enquiry line and CSACs within 20 seconds (achieved in 90 per cent and 66 per cent of cases respectively);
- it aims to reply within 10 working days of receiving a query (achieved in 35 per cent of cases);
- it is committed regularly to consult people with special needs, and their representatives, to identify better ways to meet their needs;
- staff will wear name badges and will tell callers their name on the phone and when they write;
- it aims to see people at the interview time arranged; you should never have to wait more than 20 minutes (achieved in 100 per cent of cases);
- other than information used to make a maintenance assessment, all information given will be treated in confidence;
- any written complaint will be acknowledged within two days and a full reply sent within 10 working days of its receipt (achieved in 79 per cent and 34 per cent of cases respectively).

CSA liaison meetings

As part of its charter commitments, the CSA should arrange regular meetings with people who represent client interests locally and nationally. At the local level, customer service managers will consult individuals, representatives and employers both formally and informally. If this is not already happening in your area, it may be useful for advisers to set up regular meetings with the CSA in order to take up operational issues. Effective liaison should help to improve the service and also provides another mechanism for raising problem cases.

Complaints about the CSA

There are procedures of review and appeal which allow applicants and other people affected to challenge a particular CSO decision about child maintenance (see Chapter 16). However, if a person wishes to make a complaint about the way in which matters have been handled, there are other procedures to follow. A complaint may arise about:

- failure to comply with the standards set out in the CSA charter;
- delay in dealing with an application or a review;
- lack of enforcement action or, on the other hand, lack of under-standing when negotiating arrears repayments or initiating litigation;
- poor administration – eg, difficulty in getting through on the telephone, or no one available to answer questions, lack of response to letters or failure to carry out actions as and when stated;
- the behaviour of members of staff – a complaint should be made about any rudeness, undue pressure, or any sexist, racist or other derogatory remarks;
- powers to seek or release information have been exceeded.

The CSA produces a leaflet (*Feedback*) which contains a form which can be used to make any comments either negative or positive. See p23 for the number of complaints made.

To make a complaint, follow these steps until the desired response is obtained.

- Write to the customer services manager in the CSAC or field office, marking both the letter and the envelope as a complaint; this should be acknowledged within two working days and a full reply sent within 10 working days.
- Contact the area manager responsible for the local office concerned, or the manager of the CSAC, explaining the problem as succinctly as possible and, if necessary, including a list of events in date order.
- If necessary, write to the divisional manager (for a complaint about a field officer) or operational director (see figure 2.1) with details of the complaint – this might be appropriate where the response from the area or CSAC manager promised some action which has not been carried out.
- Write to Ann Chant, the Chief Executive – a copy of the letter written

to the area or CSAC manager should suffice, with a covering note explaining why the response was not satisfactory.

See Appendix 1 for the relevant CSA addresses.

The Select Committee on the Ombudsman has suggested that an independent adjudicator be appointed to deal with complaints about the CSA; this is currently under consideration by the DSS.[28]

Complaining to an MP

If replies from the officers to whom someone has complained are not satisfactory, the next step is to take up the matter with the local MP. If the situation is sufficiently serious, the MP should be contacted if the customer services manager does not rectify the problem, and certainly it is helpful to involve the MP once the Chief Executive's office is approached.

Most MPs have 'surgeries' in their areas where they meet constituents to discuss problems. Details of these surgeries can be obtained from local libraries or citizens' advice bureaux. A constituent can either go to the surgery or write to the MP with details of the complaint. If a local address is not easily obtainable, MPs can be written to at the House of Commons, London SW1A 0AA. A copy of the complaint to the CSA is useful background, with a covering letter requesting particular action from the MP.

The MP may write to the CSA for an explanation about what has happened. The CSA has made a commitment to respond to MPs within an average of 20 working days from the date of receipt of a letter, or provide a progress report.[29] If an immediate response is required, MPs have access to a telephone 'hotline' to the CSA. If the case also involves policy issues, the MP can take this up with the Minister responsible. The MP can also refer cases of maladministration to the Ombudsman.

During 1994/95, the CSA's parliamentary correspondence unit responded to 12,374 letters from MPs and none of the 690 cases awaiting a reply were more than six weeks old; in addition, the CSACs each answer approximately 100 letters a week from MPs.[30]

The Ombudsman

If the reply from the Chief Executive is not satisfactory, the next step is to complain to the Ombudsman, via the MP. The Parliamentary Commissioner for Administration (commonly called the Ombudsman) investigates complaints made by MPs against Government departments. The Ombudsman's office will send a leaflet providing further information to the person making the complaint. If the complaint is investigated, the MP will be sent a full report. If the Ombudsman finds that someone was badly treated, s/he will recommend an apology and possibly compensation. The investigations can also lead to revised CSA guidance on procedures.

The CSA should respond to the Ombudsman within six weeks of receiving a submission on all new complaints and within four weeks of receipt of a draft report on the conclusion of an investigation.[31] However, the full investigation will take many months and quite often over a year.

Due to the number of complaints about the CSA, the Ombudsman has been limiting investigations to a number of representative cases only.[32] Further cases are taken on if they raise new issues or have caused actual financial loss. This should not deter people from continuing to send cases via their MP, as this has proved an effective way of raising issues and obtaining redress. It is important that the Ombudsman is aware of the level of complaints, even if staff are unable to carry out full investigations. Reports by the Ombudsman and the Commons Select Committee on the Parliamentary Commissioner (see p447) have highlighted the CSA's poor standards of administration and failure to achieve its Charter commitments (see p27).

Claiming compensation

Where a parent has incurred a loss as a result of the way in which the CSA has operated the child support scheme, a claim for compensation should be considered. First, there is a statutory scheme to cover reductions in assessments made as a result of the amendments to the regulations (see p165). Secondly, there are ex-gratia compensation claims; the CSA operates the general DSS arrangements for compensating actual financial losses where it is clear that these are the result of a CSA error. This would apply, for example, where it has been established that the CSA has made an error which led to the client losing money – eg, where it has significantly delayed sending a maintenance enquiry form (MEF), or where enforcement action has been delayed so long that there is less chance of recovering the arrears. The CSA has been delegated authority by the Treasury to make these payments unless the issue is considered 'novel or contentious', in which case the Treasury is consulted.[33]

The Select Committee on the Ombudsman expressed concern that compensation payments to date have been grossly inadequate and that consideration should be given to making payments for the worry and distress caused by CSA maladministration.[34] It has recommended that such payments be made in exceptional or deserving cases without the need for medical certification of harm or proven malice from officials, and without having to refer to the Treasury. This has not yet been accepted by the Government, but the DSS is reviewing the criteria for compensation. If such claims are made, they should be accompanied by as much evidence as possible of the direct effects of the CSA's activity. It is very unlikely to be sufficient to say the client found it distressing.

The first step is to write to the customer service manager explaining the full sequence of events and detailing the resulting loss. This should be forwarded to the Special Payments Unit (see p18) for consideration. If there is no satisfactory response, write to Ann Chant, Chief Executive of the CSA, with a copy to Andrew Mitchell, the government minister with responsibility for child support, at the DSS (see Appendix 1 for address). It is useful to obtain the support of the MP. It would also be helpful to send copies to CPAG as we want to put pressure on the Government to set up a formal procedure which adequately compensates clients for both financial losses and distress caused. Even in cases where the DSS is currently very unlikely to pay any compensation, it may be worth requesting compensation in order to register a protest. By the end of November 1995, 112 compensation payments have resulted from 1,182 applications.[35]

If compensation is not forthcoming, legal advice could be sought on the merits of taking the CSA to court.

4. TAKE-ON OF CASES BY THE CSA

The original four-year timetable, beginning in April 1993, for the CSA to take over all child maintenance cases from the courts has been partly abandoned due to the Agency's backlog of work. However, it is no longer possible for anyone to apply to court for a first child maintenance order (but see maintenance agreements and consent orders below).[36] Generally, once the CSA has jurisdiction in a particular case, the courts no longer deal with child maintenance, except on certain issues outside the scope of the child support scheme (see p37). A CSA assessment, once made, overrides any existing child maintenance court order (see p36).

Benefit claimants

Persons with care have their cases taken on by the CSA when they make a new or repeat claim for income support, family credit or disability working allowance (IS/FC/DWA); this means that they will be contacted initially to find out whether there is any reason why they should not apply for child maintenance (see p83). The existence of a court order for child maintenance, or a pre-April 1993 maintenance agreement (see below), does not prevent the CSA taking on the case of a benefit claimant, unless she is not the parent of the child for whom maintenance would be payable.

All existing FC/DWA claimants should have been contacted by the CSA. However, there remain some 300,000 persons with care who were in receipt of IS on 5 April 1993 but have not yet been contacted by the CSA; they will be taken on at a rate with which the CSA can cope. This may take a number of years. If such a person wishes her case to be taken on in advance of the usual procedure, she can apply to the CSA for this to happen (see p58).

Non-benefit cases

A person with care who is not receiving IS/FC/DWA can apply to the CSA as long as there is no court order for child maintenance nor a pre-April 1993 maintenance agreement (see p55). However, the parties can make or continue with a private voluntary agreement instead if they prefer; courts can still make consent orders (see p35).

Existing maintenance agreements

The existence of a pre-April 1993 written child maintenance agreement or court order prevents a case being taken on by the CSA where the person with care is not in receipt of IS/FC/DWA (for details see p54). These cases were originally due to be taken on by the CSA during 1996/97, but this has been indefinitely postponed.[37] Although the legislation can be easily amended to allow access to these cases in future years,[38] the Government has given no indication that this is likely to happen. Indeed, it is probable that these pre-April 1993 cases may never be able to obtain CSA assessments, although at some – as yet unspecified – date, they will be able to apply to the CSA for the collection and enforcement of their existing agreements/orders.

5. POWERS RETAINED BY THE COURTS

CPAG recommends seeking legal advice in connection with any court proceedings. The following is not intended to be a comprehensive guide to the law.

Generally, the courts retain jurisdiction on child maintenance issues only where the case is beyond the scope of the child support legislation. Where an assessment is made by the CSA, any court order or agreement for child maintenance ceases to have effect (see p36).

The courts retain jurisdiction for other aspects of relationship breakdown, including contact and residence orders (previously known as access and custody orders), spousal maintenance, paternity disputes (see p38) and property issues.

Where the CSA has no jurisdiction

If access to the CSA is denied because of the existence of a court order for child maintenance or pre-April 1993 written maintenance agreements (see p32), the courts retain the power to vary such orders and agreements.[39] Many courts are, in fact, using calculations according to the CSA formula presented to them as guidance when setting levels of child maintenance, and parents seeking a variation of orders should ask their solicitors to prepare such a calculation. A High Court judge has said that the figure produced should be strongly persuasive, although not binding.[40] The courts do retain the power to enforce orders.

Although courts do retain the power to revoke orders, it is not generally possible for an order to be revoked simply to gain access to the CSA.[41] However, in some cases, revocation may be granted, but those considering this option must seek advice as to the likely CSA assessment; it is not uncommon for a CSA assessment to be lower than the previous court order.

Where the CSA does not have jurisdiction because a party to an assessment is habitually resident abroad (see p47), the courts still deal with applications for maintenance. Any applications for maintenance on divorce are made to the family proceedings (magistrates) court, the county court or High Court (in Scotland, the sheriff court or Court of Session). The courts also have powers to decide issues of enforcement where an absent parent lives abroad.[42]

Where a CSA assessment is cancelled because one of the parties moves abroad (see p308), an application can then be made to the court. There is a six-month time limit on applications to backdate an order when a case moves out of CSA jurisdiction.[43]

If, in other instances, the CSA decides it does not have jurisdiction, an application could be made to court for child maintenance. Where someone wants to apply to court and there is a conflict about jurisdiction, the court staff refer the case to a district judge (or, in Scotland, a sheriff). If s/he refuses jurisdiction then there is a hearing which, if unsuccessful, means that the applicant is given written reasons, and either has to apply to the CSA or appeal to a circuit judge (or, in Scotland, the sheriff-principal or Court of Session).[44] Some people have been unable to get either the courts or the CSA to accept jurisdiction. Unfortunately, no final solution has been provided for in law; the only option, therefore, is to be persistent.

The courts can award other types of maintenance in specific situations (see p37).

Where the CSA has jurisdiction

Since 5 April 1993 the courts have no longer been able to make orders for periodical payments of child maintenance in any case where the assessment *could* be made by the CSA.[45] This applies even if, on application, a CSO would not make an assessment.[46] It is difficult to know when an assessment could be applied for but would not be made even though there is jurisdiction, other than perhaps where an absent parent could not be traced. If a CSO refuses to make an assessment, a review can be requested (see p359). Also, legal advice should be sought about making an application to court (see above). A person who wishes to obtain child maintenance should not be left without any route for doing so.

Even where the CSA has jurisdiction, there is an exception where the court is requested to make a consent order (see below). But parents who want child maintenance and cannot reach a private agreement have to use the CSA even when the court is dealing with all other aspects of the breakdown of their relationship. In limited situations, the courts can award maintenance in addition to that assessed by the CSA (see p37).

The courts have the power to revoke any maintenance order but they are unable to vary or revive an order where an application could be made to the CSA.[47] The types of maintenance order affected by this change in court powers are those orders for making or securing periodical payments to or for a child.[48]

For the very few cases where there is an application for a maintenance order made before 5 April 1993 still waiting to be heard in court, the courts still have the power to make an order up until 7 April 1997.[49] A pending application, in England and Wales, is defined as one which was filed in accordance with court rules before 5 April 1993; or, if the application was contained in a petition or answer (for divorce, nullity or judicial separation), then notice of intention to proceed had to have been given as required by court rules (forms M11 and M13) before 5 April 1993.[50] If the court makes any order, even an interim order, this would close off the possibility of an application to the CSA.

If a court order is cancelled because it was made by mistake when a CSA assessment was in force, any payments made under the order are treated as payments of child support maintenance.[51]

Once a CSA assessment is made, the courts can be involved with the enforcement of that assessment (see p415) and in hearing appeals about defective deduction of earnings orders (see p414).

The 1991 Act gives the Lord Chancellor, or the Lord Advocate in Scotland, the power to order that certain – or indeed all – appeals under the child support legislation should be made to court rather than to a child support appeal tribunal.[52] So far, this has been used for appeals against decisions about who is a parent of a child (see p38).

Maintenance agreements

Maintenance agreements for periodical payments for a child (or aliment, in Scotland) can be entered into.[53] Written agreements prevent access to the CSA only if made before 5 April 1993 (see p55).[54] Where access to the CSA is prevented, courts can increase the amount of child maintenance payable under the agreement (see p33).[55] However, where a CSA assessment could be applied for, the court can neither vary the amount of child maintenance nor insert any provisions which require the payment of periodical child maintenance for a biological or adopted child (except in the case of consent orders).[56]

Maintenance agreements cannot include any clause claiming to prevent anyone from applying to the CSA. Any such clause is void.[57]

Maintenance agreements should be considered by both parties; some parents with care are able to obtain more maintenance this way than under the CSA formula. Also, they may help while waiting for a CSA assessment, which usually takes several months.

Consent orders

Where parents make an agreement about how their finances should be dealt with on divorce, the courts can make a consent order – ie, a court order made with the consent of both parents, reflecting their agreement. This facility can be used regardless of when the maintenance agreement was entered into. Where this happens, an agreement can appear as part of a court order, as long as the court order is in identical terms to the written agreement.[58] The power to make a court order which enshrines a written agreement applies to the family proceedings court in a magistrates' court as well as to county or High Courts, or, in Scotland, the sheriff court.

Such an order – even if made after 5 April 1993 – prevents an application to the CSA, providing the parent with care does not claim IS/FC/DWA. The advantages and disadvantages of applying to the CSA now or in the future should be carefully weighed up against the wish to preserve an amicable arrangement before applying for a consent order. It is also open to benefit claimants to make such an arrangement, although IS, FC and DWA claimants would still be subject to the requirement to co-operate (see Chapter 5).

Phasing-out of court orders

When a CSA assessment is made, any existing court order or maintenance agreement either ceases to have effect or has effect in a modified form in relation to periodical payments.[59]

Once a child maintenance assessment is made for all of the children previously covered by a court order, the order ceases to have effect after two days.[60] The rules are slightly different when an interim maintenance assessment has been made, or when an order ceases to have effect before an assessment has been made (see p305). If the assessment does not apply to all the children covered by the court order, then only the amount specifically allocated to that child in the order ceases to have effect.[61] In the latter case, this amount ceases to have effect as soon as the new assessment starts – ie, two days after the assessment is made.[62] Any order made for maintenance in respect of expenses for education or training, or for a disabled child, will continue to be unaffected by any CSA assessment.[63]

Maintenance agreements become unenforceable from the effective date of any CSA assessment (see p303).[64] Again, this only applies if a CSA assessment is made which covers all of the children previously covered by an agreement. If the assessment does not apply to all the children covered by the agreement, only the amount specifically allocated to that child in the agreement becomes unenforceable. In either case, the agreement remains unenforceable until the CSO no longer has the power to make an assessment.[65] Any court order made for children not covered by the CSA assessment can be backdated to the date of the maintenance assessment.[66]

If a court order lapses as a result of a CSA assessment and a CSO then cancels the assessment because it was made in error, the court order revives, and any payments of child support maintenance will count as payments under the original maintenance order.[67]

In Scotland, if a CSO ceases to have the power to make an assessment with respect to a child, then the original order revives from the date s/he ceases to have that power.[68] Although this is not explicitly stated for the rest of Great Britain, this effect applies given that the court order has not been revoked but simply ceased to have effect for the duration of a valid CSA assessment.

Notifications

Where a CSO makes an assessment and realises that a relevant court order has been or is likely to be affected, then s/he must tell the person with care, absent parent, person treated as an absent parent under the formula, or child applicant (in Scotland only) of the assessment and when it takes effect.[69] The CSO must also give the same information to certain officers of the court in which the order was made or registered (court officers are defined below).[70]

Similarly, where a court makes an order which affects or is likely to affect a CSA assessment, the relevant officer of the court must notify the Secretary of State of this if s/he knows the assessment is in force.[71] The court officers concerned are:[72]

In England and Wales:
• the senior district judge of the High Court Family Division, or if a district registry was used, the district judge; *or*
• the district judge of a county court (or the chief clerk or other officer acting on his/her behalf);[73] *or*
• the clerk to the justices of a family proceedings (magistrates) court.

In Scotland:
• the Deputy Principal Clerk of Session of the Court of Session; *or*
• the sheriff clerk of a sheriff court.

Additional maintenance

The courts still deal with the following maintenance issues:[74]
• maintenance in respect of step-children. The courts have power to make orders in respect of children of the family[75] who are not qualifying children – ie, children who used to live with the absent parent and parent with care and who were accepted by them as members of their family;
• additional child maintenance in excess of the maximum which can be awarded by the CSA under the formula (see p234);[76]
• child maintenance to meet the expenses of education or training for a trade, profession or vocation;[77]
• maintenance to meet some or all of any expenses attributable to the child's disability – a child counts as disabled if s/he is getting disability living allowance (DLA) or does not get DLA but is blind, deaf, without speech, or is substantially and permanently handicapped by illness, injury, mental disorder or congenital deformity;[78]
• spousal maintenance (maintenance paid to a spouse, or to an ex-spouse or partner);
• maintenance orders against a person with care;[79]
• maintenance where a relevant person is not habitually resident in the UK (see p47).

It is possible to apply to increase spousal maintenance in order to preserve combined maintenance payments at the level originally considered acceptable by the court before CSA assessments were reduced as a result of changes to the formula. However, this is unlikely to be successful where the reduction in the assessment is due to a change in either parent's circumstances.[80] It is also unlikely to work where the CSA formula has led to a lower assessment than a pre-1993 order or agreement for child maintenance,[81] but may be worth pursuing where the order was based on the court's incorrect assumptions about entitlement under the CSA formula. It is advisable to seek legal advice in such cases.

Courts have powers to backdate maintenance orders to the effective date of a CSA assessment (see p303).[82] For example, orders for amounts in excess of the maximum under the formula or for increased spousal maintenance can be backdated as long as the application is made within six months of the effective date. Backdating is at the court's discretion but can help ensure that child maintenance and other related court applications are not out of step.

Parentage disputes

Where parentage has been denied, a maintenance application cannot proceed except in certain specified cases (see p41).[83] Once parentage – most commonly, paternity – has been disputed, there is provision in the 1991 Act for a reference to a court by the Secretary of State or the person with care for a declaration as to whether or not the alleged parent is one of the child's parents.[84] Any reference by the Secretary of State is at his/her discretion. If the Secretary of State or the person with care decides not to apply to the court, the CSO concerned cannot make a maintenance assessment.[85] In Scotland, the Secretary of State alone can bring an action for a declarator of parentage, and again this is at his/her discretion.[86] The Secretary of State can also decide to defend any action for a declarator of non-parentage or illegitimacy brought by the alleged parent.

Voluntary DNA testing is available from the CSA without having to go to court (see p148). However, only the courts have the power to order blood tests – including DNA tests – in any civil proceedings in which paternity is an issue.[87] Any party can request that DNA tests be taken, but authority must be given by the court. A court can direct a party to undergo a blood test, but cannot force him/her to do so. However, the court may draw its own conclusions, by inference, if s/he fails to comply, depending on all the circumstances of the case.

Courts can only order DNA or blood testing where one or other party agrees to pay. The cost is likely to be over £450. Where the CSA is asked to pay such fees by the courts, it will seek to recover them in any court costs awarded in its favour. It is usually the unsuccessful party who has to pay costs. If a person is on IS, these could be met by legal aid. Legal aid is available for CSA and court applications where parentage is disputed, but in practice is generally refused as the CSA could take the case forward (see above).

In Scotland, if an alleged absent parent takes action for a declaration of non-parentage or illegitimacy and the CSA does not defend the action, then no expenses can be awarded against the Secretary of State.[88]

According to CSA guidance, the CSA only takes cases to court where the person with care is on IS, FC or DWA.[89] If the only reason given to a person with care for not taking court action is that she is not on benefit, this could be challenged by judicial review (see p351). Even in benefit cases, the CSA appears only to take on those cases where the case against the alleged absent parent is very strong. Otherwise it will be up to one of the parties concerned to pursue the matter and they may not wish to risk the costs if unsuccessful. Paternity was established in 93 per cent of the 1,081 cases the CSA took to court in the first nine months of 1995/96, although there were some 11,500 cases involving paternity disputes outstanding at the end of November 1995 (see p149).[90]

Any appeal against a decision made about who is a parent of a child will also be dealt with by a magistrates/sheriff's court rather than by a child support appeal tribunal (CSAT).[91] A Northern Ireland commissioner has decided that any dispute about parentage should be raised in the grounds of any appeal so that a decision can be made about whether a case is to proceed to court or to a CSAT (see also p370).[92]

Property or capital settlements

Parents who separated many years ago may well have reached agreements based on, for example, the father signing over his share of the family home so that the mother and children can remain living there in return for an agreement from her not to seek maintenance. If at any time an application is made to the CSA, its assessment will override any such agreement. There is now an element in the child support formula for pre-April 1993 capital and property settlements (see p192), but not for any settlement made on or after 5 April 1993. The Government believes that the existence of the child support scheme should not result in any change in the way the courts decide property matters. However, in practice, there are signs of a return to the so-called 'Mesher' orders where the family home has to be sold when one of a number of conditions is met – eg, the children reach a certain age – often resulting in mothers being left homeless.

Attempts to overturn pre-1993 'clean-break' settlements through the courts have proved unsuccessful.[93]

CHAPTER THREE

Who is covered by the scheme

This chapter covers:

I. THE DUTY TO MAINTAIN

Both parents of a **qualifying child** (see p41) are responsible for maintaining her/him.[1]

The Child Support Agency (CSA) can only require an **absent parent** (see p45) to pay child maintenance for a qualifying child. A **parent with care** (see p45) cannot be required to pay child maintenance for the child for whom she is caring, unless that parent is treated as an absent parent because she provides care for less time than someone else or, in some cases, for the same amount of time (see Chapter 13).

A child support officer (CSO) can only make an assessment if the person with care, absent parent and qualifying child are all **habitually resident in the UK** (see p47).

2. PARENT

A parent is a person who is in law the mother or father of the child.[2] This includes:

- a biological parent;
- a parent by adoption;[3]

- a parent under a parental order made following a surrogacy arrangement.[4]

Where a person denies being the parent of a child, the CSO must assume that the person is a parent of the child in the following situations, unless that child has been subsequently adopted by someone else:[5]

- a declaration of parentage or, in Scotland, a declarator of parentage, is in force;[6]
- a declaration under s27 of the 1991 Act has been made;
- in Scotland only, where a man was married to the mother;[7]
- a man was found to be the father in certain court proceedings (including affiliation proceedings).[8]

If none of the situations above applies, then the CSO cannot make an assessment until parentage is admitted or decided by a court (see p38).

An adoption order means that a child's biological parent (including anyone assumed to be a biological parent in one of the situations above) is no longer in law that child's parent. The liability of a biological parent to maintain his child therefore ends on adoption and the parent(s) by adoption become the only people liable to maintain the child.[9]

A person who has parental responsibility under the Children Act 1989 or, in Scotland, parental rights and responsibility under the Children (Scotland) Act 1995, is not a parent for child support purposes just because of that.[10] A step-parent who is not assumed to be a parent for child support cannot be required to pay child support maintenance, but could instead be pursued in the courts (see p37).[11]

A foster parent is not a parent for child support, but s/he is a person with care if s/he has day-to-day care of a child who lives with her/him, except where the child has been placed with her/him by a local authority (see p44).

3. QUALIFYING CHILD

A **qualifying child** is a child for whom maintenance is payable. A child is a qualifying child if one or both of her/his parents are **absent parents** (see p45).[12]

A **child** is a person:[13]

- under 16;
- 16–18 years old and receiving full-time, non-advanced education (see below); *or*
- 16 or 17 years old and registered for work or youth training (see p43).

Even if a person falls into one of these groups, s/he is *not* a child if s/he is, or has been, married. This applies even if the marriage has been annulled or was never valid – eg, s/he was under 16, or not lawfully married as in bigamous or same-sex marriages.[14]

An application to the courts may still be possible in certain circumstances – eg, a dependent child at university (see p37).

Full-time, non-advanced education

A course is **non-advanced** if it is up to A level or higher level Scottish Certificate of Education (this includes a Scottish certificate of sixth year studies and a national diploma or certificate from BTEC or ScotVEC). Courses of degree level and above (including DipHE, Higher National Diploma, or a Higher Diploma or certificate from BTEC or ScotVEC) count as advanced education.[15]

The child must attend a recognised educational establishment (such as a school or college) or the education must be recognised by the Secretary of State.[16]

The CSO must treat a child as receiving full-time education if the child attends a course where contact time lasts for more than 12 hours. Contact time includes teaching, supervised study, exams and practical or project work which are part of the course. It does not include meal times or unsupervised study, whether on or off the premises.[17]

Where a child is not attending such a course – eg, where contact is for less than 12 hours – the CSO must look at all the facts and decide if the education is full time.

After leaving school or college, a child still counts as being in full-time education until the end of a fixed period after s/he leaves. The end of this period is called the **terminal date**[18] and it coincides with the beginning of the next school term. School leavers still count as children for the purposes of child support up to the Sunday following this date (see below) unless s/he is 19 before that date, when it is the Sunday following the Monday before the 19th birthday.[19]

Time of leaving school	Terminal date
Christmas	First Monday in January
Easter	First Monday after Easter Monday
May/June	First Monday in September

If a child is under school leaving age when s/he leaves school, s/he is treated as leaving school on the date s/he reaches that age. The terminal date is the next one after that date.[20] If a child is entered for an external examination before s/he leaves school, the terminal date is the first one which follows the last exam.[21]

If s/he does any paid work of 24 hours or more a week before the terminal date, s/he no longer counts as a child unless the work is temporary and expected to end before the terminal date.[22]

Breaks in full-time education

Someone at school or college still counts as a child if there is a temporary break in full-time education.[23] It does not matter whether they are under or over 16 when education is interrupted.

Any break must be reasonable in the particular circumstances of the case. The break can be as long as six months, but can only be longer if it is due to physical or mental illness or disability. The break must not be likely to be, or in fact, followed immediately by a period of time on a youth training allowance, or while receiving education because of her/his job.[24]

16/17-year-olds not in full-time education

A 16/17-year-old who is no longer at school or college full-time will still be a child for the purposes of child support if s/he is registered for work or youth training, but has not actually started either work or youth training.[25] This lasts for the **extension period**. S/he still counts as a child if s/he does paid work so long as it is for less than 24 hours a week or is temporary and expected to end before the end of the extension period.[26]

A child entitled to income support (IS) in her/his own right is not a qualifying child in this situation.[27]

The extension period begins on the day the person would otherwise stop being treated as a child (usually the terminal date – see p42). The date it ends depends on the terminal date. If the terminal date is after the end of the relevant extension period, there is no extension period.

Extension periods for 1996/97 are:[28]

Terminal date	Extension period ends
1 January 1996	31 March 1996
15 April 1996	14 July 1996
2 September 1996	5 January 1997
6 January 1997	6 April 1997

4. PERSON WITH CARE

A **person with care** is the person with whom the child has her/his **home** (see p45)and who usually provides **day-to-day care** (see below) for the child.[29] The person with care does not have to be the parent and need not be an individual but could, for example, be a children's home.

A person with care *cannot* be:[30]
- a local authority;
- someone looking after a child where the child has been placed with her/him by a local authority under the Children Act 1989, *unless* s/he is the child's parent and the local authority allows the child to live with her/him under that Act;[31]
- in Scotland, someone who is looking after a child who has been boarded out by a local authority under the Social Work (Scotland) Act 1968.[32]

There may be more than one person with care of a particular child.[33]

Day-to-day care

Day-to-day care is not defined in the Acts. It should be taken to have its ordinary, everyday meaning. A person who is responsible for a child's daily routine may be providing day-to-day care even if some things are done by another person – for example, a childminder.

For the formula and shared care regulations, day-to-day care means care of at least 104 nights per year on average.[34] The average is usually taken over a 12-month period ending with the **relevant week** (see p205). Alternatively, the amount of care can be averaged over another period which, in the CSO's opinion, is more representative of the current care arrangements (see p267).[35] For formula purposes there can be up to three persons with care.

Once care is averaged out over a year, a situation might arise where no one has day-to-day care, and no one is treated as a person with care. For more on shared care situations, see Chapter 13.

Even though this definition does not apply to the Acts, CSOs are advised to use this definition when considering whether a person is a person with care under the Acts.[36] If this makes a difference, it is important to argue that the ordinary meaning of day-to-day care should be used, not the calculation in the regulations.

For example, a mother who works night shifts may leave her son in the care of grandparents for 22 nights a month. She decides what the boy will eat and when he will go to bed, and each morning dresses him and takes him to school. Using the 104 days average, she does not provide day-to-day care, but, using the ordinary meaning of those words, she does.

In two situations the actual care being provided does not matter. Where a child is placed with his/her parents by a local authority under the Children Act 1989, the parents are treated as providing day-to-day care under the Act.[37] Where a child is a boarding-school boarder or a hospital in-patient, the person who would otherwise provide day-to-day care is treated as providing day-to-day care under the Act.[38]

Home

The person with care must have a home with the child. A home is the physical place where the child lives. It is different from a household.[39] (For a discussion of how this relates to the definition of household, see p46.) Where a child has her/his home is usually clear, but a situation may arise where a child has more than one home. The regulations explicitly refer to the fact that there can be more than one home.[40] Guidance to CSOs also makes this clear.[41] A decision as to where a child has her/his home may involve the child's own view of where it is.

Parent with care

A **parent with care** is a person with care who is also a **parent** (see p40) of a qualifying child (see p41).[42] If income support (IS), family credit (FC), or disability working allowance (DWA) is claimed by or on behalf of the parent with care, she can be required to give authority to the Secretary of State to assess and recover child maintenance.[43] Some parents are exempt from this requirement (see Chapter 5).[44]

For circumstances in which a parent with care may be treated as an absent parent, see p269.

5. ABSENT PARENT

An **absent parent** is a **parent** (see p40) who is not living in the same **household** (see below) as his child, and the child has her/his home with a person with care (see p43).[45] The most straightforward example of this is where a couple have a child and the father either no longer lives, or never has lived, with the mother and child.

A parent with care in a shared care situation can sometimes be deemed to be an absent parent (see p269).[46]

Both parents can be absent parents, in which case they can both be required to pay child maintenance.[47]

Household

The term 'household' is not defined in child support legislation. In many cases, whether people are members of the same household is obvious. A household is something abstract, not something physical like a home. It consists of either a single person or a group of people held together by social ties.[48] Where it is not obvious whether several people share a household, the following factors should be considered:

- whether they share the same physical space – eg, a house or flat;
- whether they carry out chores for the benefit of all of them (for example, cooking, shopping, cleaning).

The meaning of 'household' has been considered in family and social security cases. This case law should be used cautiously for child support purposes because the interpretation of 'household' for child support must fit with the Acts. (For the social security case law see CPAG's *National Welfare Benefits Handbook*.)

Certain guidelines from the case law are, however, clearly relevant for child support:

- there can be two or more separate households in one house;[49]
- one or more member(s) of a household can be temporarily absent from the home without ending their membership of the household;[50]
- there does not need to be a relationship like marriage for people to share a household – for example, two sisters can form a household.[51]

It is not clear whether a person can be a member of more than one household for child support purposes – for example, a father who divides his time between two women by each of whom he has a child. For social security purposes, a person can only be a member of one household at a time.[52] In the child support context, the DSS has stated that 'where the person divides his time equally between households we would consider that he is a member of each household.'[53] This appears to accept that a person can be a member of more that one household for child support purposes. This argument may be particularly important for shared care arrangements (see pp268–9).

Advisers should be careful when arguing that a supposed absent parent shares a household with a parent with care on benefit. A decision by a CSO or child support appeal tribunal that the couple share a household for child support purposes may lead to a benefits adjudication officer (AO) deciding that the couple share a household for benefit purposes.

Guidance to CSOs

CSOs are advised that 'household' and 'home' are different concepts[54] and that a single home may contain a number of households.[55] The focus should be whether the alleged absent parent and the child share a household: the other members do not matter.[56] The following questions should be considered:[57]

- Are the addresses the same?
- Does either have an alternative address?
- Do the parent and child share the same rooms?
- Who carries out the household chores?
- Who pays the utility bills?

6. HABITUALLY RESIDENT IN THE UK

A CSO cannot make a maintenance assessment unless the person with care, absent parent and qualifying child are all habitually resident in the UK.[58] The requirement for the person with care to be habitually resident does not apply if that 'person' is an organisation.[59]

The UK means England, Scotland, Wales and Northern Ireland (including coastal islands like the Isle of Wight). It does not include the Isle of Man or the Channel Islands.[60]

For child maintenance where a person is not habitually resident in the UK see p37.

Meaning of habitually resident

'Habitually resident' is not defined in the Acts. Therefore, those words are given their ordinary and natural meaning. At the time of writing (March 1996), only one decision of a child support commissioner has dealt with habitual residence.[61] The commissioner decided that habitual residence for child support was to be determined bearing in mind that the purpose of child support is the social need to require absent parents to contribute to the maintenance of their children. The commissioner appears to have decided that habitual residence means something different in child support cases than in other areas of law (for example, divorce, child abduction, income support). Unless other commissioners or courts disagree, caselaw from other areas of law will be of only limited help. 'Ordinary residence' has a similar meaning to 'habitual residence'.[62] Ordinary residence has been defined as 'residence for a settled purpose'.[63] Caselaw on ordinary residence may help to decide if a person is 'habitually resident' for child support.

While each case is different and a decision has to take into account all of the person's circumstances and intentions, some of the most important factors to consider are:

- the length, continuity and purpose of residence in the UK;
- the length and purpose of any absence from the UK; *and*
- the whereabouts of the person's possessions, family and work.

The caselaw also gives the following guidelines:

- a person can be habitually resident in more than one country or in none;[64]
- habitual residence can continue during an absence from the UK;[65]
- a person cannot be habitually resident in the UK if s/he has never been here;
- a person who leaves the UK intending never to return to reside will stop being habitually resident in the UK on the day s/he leaves;[66]
- a person who is held in a country against her/his will may not become habitually resident there, even after long residence (but see 'Children', below);[67]
- a person who is not lawfully in the UK probably cannot be habitually resident.[68]

A person returning to the UK after an absence may have remained habitually resident in the UK during her/his absence.[69] A child support commissioner has said that, when deciding whether a person has ceased to be habitually resident in the UK for child support purposes, the emphasis is on the nature and degree of past and continuing connections with the UK and intentions for the future. An absent parent employed as a UK immigration official living in India for three years, and expecting to stay there for a further two, remained habitually resident in the UK for child support purposes. It is not clear whether a person who has never been or has ceased to be habitually resident in the UK can become habitually resident from the day of arrival. A person coming to the UK to live here permanently can be ordinarily resident on the day of arrival – see, for example, *Macrae v Macrae*.[70] In *re J*,[71] the House of Lords decided that a mother returning from Australia to live permanently in the UK ceased to be habitually resident in Australia on the day that she left. The court also commented that such a person does not become habitually resident in the UK on the day of arrival, but that comment was not part of the court's reasons for its decision, nor was the court told about the caselaw on that situation.

Children

For a child, habitual residence depends on where the parent or person with parental responsibility lives. Where there are two such people who live apart, a parent should get the consent of the other parent to a change in the residence of the child, otherwise the child may be considered to have been abducted. Where there is only one person with parental responsibility the child's residence changes with that of this person.[72]

If a child has been abducted, s/he is still considered to be resident with the person s/he lives with lawfully, unless that person agrees to the change.[73] Agreement might be assumed if that person takes no action.[74] However, where an abducted child is of sufficient maturity, her/his views may prevail in a child abduction case.[75]

Guidance to CSOs

CSO guidance refers to caselaw on habitual and ordinary residence. It is crucial to argue each case on the facts. The following guidance indicates only how decisions may be made in practice.

CSOs are advised not to accept an absence of more than 12 months as temporary unless there are special circumstances causing a delay and a reasonable prospect of the absence ending.[76] Equally, a person visiting the UK from a new home abroad will not be treated as habitually resident here.[77]

CSOs are advised to consider the following factors:[78]

- the length and purpose of any absence;
- the person's intentions on leaving;
- time spent at each place (if there is more than one house);
- the location and nature of employment;
- the location of and contact with family; *and*
- number of visits to the UK.

The official guidance warns CSOs against answering hypothetical questions from someone about her/his habitual residence should s/he leave the UK,[79] but reminds them of their powers to cancel a maintenance assessment in advance. This would apply where a person plans to leave the country permanently on a certain date.[80] No special rules apply to members of the armed forces,[81] but CSOs are advised to treat Royal Navy vessels as UK territory.[82]

According to CSO guidance, the following list of people are likely to be habitually resident:[83]

- someone who has been abroad for less than three years and has now returned to the UK;
- someone working abroad for a fixed period – eg, au pairs, teachers on a year's exchange, seasonal workers or someone on a fixed-term contract (provided they return to the UK afterwards);
- someone working abroad who frequently returns, especially if they have a home in the UK;
- someone who, prior to working abroad, has always lived in the UK and is likely to return;
- someone originally from abroad who has lived in the UK for some years and is returning to their country of origin for a limited stay.

In the same guidance the following are given as examples of people not likely to be habitually resident:

- someone who has lived in the UK for a few years before moving abroad who has no definite plans to return;
- someone going to live abroad in a country where they have family ties;
- someone who buys or leases a house abroad on a long-term basis;
- someone working abroad under a series of fixed-term contracts who has rarely, or never, returned to the UK.

Although informative, this guidance should be treated with caution as it is not a statement of the law.

If the CSO decides that a case is outside her/his jurisdiction, this decision is subject to review and appeal (see Chapter 16).

7. FAMILY

A **family** is defined as a **married** or **unmarried couple** or a single person where at least one member of the couple, or a single person, has day-to-day care (see p44) of any child(ren) living with them.[84] 'Married couple' means a man and a woman married to each other and living in the same household (see p45). It includes polygamous marriages. 'Unmarried couple' means a man and woman who are living together as husband and wife. This is not defined but there is much social security caselaw which will be persuasive (see CPAG's *National Welfare Benefits Handbook*). The children living with a couple or lone parent do not have to be biological or adoptive children to count as family members. Foster children are not included. A person under 16 cannot be a member of a married or unmarried couple.[85]

For child support purposes, lesbian or gay partners do not count as a couple. A lesbian or gay man caring for a child will be treated as a lone parent family, even if s/he has a partner.

The definition of family is important for the formula. The needs of any children of an absent parent's family are taken into account in the formula when housing costs are assessed in exempt income and at the protected income stage. The latter calculation ensures that the payment of child maintenance does not reduce the income of this family below a certain level. This is the most significant point at which step-children are taken into account under the formula.

In practice, child support legislation considers a person to be part of a unit because of whom s/he *used* to be in a family with, rather than whom s/he now lives with (see figure 3.1). Child support legislation keeps these family ties through a financial commitment to child maintenance.

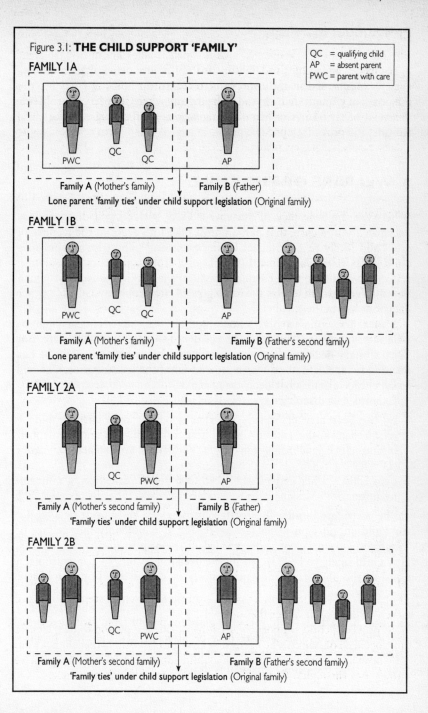

Figure 3.1: **THE CHILD SUPPORT 'FAMILY'**

QC = qualifying child
AP = absent parent
PWC = parent with care

FAMILY 1A

PWC   QC   QC   AP

Family A (Mother's family)   Family B (Father)
Lone parent 'family ties' under child support legislation (Original family)

FAMILY 1B

PWC   QC   QC   AP

Family A (Mother's family)   Family B (Father's second family)
Lone parent 'family ties' under child support legislation (Original family)

FAMILY 2A

QC   PWC   AP

Family A (Mother's second family)   Family B (Father)
'Family ties' under child support legislation (Original family)

FAMILY 2B

QC   PWC   AP

Family A (Mother's second family)   Family B (Father's second family)
'Family ties' under child support legislation (Original family)

Polygamous marriages

The child support scheme contains no special rules about how to treat polygamous marriages for liability for child support. Polygamy, however, is mentioned in the context of dividing up housing costs for the purposes of exempt income under the formula (see Chapter 9). Problems are most likely to arise when deciding who is an absent parent for child support purposes (see p45).

8. WELFARE OF THE CHILD

Whenever the Secretary of State or a CSO is making a discretionary decision about a case, that person must take into account the welfare of any child likely to be affected by the decision.[86] This also applies to a child support appeal tribunal (CSAT) or a child support commissioner, but only where the CSAT or commissioner is making a decision which could have been made by the Secretary of State or the CSO (for other decisions see below).

Many decisions involve choosing between alternatives, such as whether a person is habitually resident or not, but these are not discretionary decisions. A person has a discretion only if, once s/he has decided what the facts of a case are and what the law requires, s/he still has a choice about what decision to make.

Examples of discretionary decisions are:

- by the Secretary of State – whether a parent with care should be required to authorise the CSA to act; collection and enforcement of maintenance, including making a deduction from earnings order (DEO);
- by a CSO – whether to make a reduced benefit direction, an interim maintenance assessment or to carry out certain types of reviews.

To be considered under this welfare principle, a child must be a 'child' for child support purposes (see p41). But it is not only the welfare of 'qualifying children' or those named in the application which counts. Any child likely to be affected by the decision counts[87] – for example, a child of the absent parent's new family or one with whom the absent parent has contact.

'Welfare' includes the child's physical, mental and social welfare. For example, if a DEO would prevent an absent parent from visiting a child, that child's emotional welfare may be affected. On the other hand, a DEO may mean the parent with care has more money coming in, which may improve the child's physical welfare.

In the case of a reduced benefit diretion, where there is no risk of harm or undue distress (see p90), the welfare of the children will override the normal approach of making a direction only if there is a special factor – for example, the age or health of a child or the parent with care.[88]

The 1991 Act describes the welfare of children as 'a general principle'.[89] The High Court has said that considerable weight should be given to the welfare principle.[90] However, because there is usually no discretion about whether to make an assessment, nor about the amount of that assessment, there are only a limited number of cases in which the principle may make a difference.

CSA guidance reminds CSOs and the Secretary of State to consider the welfare of any children likely to be affected when making any discretionary decision.[91] CSA staff ought to treat the 'welfare principle' as an important part of every discretionary decision, but usually do not. Because of criticism from CPAG and others, detailed guidance on welfare of the child has been issued.[92] However, this does not advise staff on the factors to be considered but instead emphasises cases involving sick and disabled children.

The CSA normally limits its enquiries to information necessary to identify the absent parent, establish jurisdiction, collect payments and make the assessment. There is no systematic collection of evidence about the welfare of children likely to be affected.

For these reasons it is important that the CSA is given full details at the earliest stage about the effect a decision may have on a child's welfare. Where a decision has been made in ignorance of its effect on a child, the CSA should be asked to reconsider.

Although CSA staff usually claim that the welfare of the child has been considered when a discretionary decision was made, proper reasons explaining how it was taken into account are not given. Challenges to such decisions should be considered (see p351). CPAG would be interested to hear from any advisers taking such cases.

Where a CSAT or a child support commissioner makes a discretionary decision which a CSO or the Secretary of State could not take (for example, whether to adjourn a hearing) consideration must still be given to the welfare of any children likely to be affected. This is because it would be relevant to the discretion under normal legal principles.[93]

CHAPTER FOUR

Applications

This chapter covers:
1. Who can apply to the CSA (see below)
2. How to apply (see p57)
3. The maintenance application form (p61)
4. Withdrawing an application (p69)
5. Cancelling an application (p74)
6. Multiple applications (p76)

The Child Support Agency (CSA) cannot make a child maintenance assessment until an effective application has been made.

1. WHO CAN APPLY TO THE CSA

Almost anyone who is a person with care (see p43) or an absent parent (see p45) can make a child maintenance application to the CSA unless barred by an existing maintenance arrangement (see below).[1] Remember an institution or organisation, other than a local authority, can be a person with care.[2] In Scotland, children who are aged 12 or over can apply for a maintenance assessment under section 7 of the 1991 Act, provided no application has been made by the person with care or the absent parent.[3]

Parents with care who are on income support (IS), family credit (FC) or disability working allowance (DWA), or someone else who claims one of these benefits for them, *must* authorise the Secretary of State to assess and recover maintenance from the absent parent, unless they are exempt or accept the benefit penalty (see Chapter 5).[4] These applications are required under section 6 of the 1991 Act and therefore in this *Handbook* are known as section 6 applicants. The CSA tends to call them compulsory applications. Despite the fact that the CSA has now been operational for three years, not all existing IS claimants have yet been required to make an application (see p32). This requirement to co-operate is to be extended to parents with care claiming means-tested jobseeker's allowance from October 1996. See p75 for the position regarding fraudulent benefit claims.

Neither an absent parent nor another person with care can make an application for child maintenance where the parent with care or her partner is receiving IS/FC/DWA.[5] Therefore if the parent with care refuses to apply (see p101), this cannot be overturned by anyone else.

Where the parent with care is not on IS/FC/DWA or where the person with care is not the parent of the qualifying child, the application under section 4 of the 1991 Act is entirely voluntary. Such applicants tend to be called private clients or voluntary applicants by the CSA; however in this *Handbook* we refer to them as section 4 applicants. People within this group can opt to negotiate a voluntary maintenance agreement and even to apply to court for a consent order (see p35) instead of using the CSA. These agreements cannot include a provision preventing an application to the CSA at a later date,[6] although some solicitors are including contingency provisions which would take effect on a subsequent CSA application. It can be a difficult to know whether applying to the CSA is the better solution; parents should request that their solicitors calculate the amount due under the CSA formula in order to make the most informed decision. It should not be assumed that a CSA assessment will always be greater than a negotiated agreement.

On the other hand, a parent with care subject to the requirement to co-operate with the CSA can also continue with a voluntary arrangement, but only at the risk of a benefit penalty.

Where there is more than one person with the care of a qualifying child and at least one, but not all, of them has parental responsibility for the child, only those persons with parental responsibility (or parental rights in Scotland) can apply for maintenance.[7] For example, where a child is cared for partly by her/his mother who has parental responsibility, and partly by her/his grandmother, who does not have parental responsibility, only the mother can apply to the CSA. **Parental responsibility** has the same meaning as in the Children Act 1989. Parents who were married to each other when the child was born automatically have parental responsibility; this continues even after they divorce. There is also a formal procedure to acquire such parental rights by agreement – eg, between unmarried parents. In Scotland, **parental rights** are as defined in the Law Reform (Parent and Child) (Scotland) Act 1986.

An existing maintenance arrangement

An existing maintenance agreement – whether written or unwritten – does not prevent a section 6 application being required when a parent with care makes a claim for IS/FC/DWA.[8] A CSA assessment will override any pre-existing child maintenance agreement, including a court order (see p36). However, such an assessment may be phased-in in stages in order to give the absent parent time to adjust to the increase (see p300).

Access to the CSA is denied, however, to those parents with care not in receipt of IS/FC/DWA where a written maintenance agreement made before 5 April 1993 or a court order for maintenance is in force in respect of the absent parent and the qualifying child(ren).[9] This bar also applies to persons with care who are not parents of the qualifying child, whether or not they are in receipt of benefit.

Where a court decides that it does not have the power to either vary or enforce an order, an application can be made to the CSA after 22 January 1996.[10] A court order will not be considered to be in force where it has no bearing on the financial relationship between the person with care and the absent parent and could no longer be enforced by the court – for example, where the children now live with the formerly absent parent.[11] There is a long list of the different types of court order which prevent an application being made under sections 4 or 7.[12] This does not include a court order made to cover education or training, costs of a child's disability or a top-up to a maximum CSA assessment (see p37).

Therefore, in order to obtain an increased level of maintenance, a person with care prevented from applying to the CSA has to return to court to have the order varied (see p33).[13] Alternatively, if she is convinced that she would obtain a better deal from the CSA, she can try to gain access to the CSA by one of two routes, but both are unlikely to succeed. First, she can apply to have the order revoked by the court. Although one publicised attempt to have an order revoked in order to gain access to the CSA failed,[14] we understand that a minority of such applications have proved successful. An order would certainly be revoked where the person with care has changed; however such an order should not prevent an application in the first place.[15]

Second, if a claim is made for IS/FC/DWA, then a parent with care will be required to co-operate with the CSA irrespective of the written maintenance agreement or court order. However, if benefit is refused before a CSA assessment is made, then the application will be cancelled where such a court order or pre-April 1993 written maintenance agreement exists (see p74).[16] Where an absent parent believes that the parent with care has made a benefit claim entirely in order to obtain access to the CSA, it could be to his advantage not to co-operate with the CSA until the benefit claim has been determined; he may want to notify the CSA of his reasons for not co-operating.

The Government has announced that this group of persons with care not entitled to a CSA assessment will in future be given access to the collection and enforcement service of the CSA for their existing agreements and court orders, [17] but no date has been set for this.

2. HOW TO APPLY

Applications to the CSA should be made on a maintenance application form (MAF). [18] See p61 for details of how to fill one in.

Parents with care who make a claim – or whose partner makes a claim – for IS/FC/DWA are sent a letter, known as 'the declaration letter' (see p84), about applying to the CSA. The declaration letter is the beginning of the requirement to co-operate procedure and is used to establish whether the parent with care is exempt from applying (see p83).

It is Benefits Agency staff who are responsible for identifying new cases where there may be a qualifying child for CSA purposes. Claim forms for IS include a question about whether a parent of any child being claimed for is living elsewhere. This enables officers to identify qualifying children living in two parent families. Field officers are reminded not to assume that a child has an absent parent just because s/he has a different name from the parents s/he lives with.[19] Staff receive training to familiarise themselves with the naming systems of the different ethnic and religious groups.

However, if this declaration letter is delayed, as has sometimes been the case, the parent with care can contact the CSA herself and request a MAF if she wishes to speed up the application. Any delay by the CSA does not delay the benefit claim, but it does delay the date from which maintenance will be payable.

A person with care who is not the parent of the qualifying child is also contacted after making a claim for IS/FC/DWA, but should receive a different letter from parents with care making it clear that any application is entirely voluntary. Again if this is not received or if she is not claiming benefit, and she wishes to make an application, she can contact the CSA.

A parent with care not claiming IS/FC/DWA or an absent parent should contact the CSA for a MAF when wishing to make an application.

Anyone wanting a MAF should contact her field office (see p21) by telephone or in writing. If she does not know the field office address, this can be obtained from the enquiry line or the CSAC local rate line (see Appendix 1). The field officer should register the issue of the MAF on the child support computer system. If a MAF does not arrive within 10 days, this should be followed up with the field office, and a further delay may warrant a complaint (see p28).

If a CSA officer refuses over the telephone to issue a MAF – for example because there appears to be an existing maintenance agreement which would prevent a section 4 application – the person with care should follow this up in writing, giving details as to why she believes she is entitled to make an application and asking for a child support officer's decision (see p295).

When to apply

There are no time limits within which CSA applications have to be made. An application can be made as soon as someone becomes a person with care or an absent parent, or at any later date. However, there is almost no provision for backdating assessments (see p305). If the absent parent co-operates, his liability will usually begin eight weeks after he is sent a maintenance enquiry form by the CSA. There is also no provision to allow applications in advance – for example, before the birth of a baby.

Any parent with care on IS since April 1993 who has not yet been contacted by the CSA but who wishes to apply can do so at the discretion of the Secretary of State. She cannot make a voluntary application under section 4,[20] but the CSA has agreed to take such cases on under section 6 at the request of the parent with care.[21] If such a request is refused, a complaint should be made (see p28).

Returning the form

There are no specific legal time limits for returning the MAF. However, a section 6 applicant must provide authorisation without unreasonable delay.[22] Guidance to staff suggests that usually parents with care will be expected to make an application as soon as the MAF is received, but that there are exceptions, for example, where the parent with care is sick or away from home.[23] In practice, applicants are requested to return the MAF in 14 days.[24] See p103 for the procedures used if this has not occurred. If a parent with care wishes to make an application, but requires more than 14 days to complete the form, she should notify the CSA of this, giving reasons for the delay.

MAFs should be sent to the field office which covers the area in which the person with care lives. However, forms sent to a CSAC should be passed to the field office to be processed. When a form is returned by post to the CSA, the Secretary of State treats it as having been sent on the day s/he receives it but has discretion to backdate the date of receipt if there was unavoidable delay.[25] The date of the application is not usually important in itself, as liability for child maintenance does not begin until after the absent parent has been contacted (see below).

Effective applications

Only an effective application can lead to an assessment of maintenance. An application is effective only if it is made on a MAF which has been fully completed according to the instructions.[26] All applicants are under a duty to provide information to enable the absent parent to be traced and the amount of child maintenance payable by him to be assessed and recovered (see Chapter 6). If a section 6 applicant does not provide the information, she may suffer a benefit penalty (see p112). If a section 4 or 7 applicant does not supply the information, the application may be refused as ineffective (see also pp60 and 74).

Applications which are not effective are returned to the applicant by the Secretary of State, or a new form is sent out to be completed properly. Alternatively, a request for further information or evidence is sent. When a properly completed form is received within 14 days, it takes effect from the date the earlier application was treated as received by the CSA (see p77).[27]

Once an effective application has been made by an applicant, any other relevant person (absent parent or person with care) is informed that an application has been received and is sent a maintenance enquiry form (see p133).[28]

In theory, once the effective application is made it is passed by the Secretary of State to a child support officer (CSO) to make an assessment.[29] However, in practice, the information from the other party is required and the gathering and checking of all the information necessary for an assessment to be made is done by the field office. The case is then referred to a CSO, usually at the CSAC, for an assessment.

Delays in dealing with applications

There have been delays within the CSA in dealing with some applications. At the time of writing, applicants were not given regular updates as to progress with their cases, although many agencies, including CPAG, have been lobbying for this. It is advisable in the absence of these reports that an applicant requests an update from the CSA at least once a month. It is particularly important to make sure that a maintenance enquiry form has been sent to the absent parent, as any delay results in a corresponding delay in the beginning of the absent parent's liability (see p303). A claim for compensation may be made for the loss resulting from a substantial delay by the CSA (see p30).

Assessments can, of course, be held up by non-co-operation of the absent parent, but where both parents co-operate the CSA aims to complete assessments within six to 21 weeks of issuing the MAF.[30] However, even where the absent parent is not co-operating, this does not excuse the CSA of all delay as an interim maintenance assessment (IMA) can still be made (see p296). See p23 for the targets set by the Secretary of State and p26 for information on pending applications. Although the majority of new applicants should not now have to wait six months for an assessment, there are over 50,000 applications over one year old.

If the person with care is repeatedly told by the CSA that the absent parent is causing the delay by failing to provide information, she should write to the CSAC requesting that an IMA be made. If this does not happen within the next few weeks, a complaint could be made (see p28). Absent parents who have provided the necessary information but are still awaiting an assessment likewise can make a complaint.

Many CSA clients believe that applications from benefit claimants are dealt with more quickly than those from working parents with care. This is contrary to CSA stated policy; all new cases should receive the same level of attention. If any member of CSA staff suggests otherwise, a complaint should be made (see p28).

Refusing an application

The Secretary of State should not refuse to issue a MAF or to accept a completed MAF. S/he can refuse to accept an incomplete MAF as this is not an effective application (see p59). The Secretary of State must pass an application to a CSO and the decision to refuse an effective application is for a CSO to make.[31] Where an application is refused, the applicant should be notified as soon as possible and given written reasons for the refusal. In addition, an application may be accepted as valid but then the CSO may refuse to make an assessment (see p295) – for example, one of the parties is not habitually resident in the UK (see p47). These decisions can be challenged by a second-tier review (see p358).

We are aware of a case where, against the wishes of the parent with care, the Secretary of State has refused to proceed with an application on the basis of the welfare of her children (see p52). Legal advice should be sought; neither the Secretary of State has discretion to refuse to refer the application to the CSO nor the CSO to refuse to make an assessment. This is now clearly confirmed by caselaw.[32] The Secretary of State does have discretion when deciding whether to require a parent with care to co-operate with the CSA (see p82), but once an application has been accepted as effective, it can only be cancelled against the applicant's wishes in very limited circumstances (see p74).

If more than one application is made for child maintenance for the same child(ren), only one will be accepted. See p76 for the rules about which applications will go ahead.

Change of circumstances

An application can be amended at any time before a maintenance assessment is made, but not to take into account a change which occurs after the effective date of an assessment.[33] The effective date is the date from which maintenance is due to be paid (see p303). After this date, the applicant would usually need to ask for a change of circumstances review, even though no assessment has as yet been made. A delay in requesting a change of circumstances review will result in a delay in the date from which the assessment can be altered. See p355 for information on change of circumstances reviews.

In some circumstances, applications can be withdrawn (see p69).

If a benefit claim is refused before an assessment is made, a section 6 application may be cancelled by the CSA (see p74).

3. THE MAINTENANCE APPLICATION FORM

The MAF is supplied in a 'child support maintenance application pack', which contains a copy of the form along with a statement of CSA standards, an introductory leaflet and some help-notes to explain how the form should be completed. See p59 for how to obtain a MAF and p58 for returning the form.

Figure 4.1: **APPLICATIONS**

Who can apply	Type of application	Form
No benefit claim by the person with care:		
Parent with care	section 4 application	MAF CSA1
Other person with care	section 4 application	MAF CSA1
Absent parent	section 4 application	MAF CSA1(AP)
Child 12 and over (Scotland only)	section 7 application	MAF CSA1(CIS)
IS claimed by the person with care:		
Parent with care	section 6 application	MAF CSA1(IS)
Other person with care	section 4 application	MAF CSA1
Child 12 and over (Scotland only)	section 7 application	MAF CSA1(CIS)
FC/DWA claimed by the person with care:		
Parent with care	section 6 application	MAF CSA1
Other person with care	section 4 application	MAF CSA1
Child 12 and over (Scotland only)	section 7 application	MAF CSA1(CIS)

There are four types of MAF: CSA1(IS) for parents with care on IS; CSA1 for persons with care who are not on IS, or who are not parents; CSA1(CIS) for child applicants in Scotland; and CSA1(AP) for absent parents making an application.

The MAF can serve three functions:

- giving the Secretary of State the authority to pursue the absent parent for child maintenance;
- providing the details necessary for the CSA to pursue the absent parent; *and*
- authorising a representative to act on the applicant's behalf.

We deal with each of these in turn.

Providing authorisation

At the end of the MAF the applicant is asked to sign the following declaration:

- *'I declare that the information I have given on this form is correct and complete.'*
- *'I authorise the Secretary of State to act on my behalf in accordance with the Child Support Act.'*
- *'This is my application for a child maintenance assessment.'*

There is space for only one signature to confirm all three parts of this declaration.

By signing this declaration on the MAF, the person with care is giving her authorisation to the Secretary of State to pursue the absent parent(s) for child maintenance. In other words she is making an application to the CSA for child maintenance. This can be difficult to withdraw if the parent with care is a section 6 applicant (see p70). Therefore *it is important that a parent with care on IS/FC/DWA does not sign the form until she is certain that she wants to apply for child maintenance.* If she has any doubts, it is crucial that she seeks independent advice before completing the MAF.

If the person with care has provided some information on the form but wishes to withhold her authorisation, she should not sign the declaration simply to confirm the information. Even where a person with care has made it clear on another part of the MAF that she does not want to apply for child maintenance, her signing of the declaration has been taken as authorisation by the CSA; this should be challenged.

If different children of the person with care have different absent fathers and the person with care only wishes to apply for child maintenance from one of them, in order to avoid confusion, she should include only the details of the absent parent from whom she is applying.

Otherwise the declaration will be taken to apply to both of them. In the other details box she should state that she is not applying for maintenance from the second absent parent and refer to a covering letter where she makes her application for exemption from the requirement to co-operate.

Some parents with care believe that it is by withholding the name or other details of the absent parent that she will avoid the CSA pursuing him. However, she needs to be warned that if she signs the MAF without this information the CSA will interview her about the details and, more importantly, that should the CSA obtain the information from another source (see p127) – eg, the Benefits Agency – the Secretary of State then has her authority to pursue the absent parent. It is only by withholding her signature on the MAF that the parent with care can be sure of preventing the CSA from taking action to pursue the absent parent.

Applying for exemption

A parent with care should already have had an opportunity when sent the declaration letter (see p84) to provide details of any risk of harm or undue distress (see p90) which may result from an application to the CSA. If she gave reasons at that stage, she should not be sent a MAF at all while the CSA considers her application for exemption from the requirement to co-operate. However, even if she did not respond to the declaration letter or at that stage signed that she was happy to apply to the CSA, this does not prevent her refusing to authorise the Secretary of State on the MAF nor seeking exemption on the grounds of harm or undue distress.

She can provide the information about the risk in a separate letter, ignoring the MAF completely; this is usually preferable as it minimises the possibility of confusion and avoids providing authorisation inadvertently. It also protects the information from being included automatically in appeal papers should she later give her authorisation for the Secretary of State to pursue the absent parent and she or the absent parent appeals to a tribunal on a different issue.

However, if she uses the MAF and its space for additional information to apply for exemption from the requirement to co-operate, she *must not* sign the declaration at the end of the form. If a parent with care has already provided this authorisation and her application for exemption is refused, the CSA is then able to process her application for child maintenance and she is without a right of appeal to a tribunal. She should take legal advice about the possibility of a judicial review (see p351).

If a parent with care has completed and signed the MAF she can at a later date apply to withdraw the application (see p72).

Information for parents with care

Despite the fact that there is a legal requirement that the MAF should indicate in general terms the effect of completing and returning it,[34] it does not indicate the full effect of signing for section 6 applicants. There is no section about harm or undue distress on the MAF itself, but only in the help-notes and introductory leaflet and then only briefly. Applicants are referred to the relevant section of the help-notes on the front page of the MAF, but not at the back by the declaration. CPAG would like to see two signatures on the form, with authorisation being given on the front page and information being confirmed on the back. Please let CPAG know of any cases where parents with care were unaware of the implications of signing or refusing to sign the declaration on the MAF or, despite the preliminary declaration letter, the existence of the harm or undue exemption.

Information asked for on the form

Where any application for a maintenance assessment is being made, the applicant has to provide the Secretary of State or child support officer (CSO), so far as she reasonably can, with the information required to enable:[35]

- the absent parent to be traced if necessary;
- the amount of maintenance payable by the absent parent to be assessed; *and*
- the amount to be recovered from the absent parent.

Where the application is under section 7, the requirement to provide information applies to the person with care of the child and the absent parent, as well as to the child who made the application.[36]

For more about the information a person can be required to give according to the law, see pp125–7.

A section 6 applicant who fails to comply with the requirement to give information faces a reduction in her benefit, unless she is exempt (see p83).[37] However, a benefit claimant who is using the MAF to apply for exemption from the requirement to co-operate does not have to complete the full form and must be very careful not to provide authorisation by signing the declaration (see above).

The CSA stresses the confidentiality of its service and that it acts as 'a buffer' between the two parties. In the first instance, only certain information can be passed to the other party (see p157). However, persons with care completing a MAF must be warned that a photocopy of the MAF is routinely included in appeal papers should either party end up appealing to a child support appeal tribunal (see p367). These papers are sent to all parties to the assessment and therefore the absent parent will see the information provided by the person with care on the MAF. If there is information which a person with care believes is relevant to the application but which is liable to provoke the absent parent, this can be included on a separate sheet with a proviso that it should not be disclosed to him even at appeal. However, even this is not a guarantee of confidentiality at the appeal stage. It should be noted that information as to the reasons for a relationship breakdown are not relevant to a CSA assessment. Any information the CSA receives can be passed on to the Benefits Agency.

The information requested on the MAF CSA1 is set out below. The MAF for people on IS does not include the income and housing details sections. This is because this information is not needed for the formula, as IS claimants are assumed to have no assessable income (see p202).

The MAF is being redesigned from April 1996, but the information requested remains largely the same.

Section one: person with care's details

The first section asks for the following details of the applicant:

- her name and that of her partner, or any other names they are known by;
- their sex;
- their dates of birth;
- their national insurance numbers;
- her address and telephone number(s);
- whether she or her partner is registered blind and whether anyone gets invalid care allowance, disability living allowance or attendance allowance for her or her partner;
- whether there are other people aged 18 or over living in the household;
- whether she has a child or children by her new partner who lives with her;
- her marital status;
- whether she has applied to the courts for maintenance and been told to apply to the CSA.

This section also asks about use of **CSA services**:

- whether or not the applicant wishes to use the CSA collection service.

The form also asks for the following details **for each child under 19** who lives with her (the form has space for four children):

- her/his full name;
- her/his date of birth;
- her/his national insurance number (if over 16);

- her/his sex;
- her/his mother and father's full names;
- whether s/he is applying for child maintenance for this child;
- whether any other person has received child maintenance for the child within the last eight weeks;
- whether or not child benefit is in payment, and how much;
- whether the child is in full-time education;
- whether or not the child is or has ever been married;
- whether the child is registered blind or gets disability living allowance or attendance allowance;
- whether the child ever stays overnight with someone else and, if so, with whom and how often;
- whether a local authority has part-time care;
- whether s/he has any other children under 19 living with her/him (another form will be sent for details of these other children).

Absent parent's details
The form asks for the following details of the absent parent. If a section 6 applicant returns the form with this part incomplete, the CSA will request an interview to find out the reasons for her failure to complete it (for more details, see p104). The details are:

- whether the applicant wants child maintenance from more than two absent parents (the form only has space for two, so a further form would be necessary);
- his name and any other names he is or has been known by;
- his sex;
- his date of birth or age;
- his national insurance number;
- his address (present or last known address), the date he last lived at this address and telephone number;
- the names of all the children the applicant is applying to get child maintenance for from this absent parent;
- whether the absent parent was registered as the parent of these children;
- whether the absent parent knows that he is considered to be a parent of all of these children;
- whether the absent parent knows the person with care's address;
- if employed, the name, address and telephone number of any employer, and any work number, department or job title;
- if self-employed, name, address and telephone number of his business, and type of business;
- whether the absent parent is unemployed and what social security benefits, if any, he is or may be claiming;
- any other information which might help trace the absent parent;

- whether there is a court order for child maintenance and, if so, whether it covers all the children she is applying for;
- whether there is any other written voluntary or informal child maintenance arrangement with the absent parent, whether it covers all the children applied for, when it was made, the amount and how often it is paid;
- whether there has been a transfer of property or capital.

To avoid confusion, if there are two absent parents and the person with care only wishes to pursue one for maintenance, the details of the other should be omitted. However, it is advisable for section 6 applicants to enclose a covering letter explaining why they are not co-operating as regards the second absent parent in order to avoid the benefit penalty (see p112).

Section two: income details

The second section of the MAF CSA1 asks for the following information about the applicant's income details. Certain applicants are referred straight to the 'Other details' and 'Declaration' sections of the form at this point. This applies to anyone who is getting IS or who is not a natural or adoptive parent of any of the children covered by the application. The details requested from all other applicants are:

- student income, grants, loans, parental contribution and any other income;
- details of self-employment – eg, whether childminder, sole trader, sub-contractor, or partner in a business;
- whether employed or on Youth Training (if more than one employer a separate form is sent);
- employer's name, address and telephone number, work number, department or job title;
- whether the applicant works at more than one address;
- details of any travel-to-work costs and the number of round trips to work each week;
- whether the applicant works shifts or irregular hours;
- gross pay before deductions, how often paid and whether the amount on the wage slips is different from normal gross earnings (eg, due to arrears or overtime); the CSO can ask for proof of earnings for any period in the eight weeks before the relevant week (see p205) up to the date of the assessment;
- details of any bonus, commission or expenses, and whether included on the wage slips provided;
- details of any personal, company or occupational pension scheme and how it is paid;

- benefit income (except for child benefit, housing benefit and council tax benefit), how much, who it is paid to and by which office;
- benefits received by any of the children living with her;
- income from maintenance for herself (spousal maintenance) in the last 13 weeks, who from, the amount and details of any court order, voluntary or informal agreement;
- income from savings, capital or investments in the last 52 weeks, and whether derived from divorce or separation;
- child(ren)'s income from maintenance, capital or investments in the last 52 weeks;
- income from rent;
- income from board and lodging;
- other income received in the past 26 weeks.

Section three: housing details

The third section of the MAF CSA1 asks for the following housing details:

- whether the applicant or her partner lives with relatives or friends (if this is the case the applicant is directed to the section for 'Other details');
- rent and housing benefit;
- whether the tenancy is shared with anyone else;
- board and lodging payments and housing benefit;
- details of home ownership and mortgage/loan, ground rent, feu duty and service charge details;
- second mortgage or loan details;
- endowment policy details;
- whether the applicant or her partner lives in residential accommodation, a residential care home or nursing home.

A separate form is provided to send to a building society, bank or other mortgage lender for them to verify details of any mortgage or loan.

Other details

The following payment details are requested:

- whether she has any objections to being paid direct by the absent parent and for what reason;
- how she would prefer to be paid and how often;
- bank/building society account details for credit transfers;
- post office details for girocheque payment;
- whether she has her own letter box or a shared letter box.

A section is then provided for details of any representative or other person acting on behalf of the applicant (see below).

The form ends with a checklist for documents enclosed, a box in which to provide any further information, and the declaration for the person with care to sign (see p62). She must be clear that by signing the MAF she is not just confirming that the information provided is true but she is applying for child maintenance (see p86).

On the final page there is a section used by interviewing officers who have filled out the MAF on behalf of an applicant. The entries are read back to the interviewee who is asked to confirm the details as correct, by signing.

Authorising a representative

Anyone who applies can authorise a representative to act on her/his behalf, either on the form or separately in writing.[38] The representative does not have to be legally qualified. Written confirmation is not essential for legal representatives, but is required for lay representatives.[39] The authorised representative can both apply and provide information to the CSA and s/he will receive all correspondence from the CSA on behalf of the applicant, but payments of child maintenance will be sent to the applicant unless specifically requested otherwise.[40]

Other representatives are entitled to act in place of the applicant in every respect – they are: a person with power of attorney, a receiver, a Scottish mental health custodian or mental health appointee.[41] No authorisation is required and they will receive payments as well as correspondence.

4. WITHDRAWING AN APPLICATION

In this section we cover requests by applicants to withdraw their applications, as opposed to the situation where the CSO cancels the application without a request from the applicant (see p74).

It is far more straightforward to withdraw a section 4 application than a section 6 application.

Withdrawing a voluntary application

Where a section 4 or section 7 application has been made, the applicant can request that the Secretary of State stop acting on her behalf at any time.[42] The Secretary of State cannot refuse this request.[43] This applies whether or not an assessment has been made. If an assessment has been made, the applicant should specifically ask for the assessment to be cancelled as well as requesting that the CSA stop acting on her behalf.[44] (For more on cancelling assessments see p307.)

Where an application has been made by a child in Scotland, only s/he can cancel an application in this way, not the person with care.[45] Neither an absent parent nor a person with care can request that an application – nor the resulting assessment – be cancelled unless s/he is the applicant.

Withdrawing a section 6 application

If the parent on IS/FC/DWA has co-operated with the CSA but subsequently changes her mind, she is still subject to the requirement to give authorisation and is unable to withdraw her application simply because she requests it. This applies to all parents with care who have signed the MAF. If a parent has signed the MAF inadvertently or when unaware of the option of the benefit penalty (see p102), and thus wishes to withdraw authorisation, let CPAG know as we are hoping to challenge this. We are still lobbying to improve information to claimants who prefer not to apply.

The application can be withdrawn by a parent with care *only* if:[46]

- she is no longer the parent with care of a qualifying child; *or*
- IS, FC or DWA is no longer claimed by or for her, or paid to or for her; *or*
- the Secretary of State no longer requires her to give authorisation as she is exempt from this requirement on the grounds of harm or undue distress (see p90) or the Secretary of State withdraws the requirement to co-operate for some other reason – eg, if the welfare of any child is likely to be affected (see p52).[47] In fact, the Secretary of State has discretion about whom to require to co-operate and therefore in theory could cease to require a parent to co-operate on grounds other than harm or undue distress or welfare of the child. However, in practice, other grounds are very unlikely to be accepted.

As a parent with care makes an application by giving the Secretary of State authorisation to pursue maintenance, when withdrawing the application she is in effect seeking to withdraw her authorisation. However, the CSA states that a parent cannot 'withdraw her authorisation',[48] and that instead the Secretary of State is 'withdrawing the requirement to co-operate'; in other words, it is the Secretary of State's decision and not just at the request of the parent with care. This difference in wording has caused confusion and led some parents with care to believe that there is no way of withdrawing an application or cancelling an assessment. Parents with care should not let such advice from CSA staff put them off making a request to withdraw their authorisation/application.

Legally, a section 6 applicant who seeks to withdraw her application/authorisation is in fact asking the Secretary of State not to require her to co-operate under section 6(2) of the 1991 Act and to cease acting on her behalf under section 6(11). It could be helpful to quote this in the request to withdraw. This applies both before and after any assessment has been made. However, for simplicity's sake, we continue to use the phrase 'withdraw an application'.

A parent with care can make a request to withdraw the application for one of the three reasons above.[49] It should be made in writing to the field office, with a copy sent to the CSAC (see p19) if an assessment has already been made. If one of these reasons applies to her, the Secretary of State must stop taking any action.[50] As well as asking to withdraw the application, the parent with care also has to ask the CSO to cancel any maintenance assessment which has been made (see p307).[51] On any future claim for one of these benefits, she would have a further opportunity to make a decision about whether or not to give authorisation.

No longer parent with care of a qualifying child

A person may stop being the parent with care of a qualifying child (see p41) for a number of reasons. For example, the child may:

- leave school or become too old to count as a child;
- no longer qualify because her/his parents start living together;
- go to live with someone else and as a result the parent no longer counts as a person with care; *or*
- be adopted, in which case a person could cease to be the lawful parent.

Someone in this situation can withdraw an application in the same way as a section 4 or section 7 applicant (see p69). In most of these situations an assessment can be terminated without a request (see p309).

Withdrawal when benefit claim ends

If at any time a parent with care ceases to be covered by a claim for IS, FC, or DWA, then she has the same right to withdraw a maintenance application as other applicants who are not on benefit – ie, section 4 or 7 applicants. In addition, the CSA can now cancel an application in these circumstances where an assessment has not yet been made unless the parent with care states that she wishes it to continue (see p174).

A benefit award may end where the parent with care starts to receive too much income to be entitled to benefit (eg, increased earnings, the receipt of large amounts of child maintenance), begins a cohabiting relationship, or simply sends back her IS order book.

If an assessment has been made and the parent with care then comes off benefit, the absent parent will still be liable to pay the maintenance assessed unless the parent with care specifically asks the Secretary of State to stop acting on her behalf. In these circumstances the parent with care needs to ask the Secretary of State to stop acting on her behalf and to cancel the assessment (see p307) if she wishes this to happen. It will not occur automatically; the assessment remains in force until it is reviewed or cancelled.

Although in theory it is only possible to withdraw a benefit claim once entitlement has been confirmed if a claimant ceases to satisfy one of the conditions of entitlement, in practice the Benefits Agency seems to accept returned order books without seeking a reason for the terminated claim. Once the IS is no longer being cashed, the parent with care can request that the CSA application be withdrawn (and the assessment, if already made, be cancelled). Once this is confirmed by the CSA, a fresh claim for IS can be made and this time authorisation withheld (see p101). The same procedure can be followed with FC/DWA, but only at the end of the six months award of benefit.

Withdrawal due to a risk of harm or undue distress

Withdrawal of a section 6 application can take place when a parent with care has given authorisation but wishes to withdraw it on the grounds that she is now – or always was – exempt (see p83).[52] CSA guidance explains that, although a parent with care has authorised action, field officers should discuss any threats of harm or undue distress with her (see p90).[53]

Officers acting for the Secretary of State are advised to treat each case on its own merits, but it is suggested that where the absent parent does not know the parent with care's address, or where there has been no history of violence, there may be little risk.[54] Field officers are also instructed to establish a link between the authorisation given by the parent with care and the threats. Her original statements and evidence will also be looked at.[55] Much of the guidance relates only to requests for withdrawal involving threats of violence following an application or assessment. However, the same rules apply to any indications of a risk of harm or undue distress highlighted after an application has been made.

Although a request to withdraw can be made to either a CSAC or a field office, it is advisable to approach the field office as decisions on harm and undue distress are made at field level.[56] The letter should include as much information as possible about the risk and the welfare of the child(ren) involved. Supporting evidence – for example, statements from other people – are not essential but can be useful. Although a decision can be made without an interview, the parent with care will usually be asked to attend one. Therefore in urgent situations it may be advisable for the parent with care to follow the written request to withdraw with a telephone call to arrange an interview. The interview procedure is similar to that carried out when a parent with care refuses to co-operate (see p104).

At the interview, the parent with care is asked to sign a statement saying: *'If the Secretary of State decides that I am not required to continue with my application, I request that the Secretary of State ceases to act on my behalf and that no further action on my application for child maintenance be taken.'*[57] If the parent with care does not attend the interview, she should be asked if she wishes to provide more details, and if the CSA accepts her reasons she is sent a form with a tear-off slip to give this signed authority that she wishes to withdraw.[58] She has seven days in which to return it. CSA guidance reminds officers that without this slip a decision to waive the requirement to co-operate may still be made, but CSA policy is to obtain signed authority from the parent with care first in all but the most exceptional cases.[59] This is thought particularly important where the risk of harm or undue distress has been reported by a third party.

Advisers may need to remind the CSA of the procedure to waive the requirement to co-operate after authorisation is given. The instructions given to field officers are not cross-referenced to the sections of the guidance on when an application can be withdrawn.[60] CPAG would be interested to hear of any cases where there are problems as we have been lobbying for improved procedures and a right of appeal.

Before a decision has been made, the CSA will continue to act on the application and assessment (if one has already been made). In view of this fact the guidance stresses the need to deal with cases urgently.[61] If any further problems are caused to the parent with care during this period, these should be reported to the officer considering the withdrawal request and to the section whose action caused the problem – eg, the debt management section. A complaint can also be made (see p28) but tactically it may be wise to concentrate on obtaining a decision on the withdrawal request before making a complaint.

Once the requirement to co-operate has been waived, as long as the parent with care asks the Secretary of State to stop acting on her behalf, CSA action ceases.[62]

If a parent wishes to continue with an application despite the risk of harm or undue distress, then the guidance instructs the Secretary of State to consider the welfare of any child likely to be affected.[63]

Challenging a decision on withdrawal

If the Secretary of State decides that there is no risk of harm or undue distress, or refuses to waive the requirement to co-operate on the grounds of the welfare of the child, then the CSA continues to act on the original authorisation to pursue maintenance. There is no independent right of appeal against the Secretary of State's decision and the parent with care does not have the option of a benefit penalty at this stage. Legal advice could be sought on the possibility of judicial review (see p351). The argument that the CSO should not have made an assessment will fail at a tribunal.[64]

The parent's MP should be asked to intervene and raise the case with first the Chief Executive and then, if necessary, the minister responsible. This should result in the CSA reconsidering the case, and as much evidence as possible as to risk should be supplied.

Once an assessment has been made, the parent could ask that the assessment be cancelled and, on receiving a written decision, ask for a second-tier review of the CSO's decision to refuse to cancel it (see p359). This may trigger the CSA to reconsider whether there are grounds for withdrawal. If this proves unsuccessful, there is a right of appeal to a child support appeal tribunal (CSAT) against the refusal to review (see p367). CPAG is happy to advise representatives taking such cases to CSATs; they do involve complicated legal arguments.

5. CANCELLING AN APPLICATION

For information on how an applicant initiates the withdrawal of an application, see p69.

According to CSA guidance, a child support officer (CSO) can deem a voluntary application to have been withdrawn if no co-operation is received from the person with care.[65] This only applies where no 'effective application' has been made (see p59) and therefore could only apply where the person with care was the applicant. Where there is an effective application a decision must be made and notified, even if it is a decision not to make an assessment (see p295). If an effective application is deemed to be withdrawn against the wish of the applicant, advice should be sought.

A section 6 application can be cancelled without a request from the parent with care if the claim for benefit is refused or withdrawn before the assessment is made.[66] This cancellation can in fact only be carried out by the Secretary of State before the application is passed to a CSO for an assessment. CSA clients are not informed when this occurs but in some cases it can be some time before an assessment is actually made. An applicant aggrieved by such a cancellation should find out whether a CSO had become involved in the case and seek independent advice. Where there is an existing court order for child maintenance or a pre-April 1993 written maintenance agreement (see p55), the parent with care is notified that the application has been cancelled.[67] The absent parent is also notified if he had previously been contacted by the CSA and thus was aware of the application.

If there is no such existing agreement, then the parent with care will be notified by the CSA that the application will be cancelled, unless she indicates within 28 days that she wishes to continue with the application.[68]

If an assessment has already been made, this cannot be cancelled when a benefit claim is refused or an award ceases without a request from the applicant (see p307). A commissioner has recently decided that he can direct such a cancellation even though there is no express provision in the legislation.[69] If the CSA initiates such a cancellation, this should be challenged, especially in the light of the above powers to cancel applications which were only introduced on 22 January 1996.

Fraudulent benefit claims

In practice, the CSA requires all parents who claim IS/FC/DWA to apply for child maintenance (subject to the exemption – see p83) irrespective of allegations from the absent parent that the benefit claim is fraudulent. Such allegations are referred to the Benefits Agency for investigation, but do not hold up the CSA's processing of a section 6 application. However, child support commissioners have decided that the CSO, and thus a child support appeal tribunal, does need to be concerned with not just is the benefit being paid but whether it is *properly* paid.[70] This interpretation will cause practical problems for the CSA and may be further challenged. However, absent parents who want to contest an application on these grounds should see p351.

The qualifying child dies

Where a qualifying child dies before an assessment has been made, the application is treated as if it had never been made with respect to that child.[71] Any assessment made in response to the application will similarly be cancelled but only if the person with care and absent parent have not yet been notified of this assessment.

If the relevant people have already been notified of an assessment, the assessment can be reviewed (see p355), or brought to an end (see p309).

6. MULTIPLE APPLICATIONS

Where more than one application for child maintenance is made in respect of the same qualifying child, only one can go ahead.[72] If more than one person makes an application for the same child, there is an order of priority to decide which application is acted upon. Only an **effective application** (see p59) counts.[73]

The decision as to whose application goes ahead determines which applicant has the power to withdraw an application, or to request a cancellation of any resulting assessment. It does not affect the outcome of any assessment or have any effect on who is liable to pay any resulting child maintenance. Information included on any competing applications could be taken into account by a CSO.

Where the same person makes more than one application for the same child – for example, where a section 4 applicant is later required to make an application under section 6 because a claim for IS, FC or DWA has been made – usually both applications are treated as a single application (see below), unless an assessment has already been made (see p79).

The rules for which application takes priority can be divided into what happens if there is another application before a child maintenance assessment comes into force and what happens if another application is made after an assessment has been made. No section 4 application can be made at all if there is an assessment in force made in response to a section 6 application.[74]

The same rules apply when deciding the order of priority across CSA territories – ie, Northern Ireland and Great Britain.[75]

Before an assessment has been made

Where there is more than one application for an assessment to be made for the same person with care and absent parent, and no assessment has as yet been made, the applications are referred to a CSO to decide which is to have priority or whether they are to be treated as a single application.[76] If the latter applies, the application which goes ahead covers all of the children mentioned in the applications that have been made, and the effective date is decided according to which application was made first.[77]

This order of priority applies provided no request is received to withdraw all but one of the other applications.[78]

Same person applies again

If a person applies under either section 4 or section 6 and then applies again under the same section before an assessment is made, then both applications are treated as if they were the same application.[79]

If a parent with care applies under either section 4 or section 6 and then again under the other section before an assessment is made, the applications are treated as a single section 6 application.[80] This only applies where the parent with care is still required to apply under section 6.

Where more than one section 7 application is made by the same child in Scotland and maintenance has not yet been assessed, it counts as a single application so long as it is made in respect of the same absent parent and person with care.[81]

More than one applicant

Where more than one person with care has parental responsibility, there is an order of priority to decide whose application goes ahead. This depends on who is the main provider of day-to-day care.[82] The CSO first considers with whom the child spends most time and is reminded that it is the proportion of the child's time spent with each person which is relevant, not the number of nights per week.[83] If this does not determine who is the main carer, the CSO then looks at who gets child benefit.[84]

Where more than one person with care applies and each application refers to different children, then the CSO treats the priority application as the one which covers all the children mentioned in both applications.[85] Where the same person with care does not provide the principal day-to-day care for all the qualifying children mentioned in the applications, then separate assessments are made in relation to each person with care.[86]

The standard formula used to calculate child maintenance is adapted to take into account shared care (see Chapter 13). It does not necessarily follow that the parent with care who makes the application will receive the maintenance (as she may be deemed to be absent – see p269), nor that refusal of an application results in no payments (see p281 for division of the maintenance).

The CSO decides which application goes ahead according to the following criteria:[87]

APPLICANTS	PRIORITY APPLICATION
If person with care and absent parent applies.[88]	**Person with care**
Person with care or absent parent applies following an application by a child in Scotland.[89]	**Person with care/absent parent**
If there is more than one subsequent application from a person with care or an absent parent after a child has applied.[90]	**Person with care** (where there are competing applications between more than one person with care, follow the priority rules below)
Where more than one qualifying child applies under s7 in relation to the same person with care and absent parent.[91]	**Elder or eldest child**
Where both parents are absent parents and both apply.[92]	**Both treated as a single application**
If two people are to be treated as absent parents for the purposes of the formula (see p269) and both apply.[93]	**Both treated as a single application**
Where a parent with care makes a s6 application, and a person with care (with parental responsibility or parental rights) makes a s4 application with respect to the same qualifying child(ren).[94]	**Parent with care** (in fact, the other person with care is not entitled to make a s4 application where the parent with care is on IS/FC/DWA – see p55)

Priority between persons with care with parental responsibility[95]

More than one person with care with parental responsibility (or, in Scotland, parental rights) applies under s4 in respect of the same qualifying child(ren).

The application may include children not covered by the competing application, but this does not affect the order of priority.[97]

If one person is treated as an absent parent for formula purposes (see p269),[96] then the **person with care not treated as an absent parent** has priority.

Priority where more than one person with care who is not treated as an absent parent[98]

There may be cases where more than one person with care applies under s4 to cover the same qualifying child(ren) (as above), and even after one of the applicants has been deemed an absent parent under the formula, there is still more than one application. In these circumstances there is a further order of priority to decide which of the applications the CSO should proceed with. Again, this order is not affected when an application includes other children who do not appear on any competing application.

If none of the applicants has parental responsibility (or parental rights), or all do and none can be deemed an absent parent, the CSO decides who is the **principal provider of day-to-day care** in the following order of priority:[99]

- the person the child(ren) spend the most time with (decided by looking at how much time each child spends with each person); *or*
- if the time spent with each person with care is equal or the CSO cannot decide:
  - the only person with care who gets child benefit; *or*
  - the person who, in the opinion of the CSO, is the principal provider of day-to-day care.

Once the assessment is in force

Once an assessment is in force, any subsequent application for maintenance in respect of the same person with care, absent parent and qualifying child(ren) will not be dealt with (but see below) although it may, however, be treated by the Secretary of State as a request for a change of circumstances review (see p355).[100]

Section 6 application made

Any section 4 or section 7 assessment is replaced if an application is made by the person with care under section 6 and an assessment is made in response to this application.[101]

Applications for additional child(ren)

If a person with care makes an application for additional child(ren) of an absent parent when there is an existing assessment made on the request of the absent parent, a new assessment is made which replaces the existing assessment.[102] Where an absent parent makes an application for additional qualifying child(ren) cared for by the same person with care to be taken into account, any new assessment replaces the existing one.[103]

Where, in Scotland, a child has applied for a maintenance assessment and the person with care then applies under section 4 in respect of one or more children of the same absent parent in her care, then this new application replaces the original one and counts as an application for all of the children of the absent parent who are in her care.[104]

CHAPTER FIVE

The requirement to co-operate

This chapter covers:
1. Who is required to apply to the CSA (see below)
2. Harm or undue distress (p90)
3. Refusal to co-operate (p101)
4. The benefit penalty (p112)

I. WHO IS REQUIRED TO APPLY TO THE CSA

A parent with care of a qualifying child *must,* if required to do so:

• authorise the Secretary of State to take action to recover child main-tenance from the absent parent if income support (IS), family credit (FC) or disability working allowance (DWA) is claimed by the parent or on her behalf (ie, a claim for a couple made by the parent with care's partner), or if one of these benefits is paid to her or on her behalf.[1]

The requirement to co-operate will be extended to means-tested job-seeker's allowance when it is introduced in October 1996 – see CPAG's *Welfare Rights Bulletin* or the *Jobseeker's Allowance Handbook.*

Some parents are exempt from this requirement to apply for child maintenance – see p83.

Even though applications from these benefit claimants are termed compulsory by the CSA, the parent with care is perfectly entitled to refuse to give authorisation; however, she risks a benefit penalty if she does not co-operate with the CSA.[2] (For details of the **reduced benefit direction,** see pp110 and 112.) The assessment of benefit *cannot* be delayed or payment stopped if authorisation is not given to the CSA.

The requirement to give authority applies whether or not benefits are payable with respect to the qualifying child.[3] So, if a capital settlement has been made which takes the child out of the benefit calculation, this does not remove the obligation to pursue child maintenance for that child. A qualifying child should be included in any claim for benefit as non-disclosure of child benefit constitutes fraud and, anyway, any benefit penalty imposed for refusing to co-operate with the CSA will almost certainly be lower than any loss in unclaimed child allowances.

The parent with care is also required to co-operate in tracing the absent parent and to provide the information needed by the CSA to make an assessment of child maintenance (see p88).

The requirement to apply to the CSA applies even if there is an existing court order in force or she has already made a voluntary application for child maintenance which is still in force.[4]

The requirement to co-operate may not apply if the benefit claim is fraudulent. Although this argument would not be used by a parent with care as the information provided would be passed to the Benefits Agency, an absent parent can contest the validity of the application on this ground (see p75).

Non-parents

The requirement to pursue maintenance does not apply to all persons with care; it applies only to *parents* with care (for definitions, see Chapter 3).[5] In other words, the requirement does not apply to a person with care who is *not* a parent of the qualifying child. When a non-parent with care on IS, FC or DWA is sent an application form, there is a choice about whether or not to apply. A benefit penalty cannot be imposed if the person with care who is not a parent of the child decides not to apply for child maintenance. A non-parent with care who wishes to apply to the CSA needs to make a section 4 application (see p54) even if she claims IS, FC or DWA; this means she could be prevented from doing so by a pre-1993 maintenance agreement.

Secretary of State's discretion

The Secretary of State has discretion as to whether and when to require a parent with care to give authorisation. When exercising this discretion the Secretary of State must take the welfare of any child affected into account (see p52). Therefore a parent with care can make a request that the Secretary of State does not require her to give authorisation on the grounds of welfare of the child; this information could be submitted in addition to any argument that she is exempt (see p83) from the requirement to co-operate.

The Secretary of State can use her/his discretion more widely and decide not to require authorisation from certain parents with care for other reasons, and therefore as a last resort a parent with care could submit other arguments for not having her case taken on by the CSA. She may need to remind the CSA that the Secretary if State has discretion under section 6 of the 1991 Act when deciding who to require to co-operate – ie, whose case to take on. However, the only issues which it appears the Secretary of State takes into account in practice are the ability of the CSA to cope with the additional cases and the likelihood of an assessment being made.

If a parent with care is exempt from the requirement to co-operate, the Secretary of State has no discretion to override this exemption.

The take-on of existing income support claimants

The Secretary of State's discretion has primarily been used to stagger the take-on of parents with care who have been on IS continuously since April 1993. Such parents are not required to authorise the Secretary of State until contacted by the CSA.

In the first 18 months of the CSA's operations, the Secretary of State required those parents with care already receiving child maintenance to co-operate. For a year from December 1994, no further existing IS cases were required to co-operate to give the CSA time to deal with its backlog of work. The take-on of the remaining estimated 300,000 IS cases has now resumed and it appears that the CSA will target first those who are most likely to receive a significant assessment.[6] Cases where the absent parent also is on IS are to be lowest priority. The take-on is not alphabetical.

Where a pre-April 1993 claimant leaves IS either directly to claim FC or DWA or later has to make a fresh claim for IS, she will be treated like all other new claimants and required to co-operate immediately.

Young parents with care

The Secretary of State has chosen to exempt any parent with care who is under 16 years old from the requirement to give authority.[7] Similarly, dependent 16/18-year-olds who are still classed as children or young people for IS purposes are exempt – ie, if they are still at school or have very recently left school. (For a definition of who counts as a child, see p41.) No requirement is enforced even if one of the relevant benefits is being claimed for her and her child by someone else. This exemption applies until a parent with care claims benefit in her own right.

Exemption from the requirement to co-operate

A parent with care is *not* required to give authorisation if:

- the Secretary of State considers that there are reasonable grounds for believing that, if she were to comply, there would be 'a risk of her, or of any child living with her, suffering harm or undue distress as a result'.[8]

This provision removes the obligation to pursue maintenance and is often described as having 'good cause'. Where this applies, there is no question of having to apply for maintenance as no duty to give authority arises.

In practice, the CSA will want to be satisfied that the parent with care is exempt from making an application (see p83). If the CSA has accepted on a previous claim for benefit that the parent with care was exempt, she should not be asked to co-operate when she claims benefit again and if contacted by the CSA should remind it of the earlier decision. She can, of course, voluntarily apply for child maintenance if her circumstances have changed or she now wishes to.

This exemption from the requirement to give authority can only be disregarded if the parent with care specifically asks the Secretary of State to override it.[9]

For details on the meaning of harm or undue distress, see p90.

The declaration letter and claiming exemption

When a claim is made for IS, FC or DWA which includes a qualifying child, the parent with care will be contacted about applying to the CSA. This will also apply at some point to a parent with care who has been continuously in receipt of IS since April 1993 (see p32).

Usually the first contact a parent with care has with the CSA is receipt of a **declaration letter** asking whether or not she believes she is exempt from applying for child maintenance.[10] A parent with care has the option of signing and returning one of two reply slips. **Declaration Slip B** is now used to claim an exemption from the requirement to co-operate and **Declaration Slip A** is used if she does not intend to claim that she is exempt. If declaration slip A is signed and returned, a maintenance application form (MAF) will almost always be issued (see below).

It is important to read the wording of declaration slips A and B very carefully, as it may not be immediately clear which is the one that refuses the CSA permission to take action and which gives permission to go ahead. Until recently the slips were the other way round and some offices may still be using the older version. If in doubt, parents with care should seek further advice before signing.

Signing declaration slip A does not prevent a parent with care from arguing that she is exempt at any future stage. Similarly, if a parent with care has not returned declaration slip B, this does affect her right to withhold authorisation. The declaration letter assumes that any refusal to authorise will be due to a risk of harm or undue distress; however, this statement could be deleted and instead the letter could be used to refuse authority for any reason. The Secretary of State could be requested to use his/her discretion not to require the parent with care to apply to the CSA (see p82).

If declaration slip B is signed and returned, the Secretary of State has to consider whether the parent with care is exempt from the requirement to co-operate. We suggest that the parent with care sends as much additional information with declaration slip B, or instead of it, as possible to show that there is a risk of harm or undue distress. However, if she does not have time to do this straight away, she should just return declaration slip B with a brief outline of the risk in the space provided. New reasons or evidence can be supplied at any stage in the proceedings. The sooner the Secretary of State can be informed of any further information or evidence, the better. This can be done by writing to, or telephoning, the local interviewing officer or the CSO at the field office. See p99 for the evidence which is required to prove there are reasonable grounds for believing a risk exists.

The procedure for determining whether the parent with care is exempt is the same as that for dealing with parents with care who refuse to complete the MAF – see figure 5.3 on p102. The first stage is likely to be an interview with a field officer (see p104), although this is not compulsory. The parent with care may be asked to sign a MAF at the interview; she must not do so if she wishes to continue seeking exemption as she would be providing authorisation (see p87). It is advisable to seek independent advice before attending the interview.

If the Secretary of State is convinced that the parent with care is exempt from the requirement to give authorisation, she is advised of this in writing. A parent with care on IS, FC or DWA should not be given a MAF to complete if she is not required to give authorisation.[11] Once good cause has been accepted, the CSA has no power to review this decision if it has been made by the Secretary of State (in other words, the CSA interviewing officer acting on behalf of the Secretary of State). CSA staff are reminded of this in their guidance.[12] If good cause is not accepted, then the Secretary of State passes the case to a CSO after a warning notice and a six-week period (see p108).

A parent with care can claim exemption on the grounds of a risk of harm or undue distress at any stage of her contact with the CSA – eg, on receiving the MAF (see p87 for advice on how to do this). However, it is important to do this before signing the MAF if at all possible. If authorisation has already been given to the CSA by the parent with care signing the MAF, then she is in fact applying to withdraw her application on the grounds of a risk of harm or undue distress. Although this is possible (see p72), if the Secretary of State does not accept that there are reasonable grounds for believing the risk exists, then there is no right of appeal to a tribunal and the application for child maintenance proceeds.

The request for authorisation

If the parent with care on IS/FC/DWA has not claimed exemption (see above) from the requirement to co-operate with the CSA, she will be sent a MAF. A parent with care will also be asked to complete a MAF if she has requested exemption but the Secretary of State does not accept that she has reasonable grounds for believing that a risk of harm or undue distress exists.

By sending the MAF, the Secretary of State is requiring the parent with care to co-operate and requesting her authorisation to pursue maintenance. The authority must be given without unreasonable delay by completing and returning the MAF (see below for refusals to do so).[13] A signature on the MAF authorises the Secretary of State to take action to assess the maintenance payable and to recover that amount from the absent parent.

If the Secretary of State considers there are reasonable grounds for believing there would be a risk of harm or undue distress to a parent or any of the children living with her, s/he cannot ask the parent with care for the authorisation. Only if the parent asks the Secretary of State to disregard the risk can s/he proceed.[14]

No action can be taken without authorisation

If the parent with care does not sign the MAF, the Secretary of State does not have authorisation to take any action to pursue maintenance. S/he cannot trace or contact the absent parent, request any information from any party, including the parent with care, nor proceed with an assessment.[15] Therefore, even if the CSA has the necessary information – eg, the name and details of the father – no action can be taken without the written authorisation of the parent with care. The only route open to the Secretary of State is referral to a CSO for consideration of a benefit penalty after a final warning (see p109).

Some parents with care believe that if they do not provide the name of the absent parent, this prevents the CSA taking any action. However, if they have signed the MAF but left the name of the father as unknown, the CSA has their authorisation to attempt to trace the absent parent. If the CSA manages to discover the father's identity from another source – eg, a previous benefit claim, the birth register – he can then be pursued for maintenance. The only definite way to avoid pursuit of the absent parent is to refuse to give authorisation on the MAF.

It would be unlawful for the CSA to proceed with a case without the parent with care's authorisation. If the CSA does go ahead and attempt to obtain information or make an assessment, this is a serious matter and a complaint should be made (see p28) as well as the decision challenged;

advisers can contact CPAG for further information.

Absent parents cannot apply to the CSA voluntarily while the parent with care is on IS, FC, or DWA even if she refuses to apply herself or is exempt from the requirement to co-operate (see p55). A child applicant in Scotland (see p54) can apply but not where a pre-April 1993 written maintenance agreement or court order exists.

There are no plans to remove the liable relatives provisions from social security law (see CPAG's *National Welfare Benefits Handbook*). This means that, in theory, the Benefits Agency could still require a man or woman to maintain a wife or husband and any of their children who are in receipt of benefit. However, in practice, it would have great difficulty in enforcing this for child maintenance in the way it has done in the past because of the reduced role of the courts and because fewer staff specialise in liable relatives work. Instead, Benefits Agency staff direct claimants to the CSA. If Benefits Agency staff in your area use the liable relatives provisions for child maintenance, please ask an advice centre to let CPAG know.

Signing the maintenance application form

If she does not wish to apply for child maintenance, a parent with care needs to be careful to avoid giving authorisation inadvertently by signing the MAF – see p62 for the wording of the declaration. For example, if she is using the MAF to claim exemption on the grounds of risk of harm or undue distress (see p90), she must not sign the declaration at the end of the form.

It is important to note that the requirement to give authorisation is quite separate from the duty to provide information (see p88). This means that the parent with care could give authorisation without knowing any of the absent parent's details. In such a case it may be impossible for the CSA to proceed because of the lack of information, even though the parent with care has authorised. (However, even small amounts of information could lead to tracing action – see p131.) Alternatively, she might provide information while choosing to refuse to give authority to the Secretary of State and thus *must not* sign the MAF.

Once authorisation has been given, the application can only be withdrawn in certain circumstances (see p70).

Refusing to give authorisation

For parents with care required to co-operate who do not wish to apply for child maintenance, the only option is to exercise the right to refuse to authorise. The only way to do this is to refuse to sign the MAF.

A parent with care who is refusing to sign the MAF has the option of providing information about a possible risk of harm or undue distress to her or her children, and any damage to the welfare of any children affected by a maintenance application. If the Secretary of State or the CSO agrees that there are reasonable grounds for believing such a risk exists, she cannot be subjected to the benefit penalty for non-co-operation. In our experience, parents with care do have good reasons for refusing to apply for child maintenance. These reasons should be given in writing to the CSA to avoid the benefit penalty when refusing to provide authorisation. In practice, 'undue distress' can cover a wide variety of situations (see p90). If the CSA does not accept the reasons as good cause for not co-operating, there is a right of appeal against a reduced benefit direction (see p122).

Alternatively, a parent may not wish to give any reasons for her refusal to co-operate, in which case she will suffer a benefit penalty unless there is a person with a disability in the family (see p110). In the meantime, she will be contacted at a number of points for authorisation or reasons (see p101 for the full refusal to co-operate procedure).

Refusing to give authorisation to the CSA has no effect on the processing of the benefit claim by the Benefits Agency; this will proceed in the meantime. Significant numbers of benefit claimants have stopped claiming benefits during the first three years of CSA operations (see p26). There is no need to withdraw a benefit claim to avoid child maintenance being pursued. If you do not want to apply for child maintenance, **do not sign the MAF**.

The parent with care has the option of providing authorisation at any later date, but she has no right of appeal against the refusal to exempt her until a reduced benefit direction is issued (see p122). If a benefit penalty is already in place when the parent with care provides her authorisation, it will be terminated (see p119).

Providing information

The parent with care has to provide information in order:[16]

- to enable the absent parent to be traced; *and*
- for the amount of maintenance payable by the absent parent to be assessed; *and*
- for the amount of maintenance to be recovered.

For further details of the information a parent with care must provide, see pp125–7.

If a parent with care is not required to give authority (because of a risk of harm or undue distress) there is no requirement to give any information.[17] This may not be understood by all interviewing officers.

Indeed, CSA guidance sometimes refers to obtaining information or 'naming the father' without reference to the need for authority. If authorisation has been refused, the CSA has no power to pursue the parent with care for information.

If a parent with care is required to give authorisation and she refuses to provide the necessary information, she may suffer a benefit penalty, unless exempt.[18] This applies even if she has given authorisation. Before authorisation can be asked for, the risk that any harm or undue distress might result from an application must be considered. For the information requirement, consideration of this risk only takes place at a later stage (see p110).

In practice, the information is provided by the completion of a MAF (see p61). If the form is not returned, or is incomplete, the CSA will ask the parent with care to attend an interview with a field officer to discuss her reasons for failing to complete the form (see p104). It is the interviewing officer's job to ask the parent with care to comply with the Secretary of State's requirements, or to establish whether or not she is exempt from these requirements. CSA staff, including CSOs, are reminded that when requesting information or evidence they are acting on behalf of the Secretary of State.[19]

It should not be assumed that the parent with care is refusing to co-operate when she fails to provide information. Only parents who have the necessary information available must provide it. A parent with care is only expected to provide information 'so far as she reasonably can'.[20] If there is a reason for not giving the information requested, she should say so as soon as possible to avoid the benefit penalty. It is important to do this because the most likely reason for not providing information is that the parent with care simply does not know the necessary information. Parents with care who do not know who the father is should have their word accepted unless their evidence is self-contradictory or inherently improbable (see p99). In these circumstances, a parent with care has not refused to co-operate but simply cannot give any of the required information. No penalty should be applied in these circumstances as long as the parent with care is giving her full co-operation.

A lot of information may be requested by the CSA both on the MAF and at interview. However, CSOs are advised that a reduced benefit direction is not usually appropriate for failure to provide verification of earnings or housing costs if there are good reasons.[21]

Information may continue to be requested after an interview – eg, if paternity is disputed a further interview may take place (see p143). If a parent with care refuses to co-operate at this stage good cause will then be considered.[22] See figure 5.3 on p102 for the full procedure.

2. HARM OR UNDUE DISTRESS

The obligation to authorise the Secretary of State to take action to recover maintenance does not arise where the Secretary of State or a CSO considers that there are reasonable grounds for believing that if the parent with care were to give such authorisation there would be 'a risk of her, or of any children living with her, suffering harm or undue distress as a result'.[23]

This applies to *any* child living with her, not only the qualifying child – ie, includes children who are not children of the absent parent.

This exemption also applies to any failure to supply the information required by the Secretary of State or by a CSO after authority has been given.[24] (For the information that must be provided by a parent with care, see pp125–7.) In relation to the information requirement, the risk of harm or undue distress is first considered at a later stage than with the requirement to give authorisation – ie, when the CSO is deciding whether or not to issue a reduced benefit direction (see p110) and not when the Secretary of State first requests the information.

What is a risk of harm or undue distress

It is a *risk* of harm or undue distress which is relevant; there is no need for anything actually to have taken place in the past.[25] There do not need to have been threats, nor does it have to be certain or definite that the harm or undue distress *will* result in the future from an application to the CSA; there needs to be a risk that the harm or undue distress *might* occur. This point has not always been followed correctly by the CSA who may need to be referred to the caselaw.[26] In this case the commissioner decided that the tribunal had wrongly concerned itself with the question of whether harm or undue distress would actually happen; the correct test is less restrictive and involves whether there is a 'realistic possibility' of harm or undue distress being suffered. As 'risk' is not qualified by any word such as 'substantial', the risk must just be a 'real' rather than a 'fanciful' one.

The fear does not have to be of the absent parent, but must be as a consequence of the suggested application to the CSA.

For distress to be relevant it must be 'undue', but there is no such qualification in relation to harm, so that *any* harm would be sufficient. Harm is not limited to physical harm but includes psychological or emotional harm.

These terms should be understood in accordance with ordinary English usage – eg, as defined in a dictionary. In the dictionary:[27]

- 'harm' means to hurt, injure, or damage;
- 'undue' means not suitable, improper, unreasonable, excessive, unjustifiable, disproportionate, illegal, or going beyond what is appropriate, warranted or natural;
- 'distress' means strain, stress, pressure, anguish, pain, damage, danger, affliction affecting body, spirit or community, or exhausted condition under severe physical strain; distress might also mean 'lack of money or comforts'.

The commissioner in the above case did not add to the dictionary definition of 'undue' distress except to comment that on the facts of the case, if the children were likely to be distressed if their father's visits ceased or were curtailed, then it would probably follow that such distress would be undue.

Further caselaw will be covered in CPAG's *Welfare Rights Bulletin* (see p446). CPAG is happy to discuss with advisers any such cases being taken to appeal and would suggest that in the large majority of cases an argument can be put that there are reasonable grounds for believing such a risk exists. Given the falling success rate for exemption applications (see figure 5.2) and the CSA's suspicion that there is much collusion between parents with care and absent parents, there is a growing need for tribunal representation.

Requests for exemption have to be decided on a case-by-case basis according to the facts. In order to convince the Secretary of State of her reasonable grounds, a parent with care is well advised to provide any arguments, evidence or additional information from the start. This may include evidence from third parties. Although this is not a requirement, it could well avoid a lengthy dispute. Such reasons would not necessarily have to be provided on the declaration letter or the MAF (where there is little space), but could be supplied verbally or in writing. See p99 for more on the level of proof required and the right to be believed.

The policy guidelines

The DSS has published guidance on the meaning of the risk of harm or undue distress (see figure 5.1). The guidelines, although informative as to how CSA staff are likely to approach the issue, are guidance on how to interpret the exemption and not the law, and as such are not legally binding on a CSO or on a child support appeal tribunal (CSAT). They merely give an idea of the instructions that CSA staff use when reaching a harm or undue distress decision. This guidance should only be used by advisers where it is helpful to a parent with care's case. If not, it need not be referred to.

CPAG believes that 'harm or undue distress' covers a far greater number of situations than those accepted in the policy guidelines. In practice, some field officers are also applying a wider interpretation of the law than is contained in the guidelines. For example, in some cases the risk of a residency dispute or disruption of formerly amiable arrangements has been accepted as causing undue distress, as has the loss of payments in kind or presents for the children in certain situations, and the fear of inappropriate resumption of contact from the absent parent, especially one who left the parent with care when she was pregnant. In addition, there are numerous other situations which can arise which are not considered in the guidelines. A not uncommon situation is where there is a risk of contact between the absent parent and the child(ren) being reduced or lost if a CSA assessment is made; this is accepted by some, but by no means all, field officers as undue distress for the child(ren).

There might also be situations where a step-parent has been accepted in practice as the new father, or situations where a couple are attempting a trial separation and hope to be reconciled in due course. Arguments should be put forward regardless of whether or not they have been mentioned in the Secretary of State's guidance. Although additional factors may help to convince the interviewing officer – health problems, disability, financial difficulties, behavioural problems, or any other factors which the parent with care considers to be likely to increase the risk of harm or undue distress.

Because the good cause decision is discretionary and made by large numbers of field officers and area managers (see p22), rather than a specialist unit, decisions may be inconsistent; this is one of the issues being examined by the CSA (see p101). The CSA was also keen to hear of cases where good cause has been wrongly decided; CPAG will continue to pass any cases reported to us on to CSA headquarters.

Figure 5.1: **CSA GUIDANCE ON HARM OR UNDUE DISTRESS**

(This is currently in the Child Support Manual (MA) paragraphs 10761–10810 but is soon to be incorporated into the CS Requirement to Co-operate Guide. All examples are illustrative and do not represent an exhaustive list of circumstances which might arise. Each case must be dealt with on its own merits.)

10761   It is neither possible nor desirable to draw up **a definitive list** of the circumstances in which it would be reasonable to conclude that a PaWC had good cause not to co-operate in seeking maintenance but the following guidelines apply to indicative circumstances.

PaWC fears violence

10762   The PaWC's account of her reasons for fearing violence will need to be obtained. Where the AP has a history of violence to the

PaWC or her children, it may be relatively easier to reach a decision but the PaWC's fear of violence may be reasonable even where there is no history of it.

PaWC a rape victim

10763   Where the PaWC says she has been a victim of rape by the AP, interviews must be handled with the utmost tact and sympathy, though the circumstances will need to be established. It should be remembered that, even when rape has occurred, there may be circumstances in which the PaWC feels that the AP should not be freed from the responsibility to provide support for the child, particularly if she is reassured that the CSA will act on her behalf and that her address will not be revealed.

Sexual abuse

10764   A PaWC may decline to co-operate in seeking maintenance because the AP has sexually abused one of her children. This is a subject which many PaWCs will find extremely distressing and questioning should be conducted with great care and sensitivity. The PaWC should be urged to report the matter to the police if she has not done so. Even when sexual abuse has occurred there may be circumstances in which the PaWC nevertheless decides that the AP should not be freed from his responsibility to provide support for his child, particularly if she is reassured that the CSA will act on her behalf and will not reveal her address to the AP.

Child conceived as a result of sexual abuse (including incest)

10765   If the PaWC says that she does not wish to name the father because the child was conceived as a result of sexual abuse or incest, the interview must be handled with extreme tact and care, although the PaWC's account of events must be obtained and a judgement made on the consistency and plausibility of what she says. Again there may be circumstances in which the PaWC nevertheless decides that maintenance should be pursued.

10766-10769

Other circumstances

10770   There are a number of other circumstances in which the PaWC will say that she or her children would suffer harm or undue distress, where there may be less of a **prima facie** case that this would be so. The extent to which harm or undue distress would result in a particular set of circumstances will vary from case to case and it will be for the interviewing officer to decide in the light of the facts whether (s)he considers that there is in fact a risk of harm or undue distress. The situations described below are not exhaustive and each case must be considered individually.

Fear that the AP will want to see the child

10771   Some PaWCs will be afraid that if the AP is required to pay them maintenance he will demand to see the child. Sometimes the PaWC may be concerned that it will be disruptive to the child to see the AP and sometimes she herself will wish to sever all links with the AP.

10772   It is important that PaWCs are made aware that questions of contact (formerly known as access) are entirely separate from issues of maintenance. Many PaWCs and APs are known to link the two but it is important to stress that both the parents are responsible for maintaining the child subject to their financial circumstances. This responsibility is not removed because an AP no longer sees, or has never seen, the child.

10773   A belief than an approach to an AP would result in demands for contact should not on its own normally be sufficient to enable a PaWC to succeed in a claim that harm or undue distress would be caused by pursuing maintenance. If an AP subsequently sought contact, it would be for the courts to decide on the merits of the case whether it was in the child's interests for the contact to be allowed. In all cases the court would have the best interests of the child as its primary consideration and would take into account whether, for example, the AP had regular contact with the child in the past.

PaWC wishes to sever links with the AP

10774   The PaWC's wish to sever links with the AP should not normally provide grounds for her to succeed in a claim of harm or undue distress. There would normally need to be additional factors before the requirement to co-operate would be waived. The PaWC should be reminded that the CSA will not disclose her address to the AP.

No recent contact with the AP

10775   PaWCs who have older children who have no contact with the AP may refuse to co-operate because it would cause them or their children undue distress to reopen any degree of contact after a lengthy period. Again there would normally need to be additional factors before the requirement to co-operate would be waived.

10776   In many cases the child need never know about the maintenance application. The PaWC should be reminded that the CSA will not tell the AP her address and that if the AP then wants contact with the child, the matter would be for the courts who would have regard to the child's best interests.

PaWC wishes to protect the AP

10777   Sometimes a PaWC will wish to protect an AP, most usually because he is living in a stable relationship with someone else who is unaware of the child he shares with the PaWC. There may also be cases where the PaWC wishes to protect the identity of an AP who is a prominent or well known person. It would be unusual for the situation to justify a claim that co-operating would cause undue distress to the PaWC or her children, unless there are other relevant circumstances. The PaWC should be reminded that the CSA will act as a buffer between her and the AP and that the CSA's contact with the AP will be on a confidential basis. The fact that payment of maintenance may be awkward for the AP is not in itself a reason to waive the requirement to co-operate.

Juvenile PaWCs

10778   Where the PaWC is under 16 or over 16 but still classed as a child for IS purposes (ie, she is still at school) she and her child will feature on someone else's benefit claim. In these cases, although Section 6 of the Act still applies the SofS will waive the requirement to co-operate until she applies for benefit on her own account.

Juvenile AP

10779   A PaWC who is required to co-operate must do so even if the AP is aged under 16 (or was at the time that the child was conceived). For purposes of any interview, an AP under 16 must be accompanied by an adult to safeguard his position.

10780   In the case of juvenile PaWCs and APs there is a risk that one of the parents has committed a criminal offence. An older PaWC, for example, may be reluctant to name a juvenile AP out of fear that a criminal prosecution may be brought against her. A PaWC who was underage when her child was conceived may also fear that by naming the AP she might make him open to prosecution. Disclosure of information is covered by section 50 of the Child Support Act and in the Child Support (Information, Evidence and Disclosure) Regulations 1992. Other than in most exceptional circumstances, information obtained by the CSA will not be passed to the police.

10781   It is unlikely that these circumstances on their own will be sufficient to justify a refusal to co-operate.

Artificial insemination (AI) and other forms of assisted conception

10782   Where a PWC says that her child has been born as a result of artificial insemination or by placing in her of an embryo or sperm and ova, it will be necessary to establish whether there is an AP so that maintenance can be sought if appropriate.

10783   Officers acting for the SofS must first establish whether the PWC was married at the time of conception. If this is so, and the husband either consented to the treatment or accepted the child as part of his family, even if he is not the genetic father, than he is treated in law as the father and will therefore be the AP.

10784   If the above paragraph does not apply, the PWC may have been treated with a man who was not her husband. Provided that this treatment took place at a treatment centre, licensed or otherwise, and if the PWC and the man received the treatment together, then he is the AP regardless of whether or not he formally consented to the treatment or subsequently accepted the child and even if he is not the genetic father.

10785   Where neither paragraphs 10683 and 10684 applies, officers should consider the circumstances of the conception. Where, rarely, a child has been born as a result of treatment at a licensed treatment centre, and there is no legal father under the above paragraphs, then there will be no AP and no further action should be taken. This is because donors to licensed centres cannot be treated as the legal father of any child born as a result of the donation. Men who donate sperm as part of a private arrangement do not have the same legal protection. Therefore where there is no legal father under the above paragraphs and the PWC made her own arrangements or received unlicensed treatment, then the genetic father (ie, the donor of the sperm) is the AP and, if she is able, the PWC should co-operate in seeking maintenance from him unless she can show that there are reasons why harm or undue distress to her or any child living with her would result.

Test tube and donor births

10786   Where a third person has been involved in donating ova or sperm for a test tube birth, the couple to whom the child is born normally accept the child as their own, again by adoption or by registering the birth. As with AI where the husband or unmarried partner did not oppose the treatment he is treated in law as the father.

10787   As with AI, it is rare for an unmarried woman without a partner to obtain a test tube birth. Evidence should be requested when a PaWC says her child was conceived in this way.

PaWC wanted the child; AP did not

10788   A PaWC may say that she deliberately set out to conceive a child with no intention of involving the AP in her decision to have a child or in its upbringing. She may have had no intention of pursuing a relationship with the father. On its own, this is not an acceptable reason for not co-operating with the CSA. Both parents are responsible for their children.

10789   Some PaWCs may have gone on to have a child after the AP made it clear he would prefer the PaWC to have an abortion. Again, without other factors this is unlikely to provide grounds for waiving the requirement to co-operate.

Naming unlikely fathers

10790   There may be some instances where the PaWC names as the AP someone who the balance of probability suggests is unlikely to be the AP. Examples might include entertainment or sports personalities or other well-known individuals.

10791   Although the allegation may seem improbable, sufficient detail should be obtained of the circumstances to enable a judgement to be made about its validity.

10792   If the claim is judged to be improbable the PaWC may have good cause not to name the real AP. She should be reminded of the advantages to her of getting maintenance and encouraged to be open with the CSA and her real fears.

A voluntary arrangement exists

10793   The PaWC may not wish to co-operate because she considers she already has a satisfactory arrangement with the AP and does not wish to disturb it. Under the Child Support Act where the SofS requires her to co-operate, she should do so unless this would cause harm or undue distress. The disturbance of a voluntary agreement would not on its own be sufficient to justify a claim of harm or undue distress.

PaWC is mentally ill or handicapped

10794   Where a PaWC is suffering from mental distress or learning disability which prevents her from understanding what is required or leads her to seem unco-operative, officials should treat her with patience and sensitivity. She may have given as much information as she can at this time. Alternatively there may be an appointee who is able to help.

10795-10799

Other situations

10800   Other situations may arise. In each case the facts must be established and the case judged on its merits.

10801-10809

Reaching a decision

10810   Interviewing officers must start from the supposition that the PaWC is telling the truth. Their decision that harm or undue distress would not be caused by pursuing maintenance could lead

> to the loss to the PaWC of a significant amount of income; such a decision should be reached only after very careful thought and a full record needs to be kept of the PaWC's account and the officer's reasons for not accepting her argument. The officer's reasons will be considered along with any other evidence by the CSO in reaching a final decision about whether or not the PaWC has shown good cause for not co-operating.

The CSA guidance on harm or undue distress is supplemented by unpublished CSA training material. Training documents seen by CPAG initially added to our concerns about the requirement to co-operate.[28] For example, CSA staff are warned that some parents with care may claim that rape took place in order to try and avoid giving the absent parent's name. Field officers are advised that they should not assume that because the parent with care knows the rapist that the allegation is untrue. However, trainees are also advised that 'where the alleged rapist was a partner or former partner you need to decide whether the claim of rape is plausible'. Trainees are advised to ask just enough questions to satisfy themselves that the account is 'consistent and plausible' and that if a parent with care is 'obviously genuinely distressed' about talking about the situation, 'you may judge that undue distress is already evident'.

The implication that a woman is less believable if she is not visibly upset is of particular concern.Any assumption that an appearance of control means that a woman is less affected should be challenged.

Questions will be asked about the identity of the rapist, whether or not he was a stranger or someone with whom she had a previous relationship, whether or not the police were informed, and whether or not there was a court case. Trainees are advised to ask why a rape was not reported, but that a woman's story should not be rejected 'solely on that account'.

Despite this insensitive guidance, CPAG has received few complaints about requirement to co-operate interviews (see p104). This may reflect women's reluctance to make complaints in these situations for fear of exacerbating the problem and having to relive the trauma. If this is the case, it would be useful if advisers could send CPAG an anonymous summary so that we can continue to press for improved procedures.

Reasonable grounds

If IS, FC or DWA is claimed or is in payment for a parent with care, initially the Secretary of State and then the CSO has to consider whether there are reasonable grounds for believing that if the parent were required to give authorisation, there would be a risk of harm or undue distress as a result.

The reasonable grounds would relate, first, to the question of authorisation and, secondly, to the requirement to provide information. Any challenge to the duty to provide information will relate back to the issue of authority because, once a parent is under a duty to give authority, she has no option but to provide information. However, there is a second opportunity to argue harm or undue distress in relation to the information requirement itself if authorisation has already been given. After a 14-day notice has been issued by a CSO (see figure 5.3), s/he must consider the question of whether any risk might arise as a result of having to comply with either the requirement to give authorisation or the requirement to provide information.[29]

Reasons as to why the parent with care thinks she is not required to comply will be necessary to convince the Secretary of State that there would be a risk of harm or undue distress.

If the parent with care has already provided reasons for not co-operating under the old liable relatives rules and these reasons were accepted, then the same good cause may be accepted without further investigation.[30] If an exemption was accepted by the CSA on a previous benefit claim, this should still stand (except for a new qualifying child) and no further decision is necessary.[31] If this does not happen, make a complaint (see p28).

Providing evidence of reasonable grounds

It has already been established for social security purposes that corroboration of a claimant's own evidence is not necessary.[32] If given, it helps to reinforce the evidence, but it is not required. A claimant's evidence should be accepted unless it is self-contradictory or inherently improbable.

During parliamentary debates the degree of corroboration and evidence required to show reasonable grounds was discussed and the Government issued statements to say that a parent with care 'will be believed'. For example, the then Under-Secretary of State for Social Security, Alistair Burt, said:[33]

> While corroborative evidence in support of a parent's claim of good cause will be welcome, it will not be essential. A social security commissioner's decision sets out the presumption which applies in similar circumstances for benefit decisions, namely that the person concerned is telling the truth, unless there are strong grounds for thinking otherwise. The Government thinks it is right to follow such an approach for child maintenance.
>
> Suitable and comprehensive training and guidance will be given to

staff of the Child Support Agency to ensure that this sensitive area of work is handled professionally and sympathetically.

We will be able to consider the circumstances of every single case specifically. A lone parent has the right to expect that – unless it is inherently implausible – her story will be believed, if she expresses her fears to the Agency. Supporting evidence will be helpful but it will not be essential.

Please let CPAG know if the commitment made above has been breached.

The instruction to believe the parent with care unless her story is self-contradictory or improbable is repeated in a number of places in CSA guidance,[34] and this should be pointed out to CSA staff who are inclined not to believe the parent's evidence. We are concerned that the CSA's assumption that there is collusion between parents in order to avoid the involvement of the CSA is leading staff to disbelieve parents with care.[35] This, however, would be contrary to the caselaw and policy guidelines, and should be challenged should it occur in individual cases.

In some cases, while acknowledging that a parent has genuine fears that harm or undue distress would follow a CSA application, the CSA staff may not agree that these fears are realistic – ie, they do not provide the Secretary of State or the CSO with reasonable grounds for believing there is in fact such a risk. In these cases, an adviser needs to ask on what other evidence the officer has based his/her decision. The parent with care knows the people involved and their history and therefore is likely to be able to anticipate their reactions. A CSA officer cannot simply disagree with a parent with care who is neither self-contradictory nor improbable without any further evidence; his/her own opinion does not constitute evidence.

There may be circumstances where a parent with care chooses not to discuss anything with the CSA, particularly where the situation has not been discussed openly before or is especially painful – eg, rape or sexual abuse. Written communication should suffice.[36]

Evidence can be provided by someone other than the parent with care.[37] This may be provided orally or in writing. However, if the Secretary of State does not agree that there are reasonable grounds after the interview, any evidence given orally at the interview or over the telephone should be put into writing during the next six weeks (see p108).

Successful exemptions

The number of applications for exemption on the grounds of harm or undue distress has increased over the last two years, but this is unsurprising given the improved information provided to parents with care. An average of nine thousand cases are now considered for exemption each month. The success rate has fallen from about half in the first year to just over a third to date in 1995/96. Consequently, the number of reduced benefit directions is rising; this has been assumed by many parliamentarians to illustrate a high level of 'collusion' between parents with care who refuse to co-operate with the CSA and absent parents who refund the benefit penalty. This allegation was one of the main reasons for the setting up of the CSA's review of the requirement to co-operate procedures (see below). CPAG would appreciate being contacted by any adviser who notices a change in the type of cases which are being accepted as exempt by the CSA.

Figure 5.2: **APPLICATIONS FOR EXEMPTION DUE TO RISK OF HARM OR UNDUE DISTRESS**[38]

	1993/94	1994/95	April–Dec 1995
Cases considered	64,792	91,414	80,808
Good cause accepted	31,699 (49%)	41,666 (46%)	28,256 (35%)
PWCs co-operated	14,206	11,175	16,272
Good cause refused	18,857	38,573	36,280
Benefit penalties	627	17,451	21,000

The difference between the cases refused and the numbers of benefit penalties is explained by the CSA as due in part to consideration of the welfare of the child (see p52) and in part to parents with care co-operating at the end of the process.[39] However, parents should be advised not to co-operate until just after the issuing of the benefit penalty in order to obtain a right of appeal (see p122).

---

3. REFUSAL TO CO-OPERATE

The CSA is undertaking a review of its requirement to co-operate procedures. Begun in early 1995, it is due to report shortly after this handbook is published. Therefore, the procedures described in this section may be subject to change: see forthcoming issues of CPAG's Welfare Rights Bulletin. *Preliminary reports from the CSA have not found great problems with the procedures and suggest that therefore significant changes to current practice are unlikely.*

The review has involved examination of a large number of case papers, a questionnaire to staff, research using hypothetical cases for a selection of staff to adjudicate and discuss, examination of complaints,

Figure 5.3: **PROCEDURE FOR REQUIREMENT TO CO-OPERATE**

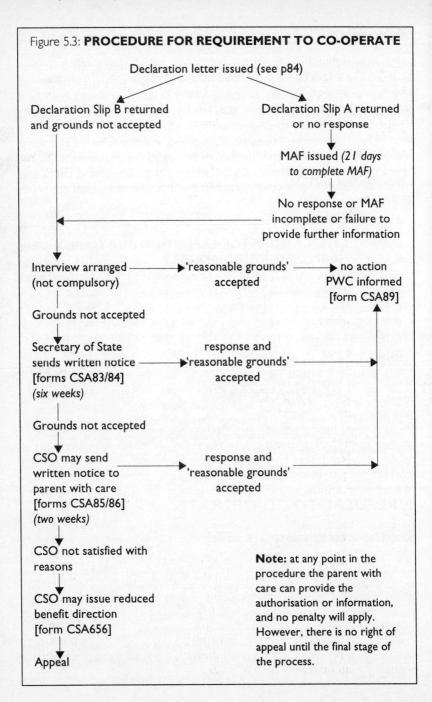

visits to 100 parents with care who had accepted the benefit penalty and requests of submissions from interested organisations. One of the main complaints highlighted so far has been the length of time which elapses between the stages of the process. Therefore, although the set six-week and two-week periods (see figure 5.3) will remain, the CSA wants to reduce the time it takes to carry out the procedure from start to finish. Delays of many months should no longer occur with the same frequency. In addition, the CSA has sometimes added additional stages to the process, such as additional reminder letters requesting completion of the MAF or a home visit to try and persuade the parent with care of the advantages of applying for maintenance. These are no longer likely to be pursued.

There were about 16,000 cases where the parents with care did not respond to the CSA on which action was suspended during part of 1994 and 1995. Some have now been returned to and the others will be followed up in due course. It should never be assumed that a lack of action on the part of the CSA means there is no longer a requirement to co-operate. If the CSA accepts that a parent is exempt, she will be notified in writing.

A parent with care who gets IS, FC, or DWA, or where someone else gets it on her behalf, is subject to the requirement to apply for child maintenance (see p81). She can refuse to co-operate but this may result in the imposition of a **reduced benefit direction**, resulting in a loss of benefit. This loss of benefit is usually referred to as the **benefit penalty**. Some families with disabilities cannot now be issued with a reduced benefit direction (see p110).

Interviews, investigations and decisions about whether someone is exempt from the requirement to co-operate are now undertaken at the field office (see p21). The procedures are very similar, irrespective of whether the parent with care seeks exemption on the declaration letter (see p84) or refuses to complete or sign the maintenance application form (MAF).

Refusing to return the MAF

See page 57 for procedures on issuing the MAF to benefit claimants.

The parent with care has to return the MAF within a total of 21 days to the appropriate office. Initially, she will be given 14 days, but if the form has not been returned in this time, a letter will be sent giving a further seven days to return it (these time limits are in guidance only).[40]

If the MAF has not been returned after 28 days, or is incomplete, or a risk of harm or undue distress is indicated, the field office will usually arrange for an interview to take place.

Posting of documents

Whenever documents are posted by the Secretary of State, they are usually treated as having been sent on the second day after the day of posting (excluding Sundays and Bank Holidays).[41] If more than one document has to be sent, or has to be sent to more than one person, and they are sent on different days, then they are treated as posted on the later or latest date.[42] When a document is returned by post it is treated as having been sent on the day the Secretary of State receives it, but there is discretion to treat it as having been sent earlier if there was unavoidable delay.[43]

Interviews

Requirement to co-operate interviews are voluntary and not compulsory; the need for them is contained in guidance only. CSA staff are reminded that if a parent does not wish to attend such an interview, she is free not to do so.[44] In these circumstances it would be advisable to send the CSA field office written reasons for not co-operating and any supporting evidence. A parent with care may want to ask the CSA for a list of questions it would like her to answer in writing. A decision can be made by the CSA on the basis of the information sent in without the need for an interview.[45]

Interviews will normally take place at the CSA field office (based at a Benefits Agency office). An interview can be arranged at another place, including the home of the parent with care if she prefers.[46]

With the notification of the interview, parents with care are issued with a copy of a leaflet called *Your Rights in the Interview* (form CSA100), which is published jointly by the CSA and the National Council for One-Parent Families. The leaflet attempts to outline what will happen at the interview, the exemption from the requirement to give authorisation and rights of review and appeal.

A parent with care should, if possible, seek advice before attending an interview and, if she wants to, she should take a friend or adviser with her. In addition to the support provided by a friend or relative, an adviser can help prevent the interviewer asking irrelevant or unnecessarily intrusive questions.

The CSA advises that the interview should not take place in the presence of a child old enough to understand what is being discussed. CSA staff should try to arrange a date when children are at school or with friends, if necessary.[47] Another view is that a child should be encouraged to have a voice in matters affecting him/her. Although clearly inappropriate in some situations, there may be cases where this is highly appropriate, especially with older children – eg, if a child is distressed at the prospect of any possible contact or alternatively the loss of contact with an absent parent.

If a parent with care has any special needs, such as the provision of an interpreter or disabled access to the interview room, the field office should be requested to arrange this. Hardly any field offices have creches or other facilities for young children and parents may want to point out the practical problems this poses for them. See below for information on travelling expenses.

If a parent fails to attend an interview, she may be telephoned, or visited at home or at her place of work.[48]

Procedure at interviews

Requirement to co-operate interviews concentrate on the question of why a parent has refused to give authorisation or has not provided sufficient information and often on the details of the absent parent. The law specifies what information must be given to the CSA (see pp125–7).[49] However, this is not relevant while a parent with care is seeking exemption from the requirement to co-operate. The interview may also involve requests to complete and sign the MAF. If the parent with care is still doubtful about the wisdom of applying for maintenance, she should refuse as otherwise she will be providing her authorisation to the CSA (see p87).

Field officers who conduct interviews have all received training from Relate and instructions on how to conduct interviews with care and sensitivity.[50] The following guidance is issued to staff:

put them at ease; you will get more information from a 'chat'.[51]

Procedures at an interview are in guidance only and there is nothing to stop a parent with care from interrupting, asking questions, taking notes or even taping the interview. A complaint should be made if procedures used at an interview are felt to be inappropriate (see p28).

The interviewing officer will point out that the CSA acts as a buffer between both parents, that the parent with care need never see the absent parent and that he will not be told of her address or even the town she lives in.[52] However, both parents may meet if an appeal against any later assessment takes place (see p377). Also, the CSA cannot prevent one parent from tracing the other.

Interviewing officers also stress the fact that paying maintenance does not give the absent parent any right to contact with the child. The advantages and flexibility of receiving maintenance will be emphasised, particularly where FC or DWA are claimed, or if she later stops claiming altogether. The officer will point out that £15 of maintenance will be ignored in calculating FC, DWA, housing benefit and council tax benefit, and that if child maintenance is paid, the CSA can collect it for her.

Guidance stresses that it is not for the interviewing officer to suggest that a parent may have good cause, but also stresses that no pressure must be applied to persuade her to provide authorisation or information.[53] Interviewers certainly should not threaten the parent with care with a benefit penalty if she does not provide authorisation or information there and then; there are several more stages in the process. Neither should s/he imply that the benefit claim would be delayed or suspended by continued non-co-operation.

Any reduced benefit direction which may be issued should not be counted in the benefit savings attributed to the CSA, so an interview should not be conducted in this context.[54] However, benefit savings (see p25) will result from any future payments of child maintenance or through someone ceasing to claim.

Information requested

It is very important that a parent with care is not pressurised into providing information she need not give. If she is adamant about refusing to co-operate, she should say this at the beginning of the interview and that she is attending only to provide information on the risk of harm or undue distress (see p90). If she has not provided her authorisation, then the CSA has no power to pursue her for information. However, if she has signed but not completed the MAF, the parent with care needs to be clear about whether she is seeking exemption from the requirement to provide the information or whether she cannot provide the information because she does not have it (see p89).

In addition to the information specified in the child support regulations (see p126), parents with care may be asked for more details, including:[55]

- alias or nickname of the absent parent;
- national insurance number of the absent parent;
- service number, if in the Forces;
- date of birth of the absent parent;
- place where the absent parent last claimed benefit;
- the couple's last address;
- address of the absent parent's parents or close relatives;
- the identity of friends who may have more information;
- the absent parent's car make, colour and registration number;
- whether the absent parent belongs to any clubs or has any hobbies;
- places where he socialises;
- details of any other family he is responsible for;

- full names of any children;
- if a parent with care does not know the absent parent's address, whom the absent parent would contact in an emergency;
- name of the absent parent's accountant;
- details of a probation officer, or any other officials.

The information which the regulations say can be requested is more limited than the above list but the CSA does have discretion to ask further questions as long as the information requested is for a specified purpose (see p125).[56] The policy guidelines say that a parent with care who only has a small amount of information about an absent parent should be encouraged to provide it, and it is pointed out that a parent who has known an absent parent for some time will obviously know more about him than if she had only had a short relationship. If she has given as much information as she can, then she has co-operated.[57]

There have been reports of direct questioning over the circumstances of conception. CSA staff are trained to ask such questions where parentage is in dispute (see p139) but not otherwise. Field officers are told to be prepared to change an interview about parentage into a requirement to co-operate interview if there appears to be good cause for withholding information.[58] (For details of the questions likely to be asked at a paternity interview, see p146.)

If questions appear to be unnecessary or intrusive, a complaint could be made to the CSA (see p28).

Travelling expenses

Travelling expenses for attending an interview at the request of the CSA can be refunded. A refund can only be given to a person getting IS, FC or DWA who has had to travel to the office on essential business[59] – eg, s/he was asked to attend. However, these payments are made at the discretion of the CSA and can also be made to someone who calls at the office uninvited because the matter could not be dealt with by telephone or letter.[60] Field officers are advised to consider whether the person concerned has difficulties with reading or writing, communicating by letter or telephone, a good command of English and access to a telephone.[61]

No refund will be made for the first pound of a fare, nor for amounts of less than 10 pence.[62] The whole fare will, however, be met for a second or subsequent call within the same week (Monday to Sunday). Fares of a companion, child or interpreter can also be met in certain circumstances – eg, the person could not travel alone due to sickness or the child would have been left alone.[63] Refundable fares are based on the cheapest return fare by public transport or the cost of petrol up to the equivalent of public transport costs, or actual costs – including taxi fares – where public transport is unavailable or the person is disabled.[64] Proof of fares is requested only if someone is suspected of being untruthful and payment is made through the Benefits Agency by cash or girocheque.[65]

Investigations

Where insufficient information has been provided by the parent with care, the CSA field officer is responsible for checking details that have been given or investigating them further. Investigations can only take place if the parent with care has given authorisation to the Secretary of State to pursue maintenance. The CSA has no powers to do so where a parent with care has refused to give authorisation.[66]

Information is likely to be obtained by telephone, letter or a visit. The information may be sought from the parent with care, absent parent (if identified) or other sources where allowed in the rules (see p127).[67] Guidance indicates that the method should be cost effective.[68] The same guidance indicates that phone calls outside office hours may prove effective, as might weekend, early morning or evening visits, or even visits during break-times at a place of work.[69] The person concerned may not necessarily be notified of the visit, particularly where the purpose of the visit is to check the address or where a notified visit has failed.[70] CPAG has heard of cases where calls have been made at inappropriate times – eg, a woman alone being visited at 9pm. A complaint should be made where such a visit causes upset (see p28).

Other examples of investigations are checking the birth register, national insurance records and benefit records (see pp131 and 150). Information gathered may be followed up – eg, by contacting anyone named as a possible witness to a relationship, or someone who might know where the absent parent lives.

For more details of information-seeking powers and investigation procedures, see Chapter 6.

Notice to comply

If the parent with care fails to give authority and the interviewing officer is not satisfied that there are reasonable grounds for her refusal, the officer (on behalf of the Secretary of State) sends her a written notice stating that if she fails to comply within six weeks, the case will be passed to a CSO to consider whether a reduced benefit direction should be imposed.[71] This is usually issued after an interview has been held.

The interviewing officer has no discretion about whether or not to issue such a notice if s/he does not believe that there are reasonable grounds (see p98). S/he must do so.

If a parent with care has given authorisation but not information, a similar notice applies. The notice is issued on form CSA83 if information has not been provided or on form CSA84 if authorisation has not been given.[72] The notice advises the parent with care to comply and should explain that the case will not be referred to a CSO until a full six weeks have expired from the date of the notice.[73] (See figure 5.3.)

Although at least six weeks must be allowed before a case is referred to a CSO, this period may be extended by the Secretary of State – eg, where someone intends to co-operate but cannot do so within the six-week period, perhaps because a friend who has more information about the absent parent is on holiday.[74]

Additional reasons for not giving authorisation or information can be provided at any stage. These must be responded to immediately by the CSA in writing even if the reasons are not accepted. This leaves the remainder of the six-week period for the parent with care to provide additional evidence.[75] A parent with care on IS should also use this time to consider whether any other deductions could be made from her benefit in order to defer the imposition of a benefit penalty (see p115).

No further action is taken if, at this stage, the CSA field officer accepts that there are reasonable grounds for believing that a risk of harm or undue distress might result from giving authorisation. The parent with care will be informed of this decision. Once good cause has been accepted by the field officer this decision cannot be reviewed either by the Secretary of State or by a CSO.[76]

If there has been no response, or the parent with care's grounds have not been accepted, the case will be referred to a CSO who is usually also the area manager. The record of any interview, together with any other representations or written evidence from the parent with care, will be given to the CSO.[77]

Final notice to comply

Once the case has been referred to a CSO, a written notice may be served on the parent with care requiring her either to co-operate or to give her reasons for failing to do so within 14 days.[78] This notice is issued on form CSA85 for failure to provide information and form CSA86 for failure to give authorisation. The CSO can use her/his discretion when deciding whether or not to issue a final notice. In exercising this discretion, the CSO must take account of the welfare of any child(ren) likely to be affected (see below and p52). If the CSO does not issue a final notice the benefit penalty cannot be invoked.[79] (See figure 5.3.)

Parents should be advised to send information during the two-week period both on the risk of harm or undue distress (see p90) and on the welfare of any child(ren) likely to be affected by any benefit penalty.

Reasons given in response to this written notice may be given orally, including by telephone, or in writing[80] by the parent with care or anyone else. These reasons must be considered by the CSO.[81] New reasons, arguments or evidence can still be put forward at this stage. If the CSO agrees that there are reasonable grounds for believing that there is a risk of harm or undue distress, s/he will notify the parent with care of this decision and take no further action.[82]

Although the 14-day period cannot be extended, there is no limit on the length of time that the Secretary of State or a CSO can take to issue a notice to comply. This means that the period allowed to make any representations, or for the Secretary of State to carry out investigations, could be extended deliberately, or through delay. In the past, this notice has not usually been sent out immediately, presumably due to the backlog of work. In future, it is more likely to happen immediately (see p101 for the review of procedures).

Reduced benefit direction

Once 14 days have expired following a final notice to comply, and the CSO is still not satisfied that the parent with care has reasonable grounds for not giving authorisation or providing information, then a reduced benefit direction may be issued.[83] (See figure 5.3.) The reduction in benefit caused by the reduced benefit direction is frequently referred to as the **benefit penalty** (see p112).

Since 22 January 1996, a CSO has not been able to issue a reduced benefit direction where:[84]

- the parent with care or her partner is paid IS which includes a disabled child premium, a disability premium or a higher pensioner premium (this applies even if it is the partner who has the disability); *or*
- the disabled child premium or the disability premium is included in the exempt income (see p183) of a parent with care in receipt of FC/DWA (this does not recognise a partner's disability).

In other cases, the CSO is not bound to issue such a direction and, in exercising this discretion, s/he must take account of the welfare of any child(ren) likely to be affected (see below). If the CSO considers that there are reasonable grounds for believing that were the parent to comply there would be a risk of harm or undue distress, s/he is bound *not* to make an order.[85]

The reduced benefit direction is signed by a CSO before sending it to the Benefits Agency and a copy is sent to the parent with care.[86] A reduced benefit direction is binding on the benefit adjudication officer and will specify by how much, from what date and for how long benefit is to be reduced.[87] It is issued on form CSA656. The benefits affected by such a direction are IS, FC or DWA (and from October 1996 will include means-tested jobseeker's allowance).

It is intended that any such direction will cover all of the qualifying children living with the parent with care at the point at which she was required to co-operate, even if they have different absent parents. This is because, in general, a reduced benefit direction applies to the parent's failure to co-operate, not to each child.[88] (For what happens in relation to any new qualifying child, see p114.)

Welfare of the child

A CSO *may* serve a final notice requiring a parent with care to comply or to give reasons for failing to do so (see p109),[89] or *may* issue a reduced benefit direction.[90] Under the 1991 Act, the CSO is not bound to do either of these, and in exercising her/his discretion should take account of the welfare of any children likely to be affected.[91]

The welfare of *any* child likely to be affected is an additional consideration for a CSO and is a separate consideration from the harm or undue distress exemption. In particular, the latter exemption looks at the possible effects of a *maintenance application*, whereas the effect of the *benefit penalty* on the welfare of the child is now considered. Many CSOs and even tribunals do not recognise that this is a second decision which is required if they do not accept that the parent with care is exempt on the grounds of harm or undue distress. It is not sufficient for a tribunal to state that it considered the welfare of the child(ren); special factors in the case must be looked for and reasons given for the decision.[92] See p52 for more on the principle of the welfare of the child.

The parent with care should submit any information about how the reduction in her income is likely to affect her children – eg, their diet, health, provision of clothing, ability to participate in school trips or other activities. These arguments are most likely to succeed where the parent is an IS claimant without any other resources (eg, earnings, capital) or where a FC/DWA claimant has a disposable income below that of IS. Particular demands on her budget (eg, debts) would also be relevant. There may be other factors which mean the mother is less able to cope with a reduction in her income – such as her own health – which will then affect the child's welfare. Although the CSA's guidance concentrates on disability in the family, this cannot be the only consideration as it is already covered in the new exemption (see p110). Furthermore, it appears that significant numbers of cases do avoid the benefit penalty on the basis of welfare of the child (see figure 5.2).

However, the child's welfare is not paramount, and any argument which is inconsistent with the principle of the benefit penalty would be unlikely to succeed. It cannot in law be assumed that the reduction in income will adversely affect the children; the specific circumstances of the case need to be explained. On the other hand, the DSS argues that as the penalty is a reduction in the parent's personal allowance, it cannot affect the children. CPAG believes this argument is unrealistic and unsustainable; any CSO who refuses to consider the effect on the welfare of the child is not exercising his/her discretion and should be challenged.

If a reduced benefit direction is in force and the Secretary of State or a CSO becomes aware that a question arises as to whether the welfare of a child is likely to be affected if the direction continues, a CSO must carry out a review.[93] The review will not be carried out by the CSO who issued the direction (see p120).

4. THE BENEFIT PENALTY

The reduced benefit direction lasts for 78 weeks in total and is based on the IS personal allowance for someone aged 25 or over (currently £47.90), whatever the age of the parent with care. The reduction in benefit is 20 per cent of the adult personal allowance for 26 weeks followed by 10 per cent for the remaining 52 weeks.[94] (Any fractions of over half a penny should be rounded up, and fractions of half a penny or less are ignored.[95]) Neither CSOs nor adjudication officers at the Benefits Agency have discretion to decrease the reduction or to shorten the period of the reduced benefit direction.

This reduction in benefit is made from IS, FC or DWA, depending on the benefit claimed or in payment for the parent with care. (It will be extended to means-tested jobseeker's allowance on its introduction in October 1996.) The reduction is made at the same rate regardless of whether a parent is on IS, FC or DWA. It is particularly punitive for 16- and 17-year-old mothers on IS who have a lower personal allowance, but who suffer the same penalty.

Benefit penalty 1996/97

Loss of benefit	Duration
£9.58	26 weeks (6 months)
£4.79	further 52 weeks (12 months)
A total penalty of 78 weeks (18 months)	

If benefit rates are increased at an April uprating during the course of a reduced benefit direction, the amount of the penalty alters. For IS, the amount of the penalty goes up from the next benefit week following the date of the uprating. For FC and DWA the penalty goes up on the first renewal claim following the date of the change in benefit rates.[96]

If applying the reduced benefit direction would reduce the amount of IS, FC or DWA to nil or to below the minimum payment for that benefit, then the penalty is itself reduced so as to leave the minimum amount.[97] The minimum amount payable is 10 pence for IS (or £5 if involved in a trade dispute), and 50 pence for FC and DWA. The penalty cannot be deducted from any other benefit which may be payable with IS – eg, unemployment benefit, incapacity benefit.

Where a reduced benefit direction is reduced in this way it does not mean that the penalty is extended to cover a longer period. A penalty should never last longer than 78 weeks, unless a further reduced benefit direction is issued for another child (see below). If other deductions are being made from an IS award, then the penalty does not take effect immediately (see p115).

If a parent with care is included in an award of FC or DWA when IS becomes payable, the penalty then applies to payments of IS instead. Where this happens, the reduction in benefit lasts for the number of weeks left to run on the penalty.[98] This is to prevent a parent who has had a reduced benefit direction applied to a FC or DWA claim from making up the loss in benefit through IS. Where the amount of IS in payment is not enough to cover the full reduction to be made, the minimum payment rule will apply, as above.

Only one penalty

Only one reduced benefit direction can be in force at any one time in relation to a parent with care.[99]

Once the full 78 weeks are up, no further direction can be given by the CSO in respect of the same child(ren).[100] This applies even if the parent with care refuses to co-operate on a subsequent claim for benefit. (For what happens if a direction has not been served in full, see pp117–18.)

More than one absent parent

If a parent with care has two or more children with different absent fathers and refuses to pursue them both, she receives only one reduced benefit direction.[101] If she pursues one but not the other, one reduced benefit direction can be imposed. Once a direction has been issued in relation to any child(ren), no further direction can be issued, unless there is a new qualifying child.[102]

New qualifying child

If a new qualifying child subsequently joins the family of the parent with care, a new question of authorisation arises. This could happen, for example, when a father has had a child living with him and the child decides to move in with her/his mother who is on benefit, when a subsequent relationship breaks down, or where a new qualifying child is born. The new child could be a child of the same absent parent, or of another absent parent.

If the new qualifying child joins the parent with care's family while a reduced benefit direction is in force and a CSO decides that a further direction should be imposed, the first direction will stop and a second one will start giving a fresh penalty of 78 weeks.[103]

A review is carried out by a Benefits Agency adjudication officer, and any new direction comes into operation on the first day of the second benefit week following the review, or what would have been the second benefit week if the penalty had not been suspended (see p117).[104] The original direction ends on the last day of the benefit week preceding the date when the new direction starts. Where the direction has lapsed because a parent has been off benefit for more than 52 weeks, the original direction is not reinstated, but is replaced by the new one (see p118).[105]

Where the new direction ends due to a review or because a parent has co-operated but an earlier direction is still in force, the reduction continues for an extended period.[106] The extended period is worked out by adding together the number of weeks for which the earlier direction was in force and the number of weeks for which the later direction was in operation, and subtracting this number from the total of 78 weeks. If the resulting direction is for more than 52 weeks it will be deducted from benefit at the 20 per cent rate for the number of weeks in excess of 52, and at the 10 per cent rate for the remaining 52 weeks. If the resulting direction is for 52 weeks or less, any reduction will be at the 10 per cent rate.[107]

When does the benefit penalty start

Once a reduced benefit direction has been issued, a Benefits Agency adjudication officer reviews the relevant benefit paid to or for the parent with care. The reduction is made to IS, FC or DWA from the first day of the second benefit week following any such review.[108]

If a recent benefit claim has been made, it should be processed as normal, and not held up while a decision is made about whether or not to impose a penalty.

Income support claimants

IS is paid for seven-day periods running from the day of the week payment is made.[109] This is known as a benefit week. A benefit week overlaps two calendar weeks (for more details, see CPAG's *National Welfare Benefits Handbook*). If a claimant's benefit week changes, then the reduced benefit direction can be modified slightly. The direction will last for between 25 to 26 weeks for the 20 per cent rate of reduction, and for between 51 and 52 weeks for the 10 per cent rate of reduction. The direction will end on the last day of the benefit week which ends before the 26- or 52-week period is up.[110] This ensures that a change in the benefit week does not result in a total penalty of more than 78 weeks.

Penalty deferred due to other deductions

A reduced benefit direction made after 22 January 1996 cannot take effect immediately if one of the following deductions is already being made from her or her partner's IS:[111]

- arrears of housing costs, fuel, water charges, poll tax or council tax;
- deductions for the payment of fines;
- repayment of overpaid benefit; *or*
- repayments of a social fund loan.

Once the deduction(s) cease, the parent with care will be notified that the benefit penalty will take effect after 14 days from the notification.[112] There is no provision to suspend a benefit penalty if any of the above deductions begin while a reduced benefit direction is in force. Therefore, a parent with care needs to have applied to the Benefits Agency – eg, for fuel direct payments – well before the reduced benefit direction is issued.

(For details of deductions made from IS, see CPAG's *National Welfare Benefits Handbook*.)

Penalty deferred until the next order book

Many IS claimants, particularly lone parents, are paid by means of an order book (rather than by girocheque). Where a parent with care is paid by order book and a reduced benefit direction would result in a small change to her benefit (ie, because of the minimum payment rule – see p113), the reduction can be deferred until a later date by the Secretary of State.[113] Any change in IS of less than 50 pence a week can be deferred up to the date when the claimant comes off benefit, or up to a week after the date of the last order in the book, whichever comes first.[114]

Family credit and disability working allowance claimants

FC and DWA claims will not be held up while maintenance is being assessed or a penalty considered. FC and DWA are usually paid for 26-week periods regardless of any changes in circumstances.[115] This means that where circumstances change during the 26 weeks – eg, income goes up or down, benefit rates change, or the claimant has another child – the amount of benefit paid continues unaffected, with very few exceptions (see CPAG's *National Welfare Benefits Handbook*).

However, FC and DWA *do* respond to a reduced benefit direction issued by a CSO. The following events count as a change of circumstances for FC and DWA:[116]

- a reduced benefit direction is issued by a CSO;
- a reduced benefit direction terminates, or is cancelled (see below);
- a reduced benefit direction is suspended because a parent is no longer the person with care, or the only qualifying child affected by a direction no longer counts as a child (see p118);
- a reduced benefit direction is again imposed because a parent or a qualifying child now counts as the person with care or a child again (see p118).

If a reduced benefit direction is given during an award of FC or DWA, the benefit concerned is reviewed and the reduction applies from the first day of the second benefit week which follows the review.[117] Benefit weeks for FC and DWA run from a Tuesday.[118] (For the date when a suspension, termination, cancellation or review decision comes into effect, see below.)

Small weekly FC/DWA entitlements (of 50 pence to £4) are sometimes paid as a lump sum instead of as weekly amounts. Where such a lump sum has been paid, the reduced benefit direction comes into force on the first day of any benefit week which follows the period covered by the lump sum.[119] If FC/DWA has stopped after the lump sum was paid and the direction cannot be imposed immediately, it comes into force if the parent with care starts getting IS/FC/DWA within 52 weeks of the original direction.[120] In such cases, the parent with care is sent a written 14-day notice to inform her that benefit will be reduced if she continues to fail to co-operate. The penalty cannot come into force until the full 14 days have expired and then it applies from the first day of the second benefit week after expiry. If IS/FC/DWA do not become payable within 52 weeks, the reduced benefit direction lapses.[121] If a parent with care starts getting IS at any stage during a period when she is covered by a lump-sum payment of FC/DWA, the reduced benefit direction and subsequent benefit penalty transfers to the IS claim immediately.[122] The benefit penalty is reduced if it would bring benefit entitlement to below the minimum (see p113).

When to claim benefits

When making a claim for IS, FC or DWA, a parent with care could consider the following points.

- There are at least 11 weeks before a reduced benefit direction can be issued (21 days to return the form, six weeks from a notice to comply, two weeks from a final notice). A claimant who is due to stop claiming IS, FC or DWA in the near future (eg, because she or her partner is about to take a better paid job) or who, for some other reason, is likely to be on benefit for only a short time, might find that they come off benefit before a reduced benefit direction can be issued.
- If a penalty is imposed and a parent is on FC or DWA, then the parent with care should ask immediately for a review of any housing benefit to take into account the reduced amount of her benefit.

If a penalty is imposed without the full 11-week procedure being followed, a complaint should be made (see p28) and a cancellation sought (see p119).

For more details of how receipt of child maintenance affects benefits, see Chapter 14.

When does the benefit penalty stop

A reduced benefit direction normally lasts for 78 weeks, but it can be brought to an end before the full period has been served in certain circumstances. A direction can be suspended, terminated, cancelled or reviewed.

Suspension means that a direction stops for a period, but the unexpired portion of the direction has to be served once the suspension is lifted. Where a direction **terminates**, it stops being in force from a specified date and the same direction cannot be resurrected.

Where a CSO **cancels** or **reviews** a direction, the direction no longer applies. The penalty is either lifted immediately and benefit repaid in full, or the direction stops being in force at the end of the week in which a change is notified.

Suspension of a reduced benefit direction

A reduced benefit direction can be suspended in the following situations.

Benefit claim ceases

If the parent with care comes off IS, FC or DWA altogether for less than 52 weeks, the direction is suspended. If she subsequently reclaims, then the unexpired portion of the reduction applies to the new benefit award.[123]

When a new claim starts, the parent is notified in writing by a CSO that the direction will continue if she fails to give authorisation again.[124] The parent with care has 14 days from the date the notice is served to decide whether or not to co-operate. If she fails to do so the direction again comes into operation. An adjudication officer reviews entitlement to benefit, and the remainder of the reduced benefit direction starts again from the first day of the second benefit week following this review.[125]

After 52 weeks off benefit the direction lapses.[126] Where a direction has lapsed and the parent concerned fails to co-operate in respect of a new claim, a new reduced benefit direction will be issued for what was left to serve of the original penalty.[127] In practice, this means that the CSA will need to go through all the stages again (from the initial request to co-operate to the final notice to comply) before any new direction can be issued for the unserved period of the earlier direction.

Parent no longer the person with care, or the child ceases to count as a child

Where the one and only child covered by a direction ceases to count as a child, or the parent stops being the person who looks after the child(ren), the direction is suspended from the last day of the benefit week in which this change occurs.[128] For example, if a child goes to live with someone else or leaves school (see p42), the direction is lifted from the end of the week this happens. The parent will be notified in the same way as when a direction lapses at the end of a benefit claim. A parent with care might be well advised to ask for a review of the reduced benefit direction in case the CSO is not aware of the change. For more on reviews, see below.

If the child starts to count as a child again, or the parent resumes the care, then the unexpired portion of the direction again applies to the benefit claim.[129]

Where the direction has been suspended for 52 weeks or more, it will lapse, as above.[130]

Parent goes into hospital, a nursing home or residential care

If a parent with care goes into certain types of accommodation or care, then the amount of her or his family's IS is worked out differently (see CPAG's *National Welfare Benefits Handbook*). This applies to private residential care and nursing homes, hospital in-patients, people detained under the Mental Health Acts and people in local authority or NHS residential accommodation.[131] If a reduced benefit direction is in operation, it is suspended for up to 52 weeks or for as long as the parent's benefit calculation is modified in this way, whichever period is the shorter.[132] Where a suspension has lasted for over 52 weeks the direction will lapse.[133]

Although the rules on suspension usually apply to temporary stays in local authority residential accommodation, they do not apply where a lone parent stays in a residential care home or a nursing home *temporarily*.[134]

Termination when a parent co-operates

If the parent with care decides to co-operate with the CSA and provide the required authorisation or information, the reduced benefit direction terminates on the last day of the benefit week in which she complies.[135] If the direction has already been suspended then it ends on the date on which she complied.[136]

Termination when someone else applies

The regulations state that if an absent parent makes an application for maintenance and it covers all of his qualifying children being looked after by the parent with care, and an assessment results, then any direction which has been imposed on the parent with care comes to an end.[137] However, the Act does not allow voluntary applications under section 4 when a parent with care is on IS/FC/DWA (see p55).[138] Therefore, if an application from an absent parent is allowed, it can be challenged by the parent with care.

In Scotland, when a child applies for a maintenance assessment which covers all of the qualifying children affected by the reduced benefit direction, and an assessment is made as a result, then the direction ends.[139]

The direction ceases to be in force on the last day of the week in which the information is given which allows an assessment to be made.[140] Where a direction has been suspended, the direction will cease to be in force on the date the necessary information is supplied.[141]

Cancellation of a reduced benefit direction

A reduced benefit direction can be cancelled where a CSO is satisfied that it was made as a result of an error made by the Secretary of State or a CSO. A direction can also be cancelled if as a result of an error it has not ended when it should have.[142] When a CSO cancels a direction in these circumstances, it is treated as if it had never been given, or as if it had been cancelled at the appropriate time.[143] This means that benefit is repaid for the whole period for which the direction has been in operation. There may be occasions where a direction has not ended when it should have. Where a direction is cancelled in these circumstances, benefit is repaid from the date the direction should have ended.

An error could be either administrative or an error in decision making. An example of an administrative error might be that information which was sent to a CSO was overlooked. A decision-making error includes where the original reasons given constituted good cause. The DSS position on this is that these circumstances could only give rise to an appeal or a request for a review.

Review of a reduced benefit direction

A reduced benefit direction can be reviewed by a CSO. A review will take place where:[144]

- a parent with care or some other person gives new reasons for failing to give authority (additional to any she gave in response to the final notice to comply); *or*
- the parent with care or some other person gives reasons why she should no longer be required to comply; *or*
- a question arises about the welfare of a child.

The CSO has to consider whether the direction should continue or stop.

If the Secretary of State becomes aware that a question arises as to whether the welfare of a child is likely to be affected should a direction continue, he must refer the matter to a CSO who must carry out a review.[145] Similarly, if it is a CSO who first realises that the question of the welfare of a child arises then, again, a review must be carried out by a CSO.[146] The review must not be carried out by the CSO who issued the original direction.[147]

In the above circumstances, a review should always be carried out. However, it appears that in practice, if the parent with care has appealed (see p123), the review does not always take place. This is incorrect in law and, if she is having to wait some months for a tribunal hearing, the parent with care should insist that the CSO carries out a review in the meantime.

The parent with care must be notified immediately about the review decision.[148] The CSO must give reasons for the decision in writing, and must also tell the parent with care about her right to appeal.[149] If a parent with care is not satisfied by the decision on review, she can appeal to a child support appeal tribunal (see p122).

If the CSO decides on review that a parent is no longer required to give authorisation or information, then the direction ends.[150] It stops being in force on the last day of the week in which the reasons are supplied which give rise to the review or in which the CSA becomes aware that a question has arisen about the welfare of a child.[151] If the direction has been suspended it ceases to be in force on the same date as the new reasons are supplied.[152]

Note: even if a parent with care is no longer getting benefit (or is in hospital or residential care) and, as a result, the direction has been suspended, she can still apply for a review to remove the direction for future claims.

Review or cancellation

In some cases the CSO has to decide whether to cancel a direction from its start or review it from a later date. This will depend on whether the reasons given for non-co-operation applied at the date of the original decision to issue a reduced benefit direction, or whether they are relate to a subsequent change of circumstance.

When first required to apply, a parent may give reasons for her belief that there is a risk of harm or undue distress which is not accepted, and a benefit penalty is accordingly imposed. If later the risk becomes reality, or new evidence becomes available which convinces the CSO that there were reasonable grounds all along, then this should arguably be treated as an example of a CSO error. For example, if a parent gave as a reason for non-co-operation that she feared violence and this was not accepted by the CSO, and later the absent parent is violent towards her as predicted, this shows that her original argument was correct from the date of the original CSO decision. In such a case she should request that the direction be cancelled. It would be advisable to make a late appeal against the original decision in case the request to cancel it is not successful. There appears to be no right to review or appeal a refusal to cancel a reduced benefit direction, as the regulations omit any such reference; judicial review could be considered (see p351).

If attempts to cancel a direction and to make a late appeal are unsuccessful, it is worth considering trying to persuade the CSA to make an ex-gratia or concessionary payment to make up for the loss of benefit. The first step is to write to the CSA asking for a refund. The intervention of an MP or the Ombudsman may help in these circumstances (see p29). Any such a payment would be made outside the usual child support rules.

Where a parent with care requests that a direction should be cancelled because she has new reasons for not giving authorisation or information to the CSA, then this request will usually be dealt with as a request to review the reduced benefit direction, not to cancel it. The disadvantage of a review decision is that the penalty is lifted only from the time the new reasons are supplied, rather than from the date of the original decision (see pp119 and 120).

If a penalty was imposed but the parent with care has since complied, she can withdraw her authority if she is able to persuade the CSO that she should no longer be required to give authorisation (see p72). Again, where a request to withdraw an application is based on new reasons, a review will result. If the same reasons applied on the date a reduced benefit direction was issued and the CSO was aware of these reasons at the time, then the parent should request that the direction be cancelled so that deductions made at the time it was imposed can be refunded. At the same time, she should appeal against the earlier decision (see below and p367).

Notice that a penalty will end

The CSO must tell the parent with care if the direction is going to stop, or in certain cases, be suspended.[153] The parent will receive a copy of a notification which has gone to the Benefits Agency adjudication officer specifying either the date the direction ceases to be in force or will be terminated, or when a suspension will start.[154] The reasons why the direction is going to stop must also be set out on the notice.[155]

This notice does not apply to cases where the direction is suspended because a parent goes into hospital, residential care or a nursing home, or where it is suspended because benefit has stopped being paid. Where a direction ends because the relevant benefit is no longer payable, a notice is not issued until a parent with care makes a new claim for IS, FC or DWA. If benefit is again payable for the parent within 52 weeks of the last claim, she will be given 14 days' notice that the direction and subsequent penalty will apply to the new claim (see p118).[156]

Appeals

A parent with care can appeal direct to a child support appeal tribunal (CSAT) against any decision to issue a reduced benefit direction,[157] or against a review decision she is not happy with.[158] This means that a parent can appeal to a tribunal without needing to apply for a review first. (For more details of appeals, see p367.)

This right of appeal applies only to a decision made by a CSO, not decisions of the Secretary of State. The reduced benefit direction is the first time in the requirement to co-operate process (see figure 5.3) that there is a right of appeal. It is therefore extremely important that a parent with care who believes there is a risk of harm or undue distress does not agree to co-operate at an earlier stage. There is no right of appeal against a Secretary of State's decision to refuse to allow the withdrawal of authorisation.

A parent with care has 28 days in which to appeal against a CSO decision to issue a reduced benefit direction. A late appeal can be allowed with the leave of the chair of the CSAT if there are special reasons (see p371).[159]

Parents with care should be careful to appeal against the original CSO decision to impose a reduced benefit direction and not against any reduction in benefit made by the Benefits Agency as a consequence. CSOs are reminded to give this advice to parents with care.[160]

While awaiting the outcome of a review or appeal, the reduced benefit direction will still be in force (unless she has co-operated in the meantime – see below). If the appeal is successful, the penalty will be lifted from the date of the original CSO decision, or – if appealing a review decision or where further information has been provided – as directed by the CSAT.[161]

Although technically the absent parent – if known – is a party to the proceedings (see p367), in practice he will *not* be contacted.

Appeal and co-operate

Parents with care whose reasons for claiming an exemption have not been accepted and who cannot afford to take the benefit penalty could opt to wait for the CSO's reduced benefit direction and then appeal immediately to the CSAT. At the same time, a parent with care could give authorisation to the CSA to act on her behalf. The benefit penalty will not then take effect (see p119), but the appeal will proceed.

The parent with care should explain that she is authorising under protest until such time as a CSAT decides the question of harm or undue distress, and that she still believes she is exempt but that she cannot afford to accept the benefit penalty. Although in these circumstances an assessment will proceed, it at least preserves the right of appeal. At present, many parents with care are missing out on this right.

Review or appeal

It is almost always advisable for a parent with care on benefit to appeal against the original decision to impose a reduced benefit direction, even if this means making a late appeal. In this way, all the lost benefit can then be repaid from when the penalty began. On review, benefit is only repaid from the week following the review (see p120). When deciding whether to continue with an appeal lodged prior to a CSO review decision, it is worth weighing up the possible gain through benefit being repaid as against the possibility that a CSAT might not make the same decision that was made on review. Although the CSAT is only re-considering the initial decision to impose the reduced benefit direction and not the favourable review decision, a dismissed appeal may trigger the CSA to look at the case again. If this happens, seek further advice as a review is only possible in the situations listed on p120.

CHAPTER SIX

Information

This chapter covers:

1. INFORMATION-SEEKING POWERS

The Secretary of State has wide powers to obtain information from (among others) parents, employers, local authorities and the Inland Revenue.[1] In addition, the Secretary of State can appoint inspectors who have extensive powers to obtain information (see p153).

The powers of the Secretary of State are exercised through the Child Support Agency (CSA) and much of the information-gathering takes place at local level. This work is carried out by local child support field staff acting in their role as representatives of the Secretary of State.[2] They are usually also responsible for any interviews or investigations which take place. Child support officers (CSOs) at the regional Child Support Agency Centres (CSACs) may ask for some information by post or by telephone, but they usually ask staff at the local level to get the information they need.

In the case of the maintenance enquiry form (MEF),[3] a request for further information in connection with a maintenance application form (MAF) which is not fully completed,[4] or for information in connection with a review,[5] the information is requested within 14 days, in the first instance. Otherwise, where information has been requested it should be provided as soon as is reasonably practicable in the particular circumstances of the case.[6] A request for information, other than a MAF or MEF, must set out the possible consequences of a failure to provide that information.[7]

In what circumstances can the CSA ask for information

The CSA can require information through the MAF or MEF (see p133). In a straightforward case almost all information will be sought through these forms. Where the information required in a MAF is not given, the application is not effective, and the applicant can be required to complete it properly (see p59). There are no regulations about what questions can be asked in the MAF. Where an applicant refuses to give information required in the MAF because it is irrelevant to the application, but the CSA refuses to accept the application without that information, she should consider challenging that decision (see p349).

Apart from this, the Secretary of State or CSO can require information only where:[8]

- an application for an assessment or for a review of an assessment has been made; *or*
- a review instigated by a CSO has not been completed.

When an assessment has been made and there is no outstanding review, there appears to be no power to require information. This seems to contradict the reference in the regulations to requiring information to collect or enforce an assessment. Whether the CSA can require information to do this is unclear.

Information can only be requested if it is necessary to:[9]

- decide whether there is a qualifying child, absent parent or person with care in relation to an application;
- decide whether the qualifying child, absent parent, or person with care are all habitually resident in the UK (see p47);
- decide which application has priority (see p76);
- identify an absent parent;
- trace an absent parent;
- assess the amount of child maintenance;
- identify how much is payable under a court maintenance order;
- collect child support maintenance or maintenance under a court order from an absent parent;
- work out interest on arrears;
- collect interest on arrears;
- identify any proceedings for a court maintenance order.

What information can the CSA ask for

Our references to information include evidence, such as statements and documents.

The regulations do not specify any restrictions on the kind of information the CSA can ask for, only on the purpose for which it is needed (see p125). The regulations state that the CSA can require information about, for example:[10]

- the habitual residence of the person with care, the absent parent and any child covered by the application;
- the name and address of the person with care and of the absent parent, their marital status, and the relationship of the person with care to any child covered by the application;
- the name, address and date of birth of any child covered by the application, the child's marital status and any education the child is undergoing;
- where there is more than one person with care:
  - who has parental responsibility (or parental rights in Scotland) for any qualifying child, *and*
  - how much time is spent by that child with each person with care;
- where parentage is disputed, who is the parent of a child and whether someone can be assumed to be a parent (see p40);
- the name and address of any current or recent employer of an absent parent or a parent with care and the gross earnings derived from any such employment;
- where the absent parent or parent with care is self-employed, the address, trading name, gross receipts and expenses, and any other outgoings of the trade or business;
- any other income of the absent parent or parent with care;
- any income of a qualifying child (except for earnings);
- how much is paid or payable under a court maintenance order or maintenance agreement;
- anyone who lives in the same household as the parent with care or absent parent, their relationship to them and to each other, and the date of birth of any child of those people;
- the employment, whether employed or self-employed, of anyone living with a parent with care or absent parent, but not of any child living in their household;
- any income, other than earnings, of anyone living with a parent with care or absent parent;
- benefits related to disability that the parent with care, absent parent or anyone living in the same household as either of them are entitled to or would be entitled to if certain conditions were satisfied;
- housing costs to calculate assessable or disposable income;
- details and statements of any account in the name of the absent parent or parent with care, including bank and building society accounts;

- whether a person counts as a child, or qualifying child, for the purposes of child support (see p41);
- information needed to decide whether an assessment should end or be cancelled (see p307);
- details of any transfer of property or capital between an absent parent and a parent with care or a qualifying child which counts as a qualifying transfer or compensating transfer under the formula (see p192).

Who has to give information to the CSA

Information can only be required from a person who has that information in his/her possession or can reasonably be expected to acquire it.[11] Information can be required from the people detailed below. Information can be given to the CSA when there is no obligation to provide it – eg, from a neighbour, GP, landlord or another organisation. Any such voluntary disclosure of information may be made without the knowledge of the persons concerned. However, there are rules and guidelines on what information can be disclosed to the parties and others (see p156).

Third-party voluntary disclosure to the CSA may break professional codes of practice, civil contracts or the Data Protection Act, depending on the circumstances. Information supplied to the CSA can give rise to a libel action.[12]

The relevant persons

The person with care, an absent parent, or parent treated as absent for the purposes of the formula and in Scotland, a child applicant, must provide the information on pp125–7 if requested.[13] They may also have to complete a MAF or MEF.

Someone who denies parentage of a child

Someone who denies parentage of a child named in a maintenance application can be required to give information *only* if it is needed:[14]

- to decide whether or not all the relevant persons are habitually resident in the UK and therefore whether the CSO has jurisdiction to make an assessment or to carry out a review; *or*
- to identify an absent parent.

This means, for example, that where the CSA only wants to identify a person as the absent parent, employment details would not normally be necessary and so should not be requested.

Employers

The current or recent employer of the absent parent or parent with care[15] can be required to give information *only* if it is needed:[16]

- to identify an absent parent;
- to trace an absent parent;
- to assess child maintenance;
- to collect child maintenance and maintenance under a court order from the absent parent; *or*
- to collect interest on arrears from the absent parent.

An employer of an alleged parent can only be required to provide information to identify and trace that parent.[17]

These rules apply where the employer is the Crown.[18]

Court officials

The following court officials[19] can be required to give information.

In England and Wales:
- the senior district judge of the High Court Family Division, or if a district registry was used, the district judge; *or*
- the district judge of a county court, or the chief clerk or other officer who may be acting on her/his behalf;[20]
- the clerk to the justices of a magistrates' court.

In Scotland:
- the Deputy Principal Clerk of Session of the Court of Session;
- the sheriff clerk of a sheriff court.

Court officials can be required to give information *only* where there is or has been a court maintenance order, or an application for such an order has been made but not determined[21] and the information is needed:[22]

- to identify how much is payable under a court maintenance order;
- to collect child support maintenance or maintenance under a court order;
- to identify any proceedings about a court maintenance order.

Government benefit departments

The DSS, including the Benefits Agency and the Contributions Agency, and the Department of Employment may give any information held for benefits purposes to the CSA.[23] This may involve, for example, the use of national insurance records from the Contributions Agency or child benefit records from the Benefits Agency. These could be used to trace an absent parent or to work out maintenance.

Local authorities

Local authorities may be required to give information but *only* if it is needed to decide whether there is a qualifying child, absent parent or person with care in relation to an application.[24] This applies only to the local authority for the area where one or more of the following resides or used to reside:

- the person with care;
- the absent parent;
- the parent treated as absent;
- the alleged absent parent; *or*
- in Scotland, a child applicant.

Local authorities must also give information to the Secretary of State which they have obtained in connection with any award of housing benefit (HB) or council tax benefit (CTB).[25] The Secretary of State gives a direction to the local authority or housing authority and, in respect of council tax, the billing authority (or levying authority in Scotland), to give this information. The information should be provided only if the absent parent or person with care is entitled to the benefit.[26] Only the following information can be requested and provided:[27]

- the amount of housing costs treated as eligible rent for the absent parent or parent with care;
- HB entitlement at the date the direction is given to the authority;
- the amount of council tax payable by an absent parent or person with care;
- CTB entitlement at the date the direction is given.

The Inland Revenue

The Inland Revenue can be required to disclose the current address or details of the current employer of an absent parent to the CSA.[28] Any information disclosed must not go any further than authorised officers, unless it is in connection with civil or criminal proceedings under the 1991 Act. Information is taken from records held in connection with the assessment and collection of income tax. It is unlawful for the Inland Revenue to give the CSA any other information.[29]

Not giving information and giving false information

Where the CSA requires information:

- not relevant to the reason for the request; *or*
- of a very different kind from the examples given in the regulations; *or*
- from a person who cannot be required to give it; *or*

- when the CSA has enough information to make a full assessment

the request should be queried. Where the CSA insists, refusal or a challenge to the request (see p351) should be considered.

Whenever a person in this situation refuses to give information, they should consider explaining that decision to the CSA, preferably in writing. A complaint to the CSA should also be considered (see p28).

The most common result of a refusal to give information is that a financial penalty is imposed, either through an interim maintenance assessment (IMA) (see p296) or through benefit. No one except an absent parent or person with care can be penalised for refusing to give information.

Where an absent parent refuses to give information which the CSO needs to make an assessment, an IMA may be made. This will usually be for a higher amount than a full assessment made using the withheld information. This can even happen where the absent parent cannot obtain the information because it is about his partner's income and she refuses to give it to him.

Where a parent with care on IS, FC or DWA refuses, a benefit penalty may be imposed (see p101). Where an absent parent refuses to give information about his partner's income and he has a joint child with that partner, a Category B IMA may be made (see p297).

Refusing to give information may lead to the CSA asking another person for that information. For example, an absent parent's employer may be asked for wages details, which may lead to the existence of the child becoming known in the workplace. Also, the person approached may provide inaccurate but convincing information – for example, a parent with care may give details about self-employed earnings which are too high. The absent parent would then need to persuade the CSA what the real figures are.

The CSA does not have to impose an IMA, but can make a full assessment if there is enough information available. This may involve making assumptions about income or housing costs which are unfavourable to one person.

Apart from where an inspector has been appointed (see p153), refusing to provide information or providing false information is not a criminal offence under the Child Support Acts. However, a person with care who gave information she knew to be false in order to get a higher assessment could be prosecuted under the Theft Act 1968 or, in Scotland, for fraud.[30] While benefits law gives the DSS the power to prosecute absent parents who fail to maintain a parent with care on IS, the DSS has assured CPAG that this will not happen where the CSA has jurisdiction (see *National Welfare Benefits Handbook*).[31]

2. TRACING THE ABSENT PARENT

The CSA may use its information-seeking powers to trace and identify the absent parent. Examples of these situations, drawn from CSA guidance, include those where:[32]

- the person with care cannot provide enough information to locate the absent parent; *or*
- the MEF has not been returned; *or*
- the absent parent stops paying maintenance and cannot be contacted; *or*
- a review form has not been returned.

In some situations parentage may also be investigated (see p139).[33]

The responsibility for tracing absent parents lies primarily with field offices.[34] There is also a special section in each CSAC to deal with more difficult cases.[35]

At the time of writing, the CSA had reported a 64 per cent success rate in tracing absent parents, which represents an average of 4,317 absent parents traced each month.[36] About 1,500 cases are abandoned each month and at the end of November 1995 there were 17,145 cases outstanding.[37]

How is the absent parent traced

The field office can undertake as many different tracing activities as are necessary to locate and identify an absent parent. All activities operate under the provisions laid out on pp124–30, with only those persons and agencies listed having an obligation to provide information. The following sequence of sources of information broadly reflects the process followed in tracing an absent parent:

- the Child Support Computer System (CSCS);
- the Departmental Central Index (DCI). This is a computer network which gives access to national insurance and Benefits Agency records. It can trace a person's national insurance number from a date of birth and the first three letters of a family name, or a full family name and first name.[38] Addresses can also be checked using the DCI system;[39]
- the Benefits Agency. The method used for tracing will depend on the benefit being claimed by the absent parent:
  - where an absent parent is on income support (IS) the CSA will check the IS computer system (ISCS). If both the CSCS and ISCS have addresses which the computer system marks as 'not confident', the CSA informs the Benefits Agency that it believes that the address may have changed and asks for any new evidence of

address held by the Benefits Agency.[40] If the Benefits Agency gets no response from the absent parent at the address held, IS is likely to be stopped;[41]

- where the absent parent is on FC/DWA, the CSA will telephone the Benefits Agency to establish the absent parent's address;[42]

- the Inland Revenue. If the absent parent is not on IS/FC/DWA and other traces have been unsuccessful, an enquiry is sent to the Inland Revenue;[43]

- the Contributions Agency. Enquiries are made to Contributions Agency Central Operations (CACO).[44] This is only done if traces so far have failed. An enquiry should not be made where the person has a common name and neither the date of birth nor national insurance number is known.[45] CACO can provide the CSA with a name and 'known as' name, benefit details, the microfilm number of employment details, the first six letters of the employer's name, any time spent in prison, dates outside the UK, employment or training services local office details and whether he has died.[46] It is also used to trace self-employed absent parents paying Class 2 contributions. Where this fails but a national insurance number is known, CACO is asked to notify the CSA of any new information coming to light. CSA action will be suspended, normally for 12 months, to await that information. The person with care will be notified that tracing action has been suspended;[47]

- the Employment Services Agency, including unemployment benefit offices;[48]

- the army, navy or RAF or Ministry of Defence if the absent parent is recently discharged;[49]

- the Prisoner Location Service;[50]

- employers. An employer should normally be contacted only after all other tracing methods have been tried. However, the employer may be contacted earlier – eg, if the DCI cannot trace the absent parent but the employer's details are on the MAF.[51] Initially, the employer will be contacted by telephone. CSA staff are instructed to be cautious when doing this, especially because the alleged parent may not be the parent. They are told to identify themselves as from the DSS, not the CSA, which is part of the DSS.[52] Employers should also be cautious about giving information in this way for reasons of confidentiality and so as not to breach data protection principles. Where contact by telephone is unsuccessful, the CSA will send the employer Form 154 requesting the person's address.[53] If the employer refuses or no reply is received, all tracing through the employer will stop.[54] Unless an inspector has been appointed (see p153), an employer cannot be penalised for refusing to provide information (see pp129–30). In any event, employers ought to check the correctness of any information with the employee before disclosing it;

- local records such as the electoral roll, legal aid office, contributions, pensions, war pensions, IS, social fund, family credit and long-term benefit records;[55]
- the person with care may be contacted at any time for information, especially if she lives in the same area as the absent parent or he visits the children.[56] The CSA will telephone the person with care:[57] if that is not possible, the CSA will write to her for information.[58] If there is no reply, an interview may be arranged.[59]

Interviews and visits may also be used. However, this appears to be an expensive method of tracing and CSA instructions are that it only be used as a last resort.[60] Interviews may be used where:[61]

- the person with care is unable to provide any new information and a visit to friends, relatives or associates may be helpful;
- no employment details are known or the employer will not co-operate;
- the person with care requests a home visit;
- the person with care cannot read or write;
- there has been no response to a CSAC enquiry – eg, the absent parent has moved.[62]

The person with care herself may be interviewed or visited.[63] The CSA asks for information about the absent parent: his last employer, officials he has to keep in touch with – eg, social worker, friends, relatives, his car, hobbies, places he socialises, his bank or any other details which could help trace him.[64]

Special section

A referral to a specialist tracing section at the CSAC will occur:

- where there is no national insurance number and a DCI specialist trace is required;[65] *or*
- where the field office is unsuccessful in tracing the absent parent.

The special section uses the same methods as the field office. A target is set for a 'confident' address to be found in 28 days.[66] The special section may refer cases back to the field office for further investigations.[67]

3. THE MAINTENANCE ENQUIRY FORM

Once an effective application (see p159) has been made, the CSA must give written notice of that to any person(s) with care, the absent parent and any person treated as an absent parent, other than the applicant, as soon as reasonably practical.[68] A MEF is sent to those notified along with a request to complete and return it within 14 days.[69] The CSA does not have to give notice or issue a MEF if it is satisfied that the application can be dealt with without a MEF.

Any notice sent to an absent parent must tell him the effective date (see p303) of any assessment to be made, and inform him about interim maintenance assessments (see p296).[70] The effective date is the date child maintenance has to be paid from.

Receipt of a MEF does not stop liability to pay maintenance under a court order or agreement. Only if and when an assessment (including an IMA) is made will a court order or agreement cease to have effect, and no earlier than the effective date (see p304). A person who is liable under an order or agreement should therefore continue payments. A person with no present liability who expects to have to pay child maintenance may wish to continue, or start, to make voluntary payments to prevent having to pay arrears later, or should put money aside regularly to pay any arrears.

CSA policy is that any child maintenance payments made before an assessment will be offset against the amounts due under that assessment (see p399). The absent parent should therefore keep records of all payments made.

Advance notice to an alleged absent parent

CSA staff are instructed to issue a MEF as soon as possible to prevent an absent parent putting off the effective date and, therefore, liability by disputing parentage.[71] However, a parentage investigation may take place before a MEF is issued, if the alleged absent parent has been named but there are insufficient details to issue a MEF or where he has not been named (see p139).

In some cases where there are insufficient details to issue a MEF, a telephone call may be made to an alleged absent parent. This happens where an alleged absent parent:[72]

- is registered as a parent of the child but is not aware that he is considered to be the child's father; or
- is neither registered nor aware that he is considered to be the father.

The call will inform the alleged absent parent that he has been named as a parent of the child and that a MEF is going to be issued.[73] If it is not possible to contact him by telephone, a card will be sent asking him to contact the CSA. The card bears only a DSS logo and contact number. A reply is requested within 14 days and, if none is received, a MEF will be issued on the assumption that the alleged absent parent has chosen not to make contact.[74]

Where the alleged absent parent denies paternity, the CSA advises him only to complete the identity details on page 2 of the MEF and the declaration.[75] If the MEF is returned fully completed and no indication is made that paternity is denied, the CSA will proceed on the basis that the alleged absent parent accepts paternity.

Authorising a representative

An absent parent can authorise a representative to act on his behalf, either on the form (which has a special section for this) or in writing. The representative does not have to be legally qualified. Written confirmation is not essential for legal representatives, but it is required for lay representatives.[76] The representative can apply for and provide information to the CSA and receive documents, notices and even payments on behalf of the absent parent.[77] Other representatives are entitled to act in place of the absent parent in every respect, such as: a person with power of attorney, a receiver, a Scottish mental health custodian or mental health appointee.[78]

Information asked for on the form

The MEF is provided along with an introductory leaflet and help-notes in a child support maintenance enquiry pack. The pack is accompanied by a letter (CSA21) which names the person with care and the qualifying children covered by an application. This may have the effect of disclosing any change of name by the person with care (and/or her children) to the absent parent.

The letter and introductory leaflet explain that the form has been issued because the person named has asked the CSA to make a maintenance assessment for the named children. They also state that people who are in receipt of IS, FC or DWA 'may be required by law to make an application to the CSA to recover child maintenance'.

The introductory leaflet outlines very briefly the assessment and payment of child maintenance and explains that there is a contribution towards child maintenance expected from some people on IS. It also explains that an interim maintenance assessment could be made if the form is not returned, a point re-emphasised in the help-notes.

There are three types of MEF. The first is for absent parents (CSA3), the second is for parents with care treated as absent parents under the formula (CSA3 (AP)), and the third is for persons with care where a child in Scotland has applied (CSA3 (CIS)).

The MEF, like the MAF, is divided into four sections. The sections ask for details of the absent parent and his family, details of income, housing details and other details.

Absent parent's details

The first section of the form asks for the following details of the **absent parent**:

- the name, address and telephone number of the absent parent and any partner;
- his sex, date of birth, and national insurance numbers of himself and his partner;
- whether he accepts that he is a parent of all, or some, of the children named in the accompanying letter;
- whether the children named live with him and stay overnight at any time;
- whether there is a court order for child maintenance for any child(ren) named and which child(ren) it is for;
- whether there is a written agreement or other arrangement for child maintenance for the child(ren) named, when it was made, the amount and how often it is paid;
- whether maintenance is paid for any other child(ren) not named;
- whether he made or agreed a settlement involving a transfer of property or capital to the person with care or a child named;
- whether he wishes to use the collection service as well as the assessment service;
- details of whether he or his partner are registered blind, or receive invalid care allowance (ICA) or disability living allowance/attendance allowance (DLA/AA) or send in sick notes for another claim;
- his marital status;
- whether anyone else over 18 lives in his household.

The form also asks for the following details of **each child under 19** who lives with the absent parent:

- her/his name;
- her/his date of birth;
- her/his national insurance number (if over 16);
- her/his sex;
- the relationship of this child to the absent parent and his partner;
- how much child benefit is paid each week and the child benefit number;
- whether the child gets DLA/AA or is registered blind;
- whether the child normally stays with someone else overnight and, if so, who;
- whether a local authority has part-time care;

- whether he has more than four children (if there are more a separate form is sent).

Income details

The second section of the form asks for details of the income from all sources (unless on IS) of the absent parent and his partner. The income of an absent parent's partner will not often affect the amount of an assessment (see p198). However, if she withholds details, a Category B interim maintenance assessment could be imposed (see p297). Advice should be sought to see whether withholding information will actually affect the assessment. People on IS are referred straight to the 'representative details' and 'declaration' sections.

The following details are requested:

- student income, grants, loans and any parental contribution;
- if self-employed, whether a sole trader, sub-contractor or partner in business (further information is requested later);
- employment details, including name and address, telephone number, and any work number, department or job title;
- whether he works at more than one address for the same employer;
- travel-to-work costs and any employer's contribution to them;
- whether he has a company car;
- how many round trips he makes weekly to work, leaving out trips during the working day and those taking less than two hours;
- whether he works shifts or irregular hours;
- how often paid, gross pay before deductions and whether the amount on the wage slips is different from normal (the CSO can ask for evidence for any period in the eight weeks before the relevant week – see p205 – up to the date of the assessment). If wage slips are not available, form CSA150 can be sent to the employer to confirm details;
- details of any bonus or commission, or expenses in the last 52 weeks;
- details of a second job;
- pension details (personal, company or occupational scheme);
- benefit income of himself and his partner and any of the children, except HB and CTB;
- income from savings, capital or investments in the last 52 weeks, and whether derived from divorce or separation;
- income from maintenance in the last 13 weeks, the amount and when paid from;
- child(ren)'s income from maintenance, capital, or investments in the last 52 weeks;
- income from rent;

- income from board and lodging;
- other income in the last 26 weeks.

Housing details

The third section of the form asks for the following details:

- whether the absent parent or her/his partner lives with relatives or friends;
- rent and housing benefit details;
- whether the tenancy is shared with anyone else;
- council tax liability or rates in Northern Ireland;
- board and lodging payments and housing benefit;
- details of home ownership;
- mortgage/loan details used for the purchase of the home or for major repairs or improvements to the home and any endowment policy, pension plan or personal equity plan linked to that mortgage/loan;
- details of any residential care home, nursing home or residential accommodation.

Other details

- whether there are any objections to paying child maintenance direct to the person named in the letter;
- whether there is any preferred method of payment;
- how often the absent parent would prefer to pay child maintenance;
- bank or building society account details in case direct debit payments are made.

A section is provided for details of any other person acting on behalf of the absent parent – eg, an appointee, custodian, receiver or attorney. Once this section has been signed, any representative who is named here, whether or not legally qualified, will be sent all correspondence, documents and notices instead of the respondent. No option is provided on the form to allow both the respondent and their representative to receive copies of the correspondence. This is followed by a checklist to show which documents are being sent with the form, and then a page which is left blank to allow the absent parent to provide any further information which he thinks might be useful. Forms CSA150 (confirmation of earnings) and CSA6 (confirmation of mortgage details) are included in the pack.

A declaration follows which says:

I declare that the information I have given on this form is correct and complete.

On the final page there is a section used by interviewing officers who have filled out the MEF on behalf of an absent parent. The entries are read back to him and he is asked to confirm the details by signing the form.

Returning the form

The MEF must be completed according to the instructions and returned to the Secretary of State within 14 days.[79] Information can be amended at any time, provided that any changes relate to the period before the effective date and an assessment has not yet been made.[80] If changes occur after the effective date (see p303) but before an assessment has been made, this can be dealt with by requesting a change of circumstances review. After an assessment has been made, any change is again dealt with by requesting a change of circumstances review (see p355).

The general rules on service of documents apply to the MEF (see p104). When a form is returned by post, the Secretary of State treats it as having been sent on the day s/he receives it, but has discretion to backdate the date of receipt if there was unavoidable delay.[81] If the MEF is not returned or is returned incomplete, further action may be taken (see below and p150).

Because returning the form within 14 days with all available information will usually delay the effective date by eight weeks (see p303), it is usually in the absent parent's interest to do this rather than wait until he has all the information requested.

4. PARENTAGE INVESTIGATIONS

Where parentage has been denied, a maintenance application cannot go ahead except where the CSO can assume parentage (see p41). In the majority of cases it will be an absent father disputing paternity.

Paternity is usually investigated where there is a paternity dispute, doubt about paternity or insufficient information to proceed. CSA guidance lists the circumstances where further investigation of paternity may take place. These are:[82]

- where there is insufficient information on the MAF;
- the MEF is not completed or returned;
- information or evidence received indicates that paternity is in doubt – eg, more than one possible father is named;
- the alleged absent parent has no contact with the child;
- the alleged absent parent denies paternity;

- the alleged absent parent is not registered as the parent of the child;
- the alleged absent parent does not know that the person with care considers him to be the parent.

Paternity investigations can take place both before and after the issue of a MEF (see p134).

Paternity may be denied after an assessment has been made or on review. The denial of paternity should mean that the assessment is suspended until the issue of paternity has been determined.[83]

Where paternity is raised as an issue during an appeal to a child support appeal tribunal (CSAT), only the issues not relating to paternity may be considered by the CSAT. The CSA will investigate paternity (see p370).

Interviews to investigate paternity can be carried out with the parent with care and alleged absent parent and, where necessary, other witnesses may be interviewed (see p148). The CSA or the person with care can make an application through the courts to obtain a declaration as to whether or not the alleged absent parent is one of the child's parents.[84] The courts can direct blood tests to be made, which could mean the use of DNA tests. It is not the CSA which orders DNA testing, though the CSA can offer reduced cost tests to alleged absent parents. For DNA tests see pp38 and 148.

If at any stage the alleged absent parent accepts paternity, a MEF is completed at an interview.[85] If there is not enough time to complete a MEF, a parentage agreement form (CSA610) is completed.

The dispute can be about one or all of the qualifying children. The CSA can proceed with the assessment for those children for whom paternity is accepted while paternity investigations are taking place for others.

Procedures for a parentage investigation

Paternity investigations are now carried out at field offices. Much of the procedural guidance on paternity investigations concerns interviewing and seeking evidence of paternity prior to the issue of a MEF, despite assurances that the issue of a MEF will not be delayed by the denial of paternity.

This part of the book describes CSA procedural guidance and is therefore not a statement of the law. Only certain people are required by law to provide information to the CSA and in certain circumstances (see pp124–9). This should be borne in mind when using this section.

According to the CSA guidance, procedures are divided into those for section 6 applicants, those for section 4 applicants who are getting IS, FC or DWA, and those for section 4 applicants who are not on these benefits. Procedures which apply after a MEF has been issued are cross-referenced to those for section 6 applicants.

Section 6 applicant

Parents with care on IS, FC or DWA are subject to the requirement to co-operate. This means that most investigations of paternity will take place when the parent with care has given her authorisation but has provided insufficient information for the MEF to be issued, or the absent parent is not aware of the existence of any children, or he denies paternity.

Initially, the CSA will check previous records and other information – eg, court orders may have been made which indicate parentage.[86] If this is unsuccessful, the field officer will interview the parent with care (see p143 for full details of interviews).[87]

Different procedures will follow, depending on her response. If she:

- provides information which identifies the absent parent and the CSA decides that her evidence is reliable, a MEF will be issued;[88]
- does not co-operate, further action may be taken under the requirement to co-operate;
- co-operates, but there is insufficient information to issue a MEF or the alleged absent parent denies paternity, a field officer will interview the alleged absent parent (see p143).[89] If the alleged absent parent denies paternity, the parent with care will be interviewed again unless a full paternity statement was taken at the first interview and no new information has arisen since.[90]

The CSA will consider court action (see p38) unless the parent with care wishes to apply to court herself.[91] The parent with care is also asked if she and the child(ren) are willing to undergo DNA tests (see p148).[92] If she refuses to go to court or to undertake testing, the CSA will consider whether or not she has met the requirement to co-operate or whether she has good cause not to (see Chapter 5).[93]

Section 4 applicant on IS, FC or DWA

Slightly different procedures apply to persons with care who are voluntary (section 4) applicants but who are getting IS, FC or DWA – eg, a sister or grandmother. In these cases there is no requirement to co-operate and the guidance suggests that paternity ought to have been established before an application was made, though why this should be so is unclear.[94]

If there is insufficient detail to issue a MEF, the CSAC will ask the person with care for more information. If the person with care does not reply, the case may be suspended or the application refused.[95]

If information is provided and the alleged absent parent is registered as a parent and aware of the child's existence, a MEF will be issued.[96] If the query cannot be resolved and further information is required, or where the alleged absent parent is not registered as the parent and is unaware of the child(ren), the person with care may be interviewed.[97]

The questions asked by the field officer will depend on how well the person with care knows the mother and the alleged absent parent and details of their relationship. The interview is intended to avoid the issuing of a MEF to someone who has no connection to the mother or child(ren).[98] For details of interviews of persons with care, see p145.

If there is insufficient information following this interview, or a MEF has been issued and paternity denied, then the alleged absent parent will be interviewed.[99] After this the person with care may be interviewed again. At this point the child's mother may also be interviewed.[100] The person with care will be asked if she is prepared for the child(ren) in her care to undertake DNA testing.[101] The Secretary of State then decides whether or not the case should be referred to court.

At any stage, the CSA may refuse to proceed or to make an assessment if the person with care refuses to co-operate or to provide information.[102] Where the CSA does not investigate properly or quickly, or refuses a person with care's request to refer to court, a complaint (see p128) or judicial review (see p351) should be considered.

Section 4 applicant not on IS, FC or DWA

A person with care who is not on IS, FC or DWA will be asked to attempt to resolve a paternity dispute herself.[103] Paternity may still be disputed by the alleged absent parent, even though this may be unexpected. If so, a MEF is issued and an interview is arranged to see if there is any information which would allow parentage to be assumed (see p41).[104] If no such assumption can be made, the person with care will be advised to contact a solicitor to make an application to court.[105]

The CSA will explain that the court decides who bears the costs. If she agrees to make such an application, she is asked to tell the CSA if and when a declaration of parentage is made. The field officer will explain that if she does not want to apply to court the CSA will be unable to proceed (but see below our comment on whether this is lawful).[106]

The case remains a 'live' case but the person with care can choose to withdraw her application. If she wishes to withdraw her application, the field officer obtains a signed statement to this effect. Field officers are told never to advise or recommend withdrawal.[107] If the person with care neither withdraws nor applies to the court, the case is suspended for three months.

If, at this point, the CSO thinks that an assumption of paternity can be made from the information given, the alleged absent parent is sent a second MEF and advised that maintenance is accruing.[108] If a declaration of parentage is subsequently received, the CSA will go ahead with any effective date being the date that the first MEF was sent.[109]

The CSA's policy of never approaching the alleged absent parent or making a court application may be unlawful. This is because the Secretary of State has a discretion to investigate or apply to court in *every* case, including those of section 4 applicants not on IS/FC/DWA. Where the CSA refuses to take action, the applicant should consider challenging that decision (see p351).

Paternity denied on the MEF

Where paternity is denied on the MEF, both the person with care and the alleged absent parent are interviewed. Both parties may be interviewed (see below).

A further MEF may be issued and filled out at an interview with the alleged absent parent, or a parentage agreement form completed.

If paternity is still denied, questioning in anticipation of court proceedings continues (as for section 6 applicants above) and there may be a further interview with the alleged absent parent. If not, the CSA will check for a full birth certificate, and if one has not been provided, a copy is requested from the registrar general's office.[110]

Interviews

It is not compulsory to attend any interview, but see pp124–9 for who can be required to provide what information. A field officer must carry an identity card at any interview. For travel expenses for attending an office interview, see p107.

Interview with an alleged absent parent

When the CSA has obtained information from the person with care (see pp141 and 145) and decides to continue with the paternity investigation, the alleged absent parent will be asked to attend an office interview. If there is a failure to respond to two interview requests, the field officer will attempt to arrange a further interview by telephone, or arrange a home visit.[111] If there is also a need to check the alleged absent parent's address or he has not responded when notified of a visit, an unannounced visit may be made.[112] For more on tracing and identifying an alleged absent parent, see p131. A paternity interview will not be carried out over the telephone, unless the alleged absent parent insists on it.[113]

Field officers are instructed to request the following details from the alleged absent parent:[114]

- whether or not he knew the mother of the child at the time of conception;
- whether he had sex with the mother of the child and if so over what period of time;
- whether contraceptives were used;
- how long the relationship lasted, and whether he lived with the woman concerned as husband and wife;
- whether or not he has had any contact with the child(ren);
- his reasons for thinking that he is not the father;
- any other information which might support his view.

The alleged absent parent is also told about the reduced-cost DNA test and asked if he would be prepared to pay for it.[115] He is given an explanatory leaflet about the test and after the interview may be offered it (see p148).

These questions are in guidance only and the information requested is not detailed in the regulations. The absent parent need only answer these questions where he denies paternity and the information is needed to decide if he is the father.

Field officers are advised not to assume that an alleged absent parent is a child's father.[116] They are also advised not to think in terms of stereotypes and to establish a good rapport.[117] Guidance suggests that more information will emerge from a 'chat' if people are put at ease.

If the alleged absent parent accepts paternity, a MEF is completed at the interview or, if there is not enough time, a paternity agreement form.[118] If paternity is still denied, the alleged absent parent is told that his version of events will be put to the parent with care and, if there is still a dispute, the matter may be referred to court.[119]

Interviewing officers take notes and after the interview (including a telephone interview) two reports are completed. One is a 'factual' report and the other is an 'opinion' report. Field officers are instructed not to put these titles on the report.[120] The factual report is completed and signed as a statement of what was said in a form which could be used in court as evidence.[121] By contrast, the opinion report represents the field officer's impressions, recommendations and views of the alleged absent parent.[122]

Interviewing young absent parents

Where an absent parent is under 16 he should not be interviewed unless he is accompanied by an adult or parent and any interview must take place at his home.[123]

Where an absent parent under 16 is asked to attend such an interview, it may be worth challenging this on the grounds that the young person concerned does not have enough income to pay any child maintenance and, once assessed, he is likely to be exempt (see p169). CSA guidance comments that normally an assessment cannot be made for an absent parent under 16, but that it can if he has an independent income.[124] This is contradicted by field officer guidance which states that while a statement of paternity is required, no maintenance assessment is implemented for the under 16s.[125] The former guidance is legally correct as there is no minimum age for an absent parent under the 1991 Act, though the assessment will be nil unless it is for more than £4.80 (see p167).

In any event, the CSA will not refer a case to court until an alleged absent parent reaches 16.[126]

Before interviewing an under-16-year-old, field officers are advised to find out:[127]

- if there is a large age difference between the alleged absent parent and the parent with care;
- whether they each have a stable parental background;
- whether he acknowledges paternity;
- if they are both 'free of a history of mental illness';
- if they are judged to be 'of low intelligence';
- if they had a stable relationship prior to the child's conception and whether they intend to marry;
- whether the parent with care or her parents object to the approach by the CSA;
- whether there is any chance of a criminal prosecution – for example, for sex with a minor; *and*
- whether he has taken any interest in the child.

No guidance is given about how to obtain this information or what use will be made of it once it has been obtained.

For 16/17-year-olds, field officers are advised to obtain a statement of paternity and the guidance again states that an assessment is not implemented.[128] The guidance also says that an alleged absent parent of this age can choose to have a parent or guardian present at the interview. Field officers are instructed never to interview an alleged absent parent at school.[129]

For enforcement of assessments for under-18-year-olds, see p415.

Interview with a parent with care where parentage is disputed

Where someone has been named as the parent of a qualifying child and he denies it or may deny it if asked or is not aware of the child's existence, the parent with care may be interviewed about this. The field officer will usually interview the parent with care before the alleged absent parent.[130] Initially, she is questioned to get enough detail about her relationship with the alleged absent parent at the time of conception to establish whether or not a MEF can be sent.[131] A 'factual' and an 'opinion' report are completed after any interview (see p144). If the parent with care is a section 6 applicant and she refuses to co-operate, the interview may become a good cause interview (see p104).[132] If the alleged absent parent continues to deny paternity at this interview (see above), a further interview may take place with the parent with care.[133] Local CSA staff are trained to ask further questions in preparation for any possible court proceedings. The CSA may ask for the following details:[134]

- her full name and date of birth;
- her present address;
- the name and date of birth of the child(ren) concerned;
- the place the child was born and whether s/he was a full-term child and if not, the reasons why;
- whether the man is named as the child's father on the birth certificate and if so, whether and why paternity is now being denied;
- when and where she first met the father and in what circumstances – eg, was he a childhood friend, did they meet casually or were they introduced and if so, by whom;
- when and where sex first took place, how often, and over what period;
- whether contraceptives were used by either of them at or about the probable time of conception;
- her address at the time the child could have been conceived;
- the date of her last period before the date of conception;
- when she first discovered that she was pregnant and whether she told the man about it and if so, when and where, and what words the man used in reply and whether there were any witnesses – eg, best friend;
- why she did not tell him, if she did not, and whether anyone else did. If so, what was his reaction and can she provide the name and address of this person;
- the following exact wording is used to ask the parent with care about DNA testing: 'If the question of paternity cannot be resolved, the case may be referred to a family court. DNA tests establish with virtually no margin for error who are the parents of a child and courts would normally expect such tests to be done, if paternity is disputed. If this happens would you be prepared for you and your child(ren) to undertake such a test?' (A person with care who is not a parent is asked if she is prepared for the child(ren) in her care to undertake such a test.);
- whether she had sexual intercourse with anyone other than the father

in the three months before or after the date of conception, what the dates were and whether contraception was used;

- whether she is single, married, widowed, or divorced, with relevant dates;
- whether they ever lived together and if so, for what period and at what address and why the relationship broke up;
- if she was married at the time the child was conceived, the date of the marriage, whether she was separated from her husband and the date of separation, or whether she was living with another man;
- if she was living with her husband or he visited her during the relevant period, by reference to some specific event, the dates when she last had sex with him, and when she last met him before the child was born;
- whether she has any letters, postcards, birthday cards, etc, from the man and whether she can identify his handwriting;
- if the alleged absent parent has made certain allegations, whether she can refute them. If he has named another possible father, whether she can give details of any relationship;
- whether there is anyone, apart from herself, who can say that she was associating with the father at a time when the child could have been conceived, when she was obviously pregnant, or after the child was born;
- whether anyone, apart from herself, could say that she was regularly meeting the father on a social basis;
- whether anyone, apart from herself, was present when the man admitted responsibility for her pregnancy or paternity of the child, or behaved as if he were responsible;
- whether she is willing to give evidence in court.

These questions are taken from guidance given to CSA staff. Not all parents with care are asked the same questions – eg, questions about living together are not asked if she has never lived with the absent parent. If the person with care is not a parent of the child, most of the questions do not apply to her. Instead, she will be asked about both the alleged absent father and mother, for details of any documents giving her care of the child(ren) and any information she has about the relationship between the father and mother of the child(ren). The absent mother herself may also be questioned; an absent mother is usually easy to trace and question as she is almost always on the child's birth certificate.

If a parent with care on IS, FC or DWA does not want the case to go to court, this may be seen as a refusal to co-operate and she will be asked to explain (see p101).[135]

Information cannot be requested other than where needed for the reasons listed on pp125–7. The guidance does not stress the need to limit enquiries to those necessary or to strike a balance between the reason for the investigation and personal privacy. Rather, some questions seem to be a 'fishing expedition'.

Where a person considers the question(s) inappropriate, she should ask the interviewer the point of the questions. If the interviewer insists, the person with care could ask to end the interview so that she can consider whether to give the information requested. She may wish to ask the interviewer to write down the questions and the reason for them. If at the interview, or later, she refuses to answer any of the questions, she should indicate that she has given all the information that is necessary to trace and identify the father. See p129 for refusal to give information.

Witnesses

If the person with care and alleged absent parent dispute parentage, or there is insufficient information on parentage, a witness may be contacted.[136] This could be a friend who can confirm a relationship between the mother and an alleged absent parent at the time of a child's conception.[137] S/he may also be asked to confirm part of a statement.

Witnesses may be asked to attend an interview, and if they refuse field officers are advised to try and find out the reasons for any refusal.[138] Only certain people can be required to give information by law (see pp127–9). At an interview the officer will seek confirmation of details already known and an opinion will be formed about whether or not the person would make a reliable witness in court.

CSA solicitors decide who to call as witnesses if a case is referred to court.[139]

DNA testing

Where there is a dispute about parentage, both the parent with care and the alleged absent parent are interviewed and asked if they will agree to undertake a DNA test before court proceedings (see pp144 and 146). They do not have to agree but, if the case went to court, inferences could be drawn from a refusal to submit to testing.

The CSA offers discounted tests (about £430 in total) to alleged absent parents.[140] This is not available to all absent parents (see below). The alleged absent parent is made aware of the availability of the discounted test and given an explanatory leaflet at a parentage interview. The CSA may contact the alleged absent parent after this to offer him the test. The alleged absent parent must agree to the results being passed to the CSA. Alleged absent parents pay the discounted fee direct to the independent testing agency.

Where the alleged absent parent is found not to be the parent, a full refund of the cost of the test will be made, except where the test is in respect of a section 4 or 7 application.

Where the alleged absent parent is shown to be the parent, the CSA will send him a MEF in order to make an assessment.

A parent with care who incurs any additional expenditure (eg, travelling expenses) in attending for the test may be able to claim a refund for these from the CSA.[141]

Where a court decides the alleged parent is the parent, the court can order him to pay costs, including the costs of any tests (see p38). If DNA tests were done in relation to the absent parent without a formal court request or direction, the CSA can recover the costs of those tests from the absent parent where the tests do not exclude that person from being the parent;[142] *and*

- *either* the parent does not now deny that he is the parent; *or*
- a court has made a declaration that he is a parent (in Scotland, a decree of declarator of parentage).

Preparation for court proceedings

When all possible action and investigation has been completed and there are no further interviews to be held with the parent with care or alleged absent parent, a CSA manager decides whether to refer the case to court for a declaration of parentage (in Scotland, declarator of parentage), or to suspend the case for 12 months.[143] A file is compiled detailing all interviews, phone calls, correspondence and investigations, including exhibits such as a birthday card from the alleged absent parent to the child,[144] and an opinion is given on the reliability of the evidence. At this stage, consideration is given to whether a section 6 applicant has co-operated (see p101).[145]

If a case is to go ahead, a proceedings file is prepared by the CSA. In Scotland, all such files are referred to the solicitors' office at the Scottish Office,[146] or in England and Wales, to the solicitors' branch (Sol B2).[147]

In England and Wales, the CSA prepares an Application and Notice of Hearing (CSA608) and the respondent's reply (CSA609).[148] In Scotland, the solicitor does this.[149] The first court hearing is a directions appointment which is an informal hearing where the parties produce the available evidence and the clerk to the court arranges procedure. The CSA interviewing officer may be required to attend.[150]

In court cases, it is the clerk (in England and Wales) or the solicitor to the sheriff (in Scotland) who decides whether or not to request blood tests and this may put off the full hearing date. It is not compulsory to submit to blood testing but inferences may be drawn from any refusal.

Notice of a full hearing at a magistrate's/sheriff's court is sent to all parties. The magistrate or sheriff then considers whether or not to make a declaration of parentage on the available evidence.

If the court decides the person is not the parent, the requirement to co-operate procedure may be considered again.[151]

5. FURTHER INVESTIGATIONS

Apart from the enquiries dealt with above – the MAF (p61), MEF (p133), tracing the absent parent (p131) and parentage investigation (p139) – the CSA may make further enquiries when considering an application or review. In practice, the CSA normally makes no further investigation where:

- parentage is accepted; *and*
- the MAF and MEF are both fully completed; *and*
- the documents requested in the MAF and MEF are provided.

Even where one parent challenges the details provided by the other, the CSA is reluctant to make any further enquiries.

Once a MEF has been returned, the CSA will check to see that it is complete. Further details may be needed – for example, if there is no national insurance number, action is taken to trace it (see p131).[152] Supplementary forms may be issued – for example, if the absent parent has more than two jobs or if additional details are needed.[153] Other details may be requested by telephone or by issuing a general enquiry form (CSA191). CSACs are advised never to return a signed MEF to the absent parent.[154] Investigations will also take place where employment details have to be checked with an employer (see pp128 and 151–2), or to check birth records if only the short version of the birth certificate is provided.

The CSA usually uses telephone investigations before considering the use of any other, more expensive method – eg, an interview or using an inspector. Field officers (see p21) normally carry out any interviews, and these usually take place at the local office or at the person's home. A 'factual' and 'opinion' report are usually completed after any interview (see p144).

More intrusive investigation might take the form of checking facts with friends and neighbours, or visiting a person's home. The CSA has said that details are not checked with neighbours and friends as they are not specified in the regulations as people from whom the CSA can get information.[155] If, in practice, such people are asked for information, it should be remembered that no one other than the people specified on pp127–9 can be required to provide information to the CSA.

An inspector may be appointed (see p153).

The need for evidence

Action to collect and verify evidence is taken by the Secretary of State, even if in practice it is carried out by an officer who is also a CSO.[156] However, the decision to require further evidence is taken by a CSO and it is up to her/him to decide when enough evidence has been gathered.[157] CSOs are advised to weigh carefully any direct, indirect or hearsay evidence – eg, documentary, written or oral evidence.[158]

Corroboration of evidence – that is, other evidence to support what the CSO already has – is not requested unless the evidence the CSO has is self-contradictory, improbable, or contradicted by other evidence.[159] For example, where a self-employed parent says s/he has done no work for six months, that will normally be accepted without any written evidence.

CSA guidance says that hearsay evidence – that is, evidence from one person of what another person has told her/him, or of what s/he has read[160] – is of limited value and should be given limited weight – for example, a report from a parent with care that an absent parent's earnings have increased.

CSOs are reminded that someone other than the applicant may have the information required – eg, when an application is made by a child in Scotland and income details are needed from the person with care.[161]

Verifying information

Verification of housing costs and earnings is automatically sought by the Secretary of State.[162] This is done in the MAF and MEF. Written details are required where possible.[163]

CSOs may request verification by telephone, by post, by computer-generated notice or by asking field officers to obtain verification on their behalf at an interview or visit.[164] Enquiries are made 'on behalf of the DSS' and written permission should be requested to contact an employer, bank or building society.[165]

CSOs are advised, where possible, to obtain signed statements.[166] Any signed statement should be accompanied by a signed and dated explanation of the circumstances in which it was made, especially if the statement is adverse to anyone's case.[167]

Verification from an employer is only requested if the employee cannot provide it (see p137).[168] A request for information from an employer should be addressed to the Personnel Officer and sent in an envelope marked private and confidential.[169] A reply is requested within

14 days. If the employer refuses to provide the information requested an inspector may be appointed by the area manager.[170]

Verification of self-employed earnings is dealt with at the CSAC by a special section. Again, evidence of income will be requested by post within 14 days.[171] Evidence is requested in the form of a profit and loss account, a trading account, or a balance sheet.[172] Alternatively, details of income and outgoings for a period of between 6 and 15 months ending in the 24 months before the relevant week are requested; where there is more than one such set of accounts, only the most recent will be examined unless this is not available for reasons beyond the control of the person;[173] or a shorter period if more recently self-employed.[174] If not supplied, a reminder is issued and a further seven days is allowed.[175] After this, an IMA may be considered (see p296), although CSOs are reminded that there may be a good reason for the delay, such as accounts being at the accountants, Inland Revenue or Customs and Excise.[176] The CSAC may check that this is the case.

Benefit details are requested direct from the paying agency, but only where there is some doubt about the amount.[177] IS details are obtained through the Income Support Computer System (ISCS). The CSA does not record details of other benefits received by IS claimants.[178]

Other income details are requested only if the CSO is in doubt about the evidence.[179] These details may also be verified during the regular verification of 2 per cent of assessments generated at random by the CSCS.[180]

Details of housing costs and council tax are requested in writing. Evidence of any other costs, such as tax-deductible expenses not met by the employer, is only requested if apparently too high.[181]

Where the CSA does not investigate

In some cases the CSA fails to investigate to the satisfaction of one party to an assessment. Except where an absent parent believes that a person with care on IS should not be entitled to IS (see p351), this situation will not usually arise until the assessment is made. This is because the parent with care is only then notified of the absent parent's income (see p300). If at any stage a person believes that the CSA ought to make more enquiries, the CSA can be asked to do so. The most effective way is for a letter to the CSA to explain all the information the person has, to ask what enquiries have already been made and to suggest further enquiries. Reference should be made to the Secretary of State's power to require information (see p124) and to appoint an inspector (see below). Where the CSA refuses to say what steps have been taken or to make further enquiries, it may be possible to challenge that by judicial review (see p351), but in practice this is unlikely to be effective. An appeal to a child support appeal tribunal (CSAT) after a second-tier review of the assessment means that the CSAT can make enquiries (see p374). The CSAT can do this as soon as an appeal is made. The CSAT has more powers than the CSA and it may be easier to persuade it to use them.

A person who is dissatisfied with CSA enquiries can also make their own enquiries and pass the information obtained to the CSA. In particular, a person with care applying for a court order for spousal maintenance (see p37) may receive information about the absent parent's income.

The inspectors

The Secretary of State can appoint inspectors in a particular case where s/he considers it appropriate to do so, for the purpose of obtaining information required under the 1991 Act.[182] However, inspectors are appointed very rarely.[183] The inspector:

- is appointed for a limited period, although this can be extended. S/he can also be appointed in relation to more than one case;[184]
- must have a certificate of appointment;[185]
- must produce the certificate when entering premises, if required to do so.[186]

The inspector will normally be an existing CSA employee. Each field office manager keeps blank certificates and a register listing the date a certificate is issued, the name of the officer to whom it was issued, the address/title of the place to be visited, the period for which the certificate is valid and the name of the person from whom the CSA wants information.[187] See figure 6.1 for a copy of a certificate.

If an office in Great Britain needs to appoint an inspector in Northern Ireland, or the other way around, an inspector can be appointed there.[188]

Powers of inspectors

Inspectors have the power to enter premises (except those used only as a home) to make enquiries, and to inspect documents.[189] The power to enter premises does not include any power to enter by force.

Inspectors also have wide powers to question people. An inspector can question any person aged 18 or over found on the premises s/he has entered,[190] and to request all such information and documents s/he might reasonably require from:[191]

- an occupier of the premises;
- an employer or employee working there;
- anyone else whose work or business is based at those premises;

Figure 6.1: **EXAMPLE OF A BLANK CERTIFICATE**

CHILD SUPPORT ACT 1991

To all whom it may concern

In accordance with Section 15 of the Child Support Act 1991; ....
(an officer of the Department of Social Security, whose signature appears below) has been duly appointed as an inspector for the purposes of the Child Support Act 1991. Inspectors so appointed have the power under Section 15:

1 to enter at all reasonable times:

   a any premises specified on this warrant, other than premises used solely as a dwelling house; and

   b any premises which are used for the purpose of carrying on any trade, profession, vocation or business, by someone specified on this warrant; and

2 to make such examination and enquiry there as may be appropriate;

3 to question any person aged 18 or over whom he finds on the premises.

If required to do so by an inspector exercising his powers, any person who is or has been an occupier of the premises in question, an employer or an employee working at or from these premises, or carrying on at or from those premises any trade, profession, vocation or business shall furnish to the inspector all such information and documents as the inspector may reasonably require to ensure that the Child Support Act 1991 is being complied with.

Under Section 15 of the Child Support Act 1991, any person shall by guilty of an offence and liable on summary conviction to a fine not exceeding level 3 on the standard scale if:

1 they intentionally delay or obstruct any inspector exercising his powers; or

2 without reasonable excuse, refuses or neglects to answer any question or furnish any information or to produce any document when required to do so under this section.

No person is required to answer any question or to give any evidence tending to incriminate himself or, in the case of a person who is married, his or her spouse.

By order of the Secretary of State for Social Security this .... day of
................................./.................... is certified by me .... Manager
.... Office to visit:

1 the employer of .... at ....

2 Mr.. at ....

   to inquire into their/............................. financial circumstances with regard to making a provision for the periodical payment of maintenance.

This warrant is valid from .... until ....

Signature of Officer named above ....

- an employee or agent of any of the above.

An inspector can enter Crown premises in order to obtain information as long as the Queen is not in residence. Crown employees or anyone carrying out Crown functions on the premises can be questioned and asked for information in the same way as anyone else.[192]

The powers of the inspectors are set out in the Act itself, and are not limited by the regulations on information (see pp124–9). In any event the information requested must be *reasonably* required.[193] The premises which may be entered must be specified in the certificate of appointment or be premises used for a trade, profession, vocation or business by a person or persons specified in the certificate. Inspectors can only use their powers when trying to enter premises or on those premises. They cannot make enquiries elsewhere, for example, door-to-door or by telephone. These enquiries would have to be made by the Secretary of State.

Deliberately delaying or obstructing an inspector carrying out her/his duties is an offence. Failing or refusing to answer a question or to provide evidence requested is an offence, unless there is a good reason for not doing so.[194] The maximum fine for such an offence £1,000.[195] However, no person is required to give any evidence or answer any question which might incriminate them or their spouse.[196]

We assume that a solicitor is entitled to claim privilege as regards information about a client's confidential affairs and can refuse to give information. The CSA has also given assurances that the powers of inspectors will not be used in relation to any other representatives, unless information is required from an employer about an employee.

CSA guidance suggests that inspectors will only be used when employers or the self-employed refuse to supply information.[197]

6. DUTY TO DISCLOSE CHANGES

There is generally no duty to volunteer information about any changes of circumstance to the CSA. However, there are some changes which must be notified. These only apply to a person with care and only when an assessment has been made, including a nil assessment.

A person with care has a duty to tell the CSA if she believes that an assessment has ceased to have effect because of one of the following:[198]

- the person with care, absent parent or qualifying child has died; *or*
- the person with care, absent parent or qualifying child is no longer habitually resident in the UK (see p47 for the meaning of habitually resident); *or*

- the absent parent and person with care have been living together for six months (see CPAG's *National Welfare Benefits Handbook* for meaning of living together); *or*
- the absent parent stops being an absent parent of the child or, if there is more than one, all the children named in the assessment – for example, because the child is adopted; *or*
- a child no longer counts as a child, or qualifying child (see p41); *or*
- a new assessment replaces an existing one in respect of any qualifying child; *or*
- if she believes an assessment should be cancelled because she has stopped being a person with care in relation to the child or, if there is more than one, all the children named in the assessment.

When informing the CSA of her belief, the person with care is also required to give the reasons for the belief. She may then be required to give further information for a decision to be made.

The person with care is not required to inform the CSA until the change has taken place. There is *no* duty to disclose information to the Secretary of State or CSO *except* in the circumstances described above. This means, for example, that a person with care does not have to disclose a change of income. This contrasts with the position for social security claims, where there is a continuing duty to disclose any relevant change of circumstances.

For the effect of not disclosing information, see p129. No person other than a person with care has a duty to disclose a change of circumstances.

7. DISCLOSURE OF INFORMATION BY THE CSA

In the course of their investigations, CSOs collect a lot of information and evidence about people affected by maintenance applications. CSOs are allowed to give out information where it is specifically required. Some forms of disclosure are part of a CSO's duties, such as giving information to courts, tribunals, the DSS or local authorities.

Each party to a maintenance assessment is given details of how the assessment has been calculated (see p299). There is some dispute about whether or not the disclosure of these details accords with the Data Protection Act. Concern over possible contraventions include the collection of excessive information, the retention for longer than necessary of personal data, and the use and disclosure of information in circumstances which may differ from the reason the details are held. However, as part of the DSS, the CSA is protected from prosecution under the Data Protection Act.

The CSA may disclose information given to it by one party to an assessment to another party in order to explain:[199]

- why an application for child maintenance or s17 or 18 review is rejected; *or*
- why an application cannot be proceeded with or why an assessment will not be made; *or*
- why an assessment is cancelled or ceases to have effect; *or*
- how an assessment has been calculated; *or*
- why a decision has been made not to arrange for, or to stop, collection of child maintenance; *or*
- why a particular method of enforcement of child maintenance has been used; *or*
- why a decision has been made not to enforce or to stop enforcement of child maintenance.

The parties to an assessment are the person with care, the absent parent and a child applicant in Scotland. Where one of those people has died, a person appointed to represent that person or a personal representative handling a review or appeal for one of those people is also a party.[200] Parties must apply for this information in writing to the CSA.[201]

The CSA must not disclose a person's address or any other information which could reasonably be expected to lead to that person being located. This disclosure can only be made when the person concerned has given written permission to that effect to the CSA. Also, the CSA must not disclose information which could reasonably be expected to lead to the identification of any person, other than a person with care, absent parent, person treated as absent or qualifying child.[202]

Regulations allow the Secretary of State or a CSO to disclose information given to the CSA for the use of local authorities in administering HB or CTB.[203] The CSA can disclose any information it has to a court, child support appeal tribunal (CSAT) or tribunal dealing with benefits, where that disclosure is for a court or tribunal case.[204] In practice, if a CSAT appeal takes place, all CSA papers (with addresses obliterated) are included in the CSO submission which is sent to every party to the appeal (see p372).

Disclosure within the DSS

Within the CSA, decisions and tasks are carried out either by a CSO or by a person appointed on behalf of the Secretary of State (see p17). Where information is held by the Secretary of State, it can only be disclosed to a CSO in certain circumstances. Similar rules apply to disclosure of information held by a CSO to another CSO or to the Secretary of State.

There are only very limited specific powers for the Secretary of State to disclose information to a CSO (see below). These do not cover disclosure to a CSO who is to make a decision on an application for an assessment or on a review. However, all applications for child maintenance are made to the Secretary of State, who must refer the application to a CSO (see p292). The CSO's job would be impossible if the Secretary of State could not pass information to her/him about the application.

There is also no specified general power for a CSO to disclose information to another CSO or for a CSO to disclose information to the Secretary of State.

However, because in practice assessments and reviews could not be carried out if this sort of disclosure were not permitted, it is very likely that a court would decide that the regulations give permission, although this permission is silent or implicit. Since the 1991 Act and regulations contain lots of references to disclosure, these implicit powers must be limited to those which are strictly necessary.

While caselaw may deal with this in the future, we believe that disclosure of information about a case can only be made between the Secretary of State and a CSO or between CSOs where a decision or investigation on that case is necessary. Disclosure outside this – for example, to an officer 'trawling' through files looking for references to a particular person – would be unlawful.

Since 22 January 1996 regulations have expressly provided for disclosure within the CSA in only one situation. Where, in one child support case, information is provided by or about a person, and that person is the absent parent, parent with care or alleged absent parent in a different, second child support case, then the Secretary of State may disclose that information to the CSO dealing with the second case and a CSO dealing with the first case may disclose that information to another CSO or to the Secretary of State.[205]

CSA guidance on disclosure

Staff at the CSA are advised that information given in confidence by a third party cannot be given to the CSO to make decisions unless that person gives permission – eg, information from a social worker without a client's knowledge, or an allegation that someone has started a job.[206]

Relevant medical evidence is taken into account even though confidential. According to CSA guidance, confidential medical evidence includes medical opinions about a person's mental health, or evidence of an incurable disease. Such information might even be disclosed to a representative at a tribunal provided s/he agreed not to inform the person concerned.[207]

CSA staff are reminded that disclosure of information about spent convictions, other than as part of an official duty, is a criminal offence.[208] Such information should only be passed to the CSO if it is considered to be essential to a particular decision – eg, it proves that an alleged absent parent cannot be a parent of a child. If a spent conviction is mentioned on another document, it should be ignored by the CSO when making a decision. The information could also be disclosed as part of a CSO's official duties – eg, for an appeal where this information happens to be included in a document.[209]

Disclosure by the CSA to other parts of the DSS

The Secretary of State can disclose information to government departments dealing with benefits, including the Benefits Agency.[210] This includes information obtained by using CSA powers or disclosed to the CSA voluntarily. This could be used to inform the Benefits Agency of any change in child maintenance, but also applies to other details. CSOs used to have the same power but this was removed on 22 January 1996.[211] However, once the file is with the Secretary of State, the information can be disclosed.

Because the Benefits Agency has close links with the Home Office, disclosure may create problems for people from abroad, in particular possible illegal entrants and those subject to the public funds requirement. If there are any doubts about whether information ought to be disclosed to the CSA, you should get advice first from a law centre or independent advice centre dealing with immigration problems or from the Joint Council for the Welfare of Immigrants (see Appendix 6). You cannot be prosecuted for refusing to give information unless it was requested by an inspector (see p153).

The Secretary of State and CSOs can exchange information with their counterparts in Northern Ireland and vice versa. Once disclosed, the information is subject to local rules about unauthorised disclosure.[212]

Unauthorised disclosure

Unauthorised disclosure of information is a criminal offence. This offence applies to anyone who is or has been a CSO, a CSA employee, a civil servant carrying out a function under the Child Support Acts (for example, a Benefits Agency officer helping the CSA make enquiries), staff of child support appeal tribunals, various ombudsmen and their staff and anyone who, though not a civil servant, is providing services to the DSS (for example, under contracted out work).[213] It does not apply to the chairs or members of tribunals or to social security commissioners.

It is not an offence to disclose information where:[214]

- the CSA can do so under the regulations for disclosure (see above);
- the CSA has already done so under those regulations;
- it is in the form of a summary or statistics and it cannot be related to any particular person; *or*
- the person to whom the information relates gives consent, or if that person's affairs are being dealt with under a power of attorney, by a receiver under the Mental Health Act, a mental health appointee or a Scottish mental health custodian, and the attorney, receiver, custodian or appointee gives consent.

A person who has broken these rules would have a defence if s/he could prove that s/he believed s/he was making the disclosure under these rules, or believed that disclosure under these rules had already been made, and had no reason to think otherwise.[215] For example, a CSO who discloses an absent parent's address under a direction from a court which is subsequently overturned on appeal, could argue that at the time of his disclosure he had no reason to doubt that he was making a lawful disclosure.[216]

The penalty for this offence is either a prison sentence, a fine, or both. On summary conviction the maximum prison sentence is six months, and the maximum fine is £5,000. On conviction or indictment there is a maximum prison sentence of up to two years.[217] At the time of writing, no prosecutions have been brought.

PART TWO

The formula

CHAPTER SEVEN

The formula in outline

This chapter covers:
1. A rigid formula (see below)
2. The five steps of the formula (p165)
3. Minimum child maintenance (p167)
4. Absent parents on income support (p168)
5. Special cases (p172)

I. A RIGID FORMULA

The Child Support Act 1991 introduced, for the first time, a statutory, non-discretionary formula for the calculation of child maintenance. A computer program is used by the Child Support Agency (CSA) for most of the calculations, which can be complicated.

The formula is contained in algebraic form in Schedule 1 to the 1991 Act and, in detail, in the Child Support (Maintenance Assessment and Special Cases) Regulations. The amount of the child maintenance assessment is not open for negotiation. There is a right of appeal against the assessment, but the child support appeal tribunal which hears the case is bound by the same law as the child support officer (see p369).

The amount of child maintenance payable depends largely on the circumstances and the income of the parents, particularly the income of the absent parent. Often parents, and therefore advisers, will not have access to all the information needed from the other parent in order to carry out an exact calculation. This will particularly affect parents with care who may well find that they have very little of the information required to predict or check the maintenance assessment.

However, understanding the way in which the formula works is important for explaining the result of an assessment as well as forecasting the effect of any change of circumstances and deciding whether to seek a review (see p350). It is also necessary to estimate the amount of child maintenance due before the CSA notification is sent in order to prevent a build-up of unmanageable initial arrears (see p398).

Deviation from the formula

A number of people have a duty to provide information to the CSA. If the CSA does not have enough information to carry out a full assessment, an interim maintenance assessment (IMA) can be imposed (see p296). These are usually penalty assessments and therefore higher than the formula assessment would be, in order to encourage absent parents to co-operate with the CSA.

The formula is not used to calculate the contribution towards child maintenance if the absent parent is on income support (see p168).

Absent parents with second families will have the assessment phased in where there would be an increase in the payments of over £20 a week compared with a pre-April 1993 maintenance agreement (see p300).

Departure

The Child Support Act 1995 introduces a system of departing from the standard formula in certain circumstances. Departure is a way of taking into account a factor particular to that family – for example, the costs of the absent parent travelling to visit the children. Although the decision as to whether or not to take into account the factor and to what extent is discretionary, an adjusted formula is then used to obtain the final assessment. Departure will take effect in the second half of 1996/97, probably from December 1996 or January 1997, but the scheme is being piloted in the south-east of England from April 1996. See Chapter 15 for details of departure.

The calculation

The formula for assessing child maintenance is based on income support (IS) components, both the personal allowances and the premiums. (For the conditions of entitlement for the IS premiums, see Appendix 2.)

The IS rates used in the calculation are those which apply on the date that the maintenance assessment comes into effect, known as the effective date (see p303).[1] The benefit rates increased on 8 April 1996. The maintenance assessment is not automatically altered at the annual April uprating of IS rates, but if a review is requested, the new rates would then be relevant. Furthermore, a periodical review of each assessment will be undertaken, usually every two years (see p353).

The child maintenance payable under the formula is given as a weekly rate and all stages of the calculation use weekly figures.[2] Fractions of a penny will be disregarded if less than one-half or rounded up to the next penny if equal to or more than one half-penny (except when calculating

70 per cent net income for the protected level (see p249), when any fraction of a penny is ignored).[3]

Accuracy of assessments

The CSA has been severely criticised for the high error rate in assessments. The CSA's target was for 75 per cent of assessments made in March 1996 to be correct, and the indications were that this would just be reached (see p24). However, this leaves approximately one quarter of new assessments incorrect, and an even higher proportion of older assessments; therefore parents should always have their assessment checked by an adviser who understands the formula.

The staff of the Chief Child Support Officer (CCSO) have the task of overseeing and monitoring the adjudication standards of the child support officers. The CCSO published his last annual report in October 1995 covering the year 1994/95:

- in 23 per cent of cases examined the assessment was incorrect;
- assessments were correct in 44 per cent of decisions examined (although in one third of these another aspect of the adjudication process was incorrect);
- in 28 per cent of cases there was too little information to know whether the assessment was correct; *and*
- the final 5 per cent involved cases without assessments where the adjudication procedure was incorrect.

The CCSO picked out earnings and housing costs as issues which were particularly prone to error.

Parents can challenge incorrect assessments by seeking a second-tier review (see p358).

Changes to the formula

Since the formula for setting assessment was introduced in April 1993, there have been two sets of changes to it – the first in February 1994 and the second in April 1995. On both these occasions all existing assessments were run through the new computer program and altered if there was a significant change.

This edition of the *Handbook* covers the formula in effect during 1996/97. Therefore, if an adviser is dealing with assessments for an earlier period, s/he must consult:

- the first edition of the *Handbook* (1993/94) for the formula from 5 April 1993 to 6 February 1994;
- the second edition of the *Handbook* (1994/95) for the formula from 7 February 1994 to 17 April 1995; *and*

- the third edition of the *Handbook* (1995/96) for a summary of the changes implemented from 18 April 1995.

Compensation for persons with care

There are no changes to the formula planned for 1996/97. However, if in the future there are further amendments to the standard formula, persons with care in receipt of family credit/disability working allowance (FC/DWA) who have their assessments reduced as a result would receive some compensation.[4] The compensation would equal half the reduction in the assessment and be paid for each week remaining in the current FC/DWA award.[5]

2. THE FIVE STEPS OF THE FORMULA

It might appear to some readers that some of the formula's steps are not always needed. However, as a note of caution, we would warn advisers not to skip steps unless they are very familiar with the formula. (See Appendix 3 for a guide to the steps and Appendix 4 for calculation sheets for each stage.)

Although only an absent parent is liable to pay child maintenance, the calculation involves the income of both parents. The term 'parent' applies to both the absent parent and the parent with care.

As elsewhere in this book, for the sake of simplicity the parent with care is referred to as 'she' and the absent parent as 'he'. However, all aspects of the formula apply if the parent with care is in fact the father and the absent parent the mother. If the person with care is *not* the parent of the child, then the income of that person with care does not affect the amount of child maintenance payable.

Step 1: The maintenance requirement

The maintenance requirement represents the minimum day-to-day expense of maintaining children. However, the maintenance requirement is neither the minimum nor the maximum amount of child maintenance payable. An absent parent might not be able to afford to pay the maintenance requirement in full or, alternatively, he may have sufficient income to pay over and above the maintenance requirement.

The main significance of this step is that an absent parent pays 50 per cent of his assessable income (see Chapter 10) in child maintenance until the maintenance requirement figure has been met. At this point he pays a lower percentage of any remaining assessable income.

For full details of the maintenance requirement, see Chapter 8.

Step 2: Exempt income

Exempt income represents the minimum day-to-day living expenses of the parent and covers the housing costs of the family s/he lives with. However, it includes only amounts for the living expenses of any of the parent's *own* children who are living with the parent, but does *not* include any such amount for a new partner or step-children. Supporting step-children is one of the grounds for departure (see p324). An allowance in recognition of property/capital settlements pre-dating April 1993 may also be included in exempt income.

Each parent is allowed to keep income equal to the exempt income before being expected to pay any child maintenance.

For full details of exempt income, see Chapter 9.

Step 3: Assessable income

Assessable income is income which is available to pay child maintenance. It is the amount of the parent's income which remains after the exempt income has been taken into account. If an absent parent has no assessable income, he may have to pay the minimum payment – see below.

For full details of assessable income, see Chapter 10.

Step 4: Proposed maintenance

Proposed maintenance is the amount of child maintenance the absent parent is expected to pay as long as it does not bring his income below the protected income level (see step 5 below).

An absent parent pays 50 per cent of his assessable income in child maintenance until he has met the maintenance requirement figure of step 1. Once the maintenance requirement is met, he pays 15, 20 or 25 per cent of any further assessable income, depending on the number of children for whom he is being assessed to pay maintenance.

The assessable income of the parent with care can reduce the proposed maintenance.

There is an upper limit to the amount of child maintenance payable under the formula. It is still possible for the parties to go to court to seek additional child maintenance (see p37).

For full details of proposed maintenance, see Chapter 11.

Step 5: Protected income

The protected income step ensures that an absent parent's disposable income does not fall below a certain level as a result of paying the proposed maintenance. At this stage the *whole* family's expenses and income are taken into account, including those related to a new partner and step-children.

In addition, no absent parent is expected to pay more than 30 per cent of his own net income.

For full details of protected income, see Chapter 12.

3. MINIMUM CHILD MAINTENANCE

There is a standard minimum payment of child maintenance that applies to absent parents where the formula results in an amount less than this minimum.[6] The minimum payment rule does not apply in exactly the same way to absent parents on IS as the formula is not applied in those cases; however, deductions from IS may be made as a contribution towards child maintenance (see p168).

The amount of the minimum payment is 10 per cent of the IS personal allowance for someone aged 25 or over, rounded to the next 5 pence, irrespective of the age of the absent parent.[7] This is currently £4.80 a week. In previous years, the minimum was 5 per cent of the adult personal allowance (ie, £2.35 during 1995/96). However, those already liable to pay the minimum payment before 8 April 1996 should not be subject to the increase until the assessment is reviewed (see Chapter 16) and replaced by an assessment with an effective date (see p357) in this financial year. Although not explicitly stated in the regulations, it is arguable that the amount of the minimum payment relates to the IS rates applicable on the effective date of the assessment.

The minimum payment must be made unless the absent parent falls into a category which is specifically excluded (see below). In other words, an absent parent who has been assessed under the formula as liable to pay less than £4.80 will have to pay child maintenance of £4.80 a week unless he falls into one of the exempt categories.

Only one minimum payment will be due where a person is the absent parent for the purposes of more than one application.[8] For example, where an absent parent has children with two or more women with whom he does not live, or where the children of his first family are being cared for by different people in different households, the minimum payment will be divided between the persons with care in proportion to the relative maintenance requirements (see Chapter 8).

Exempt absent parents

A few absent parents will not have to pay any child maintenance at all.

If an absent parent has been assessed under the formula as having to pay £4.80 or less, he is exempt from paying any child maintenance if he:[9]

- has the family premium included in the calculation or estimation of his protected income level (ie, he or his partner is receiving child benefit);
- is a prisoner;
- receives (or would receive but for failure to satisfy the national insurance contribution conditions or for receipt of an overlapping benefit) one of the following:
  - incapacity benefit or statutory sick pay;
  - maternity allowance or statutory maternity pay;
  - severe disablement allowance;
  - disability living allowance or attendance allowance;
  - disability working allowance;
  - an industrial disablement benefit;
  - a war disablement benefit;
  - invalid care allowance;
  - payments from the Independent Living (1993) Fund or the Independent Living (Extension) Fund;
- is under 16 years old, or under 19 and receiving full-time non-advanced education (ie, a child within the meaning of the Acts, see p41);
- has a net income of less than £4.80 (for details of what is net income, see Chapter 10). Youth trainees whose income consists solely of a youth training allowance, or students whose only income is a grant, grant contribution or student loan, have these incomes ignored when calculating net income purposes. Most youth trainees and students, therefore, are exempt from paying child maintenance.[10]

These exempt categories do not mean, for example, that all absent parents on incapacity benefit automatically pay no child maintenance. In order to be exempt from paying maintenance, they must first have been assessed according to the formula as only being able to afford to pay an amount of £4.80 a week or less.

4. ABSENT PARENTS ON INCOME SUPPORT

Note: from October 1996, these rules will most probably be extended to apply to means-tested jobseeker's allowance. Seek advice nearer that date.

If the absent parent is in receipt of IS, the formula is not used to assess the child maintenance payable. Instead, the Secretary of State can make a deduction from the IS of an absent parent as a contribution towards child maintenance.[11] The deduction can be made from a partner's IS if the partner of an absent parent is claiming for the couple.[12]

The parties will first receive notification of a nil assessment and then be contacted with a decision about deductions from IS.

Who can have the deduction made

Deductions cannot be made if the absent parent:[13]

- is aged under 18; *or*
- qualifies for the family premium (see p425) and/or has day-to-day care (see p44) of any child; *or*
- receives any of the following benefits or would receive one except for contribution requirements or overlapping benefit rules – statutory sick pay, incapacity benefit, severe disablement allowance, attendance allowance or disability living allowance, invalid care allowance, maternity allowance, statutory maternity pay, disability working allowance, an industrial disablement benefit, a war disablement benefit or payments from the Independent Living (1993) Fund or the Independent Living (Extension) Fund. (Thus, someone who is incapable of work but has insufficient national insurance contributions to receive incapacity benefit cannot have deductions made.)

Amount of the deduction

An absent parent on IS who is not exempt may have an amount equal to the minimum payment – ie, 10 per cent of the adult personal allowance for those aged 25 and over – deducted from his benefit by the Benefits Agency, irrespective of the age of the absent parent.[14] This is currently £4.80 a week. In some cases, half of this amount may be deducted (see below). In previous years, 5 per cent of the adult personal allowance was deducted in all cases (ie, £2.35 in 1995/96).

There will not be more than one deduction made if there is more than one person with care looking after the absent parent's qualifying children. Instead, the payment is apportioned between the persons with care in the same ratio as their respective maintenance requirements.[15]

Whether the deduction is actually made by the Benefits Agency depends upon the number of other deductions of higher priority (see p170).

What the deduction is for

Technically this deduction is not a payment of child support maintenance, but a payment in lieu of child maintenance.[16] It is not a maintenance assessment and therefore the rules which apply to assessments do not apply to these contributions. In particular, liability for the contributions will not be backdated to the effective date and arrears will not accrue if the Benefits Agency is unable to make the deduction because there are other deductions with higher priority.

In theory, deductions can also be made to recoup arrears of child maintenance which arose before the absent parent claimed IS.[17] No more than one deduction of £4.80 can be made from an IS claim at any one time.[18] In other words, the CSA will not be seeking any deductions for arrears at the same time as the current contribution in lieu of child maintenance. However, as deductions can only be made from IS while there is an absent parent with a current liability, no deduction for arrears can be made in practice. Arrears of child maintenance could still be collected by other methods (see Chapter 17). Usually the arrears will just be held in abeyance until the absent parent leaves IS.

Deductions made by the Benefits Agency

When an application is received by the CSA and it is found that the absent parent is on IS, both parties will be notified as to whether or not deductions from benefit are a possibility. If the absent parent is not exempt from deductions, the Benefits Agency will then be sent notification requesting that a deduction is made. This is binding on the adjudication officer of the Benefits Agency, unless there are other deductions being made from IS which take precedence.[19]

Direct deductions for contributions of child maintenance cannot be made from any benefit other than IS, unless unemployment benefit, incapacity benefit, severe disablement allowance or retirement pension are paid in the same girocheque or order book as the IS.[20] After the deductions are made, 10 pence a week must be left of benefit.[21]

There is a maximum amount which can be deducted from IS.[22] The total deducted for arrears of mortgage interest, rent arrears, fuel arrears, arrears of water charges, poll tax/council tax arrears, fines and contribution towards child maintenance cannot be greater than £7.20 a week. The contribution for child maintenance has a lower priority than any of the other mentioned deductions.[23] Therefore, in some cases where absent parents have other such deductions, it will not be possible to deduct the full £4.80 for the contribution to child maintenance. The Benefits Agency can deduct half of the £4.80 contribution.[24] Absent parents who are having difficulties meeting basic bills should consider requesting direct payments – eg, £2.40 for gas arrears and £2.40 for electricity arrears would ensure that only £2.40 for child maintenance is payable. If full deductions from IS are not possible, arrears of child maintenance contributions do *not* accrue.

The Benefits Agency will notify the CSA whether deductions are possible. The CSA, in turn, notifies the absent parent and the person with care that the deductions will begin on a date in the near future. The £4.80 (or £2.40) will be paid over to the person with care via the CSA.[25] The CSA will notify her of the way in which the payments will be made. If the person with care is on IS, the contribution will most probably be paid with the IS in her order book. When the person with care is not in receipt of IS, she will usually receive payments on a quarterly basis.

Reviews and appeals

As contributions to child maintenance made as deductions from the absent parent's IS are not technically child support maintenance, specific provision is made for reviewing child support officer (CSO) decisions concerning these contributions.[26] If it is the Benefits Agency adjudication officer's decision which is being contested – ie, the question being disputed is whether the absent parent can have another £4.80 deducted from his IS given his other, higher priority debts – then there is a right of appeal to a social security appeal tribunal.

A review of the CSO's decision that the absent parent is or is not exempt from IS deductions will be carried out:

- after a decision has been in force for 104 weeks;[27] *or*
- if it appears to a CSO that there has been a change which means that an absent parent can no longer have or can now begin to have deductions made from his IS; this change of circumstances review can be done at the request of one of the parties or at the instigation of the CSO;[28] *or*
- where a decision was made in ignorance of a material fact, based on a mistake as to a material fact or which is wrong in law, including at the instigation of the CSO;[29] *or*
- on request under section 18 (see p358).[30] In this case there is then a right to appeal to a child support appeal tribunal (see p367).[31]

The CSO only asks for representations in reviews concerning deductions from IS when the original CSO decision is being challenged by one of the parties.[32] The comments can be made in person or in writing. If neither written comments nor a request for an appointment are received within 14 days, the CSO can proceed with the review.[33] An appointment must be made if a person requests one in order to give comments. If the person does not turn up, another appointment must be provided if there was a good reason for missing the first.[34]

Date of effect of decision

If the decision is revised so that deductions from IS are to begin, the decision takes effect only from the date it is made.[35]

However, if the decision is that deductions should cease, this will be backdated to the change of circumstances which caused the revised decision or, in the case of an incorrect CSO decision, to the date of that mistaken decision.[36] This means that the Benefits Agency not only has to increase the ongoing IS but also has to pay the absent parent the amount deducted in the meantime. Where such payments have already been paid to the person with care, these cannot be recovered.[37]

5. SPECIAL CASES

The legislation uses the phrase 'special cases' to cover situations which are not as straightforward as where one absent parent has left one family and there is one person with care looking after all the children from that family.[38] However, in order to enable people to carry out calculations for all family situations, we have integrated these situations into the relevant steps of the formula – eg, where:

- both parents are absent (see p236);
- more than one person with care applies for child maintenance from the same absent parent (see p239);
- a person cares for children of more than one absent parent (see pp177 and 245).

Where care of a child is being shared between different people, several modifications of the formula are necessary. Shared care is, therefore, treated separately (see Chapter 13).

Shared care does not cover the situation where different children of the same family have different homes. Where the children of a family are divided between two households (eg, where one child lives with one parent and another child with the other parent), this involves two maintenance assessments. In one assessment, the first parent is the parent with care and the second parent is the absent parent. In the second assessment the roles are reversed. We have called this situation 'divided families' (see p244).

CHAPTER EIGHT

The maintenance requirement Step 1 of the formula

This chapter covers:

1. What is the maintenance requirement (see below)
2. How much is the maintenance requirement (p174)
3. Both parents are absent (p177)
4. More than one absent parent (p177)

This chapter should be read in conjunction with calculation sheet 1 in Appendix 4.

1. WHAT IS THE MAINTENANCE REQUIREMENT

The maintenance requirement is intended to represent the minimum weekly cost of caring for the child(ren) for whom child maintenance is being assessed.[1] The maintenance requirement is based on income support (IS) rates. For information on the conditions of entitlement for the IS premiums, see Appendix 2.

Both parents will contribute towards meeting the maintenance requirement if they can afford to do so. In the case of the parent with care, it is a notional contribution which may reduce the amount of child maintenance that an absent parent has to pay.

The parents may not have sufficient income to be able to pay the full maintenance requirement. If this is the case, the absent parent pays 50 per cent of his available income, known in the formula as 'assessable income'. Equally, the maintenance requirement is not the total amount of child maintenance that may be expected from an absent parent. However, once the maintenance requirement is met, the absent parent then pays a lower percentage of any further income. In other words, the maintenance requirement is the point at which the absent parent stops paying 50 per cent of his assessable income and instead pays 15, 20 or 25 per cent of any remaining assessable income (see Chapters 10 and 11).

The maintenance requirement is also used where child maintenance has to be apportioned between two persons with care. This occurs where a parent is an absent parent for two different maintenance assessments (see p239).

Interim maintenance assessments

Where a child support officer (CSO) does not have adequate information from the absent parent to carry out an assessment, s/he can make an interim maintenance assessment. This assessment is usually set at 1.5 times the maintenance requirement where the information about the absent parent's income is being withheld (see p296).[2]

2. HOW MUCH IS THE MAINTENANCE REQUIREMENT

The maintenance requirement includes an allowance for each qualifying child being looked after by that person with care. For example, if a person with care has a current partner and has a joint child with her partner, then that joint child is not a qualifying child and will not be included in the maintenance requirement. For a definition of qualifying child, see p41.

The absent parent for whom child maintenance is being assessed *must* be the parent of that qualifying child. (For definitions of these terms, see Chapter 3.) If a person with care is looking after children of different absent parents, a different maintenance requirement will be calculated for each of the assessments (see p177).

The maintenance requirement calculation

The maintenance requirement is calculated as follows:[3]

- for each qualifying child, the amount of the IS personal allowance for a child of that age; *plus*
- the amount of the IS family premium (£10.55); *plus*
- a 'parent as carer' element:
  - where at least one qualifying child is under 11 years of age, the amount of the adult IS personal allowance at the rate for a person aged 25 years or over, irrespective of the age of the person with care (£47.90); *or*
  - where none of the qualifying children is under 11 but at least one is under 14 years of age, 75 per cent of this adult allowance (£35.93); *or*
  - where none of the children is under 14 but at least one is under 16 years of age, 50 per cent of the adult allowance (£23.95); *plus*

- where the person with care has no partner, the amount of the IS lone parent premium (£5.20); this does not apply where the child is in the care of an institution; *less*
- the amount of child benefit for the qualifying child(ren).

This is the basic maintenance requirement calculation which is adapted in situations where more than one absent parent is involved (see p177).

The rates used in the calculation are the IS and child benefit rates applicable at the date on which the maintenance assessment takes effect, known as the effective date (see p303).[4] The figures given above are those for 1996/97.

Deduction of child benefit

One parent benefit is not deducted. If child benefit is not payable for a child because s/he is in the care of an institution, then an amount of child benefit will still be deducted.[5] However, in all other cases the rate of child benefit which is payable under the child benefit regulations for each child should be deducted.[6] Therefore if no one is entitled to child benefit for that child – eg, because of the residence rules, no child benefit will be deducted in the maintenance requirement.

The amount of child benefit deducted from the maintenance requirement may not always be the same amount as is actually being paid to the person with care – eg, where no claim has been made by the person with care or where the rate being paid is not correct under the child benefit legislation. The assumption in the formula is that the person with care has claimed and received any entitlement to child benefit. The entitlement to the assessed amount of child maintenance is in addition to any entitlement to child benefit. There may be cases where someone other than the person with care is receiving child benefit – eg, an absent parent. In such cases the person with care should consider claiming child benefit or asking the absent parent to make the payment of child benefit in addition to the maintenance payment (see example 8.3).

The parent as carer element

The Government has stated that the inclusion of the adult personal allowance represents the care costs of the child and that the reduction of the allowance for children over 11 years old is recognition of the reduction of the care needs as children grow up.[7] This has the effect that the maintenance requirement as a whole can reduce after a child's birthday.

The parent as carer element is not spousal maintenance – ie, maintenance for a former spouse. Spousal maintenance continues to exist and is completely separate from child maintenance calculated by the

CSA. Any application for maintenance for the parent with care will still be made to the court (see p37).

Couples

The personal allowance for couples is never included in the maintenance requirement. This is because the absent parent is not responsible for maintaining a partner of the person with care. The only acknowledgement that a person with care has a partner is that the lone parent premium does not apply.

Children's housing costs

Housing costs are not included in the maintenance requirement. The Government has stated that this is because any property settlement will be considered separately by the courts.[8]

Children with disabilities

The disabled child premium is not included in the calculation of the maintenance requirement and neither is any related carer premium. Instead, the courts will assess any top-up maintenance award in respect of a child for whom the disability living allowance is paid, or where the child is blind, deaf, without speech or otherwise 'substantially and permanently handicapped' (see p37).[9]

Example 8.1: Calculation of the maintenance requirement

(a) Anita and Bob have two children. They split up, and Anita remains in the family home with Carol (13) and David (8).

		£
Personal allowances	Anita	47.90
	Carol (13)	24.10
	David (8)	16.45
Family premium		10.55
Lone parent premium		5.20
Sub-total		104.20
Less child benefit		19.60
Maintenance requirement		84.60

(b) Five years later, Anita has remarried. David is 13 and Carol is 18 but still at school.

		£
Personal allowances	Anita	35.93
	Carol (18)	37.90
	David (13)	24.10
Family premium		10.55
Sub-total		108.48
Less child benefit		19.60
		88.88

3. BOTH PARENTS ARE ABSENT

An application for maintenance can be made by a person with care who is not a parent – eg, if a child lives with his/her grandparents or another relative (see p43). Both parents of that child are then absent parents and liable to pay maintenance. An assessment can be carried out for each absent parent if an application is made in respect of him/her, and each contributes to the maintenance requirement (see p236). An application may be made for maintenance from only one of the absent parents; in this case the assessment is made in the usual way for one absent parent – ie, the existence of another absent parent has no effect on the outcome of the assessment.

The maintenance requirement calculation is not changed if both parents are absent and the child is being looked after by a person with care who is an individual. However, if the child is being cared for by an institution, the maintenance requirement does not include any lone parent premium, but does still include the other elements.[10]

See p236 for the calculation of the proposed maintenance where both parents are absent.

4. MORE THAN ONE ABSENT PARENT

A person with care may look after qualifying children who have different parents. Therefore, there are different absent parents for the children – eg, where a mother is looking after her children who have different fathers, where a grandmother is looking after children of two of her sons, or where a lone parent is also looking after a friend's child. In these cases, if applications are made for child maintenance from each absent parent, a number of different assessments must be carried out, one for each absent parent.

The maintenance requirement for each absent parent includes only the child(ren) who are his own responsibility. However, each maintenance requirement will be adjusted, so that the amounts which relate to all the children (adult personal allowance, family premium, and any lone parent premium) are divided among the absent parents.[11] This means in proportion to the number of absent parents, and not in proportion to the number of the children who are their responsibility.[12] This apportionment should occur whether or not child maintenance is being pursued from all the absent parents.[13] For example, a person with care may apply for child maintenance from one father and not another, or one of the absent parents may be resident abroad and hence outside the CSA's jurisdiction.

The apportioned 'parent as carer' element is then further reduced if the children in the individual assessment are aged 11 or over – ie, 75 per cent of the apportioned amount is used if the youngest child is aged 11–13 and 50 per cent of the apportioned amount if s/he is 14 or 15 years old.[14] (This can mean that less than the full adult personal allowance is included across all assessments, even though it would have been included in full had the children had the same absent parent – see example 8.2b.)

See p245 for the calculation of proposed maintenance where a parent with care is looking after the child(ren) of more than one absent parent.

Example 8.2: Maintenance requirement where the children have different fathers

(a) Zoe is a single parent and has three children, all of whom live with her. Wayne is the father of Yvonne (12) and Veronica (10). Terence is the father of Samuel (3).

Wayne's assessment (maintenance requirement):		£	
Personal allowances	Zoe	23.95	(half of 47.90)
	Yvonne (12)	24.10	
	Veronica (10)	16.45	
Family premium		5.28	(half of 10.55)
Lone parent premium		2.60	(half of 5.20)
Sub-total		72.38	
Less child benefit		19.60	
Maintenance requirement		52.78	

Terence's assessment (maintenance requirement):

		£	
Personal allowances	Zoe	23.95	(half of 47.90)
	Samuel (3)	16.45	
Family premium		5.28	(half of 10.55)
Lone parent premium		2.60	(half of 5.20)
Sub-total		48.28	
Less child benefit		8.80	
Maintenance requirement		39.48	

(b) Two years later, Zoe is living with Bob and her four children. Wayne is the father of Yvonne (14) and Veronica (12). Terence is the father of Samuel (5). Bob is the father of Ricky (1). However, as Bob is not an absent parent, the apportionment occurs between Wayne and Terence only. The lone parent premium is no longer applicable.

Wayne's assessment (maintenance requirement):

		£	
Personal allowances	Zoe	17.96	(75% of half of 47.90)
	Yvonne (14)	24.10	
	Veronica (12)	24.10	
Family premium		5.28	(half of 10.55)
Sub-total		71.44	
Less child benefit		19.60	
Maintenance requirement		51.84	

Terence's assessment (maintenance requirement):

		£	
Personal allowances	Zoe	23.95	(100% of half of 47.90)
	Samuel (5)	16.45	
Family premium		5.28	(half of 10.55)
Sub-total		45.68	
Less child benefit		8.80	
Maintenance requirement		36.88	

If a person with care is looking after children of different parents, but two of the absent parents are parents of the same child – ie, the person with care is *not* a parent of that child, those two absent parents will be treated as one person for the purposes of apportioning the relevant elements of the maintenance requirement.[15]

Example 8.3: Maintenance requirement with more than one absent parent, including where both parents of one child are absent

Zoe's niece, Rebecca, who is aged 16 and still at school, comes to live with Zoe and Bob when her parents split up. Rebecca joining the household alters the maintenance requirement for the other children (see example 8.2b). For the four qualifying children Zoe is now looking after, there are four absent parents (Wayne, Terence, and both of Rebecca's parents). However, Rebecca's parents count as one unit for this purpose and therefore the amounts are divided by three.

Wayne's assessment (maintenance requirement): £

Personal allowances	Zoe	11.97	(75% of third of 47.90)
	Yvonne (14)	24.10	
	Veronica (12)	24.10	
Family premium		3.52	(third of 10.55)
Sub-total		63.69	
Less child benefit		17.60	
Maintenance requirement		46.09	

Terence's assessment (maintenance requirement): £

Personal allowances	Zoe	15.97	(third of 47.90)
	Samuel (5)	16.45	
Family premium		3.52	(third of 10.55)
Sub-total		35.94	
Less child benefit		8.80	
Maintenance requirement		27.14	

Rebecca's parents (maintenance requirement): £

Personal allowance for Rebecca (16)	28.85	
Family premium	3.52	(third of 10.55)
Sub-total	32.37	
Less child benefit	10.80	
Maintenance requirement	21.57	

An assessment will then be carried out separately for both of Rebecca's parents, each using the same maintenance requirement figure (see example 11.7).

Note: Bob is unemployed and claiming income support. Therefore, although there is a requirement for Zoe to pursue the fathers of her children for maintenance (see Chapter 5), she does not have to make an application for maintenance from Rebecca's parents. The requirement to co-operate applies only to *parents* with care. However, even if she chose not to make an application for child maintenance for Rebecca, the apportionment between three should still take place for the other two assessments.

As Rebecca is 16, no adult personal allowance is included in her maintenance requirement. Yet, because of the apportionment between the three assessments, only one third of the allowance is included in each of the other two maintenance requirement calculations and this is further reduced in Wayne's assessment where the children are over 11 years old.

We have assumed that Zoe has claimed child benefit for Rebecca, which means that under the child benefit regulations the higher rate is applicable to Rebecca and the lower rate now applies to Yvonne. The amount of child benefit deducted in the maintenance requirement follows the amount payable under the child benefit regulations.

If Rebecca's mother had continued to claim child benefit instead, then the higher rate would be payable for Rebecca as the only child for whom her mother is claiming. At the same time the higher rate will still be payable for Yvonne as she is the eldest child for whom Zoe is claiming child benefit.[16] If this were the case, the child benefit of £10.80 should be deducted for both children in calculating the maintenance requirements, even though Zoe is not actually receiving the £10.80 child benefit for Rebecca.

If Rebecca's mother did not hand over at least £10.80 each week to Zoe, whether as child maintenance or on top of the maintenance assessment, she would no longer be entitled to child benefit.[17] In this case, the maintenance requirements should be as shown above as child benefit is not legally payable to Rebecca's mother, even though in practice it is still being paid. It would be to Zoe's advantage to claim the child benefit for Rebecca. However, even where Rebecca's mother is paying £10.80 over to Zoe, Zoe would be entitled to the child benefit should she claim. As the person with whom Rebecca is living, she takes priority over the mother for child benefit purposes (see p270).[18]

CHAPTER NINE

Exempt income
Step 2 of the formula

This chapter covers:
1. What is exempt income (see below)
2. How much is exempt income (p183)
3. Housing costs (p185)
4. Pre-April 1993 property settlements (see p192)
5. Travel-to-work costs (see p196)
6. Second families (p198)

This chapter should be read in conjunction with calculation sheet 2 in Appendix 4.

1. WHAT IS EXEMPT INCOME

Exempt income is income a parent can keep for his/her own essential expenses before any child maintenance is expected. The expenses are based on income support (IS) rates but also include housing costs.

Exempt income was intended to represent the minimum day-to-day living expenses of parents and their *own* children who are living with them.[1] If the parent has a partner, the partner's personal expenses are *not* included in exempt income. The housing costs for the whole family – including any heterosexual partner and step-children – are covered in exempt income.

'Own child' means a child for whom the parent is, in law, a parent – ie, biological or adoptive parent. (For a full definition, see p41.) Exempt income does *not* include amounts for any other children in the family – eg, step-children. Allowances for other children are not even initially included if the child is the primary responsibility of the parent – eg, where the step-child's other parent is dead or cannot afford to pay any child maintenance. Later this year, in some cases departure from the assessment could be sought on these grounds (see p325).

Exempt income applies to *both* the absent parent and the parent with care as both are liable to maintain their children. However, if the parent with care is on IS, it is assumed that she has no income available for child maintenance,[2] and therefore the exempt income step is carried out for the absent parent only. If the absent parent is on IS, there is no need to calculate exempt income for either parent, as the formula is not used at all in this case. Instead, the absent parent may have deductions made from his IS as a contribution towards child maintenance (see p168).

If both parents do not receive IS, then this part of the calculation has to be done for both of them, even where one parent is the person with care. There will, of course, be no actual financial transaction between the parent with care and the children, but if the parent with care has any income available to maintain the children, this might reduce the absent parent's contribution (see Chapter 11).

If the person with care is not a parent, this step does *not* apply to them. This is because only parents have a liability to maintain their children. If the person with care is not a parent, there will usually be two absent parents and a maintenance assessment can be carried out for both parents (see p236).[3]

2. HOW MUCH IS EXEMPT INCOME

Exempt income is calculated in the same way for parents with care as for absent parents.[4] Any reference to 'parent' below applies equally to the parent with care and the absent parent.

The rates used in the calculation are the IS rates applicable on the date at which the maintenance assessment takes effect, known as the effective date (see p303).[5] The rates given below are for 1996/97. For the qualifying conditions of the IS premiums, see Appendix 2.

The exempt income calculation

Exempt income is calculated as follows for each parent:[6]

- the amount of the IS personal allowance for a single person aged 25 or over, irrespective of the age of the parent (£47.90); *plus*
- if there is a child – ie, the parent's own child (see above) – living with the parent, the amount of the IS personal allowance for a child of that age;*† *plus*

---

* Where the child's other parent also lives in the family and has sufficient income to help support the child, these amounts may be halved (see p198).

† These amounts will be included at a proportionate rate if the parent looks after the child(ren) for less than seven days but at least two nights on average per week (see Chapter 13).

- if an allowance for a child is included, the amount of the IS family premium (£10.55);*† *plus*
- if any of the children included would qualify for the IS disabled child premium (see p426), the amount of that premium for each child entitled (£20.40);*† *plus*
- if the parent would qualify for the IS disability premium (see p427) if he/she was under 60 years old, the amount of the premium for a single person (£20.40); the disability conditions must be satisfied by the parent him/herself; *plus*
- if an allowance for a child is included and the parent has no partner, the amount of the IS lone parent premium (£5.20), provided the amount of the disability premium is not included;† *plus*
- if the parent would qualify for the IS carer premium (see p426), the amount of that premium (£13.00); *plus*
- if the parent would qualify for the IS severe disability premium (see p428), the amount of that premium (£36.40); *plus*
- housing costs (see below); *plus*
- where applicable, an allowance for a pre-April 1993 property settlement (see p192); *plus*
- where the parent travels more than 150 miles a week to and from work, an amount towards travel costs (see p196); this does not apply to the self-employed.

Example 9.1: Exempt income – Bob leaves Anita

Bob and Anita have split up. Anita is looking after Carol and David, and remains in the family home. There is no need to calculate Anita's exempt income as she is in receipt of IS.

(a) Bob is living on his own in a bedsit, paying rent of £48 a week. He is not entitled to any housing benefit. He does not qualify for any premiums. He travels less than 150 miles a week to work.

Bob's exempt income is therefore:	£
Personal allowance	47.90
Housing costs	48.00
Total exempt income	95.90

(b) If Bob had moved in with his parents, his exempt income would be £47.90. If Bob was in receipt of incapacity benefit, his exempt income would then be:

	£
Personal allowance	47.90
Disability premium	20.40
Total exempt income	68.30

---

3. HOUSING COSTS

Housing costs for the parent and any of his/her family (see p50) living with him/her are included in exempt income. From later this year, where the other party believes that the parent's partner can afford to contribute to the housing costs, s/he will be able to apply for a departure direction (see p331).

Before 18 April 1995, deductions were made from housing costs where another adult was living in the parent's house on a non-commercial basis.[7] Assessments which included these non-dependant deductions do not have them removed until the next periodical, change of circumstance or second-tier review (see Chapter 15). Applications for departure will be possible on the grounds that the non-dependant is able to contribute towards the housing costs.

Housing costs which are excessive may not be included in full (see p191).

Responsibility for housing costs

Housing costs are included where:[8]

- the parent or heterosexual partner is responsible for the costs; *and*
- the costs relate to the parent's home (see p188); *and*
- the payment is made to a person who is not a member of the same household.

Therefore, where a parent moves in with a new partner, the housing costs will be accepted, even though they are the responsibility of the partner. This does not apply to homosexual couples as the definition of partner does not include gay and lesbian partners.

As well as where s/he is actually liable for the costs, a parent will be treated as responsible for housing costs in situations where:[9]

- s/he has to meet the costs in order to live in the home; *and*
- the person liable to make the payments is not doing so; *and*
- either the parent is the former partner of the liable person or is someone else whom it is reasonable to treat as liable.

Where costs are shared with another person who is not a heterosexual partner, then only his/her actual share of the costs is used.[10] For example, if three friends are joint tenants and share the rent equally, one-third of the rent will be considered to be the responsibility of the parent. If the child support officer (CSO) believes that such a division would not be reasonable – eg, the joint occupiers have unequal shares of the accommodation – a different amount can be used.[11]

The parent may be treated as responsible for housing costs that s/he shares with other members of the household (see p45), some of whom are not close relatives (see p254), even where s/he makes those payments via another member of the household.[12] This applies where:

- it is reasonable for a parent to be treated as responsible for a share of the costs; *and*
- the person with responsibility is not a close relative; *and*
- either s/he has an equivalent responsibility for those costs as the parent or s/he is meeting the costs because the liable person is not.

However, where a parent is a non-dependent member of a household (see p253), no housing costs will be included in exempt income, even if s/he is paying a contribution for housing costs to another member of the household.[13] This appears partly to contradict the last statement that a parent can be treated as responsible for costs s/he shares with another member of the household, as long as they are not close relatives, even where it is the other person who is commercially liable for the payments. Remember that in order for a parent to be a non-dependant, not only can there be no commercial arrangement, but s/he has to be a member of the same *household* as the person liable to make the payments, and this will not always be the case where a parent moves into a friend's house. However, where a parent moves in with a gay partner there can be no argument over household.

In practice it may be that no housing costs are included if payment is to a close relative, whereas the other rule is used where costs are shared with members of the household who are not close relatives. So far the interpretation has only been tested in the first situation where a parent was living with his parents as a non-dependant and therefore clearly not entitled to have his contribution to the housing costs included in exempt income.[14] However, in the second situation, if it is found that housing costs are not included in the parent's exempt income when s/he is paying half of the costs on a voluntary basis it might, depending on the circumstances of the case, be arguable that it is reasonable to treat the parent as responsible for a share of the costs. This is most likely to succeed in cases where the costs have previously been shared with someone else and the parent has taken over that person's share. However, if the parent becomes a co-owner or joint tenant, half of the housing costs will be treated as the parent's responsibility. On the other hand, if the parent became a sub-tenant, s/he would be responsible for the costs specified in the tenancy agreement.

Eligible housing costs

To be included in exempt income, housing costs must be eligible and payable in respect of the parent's home (see below).[15] It is not enough that the costs are incurred as a result of loans secured on the property; to be eligible, the costs must be in respect of the provision of the home.[16]

Eligible housing costs consist of the following and any analogous payments:[17]

- rent (net of housing benefit[18] – see below);
- mortgage interest payments;
- capital repayments under a mortgage;
- premiums paid under an endowment or other insurance policy, a personal equity plan (PEP) or personal pension plan to the extent that the policy was taken out to cover the cost of the mortgage (see below);
- interest payments on any loans for repairs and improvements to the home taken out before the maintenance application or enquiry form is sent to the parent;
- interest payments on loans for major repairs necessary to maintain the fabric of the home and for measures which improve its fitness for occupation, such as the installation of a bath, shower, wash basin or lavatory; the provision of heating, electric lighting and sockets, drainage facilities, or storage facilities for fuel and refuse; improvement to ventilation, natural lighting, insulation or structural condition; or any other improvements considered reasonable by the CSO;
- interest payments under a hire purchase agreement to buy a home;
- payments in respect of a licence or permission to occupy the home;
- payments in respect of or as a result of the occupation of the home;
- payments of ground rent or feu duty;
- payments under co-ownership schemes;
- payments of service charges if such payments are a condition for occupying the home;
- mooring charges for a houseboat;
- site rent for a caravan or mobile home;
- payments for a tent and its site;
- payments under a rental purchase scheme;
- payments in respect of croft land;
- payments in respect of a home made to an employer who provides the home;
- payments for Crown tenancy or licence;
- payments in respect of a loan that was taken out to pay off another loan (It is no longer stipulated that the original loan must have been taken out for one of the reasons given above, but, as with all eligible loans, the second must be in respect of the provision of the home; the eligible costs should not be limited to interest payments.);
- the fees (net of any housing benefit), where a parent or a partner lives in a nursing home, residential care home, local authority residential

accommodation (part III) or accommodation provided under the NHS Act 1977.[19]

Home

For the purposes of housing costs, the parent's home is either the dwelling in which the parent normally lives or, if s/he normally lives in more than one home, her/his principal home.[20] Therefore, if an absent parent is paying the costs of the family home in which the parent with care remains with the child(ren), these costs cannot be included as this is not the absent parent's own home.

The test of a principal home is not simply the parent's own view nor a calculation of the time spent at each home;[21] it has been held that an army officer's own home where he spent his leave can be his principal home over and above army married quarters. (However, the argument that the expenditure on the army accommodation should be taken into account as expenses was rejected by this child support commissioner – see p204 for details on expenses).

The only exception to the rule about only including one set of housing costs is where the parent is in a residential care home or nursing home. The fees for the residential accommodation can be included as well as the costs of the parent's own home if the parent has been in the home for less than a year or if the CSO believes that the parent intends to return home.

Where the payments for the property cover accommodation used for other purposes, eg, business use, the CSO has to identify the proportion of the cost attributable to housing.[22]

Housing benefit

Housing benefit is subtracted from housing costs only if the parent has claimed and been awarded housing benefit. If a parent delays claiming housing benefit until after completing the maintenance enquiry form or maintenance application form, full housing costs will be included as exempt income (unless they are excessive – see p91). This increases the exempt income figure.

In the case of an absent parent, the higher his exempt income, the lower the amount of child maintenance payable. In theory, an increase in the exempt income of a parent with care could increase the child maintenance payable. However, in practice, a parent with care's exempt income does not usually directly affect the maintenance she receives (see Chapter 11).

Mortgage payments

Unlike for IS, payments made towards repaying the mortgage – whether directly as capital repayments or through certain policies – are eligible housing costs for exempt income purposes.[23] Such payments are not eligible at protected income stage (see p253).

As well as endowment policies, other insurance policies taken out to pay off a mortgage on the home are considered to be eligible housing costs. These include premiums paid towards a mortgage protection policy to cover the mortgage in the event of unemployment, sickness or disability.[24] Life assurance policies taken out with the mortgage in order to discharge the debt on death are also included.[25] However, neither building nor contents insurance is included.[26]

Personal equity plans (PEPs) and personal pension plans taken out, at least in part, to discharge a mortgage on the parent's home are eligible housing costs.[27] Where a personal pension plan has been obtained both to discharge the mortgage and pay a pension, 25 per cent of the contributions made are included as housing costs in exempt income.[28]

Where the mortgage is under £60,000, all the premiums paid to an endowment policy or PEP will be eligible housing costs.[29] Where the policy was also taken out to produce a lump sum and the mortgage is over £60,000, 0.0277 per cent of the mortgage is taken to be weekly housing costs if the CSO is unable to ascertain what proportion of the premium is to cover the mortgage. Where the parent's endowment/PEP premium is larger than this 0.0277 per cent figure, it is worth pursuing the issue of how much capital is likely to be produced, especially as many endowment policies may not produce any capital in excess of the mortgage. Any payments made in excess of those required by the mortgage agreement are not eligible housing costs.[30]

Repayments made under an agreement for a loan taken out for eligible repairs and improvements (see p187) are included in exempt income as housing costs.[31]

Ineligible charges

Charges made for food, fuel, water or sewerage services do not count as eligible housing costs.[32] If the housing costs payments include an ineligible charge, an amount attributable to the service must be deducted.

If meals are provided, a standard weekly deduction is made:

	Aged 16 or over	*For each child under 16*
Full board	£17.10	£8.65
Half board	£11.35	£5.70
Breakfast only	£2.05	£2.05

If the parent provides information about the level of the fuel charge inclusive in the housing payment, this actual or estimated amount can be deducted. Otherwise a standard weekly deduction is made: heating

£9.25; hot water £1.15; cooking £1.15 and lighting 80 pence. If the parent has exclusive use of only one room, the deduction for heating, hot water and/or lighting is £5.60 a week.

Where the amount for water and sewerage charges is not separately identifiable, an amount will be attributed.

Where other service charges are included in the rent payments, they are taken into account as housing costs provided they are no more than 25 per cent of total eligible housing costs.[33] Where service charges other than food, fuel and water/sewerage do account for more than 25 per cent of housing costs, either the excess is taken into account or, if this would be less, only those which are ineligible for the purposes of housing benefit are deducted. Ineligible services include:

- personal laundry service;
- sports and other leisure facilities, including TV rental and licence fees, but excluding children's play areas;
- cleaning, other than communal areas or where no one in the accommodation is able to do it;
- transport;
- medical or nursing services; *and*
- any other charge not connected with the provision of adequate accommodation.

Weekly amount of housing costs

The amount allowed for housing costs is the amount payable at the effective date (see p303), converted into a weekly amount.[34] If the costs are monthly, the amount at the effective date must be multiplied by 12 and divided by 52. Where the housing costs are paid on any basis other than weekly or calendar monthly, the CSO considers the amount and payment period of the housing costs payable on the effective date:

- divide 365 by the number of days in the payment period, rounding to the nearest whole number;
- multiply this figure by the amount of the costs due in the payment period; *and then*
- divide this figure by 52 to give the weekly costs.

Where rent is payable to a local authority or housing association on a free week basis, the rent payable in the relevant week (see p205) is used unless that was a free week, in which case the last week which was not a free week is used.

The calculation of housing costs should be carefully checked as this is an area where the CSA often makes mistakes.

Excessive housing costs

Excessive housing costs are not generally allowed in full. However, all parents with day-to-day care of any child are exempt from the excessive housing costs restriction and therefore the rule never applies to parents with care. In addition to those with day-to-day care of a child, other absent parents who are exempt from restrictions on housing costs are those who:[35]

- have claimed or been awarded housing benefit;
- would qualify for an IS disability premium (see p427);
- remain in the former family home;
- have high housing costs because money which would otherwise be available is tied up in the former family home which is still occupied by the ex-partner;
- have been meeting those costs for over 52 weeks and the only increase in costs has been due to an increase in the rate of mortgage interest or rent;
- the costs only exceed the limit because of an increase in mortgage interest payments or rent (there appears to be no limit to how far back this can be taken).

Eligible housing costs are otherwise only allowed up to the greater of £80 or half of the parent's net income.[36] Net income is the income of the parent which is taken into account when calculating assessable income (see Chapter 10). Therefore, parents who have a net income of less than £160 are allowed to include housing costs of up to £80, while those with higher net incomes can include housing costs up to half their net income (see example 9.5).

Example 9.2: Exempt income – Bob moves in with Zoe

Bob goes to live with Zoe who has three children – Yvonne (12), Veronica (10) and Samuel (3). Zoe's rent on a three-bedroomed council house is £42 a week. They do not receive housing benefit. Even though it is Zoe who is legally liable for the rent, it is still an eligible cost.

Bob's exempt income is now:	£
Personal allowance	47.90
Housing costs	42.00
Total exempt income	89.90

Example 9.3: Exempt income of a parent with care

(a) Anita is now in paid employment and has claimed family credit. Therefore her exempt income must be calculated. She lives with her two children, Carol (13) and David (8). Her mortgage is under £60,000 and the payments, including the capital repayments, are £75 per week.

		£
Personal allowance	Anita	47.90
	Carol (13)	24.10
	David (8)	16.45
Family premium		10.55
Lone parent premium		5.20
Mortgage payment (total)		75.00
Total exempt income		179.20

(b) Anita marries Joe and together they buy a house, taking out a mortgage of £85,000. The interest payments are £495 a month and the endowment premium £108 a month – ie, £114.23 and £24.92 a week. However, as the CSO does not have information about how much of the premium is to cover the mortgage, the endowment premium is restricted to 0.0277% x £85,000 = £23.55 (see p189).

		£
Personal allowance	Anita	47.90
	Carol (15)	24.10
	David (10)	16.45
Family premium		10.55
Mortgage payment (114.23 + 23.55)		137.78
Total exempt income		236.78

The excessive housing costs rule does not apply because there are children in the family. Bob should consider seeking a departure (see p331) on the grounds that Joe can afford to contribute towards the mortgage.

4. PRE-APRIL 1993 PROPERTY SETTLEMENTS

On 18 April 1995 an allowance for certain property and capital settlements made before April 1993 was introduced into exempt income.[37] In order for an allowance to be included in exempt income, the property or capital transfer must satisfy certain qualifying criteria (see below).

Unlike other elements of exempt income, this allowance applies only to a parent with care if she was the absent parent at the time the property was transferred.[38] However, where a parent with care also transferred capital to the absent parent or the child(ren), this 'compensating transfer' may be offset against that of the absent parent's 'qualifying transfer'.[39]

There is a specialist section in each of the regional CSA centres (CSACs) which deals with this property/capital settlement allowance.

Qualifying transfer

A qualifying transfer is one which was made:[40]

- as part of a court order or written maintenance agreement which itself was made before 5 April 1993;
- when the absent parent and parent with care were living separately;
- between the absent parent and either the parent with care or a child for whom maintenance is being assessed;
- with the effect that the recipient was given the whole of the value of the transferred property; *and*
- without the entire purpose being to replace maintenance payments (either periodic or a lump sum) for the parent with care – ie, for herself as opposed to the child(ren).

For a transfer to be excluded by this final condition, there must be a specific written intention that shows that the *only* intention of the transfer was to compensate the parent with care for the right to receive spousal maintenance.[41] If there is no specific written intention or the transfer refers to another purpose in addition to the replacement of spousal maintenance, it is a qualifying transfer. The CSO will want to see the actual transfer document but, where this is not available or does not exist (eg, a transfer of cash between the parties), the CSO should treat the transfer as a qualifying transfer.[42]

It is possible for the absent parent to transfer the whole of the asset to the parent with care, but the building society insists that the absent parent's name is retained on the mortgage – eg, where the amount of the mortgage is more than the parent with care can borrow. This does not negate the fact that the whole of the asset has been transferred to the parent with care.[43] If a charge is placed on the property to benefit the absent parent, this will be deducted when calculating the allowance.

Property is defined as:[44]

- cash and savings in bank, building society or equivalent account;
- a legal estate or an equitable interest in land (or in Scotland, an interest in land);
- an endowment or other insurance policy obtained in order to discharge the mortgage or charge on a property which was also being transferred;
- a business asset, whether in the form of money, land or otherwise, which before it was transferred was being used in the course of a business in which the absent parent was a sole trader, a partner or a participator in a 'close' company.

It does not include other assets – eg, a car or contents of the home. The value of a trust fund established for the parent with care or the child can be considered.[45]

Providing evidence

Once an absent parent has notified the CSA that he wants a property/
capital settlement taken into account, he has to supply evidence within a
reasonable time.[46] The absent parent is asked to supply the evidence
within 28 days and, if this does not happen, he will be sent a reminder
giving a further 14 days. At that point, the Secretary of State will give
further time only if the parent has contacted the property settlement
section requesting this and his grounds for needing the extension are
reasonable.[47] An interview at the field office is used only as a last
resort.[48] If the evidence is not produced within this time, no allowance
will be given. If the evidence is later produced, the decision can be
reviewed, but the effective date of any revised assessment will depend on
whether there was a good reason for the delay.[49]

The absent parent must send written evidence to the CSA of:[50]

- a court order or maintenance agreement which required the transfer
  of property (this evidence must be contemporaneous);
- the fact of the transfer (this would be, for example, solicitors' or
  building society correspondence, or a copy of a Land Registry extract);
- the value of the property transferred at the date that the court order/
  written agreement was made (confirmed by a building society,
  insurance company or firm of property valuers); *and*
- the amount of any mortgage or charge outstanding at the date that
  the court order/written agreement was made (confirmed by a building
  society, bank, solicitors or accountants).

Once the CSO is satisfied that the application satisfies the qualifying
criteria, the person with care is notified of the application and asked for
any relevant information.[51] The allowance is not calculated until 14
days after the person with care has been contacted.

Calculating the allowance

Any mortgage or charge outstanding at the time of the order/agreement
is deducted from the value of land or business assets at that time.[52] Any
change in house prices since that time is irrelevant. The home is valued
on the basis that the parent with care and the child(ren) were not to
remain there.[53] The total net value is used irrespective of whether or not
the property was previously in joint ownership.

The amount transferred in the case of a bank or building society
account is the balance on the date of the order/agreement, and for an
endowment policy, the surrender value at that date.[54]

Unless the evidence produced shows that the whole of the transfer was
made in lieu of ongoing child maintenance, the value of the property is

halved to obtain the 'qualifying value'.[55] Where there has been more than one qualifying transfer, the qualifying values of the transfers are totalled.[56]

Transfers made by the parent with care to the absent parent or child(ren) which satisfy the qualifying criteria (see p193), except that they are made in the reverse direction, are called compensating transfers.[57] In addition, there is provision for the whole amount of money raised by a parent with care (eg, by taking out a loan) after the date of the court order or written agreement in order that she or her child(ren) is entitled to the whole of the property which is the subject of the qualifying transfer to be taken into account as a compensating transfer;[58] this applies where an absent parent transfers the matrimonial home to the parent with care on the condition that she buys out his interest in the property. Otherwise, compensating transfers are valued in the same way as qualifying transfers.[59]

The value of any compensatory transfer is deducted from that of the qualifying transfer to give the relevant value.[60] The allowance included in the exempt income relates to this relevant value:[61]

Relevant value	Weekly allowance
less than £5,000	nil
£5,000 – £9,999	£20
£10,000 – £24,999	£40
not less than £25,000	£60

Remember that this is an allowance in the exempt income, and therefore its inclusion does not mean that the assessment itself will be reduced by a corresponding amount.

Example 9.4: Pre-April 1993 property settlement allowance

Debbie and Steve were divorced in 1991. The family home was transferred to Debbie; at the time of the court settlement, the property was worth £58,000 and the outstanding mortgage was £22,000. Almost all the contents of the house were left with Debbie, as was the car. Instead of paying maintenance for Debbie herself, as part of the settlement, their joint savings account of £14,200 was transferred into Debbie's name. In addition, Steve gave each of the two children £3,000.

(a) The house contents and the car do not come within the definition of property. The savings account is not a qualifying transfer as it was payment in lieu of maintenance for Debbie.

The qualifying value of the transfer of the house is half of £58,000 – £22,000 = £36,000 ÷ 2 = £18,000

The qualifying value of the cash to the children is the whole actual value – ie, 2 × £3,000 = £6,000

Total qualifying value = £24,000

There is no compensating value to offset.

Therefore, as the relevant value is over £10,000 but less than £25,000, the allowance included in exempt income is £40.

(b) If the savings transferred to Debbie were only £10,000 of the £14,200 and this was not for any specified purpose, this would have been another qualifying transfer valued at £5,000. Total qualifying value = £29,000.

There is a compensating transfer with a value of £4,200 ÷ 2 = £2,100.

Relevant value = £29,000 – £2,100 = £26,900; therefore the allowance is £60.

---

5. TRAVEL-TO-WORK COSTS

Since 18 April 1995, an allowance towards travel costs has been included in exempt income for parents in employment who travel long distances.[62] It does not apply to self-employed parents.

If the parent provides the required information, an allowance towards high travel-to-work costs may be included.[63] As well as buying petrol or a ticket, travel-to-work costs include contributing to someone else's travel costs and paying someone else to provide the transport.[64] However, the allowance does not apply where the employer either provides transport which is available for any part of the journey between home and the workplace, or pays for any part of the travel-to-work cost.[65] This exclusion includes the provision of a company car, but not the situation where the employer has only made a loan to the parent, increases the amount of remuneration, or makes a payment which would be taken into account as part of net income (see p204).

Calculating the allowance

The CSO calculates or, where this is not possible, estimates:[66]

- the straight-line distance (ie, as the crow flies), rounded to the nearest mile, between the parent's home and workplace (usually by means of a computer program using UK postcodes and Ordnance Survey grid references);
- the number of journeys made between home and the workplace over a period of whole weeks which s/he thinks is representative of the parent's normal pattern of work (disregarding any two journeys made between the home and workplace within a period of two hours); *and*
- the number of journeys multiplied by the distance and divided by the number of weeks in the period used.

No allowance is included where this figure comes to less than or equal to 150 miles. However, where it is over 150 miles, 10 pence is included for each mile over 150.[67]

When determining the normal pattern of work, any days away from work due to leave or sickness are ignored.[68]

If the allowance does not reflect the real travel costs, later this year either party will be able to apply for a departure direction (see pp327 and 332).

Example 9.5: Exempt income including travel costs

Steve has remarried and has a net income for child support purposes of £380 a week. He and his wife Lisa have a mortgage of just under £60,000 and make monthly interest and endowment premium payments totalling £416 a month. They have no children.

Steve commutes five days a week to London with a straight-line distance from home to work of 80 miles. 10 journeys x 80 miles = 800 miles a week. This gives 650 miles over 150 and thus an allowance of 650 x 10 pence = £65 a week.

Steve's exempt income:	£	
Personal allowance	47.90	
Mortgage in full*	96.00	
Property settlement allowance	40.00	(see example 9.4a)
Travel-to-work costs	65.00	
Total exempt income	248.90	

* Although the housing costs are over £80, they are not considered excessive as half of Steve's net income is £190 a week (see p191).

More than one workplace

There are special rules to deal with the situation where the parent works at more than one workplace, whether for one employer or in more than one job.[69] If the pattern of work is irregular in a job, the CSO can select one of the workplaces or another location connected with the employment and assume that each day the parent travels to and from this deemed workplace.[70]

Otherwise the CSO must calculate the straight-line distances between any of the workplaces between which the parent travels, as well as between the home and each of the workplaces.[71] The pattern of journeys is obtained over a representative period as above, except that the two-hour rule only applies where the second journey is to return home. Each distance is multiplied by the number of times that journey is made over the period, and the total number of miles is divided by the number of weeks in the period.

6. SECOND FAMILIES

We use the term 'second family' loosely to describe the situation where the parent is now living with a partner and children. The children may be his/her own children and/or the partner's. We recognise that the word 'second' is not precise, as the family could be a parent's third or fourth family, or indeed a first family – eg, in the case of a married man who, despite having a child with another woman, is still living with his wife.

We have already looked at the general position of second families as regards the exempt income calculation. Partners and children who are not the parent's children are not considered when including personal allowances and premiums at this stage. However, a child of the parent is included and that child has another parent who is liable to maintain him/her. If the other parent is absent, then the child is a qualifying child and there is the possibility of receiving child maintenance.

On the other hand, if the other parent is also living in the family, then the exempt income calculation can be adjusted to recognise the other parent's liability to maintain the joint child. In other words, if a parent is living with his/her own child and the child's other parent, then the partner may be able to help support the child. This will reduce the parent's responsibility for their joint child included in exempt income. If the partner has sufficient income, this will halve the amounts for the joint child in the exempt income calculation. This is the only point at which an absent parent's partner's income can increase the assessment. Although it is taken into account at the protected income stage, a partner's income cannot increase the proposed maintenance.

The partner can refuse to disclose her income, in which case it is assumed that she can afford to help support her children and their allowances are halved. See p297 for the full consequences of the partner withholding her income details. Except for families on low incomes or where the partner has little income of her own, there is in effect no penalty for non-disclosure.

This assessment will need to be done not only where the absent parent has a second family, but also where a parent with care has had a child with a current partner. This is the only time in the formula that the income of the parent with care's partner is involved.

Can the partner afford to maintain the joint child

Before including the full allowance and premiums for a joint child in the parent's exempt income, the net income of the partner must be assessed. The partner's net income is calculated in the same way as the parent's net income when working out his/her assessable income (see Chapter

10), with just one difference.[72] The income of any of the partner's own children is *not* included. This means that maintenance for any of her own qualifying children from their absent parent – ie, step-children in the second family – is ignored.

To assess whether the partner can help support a joint child or children, compare the amount of her/his net income with the total of:[73]

- the IS personal allowance for a person aged 25 or over (£47.90); *plus*
- half the amount of the IS personal allowance for the child(ren) of that age; *plus*
- if the child(ren) would qualify for the IS disabled child premium (see p426), half the amount of that premium for that child(ren); *plus*
- half the amount of the IS family premium (except where the family premium would be payable in respect of another child who is included in exempt income – see pp183 and 425).

No personal allowances are included for any other children of the partner. This may create problems where there are step-children as well as the joint child(ren) with the current partner. The formula assumes that any step-children will be supported by their absent parent even where this is not the case or where their other parent is dead.

If the partner's net income is higher than the figure above, s/he can afford to contribute to their joint child's support. Therefore, the parent's exempt income will include only half the child's personal allowance, and half of any disabled child premium and (if there is no other child included the exempt income), only half the family premium.[74]

Example 9.6: Exempt income with a joint child

Bob and Zoe have a baby, Ricky. They are still living in the same house with a rent of £42 a week and Zoe's other three children (see example 9.2).

(a) Zoe stays at home full-time. Her only income is child benefit and maintenance for Yvonne and Veronica, both of which are ignored. Therefore, Zoe cannot afford to contribute to Ricky's upkeep and Bob's exempt income will include the full allowances for Ricky.

Bob is not the father of Yvonne, Veronica and Samuel, and therefore they are not included in the exempt income calculation.

Bob's exempt income:		£
Personal allowances	Bob	47.90
	Ricky	16.45
Family premium		10.55
Housing costs		42.00
Total exempt income		116.90

(b) Zoe begins paid work and brings home £90 a week.

Her earnings are compared with:		£
Personal allowances	Zoe	47.90
	Ricky (half)	8.23
Family premium (half)		5.28
Total		61.41

Note: Half the family premium is allowed in Zoe's means test as the family premium is only included in Bob's exempt income in respect of Ricky. There is no other child included in exempt income.

Even though the other three children in the family are Zoe's own children, they are still not taken into account at this stage. The child support formula always gives precedence to a parent's own children above step-children, and here it gives precedence to one of Zoe's own children, Ricky, above her other three children.

As her earnings are higher than £61.41, Zoe is seen as being able to contribute to the maintenance of Ricky. Therefore, Bob's exempt income is adjusted:

		£
Personal allowance	Bob	47.90
	Ricky (half)	8.23
Family premium (half)		5.28
Housing costs		42.00
Total exempt income		103.41

Family premium

If the only children who are included in the parent's exempt income are joint children with the current partner, then the question arises of whether the family premium should be included in full or halved in the exempt income. This depends solely on the net income of the partner. When calculating whether the partner can afford to help support the children, half the family premium is included in the amount with which the partner's net income is compared, as in the example above.

However, if there is another child in the family who is the parent's, but not the partner's, child, s/he will be included in the exempt income calculation of his/her parent. Therefore, the family premium is payable in full for this other child and the question of halving the family premium does not arise. The family premium is therefore excluded from the amount with which the partner's net income is compared when calculating whether she can support half the joint child.[75]

Example 9.7: Exempt income with a joint child and a qualifying child

The situation is the same as in example 9.6b except that Bob's daughter, Carol (15), has come to live with Bob and Zoe.

Zoe's earnings would now be compared with:		£
Personal allowances	Zoe	47.90
	Ricky (half)	8.23
Total		56.13

Half of the family premium is not included as Bob is entitled to the full family premium in his exempt income for Carol, and between the two partners, there cannot be more than one family premium.

As her earnings are higher than £56.13, Zoe is seen as being able to contribute to half the maintenance of Ricky. Therefore, Bob's exempt income is adjusted:

		£
Personal allowance	Bob	47.90
	Carol	24.10
	Ricky (half)	8.23
Family premium (in full)		10.55
Housing costs		42.00
Total		132.78

If Carol came to stay some of the time, but not to the extent that Bob is in receipt of child benefit for her, then the family premium would not be payable in respect of Carol (see Appendix 2 for the qualifying conditions for the IS family premium). Therefore, the family premium is only payable in the exempt income again because of the joint child, Ricky, and Zoe's means-test *would* include half the family premium. The family premium would either be included at full rate or half rate in Bob's exempt income, depending on Zoe's income.

Carol's personal allowance may be included in Bob's exempt income, but at reduced rate, depending on how often she stays with him (see Chapter 13). For a detailed explanation of the family premium in exempt income where there is a joint child and a shared care child, see p273 and example 13.4.

CHAPTER TEN

Assessable income
Step 3 of the formula

This chapter covers:

1. What is assessable income (see below)
2. What is net income (p203)
3. Calculating assessable income (p219)

This chapter should be read in conjunction with calculation sheet 3 in Appendix 4.

I. WHAT IS ASSESSABLE INCOME

Assessable income is the parent's income remaining after basic living expenses (as represented by exempt income, see Chapter 9) have been accounted for. A proportion of this remaining income is used to contribute towards child maintenance payments (see Chapter 11). In the case of the parent with care this is a notional contribution which can have the effect of reducing the maintenance payable by the absent parent.

Assessable income is the parent's net income minus exempt income.[1]

This step of the formula is carried out in the same way for absent parents and parents with care,[2] and therefore any reference to parent in this chapter applies to both. It does not apply to a person with care who is not the parent of the qualifying child.

It is useful to calculate the absent parent's assessable income first because if he has no assessable income there is no need to calculate that of the parent with care (see p219).

A parent who is in receipt of income support (IS) is treated as having *no* assessable income.[3] If only the parent with care is on IS, then this step must be done for the absent parent alone. If the absent parent is on IS, then the formula calculation is not carried out at all and instead the absent parent may have a deduction from his benefit (see p168).

2. WHAT IS NET INCOME

Net income is the total income of the parent taken into account when assessing how much child maintenance the parent can afford to pay.

Net income includes earnings, benefits and other income.[4] The types of income that come within each of these categories are clearly defined in the regulations.[5] Certain types of income are ignored in full or in part.[6] The rules about income are similar, but not identical, to those for IS – eg, there are no earnings disregards when calculating net income.

The net income of a parent's partner is calculated using these rules when assessing whether s/he can afford to contribute to the support of any joint child in the exempt income calculation (see p198).[7]

These rules for calculating net income are also used when working out the family's total income at the protected income stage of the formula (see Chapter 12). However, there are a few exceptions which are highlighted in this chapter.[8]

If any income which is normally received at regular intervals is not received, it can be treated as though it were received if there are reasonable grounds for believing that the payment will actually be made.[9]

Capital itself is not taken into account, although any income generated from the capital does count as income (see p214).

In certain cases, a parent can be treated as having income (or capital which is a source of income) which s/he does not possess if the child support officer (CSO) believes the parent deprived him/herself of it with the intention of reducing his/her assessable income (see p217).

Verification of income details is expected (see p151).

Whose income is included

A partner's income is *not* included in the net income when calculating assessable income. This is commonly misunderstood (see pp198 and 250 for the way in which a partner's income may affect the assessment). Where a source of income is held jointly and the proportions are not known or defined, then the income available will be divided equally between the people who are entitled to receive it.[10]

The income of the parent's own child living in the household can be treated as though it was the income of the parent (see p216).[11]

Earnings from employment

Earnings mean 'any remuneration or profit derived from … employment' and, as well as wages, include:[12]

• any payments for overtime;

- any bonus or commission (including tips);
- any holiday pay (except any payable more than four weeks after the job ends);
- payments in lieu of notice;
- statutory sick pay and statutory maternity pay;
- any payment for expenses not 'wholly, exclusively and necessarily incurred' in actually carrying out the job;
- allowances paid to local councillors for local authority duties, as opposed to expenses 'wholly, exclusively and necessarily incurred';
- payment for duties as an auxiliary coastguard, part-time firefighter, or with the lifeboat services, territorial army or reserve forces relating to a period of less than one year (such payments for a period of one year or more are disregarded[13]);
- awards of compensation for unfair dismissal;
- certain employment protection payments;
- any retaining fee;
- remuneration, but not share dividend or debenture interest (which is other income), paid to a director of a limited or unlimited registered and incorporated company (as opposed to a sole trader or partner who is self-employed – see p206).[14]

Earnings do *not* include:[15]

- payments of occupational pension (these count as other income – see p211);
- payments for expenses 'wholly, exclusively and necessarily' incurred in carrying out the duties of the job (see below);
- payments in kind;
- any advance of earnings or loan made by an employer to an employee (such a payment is also disregarded as other income[16]);
- payments made after employment ends which relate to a specific period of time, provided that a period of equal length has elapsed since the payment was received;
- earnings from a previous job where they are paid in a week or a period that earnings from a second job are received;
- payments made by an employer when an employee is on strike;
- the value of free accommodation provided by an employer (although the CSO may consider the issue of notional earnings – see p217 – if the actual earnings are low in relation to the job performed).[17]

A commissioner has held that payments made by the parent for expenses could be deducted from his/her earnings where the employer did not reimburse them.[18] It was emphasised that any such expenses had to be incurred 'in the performance of duties', and not just incurred in order to enable the parent's duties to be performed.

Relevant week

The concept of the 'relevant week'[19] is important in child support assessments, particularly when calculating income.

For the parent who is not the applicant, the relevant week is the seven days immediately before the date that the maintenance enquiry form (see p133) is sent to him. For the applicant, the relevant week is the seven days immediately before the maintenance application form (see p61) is submitted to the Child Support Agency (CSA).

If a periodical review (see p353) is being carried out, the relevant week is the seven days immediately preceding the date when the information is requested.

For a change of circumstances review (see p355), the relevant week is the seven days immediately before the date on which the request for the review is received at the CSA. Where a CSO initiates a change of circumstances review without a request, the relevant week is the seven days immediately before the date on which the CSO first suspected it would be appropriate to make a fresh assessment. Otherwise, where a CSO reviews an assessment, whether a second-tier review on request (see p358) or instigated by the CSO (see p364), the relevant date is the same date as for the original asessment.

Calculating normal weekly earnings

Averaged earnings are used in the child support calculation.[20] When calculating or estimating average earnings at the relevant week (see above), the CSO considers the evidence of the parent's earnings over any appropriate period, beginning no more than eight weeks before the relevant week and ending by the date of the assessment. S/he may also consider cumulative earnings to date in the tax year covering the relevant week. CSOs are advised to give reasons for the assessment period chosen for calculating earnings.[21] Although the CSO can use any period which reflects a parent's average earnings in the relevant week, s/he first considers five consecutive weeks, including the relevant week, for parents paid weekly and two consecutive months covering the relevant week for those paid monthly.[22]

Where the parent is a student (see p211 for definition of a student), earnings are averaged over 52 weeks ending with the relevant week, or as many weeks as the parent has been a student if this is a shorter period.[23]

Where the CSO believes that the amount of weekly earnings arrived at does not accurately represent the parent's normal earnings, then s/he can use any other period, taking into account earnings received and those due to be received.[24] The CSO must be satisfied that the period used reflects the parent's usual pattern of work – eg, the amount of overtime worked or sick leave.[25] A future period can be used to take into account, for example, a recent change in the number of hours worked or earnings from a job which has not yet begun. The CSO must also consider the expected duration and pattern of any employment.

Where a bonus or commission is paid during a year separately from earnings or in relation to a longer period than other earnings, the bonus/commission payments will be totalled over the year and divided by 52 weeks.[26]

The calculation of earnings is one of the areas where errors are frequently made (see p164) and therefore should be checked carefully.

Calculating net earnings

Net earnings from employment are counted as net income in full. There are no earnings disregards. Net earnings mean gross earnings less:[27]

- income tax;
- Class 1 national insurance contributions;
- one half of any contributions made to an occupational pension scheme; *and*
- one half of any contributions made towards a personal pension scheme (unless that scheme is intended partly to pay off a mortgage on the parent's home, in which case 37.5 per cent of such contributions). Certain retirement savings plans do not come within this provision.[28]

The amount of tax and national insurance actually paid is usually deducted.[29] However, where earnings are being estimated, the amount to be deducted as income tax is calculated using the personal allowances and the tax rates applicable at the relevant week (see above).[30] Similarly, the amount to be deducted as Class 1 national insurance contributions has to be calculated by using the appropriate percentage rate applicable in the relevant week.

Earnings from self-employment

For parents who are self-employed, earnings mean the gross receipts of the business. They include any business start-up grant which is paid for the same period as the receipts, unless it has ended by the relevant week, in which case it is disregarded.[31] Earnings do not include any payments received for providing board and lodging accommodation unless this is the largest part of the parent's income.[32] Where a parent is a childminder, only one third of her gross receipts count as earnings.[33]

Net earnings to be included as net income are the gross receipts of the business *less:*[34]

- income tax (calculated for the chargeable earnings at the tax rates applicable on the effective date (see p303)[35]);
- national insurance contributions (Class 2 and Class 4 contributions at the rates applicable on the effective date[36]);
- half of any premium on a personal pension scheme (unless that scheme is intended partly to pay off a mortgage on the parent's home, in which case 37.5 per cent of the contributions are deducted) or on a retirement annuity contract;
- any VAT paid in excess of VAT received in the same period as that over which the earnings are assessed;
- any expenses which are reasonably incurred and wholly and exclusively defrayed for the purposes of the business. If the CSO is not satisfied that the full expense was appropriate or necessary to the business, s/he will allow that part s/he considers reasonable.[37] Where an expense is part business and part private, eg, a telephone or a car, the CSO has to decide on the breakdown between the two uses on the evidence available.[38] They may well follow the apportionment used by the Inland Revenue. CSOs are given guidance on what may be allowable business expense.[39]

Business expenses include:[40]

- repayments of capital on loans used for the replacement or repair of a business asset (but not for loans taken out for any other business purpose);
- any income used for the repair of a business asset;
- any payment of interest on loans taken out for business purposes.

Business expenses do *not* include:

- capital expenditure;
- depreciation of capital assets;
- any sum employed in the setting up or expansion of the business;
- any loss incurred before the period of earnings being calculated;
- any expenses incurred in providing business entertainment;
- any loss incurred in any other self-employment.

There is a separate rule for share fishermen.[41]

Calculating weekly earnings of the self-employed

If a profit and loss account is provided for a period of at least six months (but no longer than 15 months) which ended within the last two years, it can be used to calculate average weekly earnings.[42] The two years end on the date on which the assessment takes effect, known as the **effective date** (see p303.) The CSO may decide to wait if accounts will shortly be available and impose a Category C interim maintenance assessment in the meantime (see p98).

If there is more than one such profit and loss account covering different periods, the account covering the latest period will be used unless the CSO is satisfied that this latest account is not available for reasons beyond the parent's control.[43] Not being available includes an accountant or another government department – eg, the Inland Revenue – holding them without a date set for their return, the Official Receiver has the accounts, or they have been destroyed, lost or stolen.

A trading account or balance sheet might be requested in addition to the profit and loss account.[44] The accounts do not need to be prepared by accountants or even typed. However, if they do not contain the required information, the CSA may request other evidence of gross receipts.

Where there is no appropriate profit and loss account available, earnings for the self-employed will be averaged over the previous 52 weeks or, if the person has been self-employed for less than a year, over the period during which the person has been self-employed.[45] In this case, the last week of the 52-week period is the **relevant week** (see p205). The self-employed person is asked to provide other evidence of business receipts and expenses, such as business books, receipts of bills sent and paid, bank statements, records of wages paid, Inland Revenue forms and VAT bills.[46]

Whatever period is used for assessing earnings, only those receipts and expenses *relevant* to that period should be used.[47] This is not necessarily the same as the payments made and received during the period.

Where the CSO believes that either or both of the above calculations produce an amount which does not accurately represent the parent's true earnings, another period can be used.[48] This may happen where there has been a major change in trading which has resulted in higher or lower earnings or where a person who has been trading for less than a year has not established a regular pattern of trading.[49]

Challenging earnings of the self-employed

Despite the fact that self-employed cases are dealt with by the Special Cases section in the regional CSA centre (CSAC), there have been particular problems with both assessment and enforcement in these cases. There have often been delays in the self-employed parent producing all the information necessary to carry out the assessment. The CSA can impose a Category C interim maintenance assessment (see p298) while awaiting the information, but this is rare. The person with care may want to request that this is done.

Many persons with care with pre-April 1993 court orders have had their maintenance reduced by the CSA where a self-employed absent parent is involved. Some persons with care allege that the self-employed absent parent, sometimes with the help of an accountant, has managed to disguise his true income. Once an assessment has been made, the person with care can seek a review (see p358) and ask the CSA to use an inspector (see p153) in order to obtain more detailed information. However, if the absent parent's accounts have been accepted by the Inland Revenue or Contributions Agency, it is very unlikely that the CSA would consider it worthwhile to undertake further investigations. The CSO may also refuse to conduct a review if the person with care cannot substantiate her allegations. This can be challenged if the belief is reasonably held as it is very difficult for one party to obtain definitive details of the other's income. The CSA is much better placed to do this.

If the person with care takes the case to a child support appeal tribunal (see p367), she will see details of the income in the appeal papers, and she may be able to argue that some of the expenses included are not reasonable or not wholly connected with the business (see above). She should also consider the notional earnings rules (see p217) and, if relevant, suggest the tribunal makes a finding on this issue. Tribunals have not had much experience of this area and, instead, may adjourn the hearing and instruct the CSA to collect further information.

Later this year, the person with care will be able to seek a departure from the assessment on the grounds that a person's lifestyle is inconsistent with the level of his income or that assets which do not currently produce income are in fact capable of producing income (see p329).

Benefits

Benefits paid by the Benefits Agency count as income for the purposes of net income, although some of these are disregarded in full or in part.[50] Remember that where IS is received by the parent or his/her partner, the parent is treated as having no assessable income (see p202).

The amount of the benefit to be taken into account is the rate applying on the effective date, the date when the maintenance assessment comes into effect (see p303).[51]

Whose benefit is it

The income of a partner is not included when working out a parent's net income. Where a couple is claiming a benefit jointly, there are rules for assigning part of the benefit to the partner. This does not apply to IS, as net income does not have to be calculated for IS claimants.

Some non-means-tested benefits contain an extra amount for a partner, called an adult dependency increase. The amount paid in respect of that dependant is treated as the dependant's income, not the claimant's.[52] This means that if the parent is the claimant, s/he is treated as not receiving the adult dependency addition. Equally, if it is the partner who is the claimant, the parent will be assumed to have income equal to the addition paid to the partner in respect of him/her.

If a parent receives a non-means-tested benefit which includes a dependency addition for a child, this addition is treated as the income of the child (see p216).

Family credit (FC) is counted as the income of the person who is working 16 hours or more a week.[53] If both members of a couple are working, then the FC is treated as the income of the partner with the higher earnings over the period used for assessing earnings for child support purposes.[54] However, where FC was calculated on the basis of a couple's earnings and one or both have since left their job, then half the FC is treated as the parent's income.[55] If the FC assessment took into account a partner's earnings and that person is no longer the partner of the parent, then FC will only be taken into account as net income if the parent is actually in receipt of the benefit.[56]

A parent may consider delaying a claim for FC until after the information regarding child support has been sought. However, there are rules concerning notional income (see p217).

Benefits ignored in full

The following benefits are ignored in full when working out net income:
- child benefit (but *not* one parent benefit).[57] Note that child benefit counts as income when calculating the total family income for protected income purposes;[58]
- housing benefit;[59]
- council tax benefit;[60]
- disability living allowance (or a mobility supplement);[61]
- attendance allowance (or constant attendance allowance or exceptionally severe disablement allowance paid because of industrial injury or war injury);[62]
- social fund payments;[63]
- guardian's allowance;[64]
- Christmas bonus.[65]

Payments made to compensate for the loss of benefits are also disregarded.[66] Special war widows' payments granted in 1990 are likewise disregarded in full.[67]

Benefits ignored in part

£10 of a war disablement pension or war widow's pension are disregarded.[68] However, only £20 in total can be disregarded from a combination of war pensions, charitable payments and student income (see below).

Other income

Unless specified below, all other income is taken into account on a weekly basis by considering the 26-week period ending in the 'relevant week' (see p205).[69] If the income has been received during each week of the period, the total received over the 26 weeks is divided by 26. In other cases, the total received is divided by the number of complete weeks for which the payment was received. However, the CSO does have discretion to use a different period if the amount produced by the above calculation does not accurately reflect actual income.

Other income includes any payments received on a periodic basis which are not covered as earnings, benefits, or a child's income,[70] as well as the following types of payment. Some payments are taken into account in full or in part, while others are ignored completely.

Payments from occupational or personal pension schemes

These and any analogous payments are taken into account in full.[71]

Income from rent

Different provisions apply, depending on the type of income from the property:

- payments made towards household expenses by a non-dependant (see p253 for a definition) are completely ignored;[72]
- the first £20 a week of a payment from a boarder are disregarded, as is 50 per cent of any amount over £20 (as long as this is not the largest part of a parent's income when it would be treated as earnings from self-employment).[73] A boarder is someone who is liable to pay for board and lodging which includes at least one meal a day;
- payments from a person who is liable to pay for accommodation in the parent's home (but who is not a lodger or a non-dependant) are treated as income. However, there is a disregard of £13.25 (or £4 if the payment is not inclusive of heating);[74]
- payments for the use of a property which is not the parent's home are taken into account as other income, unless the parent is self-employed. In this case, the income is treated as part of the gross receipts of the business. If the parent is not self-employed, the amounts to cover mortgage interest, interest on loans for repairs and improvements, council tax and water rates can be deducted from the amount received as rent.[75]

Students' income

A student is defined as someone following a full-time course of study at an educational establishment and, if under 19 years old, the course must be advanced education – ie, above A levels or Scottish Highers.[76] This can include sandwich students. There is no definition of full-time and it does not relate to the number of hours of attendance. The CSO attaches great weight to evidence from the educational establishment. Once a course has begun, a person continues to be treated as a student until either the course ends or s/he leaves the course.

Unless they have income in addition to an educational grant (including any contribution due) or student loan, students are treated as having no net income and hence are exempt from having to pay child maintenance.[77]

In other cases, income paid to a student as a grant, grant contribution, covenant income or student loan, is taken into account except to the extent that it is:[78]

- intended to meet tuition fees or examination fees;
- intended to meet additional expenditure as a result of a disability;
- intended to meet expenditure connected with residential study away from the educational establishment;
- made on account of the student maintaining a home away from the educational establishment;
- intended to meet the cost of books and equipment, or, if not specified, £278 (this goes up each September);
- intended to meet travel expenses;
- a payment from the access fund.[79]

The amount of a student's grant, covenant income and loan are apportioned equally between the weeks for which they are payable.[80] £5 of the weekly covenant income are disregarded and £10 of any loan, although not more than £10 a week can be deducted in total.[81] Any amount disregarded under this provision counts towards the £20 disregard for charitable/voluntary payments (see p214).[82]

Educational maintenance awards for courses of further education are disregarded.[83]

Youth Training allowances

Unless they have income in addition to the YT allowance, youth trainees are taken to have no net income and hence are exempt from paying any child maintenance (see p167).[84] YT trainees who are employees have their earnings taken into account in the usual way (see p203).

Training for work allowances

Training allowances are taken into account, except for the training premium, travelling expenses or any living away from home allowance.[85]

Maintenance in respect of a parent

This income is taken into account in full. There is a specific rule which applies for calculating the amount of maintenance to take into account. It is calculated by averaging the payments received in the 13 weeks preceding the assessment over the number of weeks for which a payment was due.[86]

Child maintenance

Child maintenance from an absent parent for the qualifying child for whom the assessment is being carried out is ignored when calculating the income of the parent with care.[87]

Except at the protected income stage (see Chapter 12), the CSA treats maintenance paid to a parent for any other child as income of the child. This may still be included in net income, but there are separate rules covering when and how much of the child's income can be taken into account as the parent's income (see p216).

In the calculation of protected income, any maintenance being paid for other children under a court order is deducted from the liable person's income, as long as an application cannot be made to the CSA (see pp55–6).[88] See p251 for further details.

Lump sum maintenance

There is provision to disregard other maintenance payments in full, whether child support maintenance or other forms, if they are not income.[89] However, as all payments received on a periodic basis are income, this disregard appears only to apply to irregular maintenance payments.

Payments made by a local authority under the Children Act 1989 or Social Work (Scotland) Act 1968

Payments made where the local authority is looking after a child and has placed the child with a family, relative or other suitable person, including a foster parent, are ignored completely.[90] Payments made by local authorities to promote the welfare of children being looked after, or who were formerly in their care, are also ignored.[91]

Payments made as a contribution towards the maintenance of a child living with the family as a result of a residence order under the Children Act are ignored where they exceed the personal allowances and any disabled child premium included for the child in the exempt income calculation (see p183).[92]

Adoption allowances

A payment for an adopted child is disregarded:[93]

- to the extent that it exceeds the personal allowance and any disabled child premium for the child, if child maintenance is *not* being assessed for that particular child;
- only up to the amount of any income of the child which is included as income of the parent, if child maintenance is being assessed for that child.

Income from capital

A payment of capital is not income in that it is not paid for a period and is not intended to form part of a series of payments.[94] Such capital payments are not taken into account. However, the interest, dividend or any other income produced by capital is taken into account as income and is calculated by dividing the total received over 52 weeks by 52.[95] If this gives a figure which the CSO decides is not representative of the income produced, s/he can use another period.

Where capital is jointly held and the shares are unknown, any income from the capital is divided equally between the joint owners.[96] Where capital is divided on divorce or separation and it is intended for the purchase of a new home or furnishings, then income from that capital will be ignored for one year.[97]

Although CSOs are given examples of what may constitute capital and ownership, there is no guidance on the calculation of income from different types of capital.[98]

Prisoners' pay

Unless they have another source of income, prisoners receiving only prisoners' pay will be assumed to have no net income and will be exempt from paying child support.[99]

Regular charitable or voluntary payments

These are disregarded in full if they are intended and used for any items *other than* food, ordinary clothing, household fuel, housing costs or council tax.[100] There has to be a mutual understanding between the donor and the recipient as to the purpose of the payment, but this does not need to be a formal agreement.[101] If the payment is in respect of school fees, then it is not counted as income at all even if part of the school fees relates to one of the specified items – eg, school meals.[102]

If the payment is for one of these specified items, then the first £20 will be disregarded, although no more than £20 in total can be disregarded from a student's income, a war pension and such voluntary payments.[103] This disregard was increased from £10 to £20 from 8 April 1996; however, assessments will not be reviewed just to take this into account.[104] Instead, the increased disregard will take effect when the assessment is undergoing a periodical change of circumstances or second-tier review (see Chapter 16).

This provision does not apply to payments made by absent parents which are treated as maintenance (see above).

See p219 for the position if the voluntary or charitable payment is made direct to a third party.

Other disregarded income

The following will also not be taken into account as income:

- payments in kind (except for self-employed earners);[105]
- payments made instead of milk tokens or free vitamins;[106]
- all NHS health benefits such as fares to hospital;[107]
- payments for prison visiting;[108]
- resettlement benefit paid to long-term hospital patients on their discharge from hospital;[109]
- payments made by a local education authority to help a child take advantage of a course of study or educational facilities, including a scholarship, or an assisted place;[110]
- payments under a mortgage protection insurance policy to the extent that they exceed the interest, capital payments and any further mortgage protection premiums;[111]
- payments of expenses to unpaid voluntary workers (as long as the expenses cannot be treated as notional earnings);[112]
- payments made to assist a person with a disability to obtain or keep employment;[113]
- payments made by a health authority, local authority or voluntary organisation for a person who is temporarily a member of the household in order to receive care;[114]
- compensation for personal injury and any payments made from a trust fund set up for that purpose;[115]
- payments from the Macfarlane Trust, Independent Living (1993) Fund or Independent Living (Extension) Fund;[116]
- payments from the Family Fund;[117]
- payments (other than those for lost earnings and benefits) made to jurors and witnesses for court attendance;[118]
- certain home income annuities purchased when aged 65 or over;[119]
- income tax payment or refund not already taken into account elsewhere;[120]
- charges for converting payments in another currency to sterling;[121]

- amounts payable outside the UK where transfer to the UK is prohibited;[122]
- payments to a person as a result of holding the Victoria or George Cross.[123]

Children's income

Where the parent has a child of his/her own living with him/her for at least 104 nights a year, the income of that child may be included in the parent's net income.[124] This does not have effect where the child is *not* a child (as defined by the 1991 Act) of the parent whose income is being assessed. For example, a parent of the qualifying child may have step-children living with him/her or be a person with care of another child – eg, a grandchild. The income of these children does not count in calculating net income at assessable income stage, but is taken into account at protected income stage.

The child's income is taken to be her/his own parent's income when calculating both net income for assessable income purposes and total family income for protected income purposes. However, the child's income is *not* included when calculating the net income of her/his parent's partner in order to find out whether the partner can help support a joint child included in the exempt income (see o198).[125]

What counts as the child's income

The first step is to decide how much income the child has and then, once that is done, decide how much of the child's income is to be treated as the parent's income. The child dependency additions of any benefit received by an adult is taken to be income of the child.[126]

Child maintenance received for a child is the child's income, even if it is paid to the parent.[127] Child maintenance already being received for a qualifying child who is the subject of the assessment being undertaken is ignored in full.[128]

The following are *not* included when calculating the child's income:[129]

- a child's earnings;
- interest payable on arrears of child maintenance;
- payments from a discretionary fund which benefit the child, as long as they do not cover food, ordinary clothing/footwear, household fuel or housing costs.

How much of the child's income counts

The first £10 a week of any income of a child is ignored.[130] In addition, once the child's income is treated as that of her/his parent, the same disregards apply as for the parent's own income.[131]

How much of the child's net income is taken into account as her/his parent's income depends on whether the child is the subject of the maintenance assessment. Where the child is *not* the subject of the maintenance assessment, her/his income up to the amount of the personal allowance (and any disabled child premium) included in the exempt income calculation in respect of that child is counted as the parent's income.[132] Income above that amount is disregarded.

Where the child is the subject of the maintenance assessment, the child's income counts in full if s/he is the only child for whom an assessment is being made.[133] Where there is more than one child, each child's income is counted up to the level of child's proportion of the maximum child maintenance payment (see p234) – ie, a share of the maintenance requirement plus 1.5 times the family premium and the personal allowance.[134]

At the protected income stage of the formula, the rules about how much of the child's income is taken into account are different (see p251).

Notional income

Parents can be assumed to have income which they do not possess.[135] Such notional income is treated in the same way as if it were actual income.[136] It appears that, in practice, this provision is not used often, and parents who are contesting the other party's income may want to remind the CSO at the second-tier review (see p358) that notional income should be considered.

Notional earnings

The issue of notional earnings arises where a person has done some work without being paid at all or not at a sufficient rate for the job for an employer who could afford to pay full wages.[137] This cannot apply if the employer is a charity or voluntary organisation or a member of the parent's family. The estimated foregone income is treated as earnings if a CSO decides that the principal purpose of the person doing the work without pay or for reduced pay was to reduce his/her assessable income. If the CSO decides that this is the main reason, s/he then has to consider:[138]

- does the parent perform a service from which the employer benefits?
- what is a comparable rate of pay?
- if the employer is paying less than this rate, could s/he afford to pay more for the service?

If the question of notional earnings is raised, the parent should let the CSO know his/her motives for doing the work.

Deprivation of income or capital

If a CSO decides that a parent intentionally deprived him/herself of income in order to reduce his/her assessable income, then an amount equal to that income will be included as his/her net income.[139]

This rule applies equally to capital which would have been a source of income. The CSO has to estimate a notional income from the notional capital and it is suggested that it may be reasonable to use rates of interest paid by high street banks and building societies.[140] When a CSO has decided that a certain sum is notional capital, that capital is reduced after 52 weeks by an amount equal to the income which would have been generated from that capital over the year.[141]

Deprivation refers both to income or capital that a person has disposed of and that which a person has failed to obtain – eg, by failing to apply for a benefit. However, it does not apply to one parent benefit, unemployment benefit if IS is payable, nor to a payment from a discretionary trust or a trust set up with personal injury compensation.[142] Apart from social security benefits, the other examples given to CSOs of payments which could be acquired are unclaimed councillors' attendance allowances, occupational pensions or Premium Bond wins.[143] Where income would have been available to a parent on application, an estimated amount is included as his/her net income from the date on which it could be expected to have been paid.[144]

The CSO is most likely to identify a potential deprivation of income or capital if, when reviewing an assessment, s/he finds that a source of income previously declared is not included on the review form.[145] The first question to be considered is whether the parent has actually disposed of the income or capital and the onus is on the parent to prove s/he no longer has the resource.[146] CSOs are given examples of deprivation of capital – making a lump-sum payment, putting money into a trust which cannot be revoked, gambling, using capital to fund an extravagant lifestyle or purchase personal possessions.[147] Although not mentioned in the guidance, deprivation can apply to a parent who has transferred assets to a new partner or possibly to a self-employed parent who is paying his partner a reasonable salary but not drawing much himself. Once it is shown s/he no longer possesses it, then the intention behind the deprivation has to be examined.

This rule is similar, but not identical, to those for means-tested benefits (see CPAG's *National Welfare Benefits Handbook*) and an adviser should therefore consider whether any social security commissioners' decisions could be cited as persuasive. Although it may be argued that the reduction of assessable income need not be the only or even principal motive, the CSO has to be able to show that s/he is satisfied that such an intention existed. The onus of proof remains with the CSO.[148]

When deciding whether reducing assessable income was a significant factor in the disposal of the resource, CSOs are advised to consider all the parent's reasons and the timing of the action.[149] If deprivation of capital is an issue, the CSO will consider whether the parent was aware that reducing capital would reduce the maintenance assessment.

This deprivation rule can presumably be used against an absent parent who gives up his job on finding out the size of the child maintenance expected from him, although it is unclear how long it could be assumed that such an income is still available. However, it is most probably not applicable to a case where a parent has taken out a higher mortgage to reduce his assessable income as this would not involve disposal of a *source* of income. A parent in this situation needs to consider the excessive housing costs rule (see p191). On the other hand, the use of capital as a deposit to buy a property could possibly be considered to be deprivation and motives would need to be examined.

Payments to third parties

If a payment is made on behalf of a parent or a child to a third party, it will only be treated as the parent's income if it is a payment for food, ordinary clothing or footwear, household fuel, housing costs or council tax.[150] For example, if a grandparent paid the parent's fuel bill direct to the fuel company, this would be notional income, whereas paying the telephone bill would not. Some of this notional income can be disregarded as a voluntary payment if made regularly (see p214).

3. CALCULATING ASSESSABLE INCOME

Assessable income is the parent's total net income less his/her exempt income. For details of exempt income, see Chapter 9.

If an absent parent's net income is itself less than £4.80, he is exempt from paying child maintenance and there is no need to carry on with the calculation.[151]

If the parent's exempt income is higher than his/her net income, assessable income is taken to be nil.[152] Where his assessable income is nil, the absent parent may still have to make the minimum payment of child maintenance. There is, however, no need to continue with the steps of the formula in this case as the maintenance due will either be the minimum payment of £4.80 or nil (see p167).

Where the parent with care's assessable income is nil, the proposed maintenance step is carried out with just the absent parent's assessable income.

Example 10.1: Assessable income of an absent parent

(a) Bob is living in the bed-sit on his own. His exempt income is £95.90 (see example 9.1a). His only income is £154 a week in earnings after tax, national insurance and £12 weekly superannuation contribution. Only half his superannuation is taken into account when calculating Bob's net earnings for child support purposes, which are therefore £154 + £6 = £160.

Bob's net income is therefore his net earnings: £160.

	£
Net income	160.00
Less exempt income	95.90
Assessable income	64.10

(b) Bob moves in with Zoe and her three children (see example 9.2).

	£
Net income	160.00
Less exempt income	89.90
Assessable income	70.10

(c) If Bob was in receipt of incapacity benefit of £67.60 and lived with his parents (see example 9.1b):

	£
Net income	67.60
Less exempt income	68.30
	nil

Due to his incapacity, Bob is exempt from the minimum payment (see p167). He therefore would receive a nil assessment; no further calculation is required.

Example 10.2: Assessable income of a parent with care

While Anita is on IS, she is automatically treated as having no assessable income. If she is not receiving IS – eg, she is in paid work for 16 hours or more a week – her assessable income must be calculated.

(a) Anita now earns £110 net a week. She receives child benefit of £19.60 and one parent benefit of £6.30. Bob has been paying £30.50 a week in maintenance for Carol (13) and David (8). This is not taken into account as income because it is maintenance for the qualifying children – ie, the children for whom the re-assessment is being carried out. Anita claims family credit (FC) and is awarded £42.44.

	£
Earnings	110.00
One parent benefit	6.30
Family credit	42.44
Total net income	158.74

Her exempt income is £179.20 (see example 9.3a) which is higher than her net income. She therefore has no assessable income.

(b) Anita increases her hours to 40 and is now bringing home £185 a week (after tax, NI and a £15 superannuation contribution). When her FC is re-assessed, she is no longer entitled. Only half of the superannuation payment can be taken into account – ie, £7.50 – and therefore her net earnings for exempt income purposes are now £192.50 a week.

	£
Earnings	192.50
One parent benefit	6.30
Total net income	198.80
Less exempt income	179.20 (from example 9.3a)
Assessable income	19.60

(c) Anita remarries. She is still bringing home £185 a week after tax, NI and a £15 superannuation contribution. Her husband, Joe, earns £205 a week. Net income is £192.50 (not £185 as only half the superannuation payment can be deducted from earnings). Joe's income is not taken into account.

	£
Net income	192.50
Less exempt income	236.78 (from example 9.3b)
Assessable income	nil

Example 10.3: Bob and Zoe have a baby

(a) Bob is now living with Zoe, their son Ricky and three step-children (aged 13, 11 and 4 years old). The exempt income is £116.90 (see example 9.6a). Bob's only income is now £165 a week earnings. Any income of Zoe's is not taken into account.

	£
Net income	165.00
Less exempt income	116.90
Assessable income	48.10

The CSA did not include FC as notional income. FC has not been claimed as Zoe does not want to have to apply for child maintenance from Sam's father, Terence, a married man with whom she had a brief affair. The family should be informed about the withholding of authorisation as even with a benefit penalty, the family would be entitled to some FC.

(b) Six months on, Bob and Zoe decide to claim FC as they are having trouble making ends meet. By claiming FC, Zoe is obliged to make an application for child maintenance for Sam or suffer a benefit penalty unless there is a 'risk of harm or undue distress' to her or her children (see Chapter 5). In the meantime, the FC is calculated assuming no child maintenance for Sam (see p318). Their FC award is £52.79 a week. When calculating assessable income, all the FC is assumed to be Bob's as he is the earner, even though three of the four children are not included in his exempt income. They are not entitled to housing benefit.

Zoe is receiving £20 of child maintenance from the girls' father, Wayne. The child maintenance for Yvonne (now 13) and Veronica (now 11) is the girls' income. Although this can be treated as Zoe's income as she is their mother, Zoe's income is not relevant at this stage. Yvonne's and Veronica's income cannot be treated as Bob's income because he is not their parent.

	£
Earnings (Bob)	165.00
Family credit	52.79
Total net income	217.79
Less exempt income	116.90
Bob's assessable income	100.89

(c) Zoe begins paid work, bringing home £90 a week from which she has to pay £42 childminding fees. The total net income remains at £217.79, as Zoe's earnings are not taken into account at this stage. However, her earnings have affected the exempt income (see example 9.6b) as she is now helping to support Ricky.

	£
Total net income	217.79
Less exempt income	103.41
Bob's assessable income	114.38

(d) When their FC is renewed, they are entitled to £19.19 a week.

	£
Earnings (Bob)	165.00
Family credit	19.19
Total net income	184.19
Less exempt income	103.41
	80.78

CHAPTER ELEVEN

Proposed maintenance
Step 4 of the formula

This chapter covers:

This chapter should be read in conjunction with calculation sheet 4 in Appendix 4.

1. WHAT IS PROPOSED MAINTENANCE

'Proposed maintenance' is not a term which is used in the legislation. We use it to describe the amount of child maintenance that, given the maintenance requirement and the assessable income of the parents, the absent parent would be expected to pay. There is no specific legal term for this amount; it is already referred to in the legislation as 'the amount of the assessment'. However, the proposed maintenance step is not the end of the maintenance assessment. The protected income calculation still has to be done and this may reduce the amount of child maintenance payable. Therefore a term is needed for this intermediate stage. The Child Support Agency (CSA) uses the phrase 'maintenance assessment before considering protected income' in the notifications of assessments.

Although the proposed maintenance figure may be reduced by the protected income calculation, it will never be increased. No absent parent ever pays more than the proposed maintenance figure.

There is a lot of misunderstanding about the way in which the income of a partner of the absent parent affects the maintenance assessment. At the protected income stage (see Chapter 12) the partner's income *is* taken into account in order to assess whether the family as a whole can afford the proposed maintenance. However, the partner's income *cannot* increase the proposed maintenance which is arrived at using the absent parent's net income (see p203). The income of the partner of the parent being assessed is also used to decide whether s/he can help support their own children (see p198). If the partner objects to providing income details, s/he should consider the option of withholding the information and taking a Category B interim maintenance assessment (see p297).

2. HOW MUCH IS PROPOSED MAINTENANCE

Proposed maintenance is based on the assessable incomes of both parents. In some situations a deduction rate of 50 per cent assessable income is used and in others a more complex calculation must be carried out. The 50 per cent calculation gives an amount of proposed maintenance which is smaller than the maintenance requirement figure (from step 1). The additional element calculation applies where the parents have higher income and the maintenance requirement figure is met. The calculation for proposed maintenance becomes increasingly complex with more complex situations.

To illustrate the principles of proposed maintenance, we first give an overview of the calculation in figure 11.1. To help readers through this step of the formula, we then identify the four situations, beginning with the most straightforward, in which the calculation of proposed maintenance varies. These are set out in the following figures:

- the 50 per cent calculation of proposed maintenance where the parent with care has no assessable income – see figure 11.2;
- the 50 per cent calculation of proposed maintenance where both parents have assessable income – see figure 11.3;
- the additional element calculation of proposed maintenance where the parent with care has no assessable income – see figure 11.4;
- the additional element calculation of proposed maintenance where both parents have assessable income – see figure 11.5.

These calculations are adapted if both parents are absent, or where there is more than one absent parent or more than one parent with care. These situations are explained later in the chapter.

Figure 11.1: **OVERVIEW OF PROPOSED MAINTENANCE STEP**

There are two alternative calculations:

- the 50 per cent calculation if the maintenance requirement is *not* met;
- the additional element calculation if the maintenance requirement *is* met.

To decide which to use, first try the 50 per cent calculation:[1]

- *add* together both parents' assessable incomes (if the parent with care is on income support, her assessable income is assumed to be nil);
- *take* 50 per cent of the joint assessable income;
- *compare* the figure obtained with the maintenance requirement (from step 1 as calculated in Chapter 8).

If 50 per cent of the joint assessable income is *less than or equal to* the maintenance requirement, then the proposed maintenance is 50 per cent of the absent parent's assessable income.[2]

If 50 per cent of joint assessable income is *higher than* the maintenance requirement, the additional element calculation must be done. This involves two components of proposed maintenance: a basic element and an additional element (see p230).[3] The end result is that the absent parent pays less than 50 per cent of his assessable income.

The general rule is that 50 per cent of the parents' assessable income goes towards child maintenance until the maintenance requirement is met.[4] Once the maintenance requirement is met, the absent parent continues to pay maintenance. However, only 15, 20 or 25 per cent of his remaining assessable income is paid as maintenance and up to a maximum amount.[5]

Both parents are liable to maintain their child(ren) and, therefore, both their assessable incomes must be taken into account when calculating whether the maintenance requirement has been met. Although the assessable income of the parent with care may reduce the proposed maintenance, she will never end up paying child maintenance herself.

If the assessable income of the absent parent is nil, then the proposed maintenance is nil and the minimum payment rules must be considered (see p167). The absent parent either pays £4.80 or is exempt. Similarly, if the proposed maintenance is less than £4.80, the absent parent pays the minimum payment of £4.80 unless he is exempt. In these cases there is no need to calculate the protected income level as the proposed maintenance cannot be further reduced.

3. THE 50 PER CENT CALCULATION

Once assessable income has been calculated for both parents, the next step is to check whether the 50 per cent calculation is applicable. If the parent with care has assessable income, see p228. It should not be assumed that, once a parent with care has left IS, her income will reduce the assessment. First, she may not have sufficient net income to give her any assessable income; this applies to a significant proportion of family credit claimants. Second, the assessable income may be insufficient to reduce the assessment (see example 11.2a). Remember also that a new assessment will only be made on a change of circumstances if the difference is significant, usually £10 a week (see p356).

The parent with care has no assessable income

In many cases the parent with care will have no assessable income – eg, if she is on IS. As roughly three-quarters of lone parents are in receipt of IS, this is the situation that advisers will most frequently come across. The process of calculating proposed maintenance is the same, in theory, as that where both parents have assessable income, but simpler in practice.

Figure 11.2: **50 PER CENT CALCULATION FOR PROPOSED MAINTENANCE WHERE THE PARENT WITH CARE HAS NO ASSESSABLE INCOME**

- *take* 50 per cent of the absent parent's assessable income;
- *compare* the figure obtained with the maintenance requirement (from step 1 as calculated in Chapter 8).

If 50 per cent of the absent parent's assessable income is *less than or equal to* the maintenance requirement, then the proposed maintenance is this figure – ie, 50 per cent of his assessable income.[6]

If 50 per cent of the absent parent's assessable income is *higher than* the maintenance requirement, then the additional element calculation is used to obtain proposed maintenance (see figure 11.4).

It is estimated that four-fifths of all absent parents do not meet the maintenance requirement and in these cases the proposed maintenance calculation ends at this point. These absent parents are charged 50 per cent of assessable income irrespective of the number of qualifying children. Indeed, two absent parents with the same income and out-goings, one with three qualifying children and the other with one child, would usually receive the same assessment. This is an element of the formula which continues to attract criticism.

The protected income calculation must now be done (see Chapter 12).

Example 11.1: The 50 per cent calculation where the parent with care has no assessable income

Anita is on income support and therefore has no assessable income.

(The situation would be exactly the same if Anita worked 20 hours a week and earned £110, or if she worked 40 hours a week and took home £185 a week after she married Joe. She would still have no assessable income (see example 10.2a and c) and therefore the proposed maintenance would not be affected by the fact that she is working.)

The maintenance requirement is £84.60 (see example 8.1).

(a) Bob is living on his own and has assessable income of £64.10 (see example 10.1a). As Anita has no assessable income, the first stage is to take 50 per cent of Bob's assessable income.

50 per cent of Bob's assessable income = 50% x £64.10 = £32.05

This is less than £84.60 (the maintenance requirement) and therefore £32.05 is the proposed maintenance for Carol and David.

(b) Bob is living with Zoe, three step-children and his baby son. His assessable income is £48.10 (see example 10.3a).

50 per cent of Bob's assessable income = 50% x £48.10 = £24.05

This is less than £84.60 (the maintenance requirement) and therefore £24.05 is the proposed maintenance.

(c) Bob and Zoe have now claimed family credit and been awarded £52.79. This gives Bob an assessable income of £100.89 (see example 10.3b).

50 per cent of Bob's assessable income = 50% x £100.89 = £50.45

This is less than £84.60 (the maintenance requirement) and therefore £50.45 is the proposed maintenance.

Note: as a result of the family credit payable because of the four children in Bob and Zoe's household (three of whom have not been taken into account so far in the child maintenance calculation), the proposed maintenance has risen by £26.40. Half of the family credit has been transferred into proposed maintenance for the first family. Of course, the maintenance payable may be reduced by the protected income calculation (see example 12.4c).

Where the parent with care has assessable income

Even when the parent with care has assessable income, this income does not necessarily affect the proposed maintenance. If, together, the parents do not have enough joint assessable income to meet the maintenance requirement, then the absent parent pays half of his own assessable income. This is exactly what he would have paid anyway had the parent with care had no assessable income.

Figure 11.3: **50 PER CENT CALCULATION FOR PROPOSED MAINTENANCE WHERE THE PARENT WITH CARE HAS ASSESSABLE INCOME**

To calculate proposed maintenance where both parents have assessable income:

- *add* both parents' assessable incomes to give joint assessable income;
- *take* 50 per cent of the joint assessable income;
- *compare* the 50 per cent figure with the maintenance requirement (from step 1 as calculated in Chapter 8).

If 50 per cent of the joint assessable income is *less than or equal to* the maintenance requirement:

- *take* 50 per cent of the absent parent's own assessable income to give proposed maintenance.

If 50 per cent of joint assessable income is *higher than* the maintenance requirement, the additional element calculation must be done (see figure 11.5).

A parent with care's income will not reduce the maintenance she receives unless her notional contribution towards the maintenance requirement *plus* the absent parent's proposed maintenance is over the maintenance requirement. The level of the joint assessable income is the deciding factor. The higher the assessable income of an absent parent, the sooner the assessable income of the parent with care will reduce the maintenance payable.

However, the proposed maintenance can never reduce the absent parent's proposed maintenance to zero. It just reduces the amount of the absent parent's assessable income which is needed to meet the maintenance requirement and, therefore, the absent parent begins paying at a lower deduction rate earlier than he would otherwise have done. The absent parent has to pay at least some contribution towards the maintenance requirement.

Example 11.2: 50 per cent calculation where both parents have assessable income

Anita is now working full-time and has assessable income of £19.60 (see example 10.2b).

(a) Bob's assessable income is £64.10 (see example 10.1a).
Anita's assessable income = £19.60
Joint assessable income = £19.60 + £64.10 = £83.70
50 per cent of joint assessable income = 50% x £83.70 = £41.85

This is well below the maintenance requirement of £84.60 (see example 8.1a) and so Bob pays 50 per cent of his own assessable income (assuming the protected income calculation allows it).

Proposed maintenance = 50% x £64.10 = £32.05 per week.

This is the same amount of proposed maintenance as when Anita had no assessable income (see example 11.1a). In this case Anita is earning too much to qualify for family credit, taking home £185 a week. Although this is more than Bob who takes home £154, her income still does not affect the level of proposed maintenance for David and Carol.

(b) If Bob had net earnings of £260 per week (rather than £160 as in example 10.1a), his assessable income would be £164.10.

Anita's assessable income = £19.60
Bob's assessable income = £164.10
Joint assessable income = £19.60 + £164.10 = £183.70
50 per cent of joint assessable income = 50% x £183.70 = £91.85

This is above the maintenance requirement of £84.60 (see example 8.1) and so the additional element calculation would have to be done to calculate the proposed maintenance (see figure 11.5) Therefore, Anita's assessable income, although still £19.60, would now reduce the proposed maintenance. This is because Bob's assessable income has increased and together they can meet the maintenance requirement.

4. THE ADDITIONAL ELEMENT CALCULATION

If the maintenance requirement is met in full by the assessable incomes of the parents, then the absent parent is expected to pay an additional amount over and above his contribution to the maintenance requirement. Where the 50 per cent calculation has shown that assessable income more than meets the maintenance requirement, an alternative calculation is used to obtain the proposed maintenance.

Proposed maintenance is composed of a basic element and an additional element. Likewise, the absent parent's total assessable income is composed of basic assessable income and additional assessable income.

The basic assessable income contributes towards the basic element at the rate of 50 per cent. The additional assessable income contributes towards the additional element at a lower rate up to a maximum amount. The deduction rate is 15 per cent if there is one qualifying child, 20 per cent if there are two, and 25 per cent if there are three or more qualifying children in the assessment.[7]

The assessable incomes of both parents are taken into account in calculating the basic proposed maintenance. However, to illustrate the principle of what is a complex calculation, we first address the situation where only the absent parent has assessable income.

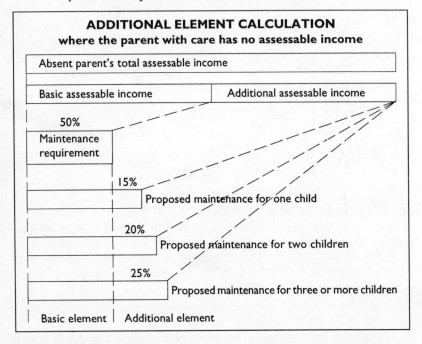

The parent with care has no assessable income

If 50 per cent of the absent parent's assessable income is higher than the maintenance requirement, ignore the 50 per cent figure and continue as below.

Where the parent with care has no assessable income, the basic element equals the maintenance requirement.[8] As basic assessable income contributes towards the basic element at the rate of 50 per cent, the absent parent must (in order to meet the maintenance requirement) use up assessable income equal to twice the maintenance requirement. Any additional assessable income which is not used up in meeting the maintenance requirement contributes towards the additional element at the rate of 15, 20 or 25 per cent.

Figure 11.4: **ADDITIONAL ELEMENT CALCULATION OF PROPOSED MAINTENANCE WHERE THE PARENT WITH CARE HAS NO ASSESSABLE INCOME**

To calculate the proposed maintenance where only the absent parent has assessable income and the 50 per cent calculation has shown that it more than meets the maintenance requirement:

- *multiply* the maintenance requirement (the basic element) by two to give the basic assessable income;

- deduct the basic assessable income from the total assessable income to give the additional assessable income;

- *take* – 15 per cent if there is one qualifying child; *or*
  20 per cent if there are two qualifying children; *or*
  25 per cent of there are three or more qualifying children
  of the additional assessable income to give the additional element;

- *add* the basic element (the maintenance requirement) to the additional element to give the proposed maintenance.

The absent parent thus pays more than the maintenance requirement, but overall less than 50 per cent of his assessable income. The overall percentage of the assessable income taken as proposed maintenance reduces from 50 per cent as income increases towards (but never right down to) 15 per cent for one child, 20 per cent for two and 25 per cent for more than two children.

When proposed maintenance has been obtained using the additional element calculation, this figure must be compared with the maximum amount (see p234).

Example 11.3: Additional element calculation where the parent with care has no assessable income

Jeremy has just left his wife, Evie, who has no income of her own other than child benefit. They have four children, Francis (14), Georgina (12), Henry (8) and Isobel (4), who are all living with Evie.

The maintenance requirement is therefore:

		£
Personal allowances	Evie	47.90
	Francis (14)	24.10
	Georgina (12)	24.10
	Henry (8)	16.45
	Isobel (4)	16.45
Family premium		10.55
Lone parent premium		5.20
Sub-total		144.75
Less child benefit		37.20
Maintenance requirement		107.55

Jeremy has an assessable income of £600 a week.
   50% x £600 = £300

This is well above the maintenance requirement of £107.55. Therefore, to calculate proposed maintenance, do the additional element calculation:

Basic element = £107.55 (the maintenance requirement)
Basic assessable income = 2 x £107.55 = £215.10
Additional assessable income = £600 – £215.10 = £384.90
Additional element = £384.90 x 25% = £96.23 (the 25 per cent deduction rate is applicable as there are four qualifying children)
Proposed maintenance = £107.55 + £96.23 = £203.78

Check whether this figure is above the maximum child maintenance payable (see example 11.5).

Where the parent with care has assessable income

Both parents contribute towards the maintenance requirement if they can afford to do so, although in the case of a parent with care this is a notional transaction. We have seen that if the parents together cannot meet the maintenance requirement, the income of the parent with care does not affect the outcome of the maintenance assessment (see p228).

However, if 50 per cent of the parents' joint assessable income more than meets the maintenance requirement, the parent with care's assessable income reduces the absent parent's proposed maintenance. Each parent contributes towards the maintenance requirement in proportion to his/her assessable income. The parent with care's notional contribution towards the maintenance requirement reduces the amount of the absent parent's assessable income which is needed to meet that maintenance requirement. Therefore, the absent parent begins paying at the lower deduction rate earlier than he would have done had the parent with care had no assessable income.

The additional element calculation is used to work out the proposed maintenance that the absent parent pays, taking into account the parent with care's notional contribution towards the maintenance requirement. The basic element does not now equal the full maintenance requirement, but only the proportion of the maintenance requirement that the absent parent has to contribute.[9] Once the basic element has been calculated, the rest of the step is the same as that which applies where the parent with care has no assessable income.

Figure 11.5: **ADDITIONAL ELEMENT CALCULATION OF PROPOSED MAINTENANCE WHERE PARENT WITH CARE HAS ASSESSABLE INCOME**

To calculate proposed maintenance where both parents have assessable incomes which jointly more than meet the maintenance requirement:

- *add* together both parents' assessable incomes to give their joint assessable income;
- *multiply* the maintenance requirement by the absent parent's assessable income divided by the joint assessable income (ie, the absent parent's proportion of the joint assessable income) to give the basic element (ie, the absent parent's contribution to the maintenance requirement);
- *multiply* the basic element by two to give the basic assessable income;
- *deduct* the basic assessable income from the absent parent's total assessable income to give his additional assessable income;
- *take* – 15 per cent if there is one qualifying child; *or*
      20 per cent if there are two qualifying children; *or*
      25 per cent of there are three or more qualifying children
  of the additional assessable income to give the additional element;
- *add* the basic element to the additional element to give the proposed maintenance.

The parent with care's assessable income can reduce the proposed maintenance below the maintenance requirement, but cannot reduce the absent parent's proposed maintenance to zero. The absent parent still pays at least some contribution towards the maintenance requirement and then a percentage of his additional assessable income.

Example 11.4: Additional element calculation where both parents have assessable incomes

Evie has now taken a paid job. Her exempt income is high as it includes allowances for the four children and a significant mortgage. Although she is earning £26,000 pa, her assessable income is only £70 a week. Jeremy's assessable income is still £600 a week.

The maintenance requirement is still £107.55 (see example 11.3)

Joint assessable income = £70 + £600 = £670

50 per cent of the joint assessable income is £335 which more than meets the maintenance requirement. Therefore, the additional element calculation of proposed maintenance has to be done:

Basic element (the proportion of the maintenance requirement that Jeremy has to pay) = £107.55 × $\dfrac{£600}{£670}$ = £96.31

Basic assessable income = £96.31 × 2 = £192.62

Additional assessable income = £600 − £192.62 = £407.38

Additional element = £407.38 × 25% = £101.85

Proposed maintenance = £96.31 + £101.85 = £198.16

Check whether this figure is above the maximum child maintenance payable (see example 11.6).

---

5. MAXIMUM CHILD MAINTENANCE

There is an upper limit on the amount of child maintenance payable for a child under the child support formula.[10] No further child maintenance is deducted from assessable income once the maximum is being paid.

When the maximum is being paid under the formula, it is open to the parties to go to court to seek any further maintenance. The courts can consider the issue of further weekly child maintenance in the context of any other arrangements which have been made for the children (see p37).

Like proposed maintenance, maximum child maintenance is composed of a basic element and an additional element. The basic element is the same as the basic element of proposed maintenance, whereas the additional element relates to the number and age of the qualifying children.[11]

Again, like proposed maintenance, the calculation varies slightly if the parent with care has assessable income.

The parent with care has no assessable income

When the parent with care has no assessable income, the basic element of maximum child maintenance equals the maintenance requirement. The maximum amount of child maintenance equals the maintenance requirement plus the additional element.

The additional element equals 1.5 times the total of the IS personal allowance for each child and the amount of the IS family premium for each child.[12]

Example 11.5: Maximum child maintenance where the person with care has no assessable income

Assuming Evie has no assessable income of her own, the maximum Jeremy would have to pay for the four children Francis (14), Georgina (12), Henry (8) and Isobel (4) is as follows:

The maintenance requirement is £107.55 (see example 11.3)

The additional element
= 1.5 [24.10 + 24.10 + 16.45 + 16.45 + (4 x 10.55)]
= 1.5 x 123.30 = £184.95

	£
The basic element	107.55
The additional element	184.95
Maximum child maintenance	292.50

Therefore, in example 11.3, the proposed maintenance of £203.78 is less than the maximum.

In order to pay the maximum amount, Jeremy would have to have an assessable income of (£107.55 x 2) + (£184.95 x 4) = £955 a week. This represents a net income of between £52,150 with no housing costs, and £104,300 with maximum housing costs, a year (assuming no second family and a journey to work of under 150 miles).

The parent with care has assessable income

The absent parent is responsible only for paying the proportion of the maximum child maintenance which corresponds to his proportion of joint assessable income.

The basic element of the maximum child maintenance is the proportion of the maintenance requirement which the absent parent must contribute. It is calculated as for the additional element calculation for proposed maintenance – ie:

- *add* together both parents' assessable incomes to give their joint assessable income;
- *multiply* the maintenance requirement by the absent parent's assessable income divided by joint assessable income.

To calculate the additional element:

- *multiply* the total of the IS personal allowance for each child and the family premium for each child by 1.5; *then*
- *multiply* this figure by the absent parent's assessable income divided by the joint assessable income.

The maximum child maintenance equals the basic element plus the additional element.

Alternatively, there is a short cut for this calculation. Multiply the maximum amount as calculated where the parent has no assessable income by the absent parent's proportion of the joint assessable income.

Example 11.6: Maximum child maintenance where the parent with care has assessable income

To check whether the proposed maintenance calculated in example 11.4 (£198.16) is above the maximum:

Evie's assessable income = £70

Jeremy's assessable income = £600

Joint assessable income = £670

The maintenance requirement = £107.55

Basic element = £107.55 × $\dfrac{600}{670}$ = £96.31 (as in example 11.4)

Additional element =

1.5 (24.10 + 24.10 + 16.45 + 16.45 + [4 × 10.55]) × $\dfrac{600}{670}$

= £184.95 × $\dfrac{600}{670}$ = £165.63

Maximum child maintenance = basic element plus the additional element = £96.31 + £165.63 = £261.94

(Alternatively, multiply the maximum figure from example 11.5 by Jeremy's proportion of joint assessable income: £292.50 × $\dfrac{600}{670}$ also gives £261.94)

Jeremy therefore pays the proposed maintenance of £198.16

---

6. BOTH PARENTS ARE ABSENT

Where the person with care is not a parent, this usually means that there are two absent parents, in which case a maintenance assessment is carried out for each absent parent. The same maintenance requirement is used in both assessments (see p177).

When calculating the proposed maintenance of each parent, the other absent parent's assessable income is used where the parent with care's income would normally be taken into account – ie, to give joint assessable income.[13] In other words, the parents will together contribute towards the maintenance requirement at the rate of 50 per cent of assessable income and, once the maintenance requirement is met, each will pay a lower percentage of their own additional assessable income.

Example 11.7: Proposed maintenance where both parents are absent

Zoe is looking after her 16-year-old niece, Rebecca, whose parents have separated. Zoe's income is not taken into account as she is not Rebecca's mother.

The maintenance requirement = £21.57 (see example 8.3)

(a) *50 per cent calculation*
Her mother's assessable income = £14.50
Her father's assessable income = £23.90
Joint assessable income = £38.40
50 per cent of joint assessable income = £19.20
This is less than the maintenance requirement.
Proposed maintenance from her mother = 50% x £14.50 = £7.25
Proposed maintenance from her father = 50% x £23.90 = £11.95

(b) *The additional element calculation*
Her mother's assessable income = £52
Her father's assessable income = £84
Joint assessable income = £136
50 per cent of joint assessable income = £68
This is more than the maintenance requirement of £21.57.
Therefore the additional element calculation has to be done as in figure 11.5. The 15 per cent deduction rate is used as Rebecca is the only qualifying child in the assessment.

Mother's proposed maintenance is:
Basic element = £21.57 x $\dfrac{52}{136}$ = £8.25

Basic assessable income = £8.25 x 2 = £16.50
Additional assessable income = £52 – £16.50 = £35.50
Additional element = £35.50 x 15% = £5.33
Proposed maintenance from mother = £8.50 + £5.33 = £13.83

Father's proposed maintenance is:
Basic element = £21.57 x $\dfrac{84}{136}$ = £13.32

Basic assessable income = £13.32 x 2 = £26.64
Additional assessable income = £84 – £26.64 = £57.36
Additional element = £57.36 x 15% = £8.60
Proposed maintenance from father = £13.32 + £8.60 = £21.92

Note: the basic proposed maintenance from both parents is the main-tenance requirement – ie, £8.25 + £13.32 = £21.57. Also, because the maintenance requirement is low and there is only one child, each parent ends up with proposed maintenance of only 26 per cent of assessable income.

The total proposed maintenance for a child with two absent parents is the same as if there were one absent parent (with assessable income equal to the joint assessable income of the two absent parents) and a parent with care with no assessable income. However, with two absent parents the total liability is split between the parents in proportion to their assessable incomes.

If the child support officer (CSO) does not have the information about the other absent parent's income within the fortnight given to provide it (see p134), it is assumed that this second absent parent has no assessable income when calculating the first absent parent's proposed maintenance.[14] When this information is available, a fresh assessment will be carried out.[15] In the meantime, the parent whose income is known could have to pay a higher amount than s/he would if maintenance was actually being assessed for both absent parents at the same time.

The regulations do not distinguish between absent parents who live separately from one another and those who, although they are no longer living with their child, still live together as a couple. Therefore, in the case of a couple being assessed, two separate assessments would be carried out following the same basic rules up to this stage – ie, net income and exempt income would be calculated separately for each parent, even though between the two assessments the same housing costs would be included twice. If Rebecca's parents were still living together, the calcu-lation of proposed maintenance would still follow that in example 11.7.

The person with care who is not a parent of the qualifying children may be looking after children who have different parents. For example, a grandmother may be looking after two grandchildren, one the child of her son and the other the child of her daughter. This involves two maintenance requirements. The proposed maintenance steps for the two children are completely separate and each is carried out for both the absent parents of each child (see above). In theory, the grandmother could receive child maintenance from four absent parents.

7. MORE THAN ONE PERSON WITH CARE

'More than one person with care' does not refer to the situation where a child is looked after for part of the time by one person and the rest of the time by another; we call that 'shared care' (see Chapter 13).

Here we cover the situation where different children of an absent parent are being looked after by different people. This includes both where the absent parent has two or more families by different women with whom he does not live and where the children of one family are split between two carers, perhaps with one child living with the mother and the other with grandparents. The absent parent is equally liable to maintain all the qualifying children and must therefore pay child maintenance to each of the persons with care who makes an application.[16]

The regulations describe this situation as 'multiple applications relating to an absent parent'. We have not used this phrase, as 'multiple applications' is also used to describe the situation when more than one application is made for child maintenance for the same child (see p76). More than one person with care involves applications for maintenance for *different* children from the *same* absent parent.

Sharing out the proposed maintenance

If the children of an absent parent are in the care of two or more people and a maintenance application has been made by more than one of those persons with care, the proposed maintenance has to be shared between the persons with care.[17] This is achieved by dividing the absent parent's assessable income between the maintenance assessments in the same proportions as their maintenance requirements.[18] Where an allowance for a pre-April 1993 property settlement has been included in exempt income (see p192), an adjustment is made when apportioning the assessable income – see below. The proposed maintenance step is then carried out separately for each application using the relevant portion of assessable income.

Only one protected income calculation (see Chapter 12) is carried out for the absent parent, using the total amount of proposed maintenance for all the assessments.[19] Where the total maintenance payable to all the persons with care is less than £4.80 (see p167), the minimum payment is divided between the persons with care in proportion to the maintenance requirements.[20]

Example 11.8: 50 per cent calculation where there is more than one parent with care

Wayne is the father of Yvonne (12) and Veronica (10) who live with Zoe. Zoe has no assessable income. She has been receiving £20 a week child maintenance from Wayne. Zoe's maintenance requirement for Yvonne and Veronica is £52.78 (see example 8.2a)

Wayne's girlfriend Lauren has recently had his baby, Keith. Wayne is not living with Lauren who is claiming income support (IS) as a single parent.

Lauren's maintenance requirement is:

		£
Personal allowances:	Lauren	47.90
	Keith	16.45
Family premium		10.55
Lone parent premium		5.20
Sub-total		80.10
Less child benefit		10.80
Total maintenance requirement		69.30

Joint maintenance requirement is £52.78 + £69.30 = £122.08

Wayne's total assessable income is £40.00 a week.

For calculating Zoe's child maintenance, Wayne's assessable income =

$£40 \times \dfrac{52.78}{122.08} = £17.29$

For calculating Lauren's child maintenance, Wayne's assessable income =

$£40 \times \dfrac{69.30}{122.08} = £22.71$ (or £40 – £17.29 = £22.71)

Proposed maintenance: 50 per cent assessable income
For Zoe: 50% x £17.29 = £8.65
For Lauren: 50% x £22.71 = £11.36

Subject to the protected income calculation, Wayne is still paying £20.01 in total, but divided between the two parents with care.

When Lauren makes an application for child maintenance, Zoe's assessment will be reduced (see below). Although her circumstances have not changed, the child maintenance Zoe can expect will be reduced from £20 to £8.65 per week. Yet Lauren does not gain as she is in receipt of IS. Zoe receives less than half the maintenance paid by Wayne, although she has two of his children and Lauren has only one younger child (see below).

By dividing the absent parent's assessable income in proportion to the different maintenance requirements, persons with care responsible for a larger number of children will usually receive a greater amount of child maintenance. However, in example 11.8, Zoe's maintenance requirement is smaller than would usually be expected for two children. She is receiving only half of certain allowances in the maintenance requirement, as another of her children, Sam, has a different absent father (see example 8.2). This reduction in the maintenance requirement for Yvonne and Veronica is unaffected by whether or not an application for maintenance for Sam has actually been made.

In the case of there being two persons with care, the division in the proposed maintenance occurs only if both of the persons with care involved actually make an application for child maintenance from the same absent parent.[21] In other words, if Lauren had refused to authorise the CSA to act, or was not in receipt of IS/FC/DWA and had chosen not to apply for child maintenance for Keith, Zoe would continue to receive £20. Where one assessment is already in force when the second application involving the same absent parent is made – eg, when his second marriage breaks down – the first assessment is reduced from the date the assessment to the second person with care takes effect (see p303).[22]

Where there is a pre-April 1993 property settlement

Before dividing the absent parent's assessable income between the persons with care, any allowance for a pre-April 1993 property settlement (see p192) is added on to the assessable income.[23] Once this has been apportioned, the property settlement allowance (if any) relevant to that person with care is deducted from her portion of assessable income.

Example 11.9: More than one parent with care and a property settlement allowance

The situation is as in example 11.8 except that Wayne has an allowance of £20 included in his exempt income in recognition of the capital settlement he made to Zoe at the time of their divorce in 1987.

Assessable income to be apportioned = £40 + £20 = £60

For Lauren's child maintenance, Wayne's assessable income =
$£60 \times \dfrac{69.30}{122.08} = £34.06$

Proposed maintenance for Lauren = 50% × £34.06 = £17.03

For Zoe's child maintenance, Wayne's assessable income =
$(£60 \times \dfrac{52.78}{122.08}) - £20 = £5.94$

Proposed maintenance for Zoe = 50% x £5.94 = £2.97

(The minimum payment of £4.80 applies only where the total payments due from an absent parent to all persons with care are less than £4.80.)

Again, Wayne continues to pay £20 a week in total, although Zoe sees her maintenance reduced from £20 to £2.97 when Lauren has to apply to the CSA.

The additional element calculation

The additional element calculation of proposed maintenance when there is more than one person with care is done in the same way as when there is only one person with care, except that a proportion of the absent parent's assessable income is substituted for his total assessable income.

Example 11.10: Additional element calculation where there is more than one person with care

Jeremy has left his wife, Evie, who has no income of her own. Of their four children, Francis (14), Georgina (12), Henry (8) and Isobel (4), the three youngest are living with Evie, but Francis is living with Jeremy's brother and sister-in-law. Jeremy has an assessable income of £600 a week.

The income of Jeremy's brother is irrelevant as he is not Francis' parent. Francis now has two absent parents who are liable to maintain him. Evie is now an absent parent in respect of Francis, but as she is on IS, she has no assessable income. Because she has children living with her, she is exempt from the deductions from IS.

Jeremy must pay his brother child maintenance for Francis as well as paying Evie child maintenance for Georgina, Henry and Isobel. Both the brother and Evie have made applications for child maintenance.

Evie: the maintenance requirement:		£
Personal allowances	Evie	47.90
	Georgina (12)	24.10
	Henry (8)	16.45
	Isobel (4)	16.45
Family premium		10.55
Lone parent premium		5.20
Sub-total		120.65
Less child benefit		28.40
Total maintenance requirement		92.25

Francis: the maintenance requirement:

		£
Personal allowance	adult (half)	23.95
	Francis (14)	24.10
Family premium		10.55
Sub-total		58.60
Less child benefit		10.80
Total maintenance requirement		47.80

(The adult personal allowance is halved since Francis, as the only qualifying child in the assessment, is 14 years old – see p174. There is no lone parent premium as the brother is living with his wife.)

Joint maintenance requirement = £92.25 + £47.80 = £140.05

Jeremy's £600 of assessable income has to be split between the two assessments in proportion to their maintenance requirements.

Evie's child maintenance

Jeremy's assessable income = $\dfrac{92.25 \times £600}{140.05}$ = £395.22

Proposed maintenance = 50% x £395.22 = £197.61
This is above the maintenance requirement of £92.25; therefore the additional element calculation must be done (as in figure 11.4):
Basic assessable income = £92.25 x 2 = £184.50
Additional assessable income = £395.22 – £184.50 = £210.72
Additional element = £210.72 x 25% = £52.68
Proposed maintenance = £92.25 + £52.68 = £144.93

When Francis leaves home, Evie's maintenance falls from £203.78 per week (see example 11.3) to £144.93.
Note: if Evie had assessable income herself, then the additional element calculation would follow figure 11.5, using £395.22 as Jeremy's assessable income.

Child maintenance for Francis

Jeremy's assessable income = $\dfrac{47.80 \times £600}{140.05}$ = £204.78

Proposed maintenance = 50% x £204.78 = £102.39
This is above the maintenance requirement of £47.80; therefore, the additional element calculation comes into effect:
Basic assessable income = £47.80 x 2 = £95.60
Additional assessable income = £204.78 – £95.60 = £109.18
Additional element = £109.18 x 15% = £16.38
Proposed maintenance = £47.80 + £16.38 = £64.18
Jeremy is paying £64.18 to his brother and £144.93 to Evie, a total of

£209.11, almost the same as the amount paid to Evie when the four children were living together. Although the total maintenance requirement is greater as Francis' maintenance requirement also includes half an adult personal allowance and a family premium, this is almost cancelled out by the use of the 15 per cent deduction rate in Francis' calculation.

However, the absent parent usually ends up paying more in total when there are two or more applications. This is because he is paying a larger amount of his assessable income at the 50 per cent rate, as he now has two or more maintenance requirements to meet before a lower deduction rate is applied.

8. DIVIDED FAMILY

We use the term 'divided family' to cover the situation where some children of a family are in the care of the mother and the others in the care of the father. This could involve two separate maintenance applications and assessments. If only one of the parents applies for maintenance, then only that application will be assessed. The calculations do not involve any variation from the basic formula.

This is not the same situation as where the care of the same child(ren) is shared between the parents (see Chapter 13).

Example 11.11: Two proposed maintenance calculations for a divided family

Carol (now 15) does not like her step-father, Joe, and decides that she wants to live with Bob and Zoe's family – Yvonne (14), Veronica (12), Samuel (5) and Ricky (1). David (10) is still living with Anita and Joe.

Therefore, Anita is the absent parent for Carol and Bob is the absent parent for David.

Maintenance requirement for Carol (15) = £47.80
Maintenance requirement for David (10) = £64.10
Although Carol is older, her maintenance requirement is lower as the carer element is halved because she is over 14.

Anita's exempt income (housing costs as in example 9.3b) = £212.68
Anita's assessable income = £270 (net income) – £212.68 = £57.32

Bob's exempt income (see example 9.7) = £132.78
Bob's assessable income = £165 (net income) – £132.78 = £32.22

Joint assessable income = £57.32 + £32.22 = £89.54
50 per cent of joint assessable income = £89.54 x 50% = £44.77

The 50 per cent joint assessable income figure (£44.77) is lower than the maintenance requirement for David (£64.10) and the maintenance requirement for Carol (£47.80).
Proposed maintenance from Bob = 50% x £32.22 = £16.11.
Proposed maintenance from Anita = 50% x £57.32 = £28.66

The protected income calculation (see example 12.8) shows that both Anita and Bob can afford these amounts, therefore Anita in effect pays Bob: £28.66 – £16.11 = £12.55 a week.

If either or both of the maintenance requirements had been lower than 50 per cent joint assessable income, then the proposed maintenance would have been obtained using the additional element calculation (see figure 11.5).

---

9. MORE THAN ONE ABSENT PARENT

A person with care may be looking after children of different absent parents. Here we look at the situation where the person with care is a parent of all the qualifying children. The situation where the person with care is not the parent of the qualifying child(ren) is dealt with on p236 – ie, both parents are absent.

If a parent with care is looking after children of different parents and applies for maintenance from more than one absent parent, then more than one maintenance assessment has to be done. If the parent with care has no assessable income, the two (or more) assessments will not alter from the basic formula already described.

Example 11.12: Proposed maintenance from more than one absent parent where the parent with care has no assessable income

Zoe has applied for maintenance from her ex-husband, Wayne, for Yvonne (14) and Veronica (12), and from Terence for Samuel (5). She is living with Bob, and has no income of her own other than child benefit. This means that her net income is nil and therefore her assessable income is nil.

Child maintenance from Wayne:
Step 1: Maintenance requirement = £51.84 (see example 8.2b)
Step 2: Exempt income:
Wayne, Zoe's ex-husband, lives on his own in a rented flat. His rent is £65 a week, but he receives £1.89 a week in housing benefit.

	£
Personal allowance	47.90
Housing costs (£65 – £1.89)	63.11
Total exempt income	111.01

Step 3: Assessable income:	£
Total net income	150.00 (net earnings)
Less exempt income	111.01
Assessable income	38.99

Step 4: Proposed maintenance: 50% x £38.99 = £19.50.
This is below the maintenance requirement of £51.84.
Therefore the proposed maintenance is £19.50.
(You may remember that Wayne had a son with Lauren. However, she has now married Sean and moved to Eire where the CSA has no jurisdiction.)

Child maintenance from Terence:
Step 1: Maintenance requirement = £36.88 (see example 8.2b)

Step 2: Exempt income:
Terence is married to Dipa and, although they have three children, only Rana, 17 and still at school, counts as dependent. They have a mortgage of £32 a week. Dipa receives invalid care allowance for looking after her mother, but this is not enough income to support half of Rana.

		£
Personal allowance	Terence	47.90
	Rana (17)	28.85
Family premium		10.55
Housing costs		32.00
Total exempt income		119.30

Step 3: Assessable income:	£
Total net income	180.00 (net earnings)
Less exempt income	119.30
Assessable income	60.70

Step 4: Proposed maintenance: 50% x £60.70 = £30.35
This is below the maintenance requirement of £36.88.
Therefore the proposed maintenance for Sam is £30.35.

The protected income calculations now have to be done to see whether Wayne and Terence can afford these amounts (see example 12.5).

Where the parent with care has assessable income

If the parent with care has assessable income and makes an application for child maintenance from more than one absent father, then a proportion of her assessable income is taken into account for each of the assessments. Her assessable income is divided between the maintenance assessments in proportion to the maintenance requirements.[24] This apportioning will only happen if an application is made for maintenance from more than one absent parent.

Example 11.13: More than one absent parent where parent with care has assessable income

Jeremy left his wife, Evie, and filed for divorce when he discovered that her youngest child, Isobel (4) was not his daughter. Evie is also looking after his three children, Francis (14), Georgina (12) and Henry (8). Evie decided to apply for child maintenance from Isobel's father, Max, as well as from Jeremy for the other three children.

Maintenance requirement for three eldest:		£
Personal allowances	Evie	23.95 (half of 47.90)
	Francis (14)	24.10
	Georgina (12)	24.10
	Henry (8)	16.45
Family premium		5.28 (half of 10.55)
Lone parent premium		2.60 (half of 5.20)
Sub-total		96.48
Less child benefit		28.40
Total maintenance requirement		68.08

Maintenance requirement for Isobel:		£
Personal allowances	Evie	23.95 (half of 47.90)
	Isobel (4)	16.45
Family premium		5.28 (half of 10.55)
Lone parent premium		2.60 (half of 5.20)
Sub-total		48.28
Less child benefit		8.80
Total maintenance requirement		39.48

Joint maintenance requirements = £68.08 + £39.48 = £107.56
Evie's total assessable income is £70. This has to be shared between the two assessments in proportion to the maintenance requirements.

Proposed maintenance from Max: 50 per cent calculation

Evie's assessable income used in this assessment = £70 x $\dfrac{39.48}{107.56}$ = £25.69

Max's assessable income is £42.50

Max and Evie's joint assessable income = £25.69 + £42.50 = £68.19

50% x £68.19 = £34.10

This is less than the maintenance requirement of £39.48.

Therefore, proposed maintenance is 50 per cent of Max's own assessable income: 50% x £42.50 = £21.25

Proposed maintenance from Jeremy: 25 per cent calculation

Evie's total assessable income is £70

Her assessable income used in this assessment = £70 x $\dfrac{68.08}{107.56}$ = £44.31

Jeremy's assessable income is £150

Jeremy and Evie's joint assessable income = £44.31 + £150 = £194.31

50% x £194.31 = £97.16

This is larger than the maintenance requirement of £68.08 and therefore an additional element calculation has to be done:

Basic element = £68.08 x $\dfrac{150.00}{194.32}$ = £52.55

Basic assessable income = £52.55 x 2 = £105.10

Additional assessable income = £150 – £105.10 = £44.90

Additional element = £44.90 x 25% = £11.23

Proposed maintenance = £52.55 + £11.23 = £63.78

Subject to the protected income stage, Evie will receive £21.25 from Max and £63.78 from Jeremy.

CHAPTER TWELVE

Protected income
Step 5 of the formula

This chapter covers:
1. What is protected income (see below)
2. Basic protected income (p253)
3. Total protected income (p255)
4. What is the maintenance payable (p256)
5. Change of circumstances (p261)

This chapter should be read in conjunction with calculation sheet 5 in Appendix 4.

1. WHAT IS PROTECTED INCOME

Protected income is income which cannot be used for paying child maintenance;[1] to this extent, the absent parent's needs take first priority. At the end of the protected income calculation, the amount of maintenance payable will be known. It will either be the proposed maintenance figure or a reduced amount. The absent parent never ends up paying more than the proposed maintenance. This step should be carried out for all absent parents. The only time is does not apply is where the proposed maintenance is £4.80 or less (see p167).

There are two forms of protection for absent parents; one prevents them having to pay an excessive proportion of their own income as child maintenance, and the other considers the needs of the whole family.

Thirty per cent cap

No absent parent has to pay more than 30 per cent of his net income (see p203).[2] Any partner's income is ignored. If the proposed maintenance is greater than this, it will be reduced to 30 per cent of net income. In other words, 70 per cent net income is a protected level of income; all absent parents (except a few of those making the minimum payment) are left with at least 70 per cent of their own net income. This applies even where an absent parent is paying more than one CSA assessment (see p259). However, if an absent parent is paying maintenance to other children, whether voluntarily or under a court order, this is not taken into account at this point (but see below).

Example 12.1

a) Bob is living with his parents, and is liable to pay maintenance for Carol and David. His net earnings are £165 a week.
Step 1 maintenance requirement: £84.60 (see example 8.1a)
Step 2 exempt income: £47.90 (see example 9.1b)
Step 3 assessable income: £165 – £47.90 = £117.10
Step 4 proposed maintenance: 50 per cent of £117.10 = £58.55 (less than the maintenance requirement)
Step 5 protected income: 30 per cent of £165 = £49.50
The maintenance is therefore reduced to £49.50, before proceeding with the rest of the protected income step.

b) Two years later, Bob is living with Zoe and her four children. His net income is £217.79 (see example 10.3b) and the proposed maintenance is £50.45 (see example 11.1c).
30% x £217.79 = £65.34
The proposed maintenance is less than 30 per cent net income and therefore remains at £50.54.

Even where the proposed maintenance has been capped at 30 per cent net income, the second protected income calculation is carried out, as the maintenance payable may be further reduced. When carrying out this second calculation which follows, substitute the capped maintenance for proposed maintenance where the latter is more than 30 per cent net income.

Total protected income

This second part of the protected income calculation is intended to prevent the absent parent and his family being left below the income support (IS) level as a result of paying child maintenance.[3] The 'family' is the same as that used for means-tested benefits – ie, the absent parent, any heterosexual partner and any children living in the same household (see p50 for a detailed definition).

What is total family income

'Total family income' includes the incomes of all members of the absent parent's family (see above).[4] The regulations and the assessment notification call total family income 'disposable income'. We do not use this term at this stage as disposable income is also used to specify the income remaining after proposed maintenance has been paid.

Income for total family income purposes is calculated in the same way as net income (see Chapter 10) except that:[5]

- child benefit is included as income;
- that part of payments under a mortgage protection insurance policy which exceed the mortgage interest repayments are disregarded; *and*
- with the exception of child maintenance, which is counted in full as the parent's income, the income of any child in the family is included as income up to the amount of the personal allowance for that child and any disabled child premium included in the protected income calculation. As at exempt income stage, children's earnings and the first £10 a week of other income is disregarded.

Where an absent parent or his partner is paying maintenance for a child under a court order where an application to the CSA cannot be made (see p56), the amount of that payment is deducted from total family income.[6] The effect is to protect the payments under the court order at the expense of the proposed maintenance resulting from the CSA application, as, if there is insufficient family income remaining to pay the latter, it will be reduced. This certainly applies where the person with care receiving the maintenance under the court order is not the parent of the child or where she is not receiving IS, family credit or disability working allowance, and we would argue that it also apples where a parent with care on benefit has refused to make an application to the CSA – eg, to preserve the court order – and the absent parent is now being assessed for his liability to maintain other children. It also applies where the absent parent or his partner is paying any child maintenance due under a court order made outside Great Britain.[7] However, no account is taken of voluntary payments, whether made in this country or abroad. In the former situation, the absent parent should consider making an application to the CSA as he may be better off with two CSA assessments.

Example 12.2: Total family income

The proposed maintenance from Bob to Anita for Carol and David is £24.05 (see example 11.1b). Can he afford it?

Bob is living with Zoe and four children – Yvonne (13), Veronica (11), Sam (4) and Ricky (baby). Bob has net earnings of £165, but no claim has been made for family credit (see example 10.3a). Zoe receives weekly maintenance of £20 for Veronica and Yvonne, and child benefit of £37.20.

Total family income:	£
Earnings (net)	165.00
Maintenance for Yvonne & Veronica	20.00
Child benefit	37.20
Total family income	222.20

What is total protected income

Total protected income is the level below which the absent parent's or second family's income must not fall. To make the calculation more manageable, we have separated the total protected income level into basic protected income (see p253) and additional protected income (see p255).

The basic protected income is based on IS rates, and it includes personal allowances, premiums, an amount towards high travel-to-work costs, housing costs for all members of the absent parent's family, and £30 as a margin above IS. The family is allowed additional protected income of 15 per cent of any family income over and above the basic protected level.

Maintenance payable

The total protected income level is compared with the family's income remaining were the proposed maintenance, or capped maintenance if it is lower, to be paid.

If the family's income would be brought below the total protected income level by paying the proposed maintenance, the maintenance due will be reduced. The child maintenance is then payable at an amount which would leave the family with disposable income equal to the protected income level.[8] However, the maintenance due cannot be reduced to less than the minimum payment[9] unless the absent parent is exempt (see p167).

If the family would have income remaining over the protected income level after paying the proposed maintenance, then the absent parent is due to pay the proposed maintenance, or the capped maintenance if that is lower. In other words, the absent parent pays the lowest of:

- 30 per cent of his net income; *or*
- the amount which would leave his family with disposable income equal to the total protected level; *or*
- the proposed maintenance from step 4.

2. BASIC PROTECTED INCOME

Basic protected income includes IS personal allowances and any relevant premiums for all the members of the family. See Appendix 2 for the qualifying conditions for the premiums. See the rates sheet at the front of this book for the 1996/97 rates of allowances and premiums.

Basic protected income is calculated as follows:[10]

- the amount of the IS personal allowance for someone aged 25 or more (£47.90) *or* if the absent parent has a partner, the IS personal allowance for a couple both aged 18 or over (£75.20); *plus*
- for each child in the family, the amount of the IS personal allowance for a child of that age;* *plus*
- the amount of any IS premiums for which the conditions are satisfied* (unlike the IS calculation, all the premiums can be added together, except that the lone parent premium cannot be included in addition to the disability premium; note that, unlike at exempt income stage, pensioner premiums are included); *plus*
- housing costs for the whole family (see below); *plus*
- council tax liability less any council tax benefit (see below); *plus*
- an allowance towards high travel-to-work costs of an absent parent (see below); *plus*
- a standard margin of £30.

*A proportion of the full rate of the personal allowances and any related premiums will be used if a child lives in the household for between two and six nights a week (see Chapter 13).

Housing costs

The rules for assessing housing costs are the same as those used at the exempt income stage (see p185),[11] except that:

- if there is a mortgage, only interest payments are allowed;[12]
- if the absent parent is living as a non-dependant in someone else's house, an amount is included as housing costs (see below);[13]
- excessive housing costs are now the higher of £80 or half total family income.[14] Housing costs will be restricted to this figure unless the absent parent is exempt from that rule – eg, because the family includes a child (see p191).

The absent parent is a non-dependant

An absent parent may be a non-dependant where he lives in a household with people who are not 'family' (see p50). He is *not* a non-dependant if he, or a partner, is:[15]

- a co-owner or joint tenant of the home;
- employed by a charitable or voluntary body as a resident carer;
- liable to make a commercial payment in order to live in the home. It will not be considered a commercial arrangement if payments are made to a close relative in the household; a close relative is a parent, son, daughter (including step-relatives and in-laws), brother and sister, and any of their partners.

The weekly amount to be included in protected income is:[16]

Circumstances of the absent parent	£
Working 16 hours or more a week and with a gross income* of	
£150 or more	32
£114–149.99	16
£76–113.99	12
under £76	6
All those not working 16 hours a week	6

* When calculating gross income, disability living allowance/attendance allowance is ignored.[17]

Council tax

Where the absent parent is the only person, other than a partner, who is liable to pay council tax in respect of the home for which housing costs are included, the weekly council tax (less any council tax benefit) is included in basic protected income. However, if there are other people resident in the home, the amount of council tax included is either:[18]

- the weekly liability divided by the number of liable people; *or*
- the weekly amount actually paid by the absent parent where the absent parent is required to pay more than his share because another liable person has defaulted.

Where the absent parent lives in Northern Ireland, liability for rates replaces council tax. Likewise, if the person with care has applied to the CSA (Northern Ireland) but the absent parent lives in Great Britain, the council tax is used.[19]

High travel-to-work costs

This allowance applies for absent parents who travel more than 150 miles a week to and from work.[20] The allowance is calculated in exactly the same way as at exempt income stage (see p196). It does not apply to partners.

3. TOTAL PROTECTED INCOME

In order to obtain total protected income, additional protected income has to be calculated. To do this, basic protected income must be compared with total family income.

Where the total family income *exceeds* the basic protected income, an addition is made to the basic protected income.

Deduct the basic protected income from the total family income to give the excess family income. The additional protected income equals 15 per cent of this excess family income.[21] This figure is added to basic protected income to give total protected income.

Where the total family income is *below* the basic protected income, there is no additional protected income. Any payment of child maintenance will bring the family's disposable income below the protected income level. Therefore, the absent parent will either pay the minimum amount (£4.80) or be exempt from paying altogether (see p167).

Example 12.3: Total protected income

(a) The situation is as for example 12.1, with Bob living with his parents. He is contributing towards the household but is not a co-owner of the home, nor liable to pay council tax. He travels less than 150 miles a week to and from work.

Basic protected income:	£
Personal allowance	47.90
Housing costs (as a non-dependant)	32.00
Margin	30.00
Basic protected income	109.90

Additional protected income:	£
Total family income	165.00
Less basic protected income	109.90
Excess family income	55.10

Additional protected income = 15% x £55.10 = £8.27

Total protected income:	£
Basic protected income	109.90
Plus additional protected income	8.27
Total protected income	118.17

(b) One year later, Bob lives with Zoe and the situation is the same as for example 12.2. Their rent is £42 a week and the council tax liability is £520 a year. Bob and Zoe are not entitled to housing benefit or council tax benefit.

Basic protected income:		£
Personal allowances	couple	75.20
	Yvonne (13)	24.10
	Veronica (11)	24.10
	Sam (4)	16.45
	Ricky (baby)	16.45
Family premium		10.55
Housing costs		42.00
Council tax liability		10.00
Margin		30.00
Basic protected income		248.85

Total family income (from example 12.2) = £222.20. Therefore there is no excess family income and no additional protected income.

Total protected income = basic protected income = £248.85.

(c) Six months later Zoe and Bob claim family credit and are awarded £52.79 (see example 10.3b). Total family income is therefore now £274.99.

Additional protected income:	£
Total family income	274.99
Less basic protected income	248.85
Excess family income	26.14

Additional protected income = 15% x £26.14 = £3.92

Total protected income:	
Basic protected income	248.85
Plus additional protected income	3.92
Total protected income	252.77

4. WHAT IS THE MAINTENANCE PAYABLE

There are two methods of calculating the maintenance payable. We cover first the full logic of the step and then a short cut.

The family's disposable income which would remain after paying child maintenance is obtained by subtracting the proposed maintenance (step 4) from the total family income. If the proposed maintenance has been capped at 30 per cent net income (see p249), this capped amount is used instead of the proposed maintenance.

If the disposable income is *higher* than the total protected income, the parent can afford to pay the full proposed/capped maintenance. Maintenance payable is the proposed/capped maintenance figure. Where the proposed maintenance has been capped, it cannot be increased back to the originally proposed level.

If the disposable income is initially *below* the total protected income, the maintenance payable is reduced until the disposable income equals the total protected income.[22] Therefore, the maintenance payable is the total family income minus the total protected income.

The minimum payment rule still applies (see p167).[23]

The alternative way of arriving at the maintenance payable is to cut out the disposable income step and in all cases to deduct total protected income from total family income to give an alternative proposed maintenance. This is compared with proposed maintenance from step 4 and also 30 per cent of net income; the absent parent pays whichever figure is smallest.

Example 12.4: Maintenance payable

(a) The proposed maintenance from Bob to Anita for Carol and David has been capped at £49.50 (see example 12.1) and Bob's total protected income is £118.17 (see example 12.3a).

	£
Total family income	165.00
Less capped maintenance	49.50
Disposable income would be	115.50

As this is below the total protected income level, the capped maintenance is reduced. Bob can only afford to pay:

	£
Total family income	165.00
Less total protected income	118.17
Maintenance payable	46.83

(b) One year later, Bob's proposed maintenance is £24.05 (see example 11.1b). As the total family income (see example 12.3b) – £222.20 – is already less than the total protected income – £248.85 – payment of any amount of maintenance would bring their disposable income even further below the protected level. Bob is therefore not liable to pay any maintenance at all; he is exempt from the minimum payment as there are children in his family.

(c) Once family credit is awarded, the proposed maintenance is £50.45 (see example 11.1c). This is less than 30 per cent net income (see example 12.1b)

	£
Total family income (from example 12.3c)	274.99
Less proposed maintenance	50.45
Disposable income would be	224.54

This is less than the total protected income of £252.77 (see example 12.3c) and therefore the proposed maintenance is reduced.

To give a disposable income equal to the total protected income level, the family can afford to pay child maintenance of:

Total family income	274.99
Less total protected income	252.77
Maintenance payable	22.22

Example 12.5: Protected income step from start to finish

A year later child maintenance from Zoe's ex-husband Wayne for Yvonne and Veronica and from Terence for Sam is being assessed (see example 11.12). The proposed maintenance from Wayne is £19.50 and from Terence £30.35. Can each of them afford it?

(a) Wayne lives on his own in a rented flat. He earns on average £150 net a week and only travels a few miles to work. His rent is £65 a week and his council tax is £6 per week. He is not entitled to any council tax benefit, but he receives £1.89 a week in housing benefit. The 30 per cent cap does not reduce the proposed maintenance as: 30% x £150 = £45.00. Therefore, the proposed maintenance remains at £19.50.

	£	£
Basic protected income:		
Personal allowance	47.90	
Housing costs	63.11	
Council tax	6.00	
Margin	30.00	
Basic protected income	147.01	147.01
Total family income	150.00	
Less basic protected income	147.01	
Excess family income	2.99	
Additional protected income = 15% x £2.99 =		0.45
Total protected income		147.46

Payment of the proposed maintenance of £19.50 would leave Wayne with a disposable income of £130.50, below his total protected income.

	£
Total family income	150.00
Less total protected income	147.46
	2.54

However, Wayne is not exempt from the maintenance payment and therefore he is liable to pay £4.80 a week.

(b) Terence is married to Dipa and they have one dependent daughter, Rana (17), who lives with them. Their mortgage is £32 a week, half of which is capital repayments. Their council tax is £9 per week. Terence is self-employed and his net earnings average £180 a week. Dipa receives invalid care allowance of £36.60 and child benefit of £10.80 a week.

The 30 per cent cap does not reduce the proposed maintenance as: 30% x £180 = £54.00. Therefore the proposed maintenance remains at £30.35.

Basic protected income:		£	£
Personal allowances	couple	75.20	
	Rana (17)	28.85	
Family premium		10.55	
Carer premium		13.00	
Housing costs (mortgage interest)		16.00	
Council tax		9.00	
Margin		30.00	
Basic protected income		182.60	182.60

Total family income:	£	
Net earnings	180.00	
Invalid care allowance	36.60	
Child benefit	10.80	
Total family income	227.40	
Less basic protected income	182.60	
Excess family income	44.80	
Additional protected income = 15% x 44.80 =		6.72
Total protected income		189.32
Total family income	227.40	
Less proposed maintenance	30.35	
Disposable income	197.05	

As disposable income is above the total protected income, the maintenance payable is the proposed maintenance of £30.35.

More than one person with care

Where an absent parent is being assessed to pay child maintenance to two or more persons with care for different qualifying children, only one protected income step is carried out on the total proposed maintenance. Both the 30 per cent cap and the total protected income check will be carried out for this total.[24] If the absent parent cannot afford the total proposed maintenance, the amount he can afford is divided between the persons with care in proportion to their proposed maintenance.

Example 12.6: Protected income step for more than one person with care

Lauren has left her husband and returned to the UK. She claims IS and applies for child maintenance for Wayne's son, Keith. Wayne is also the father of Zoe's daughters. His net wages are now £170 a week and he is no longer entitled to housing benefit on his rent of £65 (see example 12.5). He lives 17 miles as the crow flies from his new workplace.

Step 1 maintenance requirement: £

Zoe's   51.84 (see example 8.2b)

Lauren's   69.30 (see example 11.8)

Total   121.14

Step 2 Wayne's exempt income: £114.90

Step 3 Wayne's assessable income: £55.10
(Neither parent with care has any assessable income.)

Step 4 proposed maintenance:

Zoe $\dfrac{51.84 \times £55.10 \times 50\%}{121.14} = £11.79$

Lauren $\dfrac{69.30 \times £55.10 \times 50\%}{121.14} = £15.76$

Total proposed maintenance = £11.79 + £15.76 = £27.55

Step 5 protected income:

Check whether the total proposed maintenance is more than 30 per cent net income: 30% x £170 = £51.00

The total proposed maintenance of £27.55 is less than this and therefore does not need to be capped. Now carry out the second protected income calculation.   £

Personal allowance	47.90
Housing costs	65.00
Council tax	6.00
Travel-to-work costs	2.00
Margin	30.00
Basic protected income	150.90

Total family income	170.00
Less basic protected income	150.90
Excess family income	19.10

Additional protected income = 15% x £19.10 = 2.87
Total protected income = £150.90 + £2.87 = £153.77

Total family income	170.00
Less total proposed maintenance:	27.55
Disposable income	142.45

This is below the total protected income (£153.77), so Wayne cannot afford to pay the proposed maintenance.

Total family income	170.00
Less total protected income	153.77
Maintenance payable	16.23

The maintenance is split between Zoe and Lauren in proportion to their proposed maintenance:

Zoe's $\frac{11.79 \times £16.23}{27.55} = £6.95$

Lauren's $\frac{15.76 \times £16.23}{27.55} = £9.28$

Note that Lauren ends up with a greater proportion of the maintenance, even though she has one young child and Zoe has two older children. In this case, as neither of them has assessable income, the difference is entirely due to the maintenance requirement rules.

---

5. CHANGE OF CIRCUMSTANCES

An increase in the total family income of a second family on the protected income level can result in an increase in the maintenance payable to the first family. This arises because the total protected income level only increases by 15 per cent of any increase in family income. The net effect of a £1 a week increase in total family income is an 85 pence increase in the child maintenance payable to the first family. This begins as soon as the maintenance payable is £4.80 a week and only ceases once the maintenance due reaches the capped or proposed maintenance level.

This recycling effect is the same irrespective of whether the income is the absent parent's or a partner's. There is even no exception for income specifically meant for step-children in the second family – eg, child maintenance paid for them. The theory is that an increase in the income of the absent parent's partner means that she is better able to support herself and her own children. This in turn releases more of the absent parent's income away from supporting his partner and his step-children and into paying maintenance to his own children. However, this distinction has certainly not been obvious to second families.

Once the proposed maintenance level is due, a £1 increase in the absent parent's income results in an increase of between 50 pence and 15 pence in the maintenance assessment. The partner's income then no longer increases the assessment at all (except to a limited extent in some instances where there is a joint child – see p198).

If the proposed maintenance has been capped, then increases in the partner's income do *not* increase the maintenance payable. While the maintenance remains capped, a £1 increase in the absent parent's own net income produces a 30 pence increase in the assessment.

Example 12.7: Change in total family income

Zoe decides to take a job, earning £90 net a week. Bob is still taking home £165 a week. When their family credit award is renewed, they are now entitled to £19.19 a week (see example 10.3d). Zoe now begins to receive child maintenance as assessed in example 12.5.

Step 1 Maintenance requirement: £84.60 (see example 8.1a)

Step 2 Bob's exempt income: £103.41 (see example 9.6b)

Step 3 Bob's assessable income: £80.78 (see example 10.3d)

Step 4 Proposed maintenance: 50% of £80.78 = £40.39
(Anita has no assessable income)

Step 5 Protected income:
To check whether the proposed maintenance is less than 30 per cent net income (see example 10.3d): 30% x £184.19 = £55.26.
Therefore the proposed maintenance remains at £40.39.

	£
Bob's earnings	165.00
Zoe's earnings	90.00
Maintenance from Wayne	4.80
Maintenance from Terence	30.35
Child benefit	37.20
Family credit	19.19
Total family income	346.54
Less basic protected income	248.85 (see example 12.3b)
Excess family income	97.69

Additional protected income = 15% x £97.69 = £14.65
Total protected income = £248.85 + £14.65 = £263.50
If the proposed maintenance were paid, disposable income would be:

Total family income	346.54
Less proposed maintenance	40.39
Disposable income	306.15

This is higher than the total protected income (£263.50) and therefore the proposed maintenance is the maintenance payable. Bob is now paying Anita £40.39 instead of £22.22 (see example 12.4c). Although Bob and Zoe's total family income has increased by £71.55, their disposable income after maintenance has been paid has increased by £53.38 which does not quite cover Zoe's childminding and travel-to-work costs. Now that the proposed maintenance is being paid, any further wage increase of Zoe's will not increase Bob's maintenance assessment any further.

It would certainly not be to Bob's advantage to ask for a review of the maintenance assessment on the grounds of change of circumstance! However, he would not be able to avoid a periodical review (see p353).

In practice, not every change of circumstance will immediately affect the amount of child maintenance payable, for two reasons. First, the person concerned does not have to request a review if there is a change in their circumstances. It is optional. Second, if a review is requested and undertaken, the general rule is that the maintenance in payment will only be altered if the new assessment is at least £10 more or less than the assessment in force. However, a new assessment which is reduced by only £1 or more or increased by £5 or more from the previous assessment will always take effect if it leaves the absent parent's family on protected income level (see p356). Therefore, cases which involve an absent parent on the protected income level will be more frequently changing than cases where the full amount of the proposed maintenance is being paid.

Example 12.8: Change in family composition

Bob's daughter Carol (now 15) moves, leaving Anita to live with Bob and Zoe. The four other children are now Yvonne (14), Veronica (12), Sam (5) and Ricky (1). Zoe receives weekly maintenance of £4.80 for Veronica and Yvonne, and £30.35 maintenance for Sam. Child benefit increases to £46 when Carol becomes part of the family. Bob has lost his overtime and again has net earnings of £165. Zoe has net earnings of £90 and incurs £42 of childminding costs while she is at her paid job.

David (10), Bob's son, still lives with Anita and her husband, Joe. Anita has net earnings of £270 and Joe has net earnings of £295. Anita's child benefit entitlement is now £10.40. Their mortgage interest payments are £114.23 a week, the endowment policy premium £24.92 a week, and council tax £14.50 a week.

See example 11.11:

Proposed maintenance from Anita for Carol: £28.66

Proposed maintenance from Bob for David: £16.11

Protected income calculation for Bob

The 30 per cent cap does not reduce the proposed maintenance as:

30% x £165 = £49.50.

Basic protected income:		£
Personal allowances	couple	75.20
	Carol (15)	24.10
	Yvonne (14)	24.10
	Veronica (12)	24.10
	Sam (5)	16.45
	Ricky (1)	16.45
Family premium		10.55
Housing costs		42.00
Council tax liability		10.00
Margin		30.00
Basic protected income		272.95

Total family income:

£346.54 (see example 12.7) + £8.80 (child benefit) = £355.34

Excess family income = £355.34 – £272.95 = £82.39

Additional protected income = 15% x £82.39 = £12.36

Total protected income = £272.95 + £12.36 = £285.31

	£
Total family income	355.34
Less proposed maintenance	16.11
Disposable income	339.23

This is above the total protected income of £285.31 and therefore Bob can afford to pay the proposed maintenance.

Protected income for Anita

Basic protected income:		£
Personal allowances	couple	75.20
	David (10)	16.45
Family premium		10.55
Housing costs (mortgage interest only)		114.23
Council tax liability		14.50
Margin		30.00
Basic protected income		260.93

Total family income:	£
Anita's earnings	270.00
Joe's earnings	295.00
Child benefit	10.80
Total family income	575.80
Less basic protected income	260.93
Excess family income	314.87

Additional protected income = 15% x £314.87 = 47.23
Total protected income = £260.93 + £47.23 = 308.16

	£
Total family income	575.80
Less proposed maintenance	28.66
Disposable income	547.14

This is well above the total protected income of £308.16 and therefore Anita can afford to pay the proposed maintenance.

Note that the formula works in such a way as to leave Anita and Joe with disposable income of £547.14 when they have the care of one child, whereas Bob and Zoe are left with £339.23 when they are looking after five children and this takes no account of Zoe's childminding expenses.

CHAPTER THIRTEEN

Shared care

This chapter covers:
1. What is shared care (see below)
2. Care shared between separated parents (p268)
3. Care shared between a parent and another person (p279)
4. Care shared between two people who are not parents (p283)
5. Three persons with care (p283)
6. Care provided in part by a local authority (p284)
7. Maintenance requirement is met in full (p285)

1. WHAT IS SHARED CARE

We use the term 'shared care' to describe a situation where there is more than one person looking after a particular child and those people live in different households. If the people providing care live in the same household (see p45), then this is not shared care.[1] The legislation only acknowledges shared care where more than one person has day-to-day care of a child.

What is day-to-day care

When deciding whether someone is a person with care under section 3 of the 1991 Act, there is no definition of day-to-day care. Therefore an everyday definition can be used (see p44). A person who is not a parent can apply to receive child maintenance only if s/he has day-to-day care of a child. Parents with care and absent parents can both apply for a maintenance assessment, although there are some exceptions (see p54) as well as rules governing which application takes precedence (see p76). There can be more than one person with care of a child.

For the purposes of the formula and shared care regulations, a person will be treated as having day-to-day care of a child only if s/he cares for the child for at least 104 nights in the 12-month period ending with the relevant week.[2] See p205 for a definition of relevant week; in addition, where the absent parent and the person with care receive requests for information for a periodical review (see p353), the relevant week is the seven days immediately before the later request for information.

The child support officer (CSO) can use another period, ending with the relevant week, which s/he thinks is more representative of the current arrangement.[3] The number of nights of care in that period must be in the same ratio as 104 nights is to 12 months – ie, 52 nights in six months, 26 nights in three months, 13 nights in two months, nine nights in a month. Examples are given to CSOs of situations where it might be appropriate to use a period other than 12 months because the care arrangements have recently changed – due to a relationship breakdown, a court ruling on residence or contact, or the person now providing day-to-day care has been abroad, in prison, in hospital, away from home or otherwise unable to provide care.[4] If the arrangement has simply been renegotiated between the two parents, written acceptance of this should be provided so that the CSO knows that this is now the current arrangement and not a temporary change. A future period cannot be used; the period has to *end* with the relevant week.

If a parent is providing some care but to an extent less than that described as day-to-day care, he is not only still liable to pay child maintenance but also the level of care he provides is not acknowledged by the child support formula. Therefore, such an absent parent is expected to contribute the same amount of child maintenance as if he were not looking after the child at all. This means, for example, that fathers who have the children to stay every other weekend will pay the same level of maintenance as those who do not.

A father who looks after the children for all of the school holidays would not be accepted as a person with care if the time spent with the children was assessed over 12 months. However, the father could request a review during the summer holidays on the ground that he is now a parent with care and a shorter period should then be used to calculate who has day-to-day care in order to reflect the current arrangement. It is arguable whether this would be grounds for review if the six-week period had already been taken into account when averaging over the year for the first assessment. However, if the arrangement for the holiday had not been known at the time of the original assessment, this may be successful. If not, an appeal should be considered (see p367).

If day-to-day care were to be re-assessed over this shorter period, then the father would become the parent with care and the mother the absent parent. Indeed, the father could then apply for maintenance from the mother. (Note that the period used to assess day-to-day care ends with the relevant week which precedes the request for the change of circumstance review – see p205. Therefore the request should not be made right at the beginning of the summer holiday.)

On the other hand, if it is held that such a review cannot take place, such a father technically remains the absent parent over the holiday when he has the child(ren) full-time. He would be liable to continue paying the mother the full level of maintenance even for those weeks the children spent with him. The parents may come to some voluntary arrangement whereby the mother would forgo the maintenance due, but this may not be financially possible, especially if she is in receipt of income support (IS).

More than one person with care

Where there are two people in different households who both have day-to-day care of a qualifying child, either can make an application for child maintenance as long as both or neither has parental responsibility or rights over the child.[5] If only one of them has parental responsibility/rights, then the person with that responsibility must be the applicant. This means that if the person with parental responsibility/rights decides not to apply, the other person with care could lose out on child maintenance.

If both persons with care can and do make an application, then only one will be accepted (see p76).[6] Which application is accepted is largely a technicality, however, as this does not change the status of the people involved nor the way in which the assessment is carried out (see below). It does, though, affect who can cancel the assessment (see p307).

The basic formula is varied to take into account the fact that there is more than one person with care. The way in which the formula is adjusted depends on which people share the care.

2. CARE SHARED BETWEEN SEPARATED PARENTS

Under the 1991 Act, where both the parents are accepted as having day-to-day care, there is initially no one who can be assessed as having to make child maintenance payments in order to discharge liability to maintain the child. Therefore, in order to make an assessment, one of the parents with care has to be treated as an absent parent. The regulations provide that one of the parents with care is deemed an absent parent and is assessed to pay child maintenance.[7] It is arguable that the regulations cannot – and in fact do not – overrule the Act under which only absent parents, and not parents with care treated as absent, are liable to pay child support maintenance.[8] This could mean that the legislation has not been drafted in such a way as to achieve the intended shared care rules described in this chapter. CPAG is currently taking a case to the child support commissioners (see p382) to test this point but does not expect a decision until towards the end of 1996/97. Anyone else who wishes to challenge the shared care rules in the meantime should take their case to a child support appeal tribunal (see p367) and, on receiving the tribunal's decision, contact CPAG for advice on seeking leave to appeal to the commissioners.

Only a parent who provides day-to-day care as defined by the regulations – ie, care of at least 104 nights out of 12 months (see above) – can be deemed absent. In almost all cases the parents with care will both be providing care for at least 104 nights out of 12 months and therefore one will be deemed absent (see below). However, a different definition of day-to-day care could have been used under the 1991 Act (see p44). For example, if the mother provides care during the day but the children sleep at the father's home, each cares for the children an equal number of hours a week and, although there are two parents with care, the shared care rules (deeming one parent absent) cannot be used. No maintenance assessment could be carried out. CSOs may refuse to use a broader interpretation of day-to-day care possible under the Act in order to avoid this problem; an appeal should be considered by the parent who has not been seen as a parent with care. For advice on how to proceed, contact CPAG.

In cases where a parent with care is treated as absent, an assessment is carried out to find out how much child maintenance has to be paid to the other parent. As the remaining parent with care does not have to discharge her responsibility under the Act by paying child maintenance, this assignment of absent parenthood can result in one parent paying child maintenance to another who has equal responsibility for the child. Even though the assessment is reduced to acknowledge the care provided by the deemed absent parent, the end result may be considered ureasonable.

Who is treated as the absent parent

The parent who provides day-to-day care to a **lesser extent** is treated as the absent parent.[9] A lesser extent could be interpreted as meaning either for fewer *nights* per week on average or fewer *hours* per week on average. The number of nights will be considered first by the CSO, but it should be argued on the basis of hours if this would give a fairer result. Indeed, it could even be said that nights involve less care than days. For example, if one parent had the child from 4pm Friday to 8.30am Monday (three nights), this could be argued to be as much care as the other parent who is with the child from 4pm Monday to 8.30am Friday (four nights). It might be possible to argue that the degree of responsibility, as well as the amount of time, is relevant to determining the extent of the care – eg, who buys the child's clothes, who attends school functions, who organises leisure activities or visits to the dentist. These issues need not be raised if both parents agree that the number of nights of care fairly determines the question.

It is helpful if parents keep a record of the time the children spend in each household, especially if there are changes to the usual pattern of care. The extent of day-to-day care is measured over the period explained on pp266–7 – either the previous year or since a change in the arrangements. The current arrangement is considered, but not a future change, which can be dealt with by a change of circumstance review (see p355).

If the parents provide care for an equal amount of time, the parent who does *not* receive child benefit is treated as the absent parent.[10] As the right to receive child maintenance follows the receipt of child benefit, this may lead to competing claims for child benefit. Where more than one person who would otherwise be entitled makes a claim for child benefit, the following order of priority is used to determine who is to be awarded the benefit:[11]

- the person having the child living with her/him;
- the wife, where she is living with her husband (this continues for 13 weeks of a permanent separation);
- a parent, including a step-parent;
- the mother, if the parents are unmarried and living together;
- a person agreed by those entitled;
- failing all the above, the person selected by the Secretary of State.

Priority can be conceded by a higher priority claimant to someone else in writing. For more information on entitlement to child benefit, see CPAG's *Rights Guide to Non-Means-Tested Benefits*.

If care is shared equally and neither parent receives child benefit, the CSO decides who is the principal carer.[12] CSOs have not been given any guidance on this point.

Example 13.1: Shared care and a deemed absent parent

Marcia and Nathan are divorced. They have two children, Oscar (7) and Patrick (5). Every fortnight the children spend five nights with Nathan. The rest of the time they live with Marcia.

Do both parents have day-to-day care? Yes.

Marcia has the children 9 out of every 14 nights = 234 nights a year.

Nathan has the children 5 out of every 14 nights = 130 nights a year.

Marcia, therefore, remains a parent with care and has no liability to pay child maintenance.

Nathan is deemed an absent parent and therefore an assessment is carried out to decide how much child maintenance he should pay to Marcia.

For the purposes of simplicity in this chapter, it is assumed that the parent who remains the person with care is the mother and the deemed absent parent is the father.

There may be cases where each child of a family spends a different amount of time with the two parents – ie, the mother may be deemed the absent parent for one child and the father for the other. If this is the case, the situation is similar to that of a divided family in which different children live full-time with different parents (see p244). Two completely separate assessments are carried out: if the mother cares for the daughter for the greater amount of time, the daughter's child maintenance will be assessed with the father as the deemed absent parent; child maintenance for the son, who spends more time with the father, will be assessed with the mother as the deemed absent parent.

Calculating child maintenance

When two parents share care, there is a remaining parent with care and a deemed absent parent (see above). The five steps of the formula as described in Chapters 7 to 12 are still applicable in calculating how much maintenance the deemed absent parent must pay. However, the standard formula is adjusted to take into account the fact that the so-called absent parent does care for the child(ren) for a proportion of the time.

Step 1: Maintenance requirement

Only one maintenance requirement is calculated (see Chapter 8). When deciding whether to include the lone parent premium, the parent who remains the parent with care is considered. (Although it may appear from the legislation that a maintenance requirement is needed for each parent in order to calculate the deemed absent parent's proposed maintenance – 'X' in the regulations – and the parent with care's notional maintenance – 'Y' – in practice, the same maintenance requirement is used for both calculations.[13])

Example 13.2: Maintenance requirement

The situation is as described in example 13.1. Marcia has remarried and looks after Oscar (7) and Patrick (5) for nine nights every fortnight.

Maintenance requirement with Marcia as parent with care:		£
Personal allowance	Marcia	47.90
	Oscar (7)	16.45
	Patrick (5)	16.45
Family premium		10.55
Sub-total		91.35
Less child benefit		19.60
Maintenance requirement		71.75

Step 2: Exempt income

When calculating the exempt income of the parents, a proportion of the personal allowance for the child (plus any disabled child premium) is included to reflect the average number of nights a week the parent does have care of the child.[14] Similarly, only a proportion of the family premium and, if applicable, the lone parent premium is allowed unless another of the parent's children lives in the household all week (see below for the situation where there is another child).[15] See example 13.10 for the situation where the care of more than one child is shared but the children spend a different number of nights with the parent.

Full housing costs are included. For full details of exempt income, see Chapter 9.

Example 13.3: Exempt income for shared care when no child lives in household for seven nights a week

Marcia looks after Oscar and Patrick for an average of 4.5 nights a week. Nathan looks after Oscar and Patrick for an average of 2.5 nights a week. Marcia married Gareth recently. Their mortgage payments are £120 a week.

Marcia's exempt income:		£	
Personal allowance	Marcia	47.90	
	Oscar (7)	10.58	(for 4.5 days)
	Patrick (5)	10.58	(for 4.5 days)
Family premium		6.78	(for 4.5 days)
Housing costs		120.00	
Total exempt income		195.84	

Nathan lives on his own when the children are not with him. His privately rented flat costs £75 a week. He lives within a few miles of his work.

Nathan's exempt income:		£	
Personal allowance	Nathan	47.90	
	Oscar (7)	5.88	(for 2.5 days)
	Patrick (5)	5.88	(for 2.5 days)
Family premium		3.77	(for 2.5 days)
Lone parent premium		1.86	(for 2.5 days)
Housing costs		75.00	
Total exempt income		140.29	

See example 13.10 for the apportionment of premiums where the children spend a different number of nights with each parent.

Premiums where there is a shared-care child and another child

Only read this section if there is a child who lives in the household all week, as well as the child(ren) there part-time. If the household includes only the children whose care is shared and/or step-children, the premiums are apportioned as above; go to step 3.

Where another child of the parent lives in the household for seven nights a week, this child can either be another qualifying child or a joint child with a new partner. The lone parent premium is included in full if there is no new partner. The family premium will either be included in full or halved.[16] It will be included in full if:

- the parent qualifies for the family premium for the shared child(ren) – ie, receives child benefit for her/him, or where no one receives child benefit, or has claimed child benefit or is the person with whom the child usually lives – hereafter referred to as 'with child benefit', *or*
- there is another qualifying child (of that parent) in the household, *or*
- the new partner cannot support the joint child (see p198).

The following briefly outlines the various permutations and whether or not the premiums are included in full.

- A lone parent with shared-care children (with child benefit) and another qualifying child – full family and lone parent premiums are included.
- A lone parent with shared-care children (no child benefit) and another qualifying child – full family and lone parent premiums.
- A parent with shared-care children (with child benefit) and a joint child with a new partner – full family premium. (**Note:** the personal allowance for the joint child is halved if the new partner can contribute to her/his support.)

- A parent with shared-care children (no child benefit) and a joint child with a new partner – the family premium is halved if the new partner can contribute to the support of the joint child.

For example, a divorced man has his son to stay for two nights a week; his exempt income includes two-sevenths of the son's personal allowance, two-sevenths of the family premium and two-sevenths of the lone parent premium. He later remarries and has a daughter by his new wife. At this point, his exempt income still includes the two-sevenths allowance for the son, but as his ex-wife receives the child benefit, he is not entitled to the full family premium for his son. Therefore, a means test is carried out on his wife's net income and either the full personal allowance for the baby and a full family premium is included (if his wife has insufficient income to support half her daughter) or half the baby's personal allowance and half the family premium.

Example 13.4: Exempt income where there is shared care and a joint child

Marcia still has the qualifying children, Oscar and Patrick, 9 out of 14 nights (an average of 4.5 nights a week) and receives child benefit for them. Marcia and her husband, Gareth, now have a baby daughter, Megan. Gareth earns £450 a week. Their mortgage payments are £120 per week.

Marcia's exempt income:		£	
Personal allowance	Marcia	47.90	
	Oscar	10.58	(4.5 days)
	Patrick	10.58	(4.5 days)
	Megan (half*)	8.23	
Family premium (in full**)		10.55	
Housing costs		120.00	
Total exempt income		207.84	

* As Gareth earns £450 a week, he can afford to contribute to his daughter's maintenance and therefore only half of Megan's personal allowance is included (see p198 for details of the means test).

** Because Megan lives in the household all week, the family premium is not apportioned according to how many nights Oscar and Patrick stay. Instead, consideration has to be given to whether Marcia is entitled to the family premium as a result of looking after Oscar and Patrick. As she receives child benefit for them, she is entitled to the full rate of the premium. (If her ex-husband received the child benefit, Marcia would not be due the full family premium for them. Consideration would then be given to Megan and, since Gareth can afford to maintain half of Megan, the family premium would be halved.)

Step 3: Assessable income

This step is exactly the same as for other situations (see Chapter 10).

Example 13.5: Assessable income

Before the birth of her daughter, Marcia's income is net earnings of £145 a week and child benefit of £19.60. Her husband's earnings are not taken into account in the net income calculation and neither is the child benefit.

Marcia's assessable income:	£
Net income	145.00 (net earnings)
Less exempt income	195.84 (from example 13.3)
Assessable income	nil

Nathan takes home £220 a week, after £40 has been deducted as superannuation. Only half of the superannuation is taken into account (see p206).

Nathan's assessable income:	£
Net income	240.00 (net earnings)
Less exempt income	140.29 (from example 13.3)
Assessable income	99.71

Step 4: Proposed maintenance[17]

The proposed maintenance step is carried out in full for each parent in order to obtain both the proposed maintenance from the deemed absent parent and a notional proposed maintenance from the remaining parent with care. When calculating the proposed maintenance from each parent, the assessable income of the other parent is taken into account in the same way as if both were absent parents (see example 11.7).

The amount of the deemed absent parent's proposed maintenance and the notional amount of proposed maintenance from the remaining parent with care are then added together to give joint proposed maintenance.

The deemed absent parent is taken to have already contributed a proportion of the total proposed maintenance in kind. His assumed contribution is the proportion of the joint proposed maintenance that is equivalent to the proportion of time the children spend with him. The proportion of time the parent spends with his children is given in terms of the average number of nights per week divided by seven. The average number of nights per week does not have to be a round figure; it is calculated to two decimal figures. For example, if a deemed absent parent has the child one week in three, the average number of nights per week is 2.33. If there is more than one child, the total average number of nights per week is divided by the number of children. For example, if a father has one child two nights a week and another child four nights a week, the average number of nights per week is three.

This contribution in kind is then subtracted from the absent parent's proposed maintenance to give an adjusted proposed maintenance figure. If this produces a figure less than zero, no child maintenance is payable.[18] The absent parent has more than contributed his proportion of the total proposed maintenance in kind by providing a certain amount of care.

The minimum payment rule (see p167) applies to an adjusted proposed maintenance figure of between £0 and £4.80.[19]

Example 13.6: Proposed maintenance from Nathan

As Marcia has no assessable income, the proposed maintenance is 50 per cent of Nathan's assessable income (see example 13.5):

50% x £99.71 = £49.86

This is less than the maintenance requirement of £71.75 (see example 13.2), so £49.86 is the proposed maintenance.

As there is no proposed maintenance from Marcia, the joint proposed maintenance is £49.86.

Nathan contributes a proportion of the care:

$$= \frac{2.5 + 2.5 \text{ nights in the average week}}{7 \times 2} = 35.71\%$$

(2 represents the number of children for whom care is shared)

As he contributes 35.71 per cent of the care, he is taken as contributing 35.71 per cent of the joint proposed maintenance in kind:

35.71% x £49.86 = £17.81

Nathan is deemed to have contributed £17.81 and is therefore due to pay the remainder of his proposed maintenance (if protected income allows).

Adjusted proposed maintenance = £49.86 – £17.81 = £32.05

If the caring roles had been reversed and Nathan had the children for 4.5 nights a week, then the proposed maintenance from Marcia, as a deemed absent parent, to Nathan would have been nil, as Marcia has no assessable income.

Example 13.6 gives the most straightforward shared-care situation where only the deemed absent parent has assessable income and even then not enough to meet the maintenance requirement. See example 13.10 for an example of the additional element calculation where both parents have assessable income.

However, any of the situations explained in Chapter 11 can apply to the assessments carried out for parents sharing care. In effect, two separate assessments are being carried out up to step 4 to give a proposed maintenance from the deemed absent parent and a notional proposed maintenance from the parent with care. First, arrive at the proposed maintenance for each parent in the same way as for absent parents before adding together the two amounts of proposed maintenance to give the joint proposed maintenance. Only at this stage is the absent parent's proposed maintenance reduced in recognition of his payment in kind.

The shared care calculation is complicated, but there is a certain amount of logic to it. Both parents have a liability to maintain and therefore, in theory, maintenance is due from each of them for the nights that the child spends with the other parent. For the child there is then a notional amount of maintenance available per week. Imagine the total proposed maintenance divided by seven to give a daily rate of maintenance. Each night of care provided is equivalent to having paid this amount of maintenance. A deemed absent parent will end up having to make payments of child maintenance if the amount equivalent to the number of nights' care he contributes does not exceed his portion of the proposed maintenance.

However, the calculation can mean that the parent with a lower income who has the child for less time can end up handing over maintenance to a parent with a higher income. Although this is equally true in standard cases, in cases of shared care the deemed absent parent may find that he does not have what he considers to be sufficient income left for those days when he is responsible for the child.

Even more difficult to explain is the fact that a deemed absent parent on a low income will never receive any maintenance from a remaining parent with care with a higher income. This may appear particularly galling when the care is shared equally. It may lead to competing claims for child benefit as this will be the determining factor in who receives the child maintenance.

It is also rather bizarre that a parent with care on IS, family credit (FC) or disability working allowance (DWA) who is required to apply for maintenance can be deemed an absent parent and thus not entitled to any child maintenance at all. A parent with care who is deemed to be absent does not, however, have deductions for contributions to child maintenance from IS.

Step 5: Protected income

Protected income is still the final stage of the calculation (see Chapter 12).[20] The deemed absent parent may not be able to afford the proposed adjusted maintenance. When assessing the basic protected income, the allowances for the child are adjusted as for exempt income – see p272 – to represent the proportion of the average week that a child spends with the absent parent.[21] If there is more than one shared-care child and they spend different nights with the family, the family premium and any lone parent premium is included in proportion to the average number of nights per week that a child is in the household.[22] If another child lives in the household full-time, these premiums are included in full.

Example 13.7: Shared care and protected income

Nathan lives on his own, when the children are not with him. His privately rented flat costs £75 a week and his council tax is £300 a year. He earns £240 net a week. He has Oscar and Patrick for five nights per fortnight.

Can Nathan afford to pay the proposed maintenance of £32.05 (see example 13.6)?

The 30% cap does not reduce the proposed maintenance as:

30 per cent x £240 = £72

Therefore the proposed maintenance remains at £32.05.

Basic protected income:		£
Personal allowance	Nathan	47.90
	Oscar (7)	5.88 (for 2.5 days)
	Patrick (5)	5.88 (for 2.5 days)
Family premium		3.77 (for 2.5 days)
Lone parent premium		1.86 (for 2.5 days)
Housing costs		75.00
Council tax		5.77
Margin		30.00
Basic protected income		176.06

Additional protected income:	£
Total family income	240.00 (net earnings)
Less basic protected income	176.06
Excess total family income	63.94

15% x £63.94 = £9.59

Total protected income = £176.06 + £9.59 = £185.65

	£
Total family income	240.00
Less proposed maintenance	32.05
Disposable income	207.95

This disposable income is above the total protected income level of £186.65. Nathan can pay the proposed maintenance of £32.05 a week.

---

3. CARE SHARED BETWEEN A PARENT AND ANOTHER PERSON

The way in which this situation is dealt with depends on which person has the child for the greater length of time. Once again, both the parent and the other person involved must provide day-to-day care (see p266) and live in different households. The way in which this situation is treated depends upon which of the persons with care provides day-to-day care to the lesser extent (see pp269–70).

The parent provides care for less time

Although there are two persons with care as defined by the 1991 Act, the parent with care, for the purposes of the formula, is again deemed by the regulations to be absent, as she provides day-to-day care for less time.[23] Therefore, there is no longer a parent with care, but a person with care and a deemed absent parent.

In most cases, the second parent will also be involved as an absent parent. For example, the grandmother has the child Monday night to Thursday night (the person with care), the mother has the child Friday to Sunday nights (deemed absent parent) and the father has the child for only two weeks in the summer (absent parent).

Both absent parents are liable to pay maintenance to the person with care. Therefore, two separate assessments have to carried out, one for each of the liable parents (assuming an effective application has been made in each case). Remember, the person with care who is actually going to receive the child maintenance cannot apply if she (the grandmother) does not have parental responsibility/rights while the deemed absent parent (the mother) does have that responsibility (see p55). Because the deemed absent parent is a parent with care under the Act, she is required to co-operate if she is on IS/FC/DWA (see Chapter 4). However, if she is on IS, she will *not* have deductions made from her benefit.

How is child maintenance calculated

In the case of the absent parent who does not participate in the caring of the child, the assessment is exactly the same as it would be if there were no shared care arrangement. The fact that the care of the child is shared between two people does not affect the amount that the absent parent can afford to pay. At the proposed maintenance step of the calculation, the assessable income of the deemed absent parent is added to the absent parent's assessable income to give the parents' joint assessable income, in the same way as if both parents were truly absent (see p236).

The deemed absent parent's calculation follows that described above for a deemed absent parent sharing care with the other parent. The only difference is that instead of adding a notional proposed maintenance for the parent with care, the actual proposed maintenance of the absent parent is used to obtain joint proposed maintenance.[24] Where there is no absent parent – eg, he has gone abroad or is deceased – or where the absent parent's assessable income is unknown – eg, he has not been traced – the deemed absent parent just pays child maintenance for those days for which she is not caring for the child(ren).[25]

Example 13.8: Care shared between a parent to a lesser extent and another person to a greater extent

Gran, who is a widow, has Beverley (15) for four nights a week and her mother has her for the remaining three nights. As the mother looks after Beverley for less time than the Gran, the mother is deemed to be absent. The mother has parental responsibility and receives child benefit.

Maintenance requirement:		£
Personal allowance	Gran	23.95 (half – see p174)
	Beverley (15)	24.10
Family premium		10.55
Lone parent premium		5.20
Sub-total		63.80
Less child benefit		10.80
Maintenance requirement		53.00

The mother's assessable income is £42 a week. (When working out her exempt income, 3/7ths of the personal allowance for Beverley, 3/7ths family premium and 3/7ths of the lone parent premium would have been included.)

(a) The absent father's assessable income is £57.

Parents' joint assessable income = £42 + £57 = £99

50% of joint assessable income = £49.50

This is below the maintenance requirement and therefore the 50 per cent calculation applies to each parent.

Father's proposed maintenance = 50% x £57 = £28.50

Mother's proposed maintenance = 50% x £42 = £21

Joint proposed maintenance = £28.50 + £21 = £49.50

The mother provides three out of seven nights' care = 42.86%

This is equivalent to paying 42.86% x £49.50 = £21.21 a week maintenance.

The mother's adjusted proposed maintenance: £21 – £21.21 = nil

As she is exempt from the minimum payment, she is not liable to pay any child maintenance as her contribution in kind outweighs the financial contribution.

Assuming the protected income calculation allows it, the father pays £28.50 a week to the grandmother, but nothing to the mother.

See example 13.11 for the assessment where the parents have higher assessable incomes.

(b) If the father emigrated, the mother would pay 4/7ths of her proposed maintenance to the grandmother, assuming that the protected income calculation did not reduce this.

The mother's proposed maintenance would still be £21. She is still providing care three nights a week or 42.86 per cent of the proposed maintenance in kind: 42.86% x £21 = £9.

This leaves her with adjusted proposed maintenance of £21 *less* £9 = £12 per week to the grandmother. The protected income calculation has to be carried out and would include 3/7ths of Beverley's personal allowance, 3/7ths family premium and 3/7ths lone parent premium.

The mother, as someone not in receipt of IS/FC/DWA, may now decide to cancel the assessment! Gran can only apply if she has parental responsibility for Beverley.

The regulations do not allow for the maintenance paid by the absent parent to be split between two persons with care where one is a deemed absent parent. The entire amount of child maintenance from the absent parent is paid to the remaining person with care. In other words, the parent with care who shares care for the lesser time can never receive child maintenance from an absent parent, no matter the size of the bill being paid.

This may seem illogical, not to say unfair, particularly where the application has been made by the parent with care or where – although applications have been made by both persons with care – the application from the parent has been given priority (see p76). For example, where the parent with care is in receipt of IS/FC/DWA and so has to make an application under section 6 of the 1991 Act, she will not receive any child maintenance where another person is providing a greater amount of care.

Parent provides care for greater amount of time

If a parent does a greater proportion of the caring than another person with care, then she remains a parent with care for the purposes of the maintenance assessment.[26] This also applies where the parent provides care to the same extent as someone else, but the parent receives the child benefit. There is no deemed absent parent. Instead there is usually a parent with care, another person with care and an absent parent. It can also cover the rare situation where a person is not technically a person with care under the Act (see p54) even though s/he is providing care of at least two nights a week on average.

If only one of the persons with care has applied for a maintenance assessment, that person will receive all the child maintenance payable by the absent parent.[27] This also applies where both persons with care have made an application, but only one has been accepted. There is an order of priority as to which application will be accepted (see p76). It also covers cases where the second carer cannot make an application – eg, s/he does not have parental responsibility or s/he does not share a home with the child.

However, if a request is made to the Child Support Agency (CSA) by *either* of the people looking after the child(ren), the child maintenance may be divided between the two of them in proportion to the day-to-day care provided.[28] The ratio of care provided does not have to be calculated on the basis of the number of nights a child spends with the carer. An alternative method could be argued for if this were to give a fairer division of the maintenance (see pp269–70).

It is not specified in the regulations what form such a request needs to take. Presumably, simply stating on the maintenance application form or in a letter that part of the maintenance should go to another person should suffice. There is no time limit for making the request. In theory, it is arguable that the request could be verbal, but we suggest that in case of disputes, such a request should be put in writing.

The decision to share the child maintenance assessment between the persons with care is a discretionary decision made by the Secretary of State. The Secretary of State must consider the interests of the child, the current care arrangements and all representations received about the payment proposals.[29]

The alternative is for the persons with care to come to a voluntary arrangement, but this may not be feasible where the person who is the applicant for the CSA purposes is in receipt of a means-tested benefit.

Example 13.9: Care shared between a parent to a greater extent and another person to a lesser extent

If the caring responsibilities of the grandmother and mother in example 13.8 are swapped, so that mother has Beverley for four nights a week, the calculation is as follows:

The mother now remains the parent with care and the grandmother is still a person with care. (This also applies where care is shared equally but the mother is in receipt of child benefit.)

The father's proposed maintenance remains £28.50 a week.

However this time the mother will receive the full amount if she makes the application for maintenance and there is no request to split the payment. If there is such a request and it is granted, then the mother will receive 4/7ths – ie, £16.29 – and the grandmother the remainder – ie, £12.21 a week.

4. CARE SHARED BETWEEN TWO PEOPLE WHO ARE NOT PARENTS

The situation may arise where two people living in different households each have day-to-day care (as defined in the regulations – see p266) of a child of whom neither is the parent. The same rules apply here as where care is shared between a parent for the greater part and another (see above)[30] – ie, if a request is made by either person, the maintenance payable by each absent parent may be divided between the carers in proportion to the amount of care being provided. If no request is made, then the full amount goes to the applicant.

In this situation it is likely that there are two absent parents and therefore maintenance could be paid by both absent parents. If one of the persons with care chooses to apply for maintenance from only one of the absent parents, there is no reason why the second person with care cannot apply for child maintenance from the other absent parent.

5. THREE PERSONS WITH CARE

As a person with care has to look after the child for a minimum of two nights a week on average, there can be no more than three persons with care for any child. However, there may be a combination of parents and others providing the care as follows (in each case the first person provides the greatest amount of care and the third, the least):

- parent, parent, other person – this situation is not covered specifically, although the intention must be to deem the second parent absent and for maintenance to be paid by him to the applicant;
- parent, other person, parent – second parent is deemed absent and maintenance is paid by him to the applicant;
- other person, parent, parent – second parent is deemed absent and maintenance is paid by him to the applicant;

- parent, other person, other person – applicant receives maintenance from the absent parent or it may be apportioned on request;
- other person, parent, other person – this does not appear to be explicitly covered by the regulations, but we presume that the intention is that the parent would be deemed absent; there would, of course, be a second parent who is absent;
- other person, other person, parent – parent with care deemed absent and other parent absent are both liable;
- three other people – maintenance from both absent parents may be apportioned on request.

6. CARE PROVIDED IN PART BY THE LOCAL AUTHORITY

A local authority cannot be a person with care.[31] Therefore, if a child is in the care of the local authority for seven nights a week, no child maintenance is payable by the absent parents. There may be cases where a child is not being provided with care by the local authority all the time, but only for part of the time. If the local authority care amounts to less than day-to-day care (see p266), such a level of care can be ignored.

However, if the element of care provided by the local authority amounts to day-to-day care, child maintenance is not payable for any night that the child is in that local authority care.[32] Instead, the person with care who looks after the child for the remainder of the time receives reduced child maintenance from the absent parent. The maintenance payment is reduced to correspond to the number of nights per week that the child is in that person's care – eg, if the child is in local authority care for five nights a week, the person with care will receive two-sevenths of the amount of the maintenance assessment from the absent parent.

Where there is more than one qualifying child and the local authority provides some day-to-day care, for at least one of the children, again the maintenance payable is reduced.[33] For example, a person with care looks after two children; one spends the whole week with the person with care, the other child spends four nights in local authority care and three nights with the person with care. To work out the maintenance payable in this circumstance, calculate the total number of nights spent with the person with care per week, and divide this by seven times the number of qualifying children. In this case 10 (7+3) out of 14 (7x2) nights are spent with the parent with care. The maintenance payable is ten-fourteenths (or 71.43 per cent) of the maintenance assessed.

7. THE MAINTENANCE REQUIREMENT IS MET IN FULL

The calculations described earlier in the chapter hold true when the maintenance requirement is met in full. If 50 per cent of the parents' joint assessable income is greater than the maintenance requirement, the additional element calculation has to be used for proposed maintenance. For a full explanation of the additional element calculation, see Chapter 11.

Example 13.10: Care shared by parents

This is the same family as in examples 13.1 to 13.7.

Oscar (now aged 9) now spends every other week with Nathan, while Patrick (6) still spends five days a fortnight with him. Marcia still receives child benefit for both boys and therefore Nathan is still deemed to be an absent parent in respect of Oscar as well as Patrick. A calculation, therefore, has to be done to assess how much Nathan pays Marcia. However, in assessing Nathan's actual contribution, a notional contribution from Marcia has to be calculated.

Nathan's take-home earnings have risen to £238 a week, and his super-annuation contribution is now £44 a week.

Marcia has increased her hours and now earns £240 net a week. Her husband, Gareth, earns £450 net a week. Their mortgage payments are £120 a week. Their daughter Megan is two years old.

Step 1: The maintenance requirement £71.75 (see example 13.2)

Step 2: Exempt income

Marcia's exempt income:		£	
Personal allowance	Marcia	47.90	
	Oscar	8.23	(3.5 days)
	Patrick	10.58	(4.5 days)
	Megan (half)	8.23	
Family premium		10.55	
Housing costs		120.00	
Total exempt income		205.49	

(See example 13.4 for comparison)

Nathan's exempt income:		£	
Personal allowance	Nathan	47.90	
	Oscar	8.23	(for 3.5 days)
	Patrick	5.88	(for 2.5 days)
Family premium*		5.28	(for 3.5 days)
Lone parent premium*		2.60	(for 3.5 days)
Housing costs		75.00	
Total exempt income		144.89	

* The premiums are included in proportion to the average number of nights a week that care is provided for a child. In this case Patrick stays with Nathan on nights that Oscar is there – ie, care is provided for at least one child for an average of 3.5 nights a week and for the other 3.5 nights Nathan is a single man. However, if the children stayed different nights, 6/7ths of the premiums would be included.[34]

Step 3: Assessable income

Marcia's assessable income:		£
Net income	Earnings	240.00
Less exempt income		205.49
Assessable income		34.51

Nathan's assessable income:		£
Net income	Earnings*	260.00
Less exempt income		144.89
Assessable income		115.11

* Only half of the superannuation is taken into account.

Step 4: Proposed maintenance

Joint assessable income: £34.51 + £115.11 = £149.62

50% x £149.62 = £74.81

This is above the maintenance requirement of £71.75 and therefore an additional element calculation must be done (see figure 11.5).

Marcia's notional proposed maintenance:

Basic element = £71.75 x $\dfrac{34.51}{149.62}$ = £16.55

Basic assessable income = £16.55 x 2 = £33.10

Additional assessable income = £34.51 – £33.10 = £1.41

Additional element = 20% x £1.41 = £0.28

Notional proposed maintenance = £16.55 + £0.28 = £16.83

Nathan's proposed maintenance to Marcia:

Basic element = £71.75 x $\frac{115.11}{149.62}$ = £55.20

Basic assessable income = £55.20 x 2 = £110.40

Additional assessable income = £115.11 – £110.40 = £4.71

Additional element = 20% x £4.71 = £0.94

Proposed maintenance = £55.20 + £0.94 = £56.14

Joint proposed maintenance = £16.83 + £56.14 = £72.97

Nathan contributes in kind = $\frac{3.5 + 2.5}{7 \times 2}$ = 42.86% of the care

This is equivalent to £31.27 (42.86% x £72.97)

Nathan's proposed maintenance after taking into account his portion of the care = £56.14 – £31.27 = £24.87 per week.

Step 5: Protected income

This follows example 13.7, except that now half Oscar's personal allowance and half both the family and lone parent premiums are included (see p278). The protected income calculation shows that Nathan can afford the proposed maintenance of £24.87. He may not be very happy about this as he has the children for almost as much time as Marcia, Marcia has the child benefit, her take-home pay is similar to his, and her husband has a significant salary.

There could be times when there is more then one child and because the care is shared in different ways for the different children, each parent would be the person with care for one child and the deemed absent parent for the other. In this case, two shared care calculations would have to carried out. This would happen in the situation described in example 13.10 if Nathan was in receipt of the child benefit for Oscar.

Example 13.11: Care shared between a parent and another person

Gran has Beverley (15) for four nights a week and her mother has her for the remaining three nights. The mother is therefore deemed to be an absent parent. When the mother's assessable income was £42 and the father's was £57, the mother's child maintenance liability was nil while the father's proposed maintenance was £28.50 (see example 13.8).

(a) The mother's assessable income has doubled to £84

Joint assessable income = £84 + £57 = £141

50 per cent of joint assessable income = 50% x £141 = £71

This is above the maintenance requirement of £53 (see example 13.8) and so an additional element calculation has to be done.

Father's proposed maintenance:
Basic element = £53 x $\frac{57}{141}$ = £21.43

Basic assessable income = £21.43 x 2 = £42.86
Additional assessable income = £57 – £42.86 = £14.14
Additional element = £14.14 x 15% = £2.12
Proposed maintenance = £21.43 + £2.12 = £23.55

Mother's proposed maintenance:
Basic element = £53 x $\frac{84}{141}$ = £31.57

Basic assessable income = £31.57 x 2 = £63.14
Additional assessable income = £84 – £63.14 = £20.86
Additional element = £20.86 x 15% = £3.13
Proposed maintenance = £31.57 + £3.13 = £34.70

Joint proposed maintenance = £23.55 + £34.70 = £58.25
The mother provides care three out of seven nights = 42.86% of the care.
This is equivalent to paying 42.86% of £58.25 or £24.97 a week maintenance.
The mother's adjusted proposed maintenance = £34.70 – £24.97 = £9.73

Assuming the protected calculations allow these figures, Gran now receives £9.73 from the mother and £23.55 from the father, a total of £33.28 instead of the £28.50 from the absent father. The mother may have applied for child maintenance hoping to receive something from the father. Given the result, she may decide to cancel the assessment. Gran could only apply for maintenance if she had parental responsibility.

(b) The absent father's assessable income has now doubled to £114 and the mother's remains at £84 a week.
Parents' joint assessable income = £84 + £114 = £198
50 per cent of joint assessable income = 50% x £198 = £99
This is above the maintenance requirement of £53 and therefore an additional element calculation has to be done.

Father's proposed maintenance:
Basic element = £53 x $\frac{114}{198}$ = £30.52

Basic assessable income = £30.52 x 2 = £61.04
Additional assessable income = £114 – £61.04 = £52.96
Additional element = £52.96 x 15% = £7.94
Proposed maintenance = £30.52 + £7.94 = £38.46

Mother's proposed maintenance:
Basic element = £53 x $\frac{84}{198}$ = £22.48

Basic assessable income = £22.48 x 2 = £44.96
Additional assessable income = £84 – £44.96 = £39.04
Additional element = £39.04 x 15% = £5.86
Proposed maintenance = £22.48 + £5.86 = £28.34

Joint proposed maintenance = £38.46 + £28.34 = £66.80
The mother provides care three out of seven nights = 42.86% of the care. This is equivalent to paying 42.86% x £66.80 = £28.63 a week maintenance. The mother therefore does not have to pay any maintenance as her contribution in kind (£28.63) just outweighs her financial liability (£28.34). Despite the fact that her assessable income is the same as in (a), her liability has been reduced as a result of the increased liability of the father.

The father still has to pay his proposed maintenance, assuming this does not bring his disposable income below the protected income level. The maintenance of £38.46 is paid to the grandmother.

PART THREE

The assessment and after

Assessments

This chapter covers:

I. MAKING ASSESSMENTS

Once an effective application has been made – ie, a maintenance application form (MAF) has been fully completed (see p59) – and the Child Support Agency (CSA) has obtained or tried to obtain the information necessary, a child support officer can make an assessment.

Who makes the assessment

The Secretary of State must refer each maintenance application to a child support officer (CSO).[1] The only exception to this is where a parent with care has applied under section 6, but the income support (IS), family credit (FC) or disability working allowance (DWA) claim has been refused or withdrawn (see p74). Only a CSO can make or refuse to make an assessment.

In practice, most assessments are made by the CSA computer without a CSO bring involved.[2] It is doubtful whether this is lawful, though the CSA thinks it is.[3] A CSO will accept responsibility for any assessment made by computer as if it had been made by a CSO. Most assessments are done at the CSA regional centre (CSAC) which deals with the person with care's area of the country (see p19). At the time of writing, the CSA is conducting a pilot for assessments done at field offices.[4]

The Secretary of State checks the papers and, if s/he considers that the CSA has all necessary information and that the case is straightforward, puts the details into the computer. The computer then makes the calculations and produces an assessment.[5]

Alternatively, the application is passed to a CSO if the Secretary of State thinks that more information is needed or that the case is not straightforward or is of a kind which the computer cannot deal with. The CSO then decides to either:

- seek further information (see Chapter 6);
- calculate the assessment (see Chapters 8–12);
- make an interim maintenance assessment (IMA) (see p296); *or*
- refuse to make an assessment (p295).

The following cases are clerically assessed, presumably because the computer cannot cope with them:[6]

- one of the parties does not have a national insurance number and refuses to be given one;
- one or both parents are aged 16 or less;
- a parent with care is also looking after another child of the absent parent who is not her child;
- the person with care is an organisation, eg, Barnardo's;
- the parents of the child are of the same sex;
- the system would not accept the case because of a fault;
- shared care cases where the average number of nights a week that the deemed absent parent looks after the child(ren) is not a whole number or where children are cared for by that parent on different nights.

Other cases may be assessed clerically in part – eg, the calculation to establish whether housing costs are excessive (see p191) has to be carried out clerically.[7]

Checking assessments

Two per cent of all assessments made are randomly selected for a checking procedure.[8] This involves first seeking verification of all financial details that were not checked before the assessment and then referring the case to management. This can cause a delay in notification of the assessment as written evidence is usually requested.

Relationship with CSA Northern Ireland

For child support cases, there are two 'territories': Great Britain and Northern Ireland. If the person with care, absent parent and qualifying child do not all reside in the same territory, the application will be dealt with by the CSA of the territory where the person with care lives.[9] If more than one application is made naming the same absent parent, those applications will be dealt with by the CSA of the territory where the person with care lives who was named in the first application received by the CSA.[10] Where a case has been allocated to a CSA by these rules and the person with care applies again, naming a further absent parent, that application will be dealt with by the CSA already dealing with the earlier case(s).[11]

These rules do not apply where an application is made under section 7 by a child in Scotland (see p54). In that case the application and any others naming the same absent parent will be dealt with by the CSA for the territory where the person with care of the child applicant lives.[12]

Any assessment made under these rules must take into account the rules of the other territory.[13] Because the rules for the two territories are very similar, this should not make any difference.

Waiting for the assessment

The CSA originally intended that most cases would have an assessment within six to 12 weeks of the application. This does not happen in practice (see p24 for current waiting times).

Delays caused by the parties returning forms and providing further information are compounded by the backlog of work at the CSA. Delay does not normally put off the starting date of any maintenance assessment, but the date of the decision on maintenance is delayed. Liability under an order or agreement continues and absent parents should consider starting or continuing voluntary payments or putting money aside (see p134).

Withdrawing the application

Where an application is withdrawn (see p69) before the CSO makes or refuses to make an assessment, the CSO cannot make an assessment. Where an assessment is made in these circumstances, it can be challenged (see Chapter 16).

Where an assessment is made, the application cannot be withdrawn because it has already been dealt with, but the assessment can be cancelled (see p307) or reviewed (see Chapter 16).

Change of circumstances

The person with care does not have to inform the CSA of any change of circumstance which happens after the MAF is returned but before the assessment is made. She can do so, and may want to, where an assessment could now be made (eg, the absent parent is now living in the UK) or the amount of an assessment would be increased (eg, her earnings have fallen). The absent parent may also want to tell the CSA about any changes but he does not have to.

Any party may also want to tell the CSA of new information about the case which relates to the details given in the MAF or maintenance enquiry form (MEF). For example, the parent with care may have discovered that the absent parent has a second job which she believes he has not disclosed to the CSA.

Where the CSA is told about a change or given new information before an assessment is made, it is not necessary to ask for a review. Any new information may be taken into account in the assessment or may lead to two assessments, one taking over from the other at the date of the change.[14]

Once an assessment is made, the person with care has a duty to notify the CSA of certain changes (see p155).

Refusal to make an assessment

The CSO will refuse to make an assessment where:

- the application was made by a person who is not an absent parent, person with care or a qualifying child aged 12 or over in Scotland (see p54);
- the application is under section 4 or 7 and there is a court order or written agreement (see p56);
- the application is under section 4 and the parent with care is on IS/FC/DWA (see p55);
- not all the parties are habitually resident in the UK (see p47);
- there is no absent parent, either because both parents live in the same household as the child (see p45), or because the CSO does not accept that the person named is a parent of the child (see p40); *or*
- there is no qualifying child (see p41).

Where there is a change of circumstance so that one of these situations applies but only for a period beginning after the effective date (for meaning of effective date, see p303), the CSO should make an assessment which ends on the date of the change.

Where one of these situations applied on the effective date but a change of circumstance means that it no longer applies, the CSO should make an assessment from the date of the change.

Where the child (or all the children) named in an application die(s) before the assessment is made, the CSO treats the application as if it had not been made and no decision is given.[15]

The CSO must still make an assessment when the absent parent is exempt from paying the minimum payment (see p167) and the assessment is therefore nil.[16] The parties must still receive a notification (see p299).

If the CSO refuses to make an assessment, the applicant and, if the applicant was a child in Scotland, any person with care or absent parent who had been notified of the application, must be informed as soon as possible, in writing, of the reasons and how to seek a review.[17]

A second-tier review of a refusal to make the assessment can be requested (see p358). A fresh application could also be made, for example, if, after the refusal, the person with care's income falls so that an assessment would be made.

2. INTERIM MAINTENANCE ASSESSMENTS

Where a CSO considers that s/he does not have enough information to make a full assessment using the formula on an application, or enough to conduct or complete a review (see Chapter 16), s/he may make an IMA rather than a full assessment.[18] A CSO has only had the power to make an IMA on a review of a full assessment since 22 January 1996.[19] The decision whether to make an IMA is discretionary so the CSO must take into account the welfare of any child(ren) the decision may affect (see p52). CSA guidance states that an IMA will not be imposed on:

- an absent parent under the age of 16; or
- an absent parent who cannot be traced.[20]

An IMA will almost always be higher than child maintenance calculated under the formula, penalising the absent parent until the necessary information is provided. This is to ensure that the person with care gets maintenance as speedily as possible.[21] CSOs are reminded to delay the making of an IMA if the absent parent is making every effort to obtain the information needed and the delay is unavoidable.[22] CSOs sometimes delay making an IMA even though the absent parent is not co-operating with the CSA. Parents with care who are losing out in this situation should ask the CSO to make an IMA or explain why this is not being done. If an IMA is cancelled, there may be an overpayment of child maintenance which has to be repaid (see p393).

Before making an IMA, the CSO must give the absent parent, parent with care and Scottish child applicant written notice of her/his intention to do so, unless that is not reasonably practicable.[23] The notice gives the absent parent 14 days to comply: this period starts from the day the notice was given or sent by the Secretary of State.[24] This is one occasion where a notice is *not* treated as sent on the second day after posting.

After those notices are sent, the CSO may give a person more time to provide the information required or may decide to stop considering making an IMA. Where this happens and the CSO then decides to make an IMA, CSA guidance says that written notice of intention must be given again.[25]

There are four types of IMA: Category A, Category B, Category C and Category D (see below).[26] Category C and D were added from 18 April 1995. For further information on IMA commencement, cancellation and review, see pp306 and 311 and Chapter 16.

Category A interim maintenance assessments

A CSO may make a Category A IMA where an absent parent has failed to provide information which a CSO requires from him to make an assessment (eg, information about income or housing costs).[27] The absent parent must have the information or can be reasonably expected to get it. A Category A IMA cannot be made where the information not provided relates *only* to the income of the absent parent's partner or the person with care's partner or another member of the absent parent or person with care's family.

A Category A IMA is set at *one-and-a-half times* the maintenance requirement.[28] For how the maintenance requirement is calculated, see Chapter 8.

Category B interim maintenance assessments

A CSO may make a Category B IMA where s/he needs information about the income of the absent parent's partner or parent with care's partner, or other member of the absent parent or parent with care's family, and it has not been provided.[29] The partner or family member concerned must have the information or can be reasonably expected to acquire it, or the absent parent/parent with care has been given the information by the partner or family member but has not provided it to the CSO. This includes the situation where the absent parent does not ask his new partner for details of income because his partner does not know of the existence of the child.

No partner or family member has a duty to provide this information, but without it a full assessment cannot be made. In these circumstances a Category A IMA is not appropriate. A Category B IMA will mean that the calculation of exempt income and protected income will be affected (see below).

Partner expected to help maintain a joint child

Where an absent parent or a parent with care has a partner, any joint child of theirs is included in the exempt income calculation (see p198).

Information is needed by the CSO in order to decide whether the partner can afford to help support the joint child and, if so, reduce the amount included in the exempt income calculation for that person.

Where the CSO cannot make a decision on this because the information has not been provided, s/he calculates child maintenance in the usual way, but halves the child's personal allowance, any disabled child premium and (where no other child is included in exempt income) the family premium, when calculating exempt income.[30] The partner is assumed to have enough income for half the child's needs. If this is the case the family does not lose out by having a Category B IMA. Where the new partner's income is too low to help support the joint child, the family may lose out if a Category B IMA is imposed.

Second family's total income unknown

Where the CSO does not have the income details of the absent parent's partner or other family members, s/he will be unable to carry out the protected income calculation (see p250). This calculation is intended to ensure that the disposable income of the second family of an absent parent does not fall below a certain level as a result of paying maintenance.

Where the income of his second family is not known, the Category B IMA is the amount of proposed child maintenance calculated in steps 1 to 4 of the formula (see Chapters 8–11).[31] Where this amount is greater than 30 per cent of the absent parent's net income, the amount of the Category B IMA will be restricted to 30 per cent of net income (any fraction of a penny will be rounded down).[32] Middle-income families who will not fall below the protected income level can afford to withhold information without this affecting their assessment. They would not be penalised by a Category B IMA.

Category C interim maintenance assessments

A Category C IMA may be made where the absent parent is self-employed and is unable to provide information about earnings, but has said he expects to be able to do so within a reasonable time.[33] If a court order or written agreement for maintenance is in force for any of the child(ren) named in the application, a Category C IMA cannot be imposed.[34] Category C IMAs are very rare: only five had been made in the ten months after they were introduced.[35]

The amount of a Category C IMA is normally £30 but the CSO can set a lower amount than this, or nil, if s/he thinks that this is reasonable.[36] The person with care is notified if the CSO is considering setting an amount lower than £30, and her representations will be taken into account when deciding whether to do that.[37]

The protected income calculation (step 5 of the formula, see Chapter 12) does not apply to a Category C IMA.[38]

Category D interim maintenance assessments

Where a Category IMA is in force, a CSO may make a Category D IMA instead, where it appears to her/him, on the basis of the available information about the absent parent's income, that a full assessment (ie, steps 1 to 5 of the formula) would be higher than the existing Category A IMA.[39] This is to prevent an absent parent from being better off with a Category A IMA than if properly assessed and so benefiting from non-co-operation.

The amount of a Category D IMA is calculated in the same way as a full assessment, except:[40]

- no protected income is calculated, nor is there the 30 per cent cap (see Chapter 12);
- no housing costs are allowed;
- only the adult personal allowance is included in exempt income (see p183); *and*
- when working out income, no allowance is made for payments to personal or occupational pensions or to pension schemes intended to provide capital sums to discharge a mortgage.

The CSA may use its powers to obtain information about the absent parent's earnings or income.[41] The CSA says that it will pursue all reasonable lines of enquiry, including the inspectors (see p153). The person with care may be contacted to see if she can provide wage slips or bank statements showing salary payments.

If the absent parent is an employee and it is not possible to work out his earnings, the CSO can make an estimate (see p206).[42] The absent parent's other income can also be estimated if the CSO cannot calculate it.[43]

Before imposing a Category D IMA the CSO should, whether or not the absent parent is an employee or self-employed:[44]

- be satisfied that the income details obtained are a reasonable representation of the absent parent's current income; *and*
- consider whether the absent parent's employment or income status has changed since the period covered by those details.

3. NOTIFICATION OF ASSESSMENTS

The CSO must notify the person with care, absent person and Scottish child applicant that an assessment has been made as soon as possible after the decision.[45] This applies to full assessments, IMAs and assessments made after review. The notification *must* include:[46]

- the effective date;
- the maintenance requirement;
- the absent parent's net and assessable income;
- the absent parent's protected income level and the amount of the assessment before the protected income adjustment (if relevant);
- the absent parent's housing costs (if relevant);
- the parent with care's assessable income;
- details of any apportionment (in cases of shared care or where more than one person with care has applied for child maintenance for different children of the same absent parent);
- where phasing-in applies (see below) the amount which was payable under the order(s)/agreement(s);[47] *and*
- how to seek a review.[48]

Notification must also be given of any adjustment made to the assessment in order to recoup an overpayment, including the amount and period of the adjustment (see p394).[49]

Where the assessment is a Category B IMA, the absent parent's assessable income is included only where it is known.[50] Where the assessment is a Category A, C or D IMA, only the effective date and the maintenance requirement needs to be notified.[51]

Parties may be unhappy with the financial details disclosed by the CSA. For example, the absent parent may feel his housing costs should be confidential. On the other hand, it is often impossible to see from the assessment notice whether the figures given by the absent parent for his earnings and housing costs fit with the information known to the parent with care. As a result, reviews and appeals are often sought so that the CSA will provide the full details it holds (see Chapter 16). For disclosure of addresses and names see p157.

On receiving the notice the parties should check for any mistakes. If you are unhappy and want advice you should seek it quickly. In particular, because a Category A or D IMA will almost always be higher than a full assessment, an absent parent should seek advice if one is made.

4. PHASING-IN OF ASSESSMENTS

Because the formula for assessing child maintenance usually results in larger payments than under old court orders or agreements, assessments which would mean significant increases can sometimes be introduced in up to four stages. An assessment may *only* be phased in if:

- there was a court order or agreement for maintenance in force on 4 April 1993 and continuing from then until the date the assessment is made;[52] *and*
- the assessment exceeds the old agreement by more than £20 a week.[53] Any payments in kind or payments to third parties are ignored when determining the old amount.[54]

Type A phasing

Called type A by the CSA,[55] this has existed from April 1993 and the reduced amount payable is known as the modified amount.[56] It does not apply to a Category A IMA.[57] It applies where:[58]

- the old maintenance order/agreement covered all the children named in the assessment; *and*
- the absent parent is responsible for maintaining a child living with him who is not named in the assessment (for definition of child, see p41); *and*
- the assessment is £60 or less.

The weekly modified amount is the amount under the old order/agreement plus £20.[59] This continues for a year but will end before that if one of the above conditions is no longer met.

Type B phasing

Called type B by the CSA,[60] this was introduced on 7 February 1994 and the reduced amount payable is known as the transitional amount.[61] It does not apply to a Category A or D IMA.[62] It applies where:[63]

- the old maintenance order/agreement covered at least one child named in the assessment; *and*
- the absent parent was a member of a family (see p50) which included at least one child on the effective date (see p303) (or on 7 February 1994 if that was later) and is still a member of a family with a child; *and*
- type A phasing does not apply;[64] *and*
- the assessment does not replace a Category A or D IMA made after 22 January 1996.[65]

Where the assessment is £60 or less, the transitional amount is the amount under the old order/agreement plus £20.[66] This lasts for 52 weeks from the effective date or 7 February 1994, whichever is the later.[67]

Where the assessment is more than £60 a week, the transitional amount is:[68]

- for the first 26 weeks, the old amount *plus* the greater of £20 and a quarter of the difference between the assessment and the old amount;
- for the next 26 weeks, the old amount *plus* the greater of £40 and half of the difference between the assessment and the old amount; *and*
- for the last 26 weeks of the phasing-in period, the old amount *plus* the greater of £60 and three-quarters of the difference between the assessment and the old amount.

The maintenance payable becomes the assessment amount if the transitional amount would be larger than that. Therefore, it is only where the difference between the old amount and the assessment amount is more than £60 a week that the phasing-in period lasts the full 18 months.

Which type of phasing applies

Transitional protection is calculated automatically by the CSA, except where the assessment was made before 7 February 1994.[69] CSOs are instructed to consider only type B phasing-in cases where the effective date (see p303) is after 7 February 1994.[70] This is wrong, because the regulations say that type A takes precedence.[71] In most cases this will not matter, because both types of phasing would be the same. However, an absent parent may lose out where a Category D IMA is made or a full assessment is made which replaces a Category A or D IMA, because only type A phasing can apply. If phasing is not applied, a second-tier review can be sought (see Chapter 16).

Previous maintenance arrangements

The absent parent is asked to provide a copy of any order or agreement. This is accepted by the CSA as evidence of a maintenance agreement even if it was not drawn up by a solicitor and is unsigned and unwitnessed. If the absent parent does not have a copy of a written agreement, he should obtain a copy from the court or solicitor or, in the case of an agreement drawn up by the two parties, the CSA will ask the person with care to confirm the agreement. The CSA can obtain evidence of an arrangement negotiated with the Benefits Agency from them. If the arrangement was a verbal one and the absent parent cannot produce evidence of payment – eg, cheque stubs, bank statements – the person with care is asked to provide written confirmation of the existence of the arrangement.[72] If payments had not been made regularly or she had not agreed to the amount paid, the person with care can challenge the phasing-in on the ground that the agreement was not 'in force' over the period. For more details, see p55.

Reviews where phasing-in applies

Where type A phasing applies and a second-tier review (see 358) or a review instigated by a CSO (see p364) is done and the conditions for phasing are still met, phasing will continue until the 52-week period ends.[73]

Where type A applies and a change of circumstances review (see p355) is made, or where type B applies and any review is made, then the following amount is payable:[74]

- where the fresh assessment is less than the modified or transitional amount, the fresh assessment;
- where the fresh assessment is less than the previous assessment but more than the modified or transitional amount, the modified or transitional amount;
- where the fresh assessment is higher than the previous assessment, the modified or transitional amount is increased by the same amount as the increase between the two formula assessments. For example, the court agreement was £15 a week and the first formula assessment is £40, then the modified amount actually paid is £35. If the fresh assessment after the change of circumstances review is £52 – ie, an increase of £12 over the first assessment, the modified amount is increased by £12 from £35 to £47.

5. WHEN DOES AN ASSESSMENT BEGIN

The date an assessment made by the CSA takes effect is called the effective date.[75] There are separate rules for the effective dates after reviews (see Chapter 16) and, in some cases, for IMAs (see p306).

For arrears before an assessment is made, see p398. For overpayments, see p393.

The effective date is important in that it is often used as a reference point when calculating the assessment – eg, for the benefit rates used in the calculation (see p175) and for assessing certain income, for example, benefits (see p209).

The effective date

Unless there is or has been a court order in force (see below), where the application was made by the person with care or a Scottish child applicant, the effective date of the first assessment, is:[76]

- eight weeks from the date on which the MEF is given or sent to an absent parent as long as:

- within four weeks of being sent the MEF, it is returned with his name, address and written confirmation that he is the parent of the child(ren) named in the MAF; *and*
- the MAF was issued on or after 18 April 1995; *or*
- the date the absent parent was actually given or sent the MEF.

Where the absent parent made the application, the effective date of the first assessment is:[77]

- eight weeks from the date on which the application was received by the CSA as long as:
  - the absent parent provides his name, address and written confirmation that he is the parent of the child(ren) named in the MAF as part of the MAF or within four weeks of the date of the application; *and*
  - the application is recorded as received on or after 18 April 1995; *or*
- the date an effective MAF (see p59) is received.

Where the absent parent takes more than four weeks to supply his name, address and confirmation of paternity, he can argue that the delay was unavoidable. If the CSO accepts this, s/he may apply the eight-week extension above.[78] The person with care can contest this by seeking a second-tier review (see p358).

Although other documents sent by the CSA are treated as being given or sent two working days after posting, this rule does not apply when fixing the effective date.[79] If the MEF is sent to the wrong address, it should be reissued to the correct address and the effective date relates to the date that the second MEF was correctly sent.[80] On the other hand, if the absent parent has deliberately avoided receipt of the MEF, then the CSO can determine the date that the MEF would have been given or sent had that not happened.[81] Then that is the effective date.

If the person with care loses out financially because the CSA delays in sending the MEF to the absent parent, she can complain and seek compensation (see p30).

The absent parent cannot delay the effective date of an assessment by disputing paternity, unless he delays the issue of the MEF. The CSO will not make an assessment until the issue of paternity is resolved (see p40), but, if the CSO later decides that the alleged absent parent is the father, the assessment will be backdated to these same dates.

If there are multiple applications for child maintenance and these are treated as a single application (see p76), the effective date is fixed using the earlier or earliest application.[82]

Court orders

Where there is or has been a court maintenance order for at least one of the children named in the assessment, the following rules apply whether the assessment is a full one or an IMA.

Where the order is in force on the date the assessment is made, the effective date is two days after that date.[83] The order ceases to have effect from the effective date (see below).[84]

Where a full assessment replaces an IMA which was made when an order was in force, the effective date of the full assessment is the same as the replaced IMA.[85]

There are special rules where the order stops being in force while the CSA is considering the maintenance application. These are, that where, on or after 18 April 1995, an order stopped being in force before the full assessment is made, and:

- that was not because an IMA was made; *and*
- the date the order stopped being in force was after the MEF was actually given or sent to the absent parent or, where the absent parent is the applicant, after an effective MAF (see p59) was received

then the effective date is the next day after the court order stopped being in force, regardless of when the assessment is made.[86] Otherwise, the effective date is fixed by the usual rules for assessments (see above).

Liability for maintenance continues until the order stops being in force and the absent parent should continue making payments while awaiting the assessment. For collection and enforcement of arrears see p397.

Backdating assessments

An assessment begins earlier than the date on which the absent parent was sent the MEF or sent a MAF to the CSA, where:

- an assessment is in force for an absent parent and a different person with care applies for child maintenance and a second assessment is made then, except where the second assessment is an IMA or a full assessment replacing an IMA (for which see pp311-14), the effective date of the second assessment is the first day of the maintenance period (see below) beginning seven days or less after the parties are notified of the second assessment;[87]
- an assessment has been in force for a qualifying child, but has been terminated because there has been a change of person with care and an application naming the new person with care has been made;[88]
- a section 7 assessment has been cancelled at the request of the Scottish child applicant or because s/he is no longer a child, and an application for children who were qualifying children under the previous assessment has been made.[89]

In these two cases, the Secretary of State may treat the new application as received up to eight weeks earlier than the date it was actually received by the CSA but no earlier than the date on which the previous assessment ended.[90] The effective date is then fixed by the normal rules.

Maintenance periods

Child maintenance is calculated on a weekly basis, although it is not always paid on a weekly basis (see p392). It is payable in respect of successive seven-day periods with the first period beginning on the effective date.[91] The only exception is where there is an assessment in force for the same absent parent to pay for a different child to a different person with care. In that case, the maintenance period of the new assessment begins on the same day of the week as the existing assessment.[92]

The main significance of the maintenance period is that, after a review, any fresh assessment comes into effect on the first day of the maintenance period (see pp357, 363 and 366).

Effective dates of interim maintenance assessments

For details of the four categories of IMAs, see p296. For effective dates of IMAs where a court order exists, see p304. For effective dates after a review, see Chapter 16. For effective dates of Category D IMAs and where an IMA replaces another IMA, see pp312-14.

The effective date of a Category A IMA is the first day after it is made which falls on the same day of the week as the day the MEF was actually given or sent to the absent parent or, where the absent parent is the applicant, the day the MAF was received by the CSA.[93] For example, if the MEF had been sent on a Monday and the IMA was made on a Thursday some months later, it would take effect on the first Monday following that Thursday.

The effective date of a Category B IMA made after 22 January 1996 and a Category C IMA is the date the MEF was actually given or sent to the absent parent or, where the absent parent is the applicant, the day the MAF was received by the CSA.[94] For Category B IMAs made before 23 January 1996, see 1995/96 *Child Support Handbook*, p313.

However, for Category A, B or C IMAs where the effective date fixed by these rules would be less than eight weeks after the MEF was actually given or sent to the absent parent or, where the absent parent is the applicant, the day the MAF was received by the CSA, and:

- the absent parent has provided his name, address and confirmation of paternity within the four week period; *or*
- the CSO considers the delay in providing those details was unavoidable; *then*

the effective date is fixed using the rules for full assessments (see p303).[95]

6. WHEN DOES AN ASSESSMENT END

An assessment continues until a CSO:

- cancels it (see below);
- accepts it has ceased to have effect (see p309);
- sets it aside (see p352); *or*
- reviews it (see Chapter 16).

Some assessments are replaced by another while in other cases no further assessment is made. Where arrears remain after an assessment ends, the CSA may still collect arrears. The person with care should make it clear to the CSA whether or not she wishes the CSA to collect and/or enforce arrears. If she refuses to authorise the CSA to collect and/or enforce, the CSA cannot do so. This is the case even for section 6 applicants whose assessment has been cancelled. Please let CPAG know of cases where the CSA ignores the person with care's instructions.

Requests to cancel assessments

Where an application was made under section 4 (ie, voluntarily, see p55) or under section 7 (ie, by a Scottish child applicant, see p42) the assessment (including an IMA) must be cancelled if the applicant requests it.[96] No reasons have to be given for the request.

Requests from section 6 applicants

A section 6 applicant – ie, a parent with care in receipt of income support (IS), family credit (FC) or disability working allowance (DWA) – may want to withdraw from the child support scheme. For cases where the assessment has not yet been made, see p70. A CSO must cancel an assessment (including an IMA) on a section 6 applicant's request if:[97]

- she is no longer on IS/FC/DWA (for coming off benefit to get an assessment cancelled see p71); *or*
- the Secretary of State allows her to withdraw authorisation (see p72).

A CSO may cancel an assessment if the applicant is no longer the person with care of all of the children named in the application, even if she is still the person with care of some of those children.[98]

Living together

A CSO *may* cancel an assessment if the parent with care and absent parent are living together and they both request a cancellation.[99] 'Living together' is not defined in the Acts or regulations. It does not mean the same as 'living together as husband and wife', a different phrase used in some child support regulations.[100] CSO guidance states that the main factor is whether the absent parent and the parent with care share the same household (for 'household', see p45).[101] Once the absent parent and parent with care have lived together continuously for six months, the assessment ceases to have effect (see p309).

In practice, where the parties all share the same household, the absent parent will no longer be absent (see p45), so the child will no longer be a qualifying child and the assessment ceases to have effect anyway (see p309).

Other cancellations

Some changes of circumstance lead to a cancellation whether or not a request is made. The CSA may be aware of a change from a request, a notification by the parent with care under her duty to do so (see p155) or from the DSS computer.[102] A CSO *must* cancel an assessment (including an IMA) where:

- the person with care, absent parent or qualifying child is no longer habitually resident in the UK (see p47 for 'habitually resident');[103] *or*
- a Scottish child applicant ceases to be habitually resident in Scotland.[104]

Date of cancellation

An assessment is cancelled with effect from the date the request was received or a different date determined by the CSO. Where the CSO can choose to fix the date of cancellation, that is a discretionary decision, so the welfare of any children must be taken into account (see p52).

Where an assessment is cancelled because the absent parent and parent with care are living together, the cancellation will usually be from the date they started living together, but it can be any other date.[105]

The assessment is cancelled from the date of the change of circumstance where:

- the person with care is no longer person with care for all the children named in the assessment;[106] *or*
- a party is no longer habitually resident in the UK;[107] *or*
- a Scottish child applicant is no longer habitually resident in Scotland.[108]

In all other cases, except Category A or D IMAs, the assessment can only be cancelled from the date the request to cancel was received or a later date.[109] There are no rules for Category A or D IMAs except those above.

A later date may be appropriate where an applicant has requested that the assessment end on a later date or a benefit claimant has requested cancellation on the grounds that she is coming off benefit soon.[110]

In a case where the CSO must cancel the assessment on request (see p307) these regulations may not be lawful. This is because the 1991 Act does not clearly allow the CSO to delay the date of cancellation in these cases.[111] If you lose out in a case like this because the CSO set the cancellation date at later than the date the request was received, seek advice.

The full weekly amount of the assessment is due for the maintenance period (see p306) in which the cancellation date falls,[112] except where a Category A or D IMA is cancelled, when it is only due to the cancellation date.[113]

Notification of cancellation

When a CSO cancels an assessment, s/he must notify the absent parent, person with care and Scottish child applicant of the decision, if this is reasonably practicable, giving reasons and explaining how to seek a review.[114] The only exception to this is where a Category A or D IMA is cancelled on the request of the absent parent, when only the applicant need be informed.[115]

Refusal to cancel an assessment

A CSO who refuses a request to cancel a maintenance assessment must notify the applicant as soon as possible, giving reasons and explaining how to seek a review.[116]

Assessments ceasing to have effect

An assessment (including an IMA) ceases to have effect:[117]

- when there is no longer a qualifying child – eg, the youngest child reaches 19 or the only qualifying child dies;
- when the absent parent ceases to be a parent of the child or all the qualifying children – eg, the child is adopted;
- on the death of the person with care or the absent parent;
- when the absent parent and the parent with care have been living together for a continuous period of six months; *or*
- when a new maintenance assessment is made for the qualifying child.

The CSO must decide whether the assessment has ceased to have effect.[118]

Figure 14.1

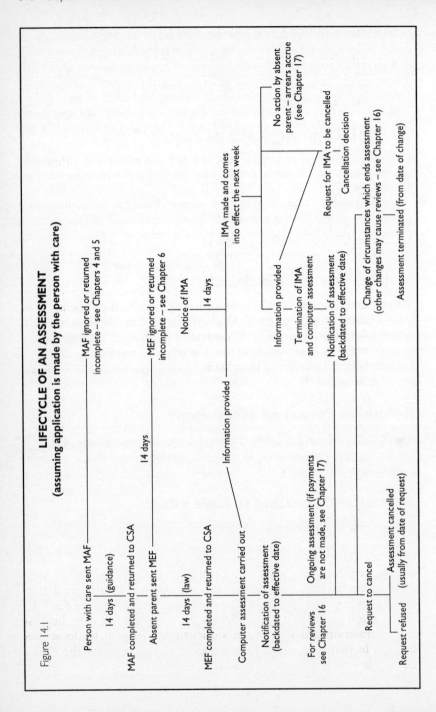

LIFECYCLE OF AN ASSESSMENT
(assuming application is made by the person with care)

Notification of CSO decision on ceasing to have effect

A CSO who makes a decision on whether an assessment has ceased to have effect must notify the absent parent, person with care and Scottish child applicant as soon as possible, giving reasons and explaining how to seek a review.[119]

Ending interim maintenance assessments

The rules above apply to all IMAs, except where we note otherwise. Guidance to CSOs states that Category A, C and D IMAs can *only* be ended in the circumstances below,[120] but we disagree.

A CSO may cancel an IMA and:

- make a full assessment; *or*
- make an IMA of the same category; *or*
- make an IMA of a different category; *or*
- make no assessment.

The rules (see below) enable a CSO to adjust maintenance payable to reflect mistakes, changes of circumstance and the non-co-operation or co-operation of the parties. A CSO is only required to end an IMA where s/he receives enough information to make a full assessment. Apart from that case, the CSO has a discretion whether to cancel an IMA, whether to make a new IMA and (in some cases) to fix the effective date of the cancellation. When making those decisions, the CSO must consider the welfare of any children involved (see p52).

Whether the total amount payable will be less or more once a full assessment is made depends on the circumstances of the case. Where a full assessment is made after an IMA, the amount due under that IMA from its effective date becomes the amount of the new assessment,[121] even though this may be before the effective date of the new assessment. There are two exceptions where the amount due does not change before the effective date of the full assessment:

- the full assessment is for minimum child maintenance (see p167);[122] *and*
- for any period before 19 April 1995.

Child maintenance is payable at the rate set in the full assessment for the period from the effective date of that assessment to the effective date of the IMA where that is later.[123] The exception to this is where the CSO makes a full assessment, but not from its usual effective date, because the information provided is not sufficient for her/him to do so (see below). In that case, child maintenance is not payable for the period before the effective date of the IMA.[124]

The amount owed for the past period may go up or down when a full assessment is made. The full assessment will almost always be less than a Category A or D IMA (see pp297 and 299). However, the effective date of the full assessment will usually be at least several weeks earlier than that of the IMA. So, the weekly amount due will usually be lower but for a longer period. There may be an overpayment (see p393).

CSO has enough information

Once the CSO has enough information to make a full assessment for all the children named in the IMA, then, regardless of how that information was obtained, the IMA ceases to have effect in the following way.

Where the IMA was made following an application and the CSO:

- has enough information to make the assessment for the whole of the period beginning with the effective date of the full assessment (see p303), the IMA ceases to have effect on the first day of the maintenance period in which the CSA received the information;[125] *or*
- has only enough information to make a full assessment for part of that period then the IMA ceases to have effect:[126]
  - where the CSA had that information by 18 April 1995, on that date; or, if not,
  - on the first day of the maintenance period in which the CSA received the information.

Where the IMA was made because the CSO did not have enough information to carry out a review (see p296) and s/he now has that information, the CSO must, as soon as practicable, cancel the IMA from its effective date.[127]

Example 14.1: Cancellation of an IMA and replacement with a full assessment

A Category A IMA for one 15 year old is £79.50 (the maintenance requirement is £53 – see example 13.8).

Beverley's father completely fails to respond to the MEF sent to him on Wednesday 15 May 1996, and to subsequent reminders. The IMA of £79.50 is made on Friday 19 July with an effective date of Wednesday 24 July.

After seeking advice, the absent parent provides the full information needed for the assessment by Monday 12 August. The IMA is cancelled from Wednesday 7 August. The replacement assessment of £28.50 a week made on Friday 23 August has an effective date of Wednesday 15 May.

As no payments have been made during the period, the initial arrears are 18 weeks at £28.50 = £513.

Unavoidable delay

The CSO may cancel an IMA where the absent parent's delay in returning the MEF or providing information required to make an assessment or carry out a review was unavoidable.

Where the delay was unavoidable for the whole period the IMA was in force, the IMA will usually be cancelled completely.[128] A full maintenance assessment may then be made from the usual effective date (see p303). It is doubtful whether a further IMA can then be made, though one could be made on a later review (see p296).

The CSO may replace a Category A, B or D IMA with *another IMA of the same category* which starts from a later date where the delay was only unavoidable for part of the period of the replaced IMA (see below and example 14.2). Maintenance will then only be payable from the effective date of the replacement IMA. The exception to this is a Category A or B IMA in force before 18 April 1995 where the delay became avoidable before 18 April 1995.[129] In that case, the IMA cannot be cancelled before the date the delay became avoidable.

Where the cancelled IMA was made after 17 April 1995, the effective date of the new IMA is, for:

- **Category A or D**, the first day of the first maintenance period after the maintenance period in which the delay became avoidable;[130] *or*
- **Category B**, where the replacement IMA is made after 22 January 1996, the date the MEF was actually given or sent to the absent parent or, where the absent parent is the applicant, the day the MAF was received by the CSA;[131]
- **Category B**, where the replacement IMA is made before 23 January 1996, the same date as for a Category A IMA.[132]

However, where the cancelled Category A or B IMA was made before 18 April 1995 the effective date cannot be before 18 April 1995. If this would be the effect of the above rules, then instead the effective date is the first day of the first maintenance period which begins after 17 April 1995.[133]

Replacing an IMA with one of a different category

The CSO may replace any IMA with *an IMA of a different category* (see also example 14.2). This may alter the rate of maintenance from the effective date of the replacement IMA.

Where the new IMA is a Category A, C or D IMA, the effective date of the new IMA is the later of the first day of the maintenance period in which the CSO decides to make the new IMA *and* the first day of the maintenance period which begins after 19 April 1995.[134] The old IMA is cancelled with effect from the effective date of the new IMA.[135]

Where the new IMA is a Category B IMA, then the old IMA and any earlier IMA which it immediately followed is cancelled with effect from the later of its effective date *and* 22 January 1996.[136] The effective date of the new IMA is:

- where the cancelled IMA (or the first of the two cancelled IMAs) had caused a court order to cease to have effect (see p304), the effective date of that IMA;[137] *or*
- otherwise, the date the MEF was actually given or sent to the absent parent or, where the absent parent is the applicant, the day the MAF was received by the CSA.[138]

Example 14.2: Cancellation of an IMA, replacement by another IMA and overpayments

Jack's father fails to respond to an MEF issued on Friday 2 February 1996 and to subsequent reminders. On 16 April the CSO makes a Category A IMA of £103.95 (the maintenance requirement is £69.30) with an effective date of Friday 19 April.

The absent parent returns the MEF to the CSA on 10 June, explaining that he was in hospital from January 1996 until 26 May and that he has only just got his affairs in order. He refuses to give details of his income.

After issuing a further warning notice which is ignored, the CSO accepts there was unavoidable delay in returning the MEF until 10 June, but decides that the delay in providing the details requested became avoidable on that date. The CSO cancels the IMA completely, but a fresh Category A IMA of £103.95 is made with an effective date of Friday 14 June 1996.

On 15 July the CSA receives a letter from the absent parent explaining that he is self-employed receiving about £80 a week and has no accounts but will have them soon. On 3 September the CSO accepts this and cancels the second Category A IMA with effect from 30 August and makes a Category C IMA of £30 with effect from Friday 30 August.

On 5 September the absent parent's total liability is £1,173.45:

14 June – 29 August 1996	11 weeks at £103.95 a week
30 August 1996 – 5 September	11 weeks at £30 a week

The absent parent pays £500 towards arrears from his savings and makes weekly payments of £30.

In October he provides accounts. On 31 October the CSO makes a full assessment of £16. The effective date is 29 March, eight weeks after the MEF was issued (see p303).

The total amount of child maintenance at 31 October is 31 weeks at £16 a week = £496.

The absent parent has paid £740 so there is an overpayment of £244. The assessment is adjusted to £4.80 for 21 weeks to recoup the overpayment (see p394).

Procedural error or no jurisdiction to make an IMA

A CSO may cancel an IMA because there was a material procedural error in connection with the making of the IMA.[139] This applies, for example, where the warning letter was not sent to the absent parent.[140]

A CSO may cancel an IMA because there was no jurisdiction to make it in the first place or there would no longer be jurisdiction to make it.[141] This applies, for example, where the absent parent was never habitually resident in the UK or where he once was, but is no longer.[142]

Where a CSO cancels an IMA for one of these reasons, s/he can choose the date that cancellation has effect.[143]

Request to cancel

An absent parent may apply to have a Category A or D IMA cancelled.[144] The application must be in writing, giving reasons for the request – eg, that the absent parent disputes parentage.[145] The CSO has discretion whether to cancel the IMA and if so from what date, as well as whether a new IMA or full assessment should be made.[146]

Once a CSO has made a decision, s/he must notify the absent parent as soon as possible, giving reasons and explaining how to seek a review.[147]

7. HOW AN ASSESSMENT AFFECTS BENEFIT

In this section, we cover the effect of *receiving* child support maintenance on means-tested benefits: income support (IS), family credit (FC), disability working allowance (DWA), housing benefit (HB) and council tax benefit (CTB). Other social security benefits are not affected. Child maintenance *paid* by an absent parent is not taken into account when calculating his, or his partner's, means-tested benefits.

For full details of how means-tested benefits are calculated, including the effect of other maintenance payments, see CPAG's *National Welfare Benefits Handbook*.

For details of the benefit penalty, see p112.

For details of the deductions from IS for contributions to child maintenance, see p168.

Income support

Payments of child maintenance may be made direct to the person with care (see below) or via the CSA (see below). From April 1997, parents with care who are not lifted off IS by receipt of child maintenance will build up a 'maintenance bonus' of £5 a week (or maintenance paid if that is less). This bonus will be paid as a lump sum if she leaves IS to take up work of 16 hours or more a week.[148]

Payment direct to the person with care

Payments of child maintenance are treated as income and are taken into account on a weekly basis.[149] Payments are treated as income in the week they are received by the parent with care, except that child maintenance due before the IS claim, but paid during the claim, is treated as paid in the week it was due.[150] Lump sum payments are always treated as income not capital.[151]

Payments of child maintenance made regularly have to be converted into a weekly amount in order to be taken into account in the IS calculation – eg, where payments are made monthly, multiply by 12 and divide by 52.[152] Where payments are made at irregular intervals, each payment is divided over the weeks since the last payment.[153]

There is no disregard for child maintenance when calculating IS, so the amount received is taken into account in full as income.[154] This is so even if the child maintenance is paid to the child, since it is counted as the income of the claimant.[155] IS will, therefore, be reduced by this amount.

The Benefits Agency should not assume that child maintenance payments are being made as soon as the CSA sends notification of the assessment. If the Benefits Agency asks for a person with care's IS order book to be returned before payments begin, she should contact the Benefits Agency to explain the situation. Her IS should not be reduced until payments are made.

If, after her IS has been reduced, one of the payments due from the absent parent direct to the person with care is missed, she should contact the Benefits Agency to request that the extra IS be paid for that period. The Benefits Agency should do this without waiting for the CSA to enforce the payment of maintenance.

The person with care can contact the CSA to take enforcement action to chase missing payments and to have payments made to the CSA. For CSA collection and enforcement, see Chapter 17.

Payment to the Child Support Agency

The CSA can arrange to collect maintenance so that the absent parent does not have to pay direct to the person with care. For details of when this may happen, see p388. The CSA can keep any payments made by the absent parent to the CSA for a person with care on IS.[156] When the CSA does this the Benefits Agency does not take that payment into account.

Alternatively, the payment is made via the Benefits Agency to the person with care in the IS order book or girocheque.[157] However, this has the same practical end-result as there is one order/girocheque per week, which is part IS and part child maintenance. If the absent parent does not make the payment one week, the person with care can still cash the full amount of the order/girocheque, but it will all be IS.[158] If the missed payment of child maintenance is later made by the absent parent to the CSA, it will be retained by the CSA.[159]

Payment of arrears

The CSA intends that arrears payments should be made by the absent parent to the CSA. In these cases, the CSA retains the arrears equal to the overpayment of IS which has occurred because the maintenance was not paid on the due date.[160] If a payment of child maintenance is made late, but the person with care has not had her IS made up, there is no need for any adjustment to her benefit and, if collected by the CSA, the arrears should be passed on to the person with care.

There are usually arrears at the beginning of an assessment (see p398). Again, these arrears will almost always be paid to the CSA where the person with care is on IS. If the payment is made to the person with care, the full amount of the overpaid benefit for the past period can be recovered by the Benefits Agency.[161]

Loss of income support

Persons with care lose entitlement to IS when the child maintenance due increases their income over the IS applicable amount. If the person with care is only a few pounds over the IS level, she may find herself worse off because of the loss of passported benefits – eg, free school meals, full health service benefits (see p321) and access to the social fund.

A person with care who is not a parent of the qualifying child is a section 4 applicant and can therefore ask for the assessment to be cancelled (see p307). On reclaiming IS the issue of notional income may arise (see CPAG's *National Welfare Benefits Handbook*). We do not know of any cases where this has happened, but please let us know if it does.

The loss of these benefits, particularly in families with school age children, could have a greater effect than the benefit penalty (see p112). However, when deciding whether to withhold authorisation from the

CSA, the parent with care is unlikely to have the information needed to calculate the assessment. A section 6 applicant who finds herself in this situation should consider requesting the cancellation of the assessment on the grounds that she is no longer in receipt of IS (see p71). On re-applying for IS, she can withhold her authorisation from the CSA and argue that the family is at risk of undue distress. If this is not accepted, she can take the benefit penalty and appeal (see p112).

If a payment of maintenance is not made on time, an IS claim can be made. If the Benefits Agency delays in adjudicating the claim while the CSA enforces the child maintenance, make a complaint and let CPAG know. The Benefits Agency cannot take into account child maintenance due under an assessment but which has not been paid (see p316).

Reclaiming income support

Full mortgage interest is not usually included in the IS calculation for the first 26 or 39 weeks of any IS claim (depending on circumstances): see the *National Welfare Benefits Handbook* for details. The IS calculation includes 100 per cent of eligible mortgage interest where:[162]

- a person with care stops being entitled to IS as a result of receiving child maintenance; *and*
- at the time that happened, she was receiving 100 per cent eligible mortgage interest; *and*
- her maintenance assessment is then reduced or ended because:
  - the child support regulations are changed on or after 18 April 1995, for example, a change in the formula; *or*
  - the assessment is an IMA and it is ended and not replaced *or* is replaced by another IMA or by a full assessment; *and*
- she claims IS within 26 weeks of the date she stopped being entitled to it.

Family credit and disability working allowance

To be entitled to FC or DWA, a claimant or her/his partner must be in paid work of 16 hours a week or more. For details of all the conditions of entitlement, see CPAG's *National Welfare Benefits Handbook*.

No child maintenance at time of claim

If a person with care makes a claim for FC/DWA, and she has not already applied for child maintenance, she will be contacted by the CSA. The FC/DWA claim is not held up for the CSA assessment. Any FC/DWA award is not affected by any later assessment or payment of child maintenance.[163]

Child support maintenance due

If payments of a regular amount are being made regularly at the date of claim, including any renewal claim, the weekly equivalent of the payment counts as income.[164] If the person with care was notified (see p299) of an assessment in the 13 weeks ending with the week before the week in which the claim was made, weekly income is total payments received from the week of the notification to the week before the week of claim, divided by the number of weeks in that period.[165] If neither of these is the case, weekly income is total payments received in the 13 weeks ending with the week before the week of the claim, divided by 13.[166] For these purposes, weeks begin on a Sunday.[167]

If this calculation gives a weekly figure higher than the amount of the assessment, then the assessment figure is used.[168] This may happen where arrears are being paid off. It may also apply where the assessment is reduced between the benefit claim and the decision on that claim.

Where arrears are paid in a lump sum, that may count as capital.[169] Unless that takes the claimant over the capital limit (FC – £8,000, DWA – £16,000), s/he may be better off by persuading the Benefits Agency to regard the arrears as capital.

Maintenance disregard

£15 a week maintenance is disregarded when calculating FC/DWA.[170] Only £15 is disregarded from total maintenance received, including other forms of maintenance such as spousal maintenance.

Where the claimant's or partner's child support assessment ends because the child(ren) named in the assessment no longer live with her or are no longer qualifying children (see p41) and a FC/DWA claim is made, the disregard will only apply to any payments of arrears if the absent parent was once the partner of the claimant/claimant's partner (and, for DWA, a child still lives with the claimant).

Changes of child maintenance

FC/DWA is awarded for a period of 26 weeks and the award is not altered because of changes of circumstance.[171] This rule does not apply to the application of the reduced benefit direction (see p116).

On the first application to the CSA, most persons with care on FC/DWA gain, because maintenance paid does not affect the FC/DWA award until the six-month renewal. Similarly, any child maintenance review which increases the amount due during that time is to the person with care's advantage.

However, if, during the period of of an FC/DWA award which took into account payments of maintenance, either payments are missed or the amount of the maintenance assessment falls as a result of a review, the FC/DWA is not increased to compensate for the loss of that income. CPAG has lobbied (unsuccessfully to date) for a system to ensure that FC claimants do not suffer as a result of missed payments, and we want to hear of any such cases where difficulties are caused.

The DSS pays some compensation to persons with care on FC/DWA who have their assessments reduced as a result of the 18 April 1995 changes or any later changes in child support legislation. See p165 for details.

Housing benefit and council tax benefit

There are no special rules for child maintenance when calculating HB/CTB, except that £15 weekly is disregarded when calculating HB/CTB for persons with care who are not in receipt of IS.[172] The disregard applies to all forms of maintenance paid by a former partner or a parent of a child, but only if there is a child in the family claiming HB/CTB. Even if there is more than one type or source of maintenance, only £15 is disregarded from the total.

If there is a change in the amount of child maintenance received, the person with care should notify the local authority benefits section. Reviews of HB/CTB should also be requested by FC claimants who suffer a benefit penalty.

In theory, a reduction in a parent with care's HB caused by receipt of maintenance could, in turn, increase the maintenance payable by the absent parent. However, in practice this is extremely unlikely to occur, because the majority of parents with care have insufficient income to affect the assessment at all and, where there is an effect, it is most probably too small to trigger a change of circumstance review (see p355).

There is no obligation for HB/CTB claimants not on IS/FC/DWA with qualifying children to apply to the CSA. However, a local authority might use the notional income rules and decide that claimants who opt not to apply have deprived themselves of income.[173] This would be extremely difficult in practice, as local authorities will not have enough information to calculate the maintenance which would be assessed.

The notional income rule is used for claimants who decide not to apply for FC but claim HB/CTB. Therefore, if persons with care working 16 hours or more a week decide not to claim FC in order to avoid having to apply for child maintenance, the local authority may treat them as receiving an amount of FC. The alternative is to apply for FC, accept the benefit penalty and then ask for HB/CTB to be reviewed.

For details of the notional income rules, see CPAG's *National Welfare Benefits Handbook*.

Health service benefits

People who are not on IS/FC/DWA or are on DWA but have more than £8,000 capital are not automatically exempt from all NHS charges. They may be entitled to full or partial reductions of charges on low income grounds. This covers prescriptions, dental treatment, sight tests, glasses, wigs, fabric support and fares to hospital. For these purposes, where child maintenance payments are made:

- regularly, income is the weekly equivalent of payments; *and*
- not regularly, income is total payments in the 13 weeks before the claim, divided by 13.

There is no disregard. For full details see CPAG's *National Welfare Benefits Handbook*.

8. TAXATION OF CHILD MAINTENANCE

Person with care

Child maintenance is not taxable income.

Absent parent

Child support maintenance qualifies for tax relief, but only where the parties were married or are still married. The relief ends if the ex-spouse remarries.

The absent parent makes payments gross and then claims tax relief up to the level of the married couple's tax allowance, currently £1,790 a year. The amount of maintenance due in the tax year up to this limit is deducted from the absent parent's taxable income. This relief was restricted to 15 per cent from April 1995.

Departures

This chapter covers:

The information in this chapter is based on early sources and therefore is subject to change, particularly for the full scheme. The regulations for the pilot scheme became available just before we went to press: The Child Support Departure Direction (Anticipatory Application) Regulations 1996. However, it was not possible to include the full contents of the regulations and therefore details must be checked when advising on a particular case. CPAG's Welfare Rights Bulletin *(see Appendix 8) will contain updates, including details of the full scheme when it is finalised. The next edition of this* Handbook, *planned for April 1997, will include full details of departure.*

The Child Support Act 1995 introduces a system of 'departure' from the standard formula. This means that a degree of flexibility will now be available when setting child maintenance levels, and, in specified situations, an alternative formula, taking into account additional costs or information, can be used to recalculate the assessment. The standard formula will be 'departed' from where the Secretary of State believes there are grounds for doing so. The DSS is expecting that departure will not be common, but estimates about 20 per cent of cases will apply for departure and about half will be successful.

1. DATE OF IMPLEMENTATION

Although there is no definite date for the full introduction of departure available to all Child Support Agency (CSA) clients, it is likely that the scheme will be up and running in December 1996. In addition, in order to prevent the CSA being swamped with applications on the first day of the departure scheme, the CSA has the power to take on cases in batches.[1] The take-on process will not be set until after the results of the pilot project, but it is likely that the oldest cases will be assessed first. It is most probable that all directions would take effect from the start date of the scheme, irrespective of their place in the queue.

The pilot project

The departure scheme will be piloted for six months, beginning on 9 April 1996.[2] The experience from the pilot should enable the DSS and CSA to correct any deficiencies in the regulations, the procedures or the computer programs before the full scheme takes effect. However, any departure directions awarded to those people who opt to take part in the pilot project will only take effect from the implementation of the full scheme.[3] Therefore the only advantage to parents who do take part in the pilot is that their applications will be processed in advance and they will be aware of the outcome before it takes effect. These directions will be reviewed just before implementation later in the year to take into account any relevant change of personal circumstances or in the regulations.

The pilot will take place primarily among cases where the person with care lives in the south-east of England. A random selection of parents with care with assessments made by Hastings CSAC and their respective absent parents will be contacted by the CSA in mid-March 1996 and invited to apply for departure. This is to be repeated until sufficient applications are received. The pilot needs to cover all the different grounds (see below) for departure, and therefore, if the Hastings CSAC cases do not provide sufficient cases in certain categories, these will be sought in other regions. Do not contact the CSA to take part in the pilot unless an invitation is received; the CSA wants the pilot to be representative of their caseload and not self-selecting. If a parent does not respond to the invitation to take part in the pilot, s/he may apply under the final scheme.

2. GROUNDS FOR DEPARTURE

The grounds on which departure can be considered fall into three categories:[4]

- a parent has expenses which the standard formula has not recognised – these will more often be applied for by an absent parent;

- the formula has been over-generous in allowing certain costs or the parent appears not to be disclosing all his income or utilising his capital to produce income (see p329) – these will more often be applied for by a person with care; *and*
- pre-April 1993 property or capital transfers (see p332).

There is the power both to introduce further grounds using regulations at a later date and to decide not to implement some of the grounds contained in the 1995 Act. These issues will be examined during the pilot and therefore parents who believe their assessment is unfair for a reason other than those already included in the departures scheme could let the CSA know.

Special expenses

Departure is possible where the applicant has:[5]

- costs of keeping in contact with the child(ren) for whom the assessment is payable;
- costs of supporting a step-child and other children in the family;
- travel-to-work costs not taken into account in the assessment;
- costs resulting from a long-term illness or disability of the applicant or a dependant;
- debts incurred before the couple separated which were for the benefit of both parents or a child; *or*
- pre-April 1993 financial commitments from which either s/he cannot withdraw or it would be unreasonable to expect her/him to withdraw.

With the contact costs, travel-to-work costs, debts and pre-1993 financial commitments, the first £15 of the combined costs will be disregarded. Although there is the power to limit to a maximum amount how much can be included as special expenses,[6] this is not to be used in the first instance. However, consideration will be given as to whether the expense is reasonable. There are other factors which must be or cannot be taken into account when considering a departure application (see p337).

Contact costs

Only travel costs to visit children or for the children to visit their absent parent will be covered, not the costs of treats or overnight stays. Either the cost of fuel on the most economical route or second-class rail fares will be covered. The costs will be based on actual visits made in a previous period or proposed in a future period where there is a recent separation, a change of arrangement or where the absent parent claims that he has been unable to make the desired visits because of a lack of money. If the visits are not kept up – whether due to the absent parent's failure or to the person with care preventing contact – any departure direction can be cancelled (see p347). Any court order concerning contact would be used by the CSA when considering what is reasonable contact. Other factors will also be taken into account when deciding what are reasonable costs – for example, if the absent parent moves further away from the children without any good reason.

This ground will not apply at all to parents who share care of the qualifying children to the extent that they have day-to-day care (see p267), as this is in theory taken into account in the formula. It also does not apply to a person with care who is an absent parent of another child with whom she has contact.

Costs of supporting a step-child

The costs of supporting a child in the family who is not the parent's own child can be considered – see p40 for definition of a parent. This includes children of a current or former partner whether or not the applicant is married to their parent, but not other children who may be living as part of the family – for example, the grandchild of the parent being assessed for child support. However, we use the phrase 'step-child' here for simplicity. This ground cannot apply to Category B interim maintenance assessments (see p297).

Although it is not included in the Act nor mentioned in the parliamentary debates, it is now intended that this ground will only apply to step-families formed before April 1993. The DSS argues that any step-families formed after that date did so in the knowledge of a child maintenance liability and that they are covered by protected income calculation (see p253). However, we suggest that any other step-families should submit information of hardship to the CSA in the hope of influencing this policy decision at the end of the pilot.

A calculation will be performed to determine the extent of the resources available for any step-child(ren) who was before April 1993, and still is, part of the family. This will first compare any child maintenance due for the child(ren) with his/her income support (IS) personal allowances and any relevant premiums not already included in exempt income (see p183). If the child maintenance due is more than the IS equivalent, the departure application fails.

If the child maintenance is lower than the IS equivalent, then the child(ren)'s other parent – where she is the partner of the parent being assessed for child maintenance – is means-tested to see to what extent she can afford to support her children. This is similar to the means test for the support of any joint children (see p198); her net income is compared with her own personal allowance, any contribution towards a joint child (as assessed under the formula) or towards housing costs (as set by a departure direction – see p331) and the remaining allowances for the step-children. If her income is above this amount, she is deemed to be able to support her children. If not, the remaining allowances for the step-children are included in her partner's exempt income.

Example 15.1

a) Bob has been assessed to pay £30.24 for his two children, Carol and David. However, he lives with his partner, Zoe, their child, and three step-children: departure would only be possible if the step-family had been formed before April 1993. Zoe receives child benefit and maintenance of £20 a week for Yvonne (12) and Veronica (10), but nothing for Sam (4). The departure officer may well consider it unreasonable to give a departure direction if, for example, Zoe had refused to accept maintenance for Sam. However, if her CSA assessment was nil, the following calculation would be carried out:

		£
Personal allowances:	Yvonne (12)	24.10
	Veronica (10)	16.45
	Sam (4)	16.45
Total *		57.00
less maintenance due		20.00
Allowances outstanding		37.00

* no family premium applies as it is already included in Bob's exempt income for the joint child (see example 9.6).

Can Zoe afford to contribute £37 for the children as well as £47.90 for herself? As her only income is child benefit, she cannot support even herself, let alone her children. (Although the family receives family credit, this cannot be set against the children's allowances as it has already been taken into account in full as Bob's income.) A departure direction for a special expense of £37 can therefore be made if it would affect the assessment – see example 15.6.

It is very nearly Veronica's 11th birthday, which will increase her personal allowance by £7.65; this should be taken into account by the departure officer who can decide that this is a change of circumstances at which the direction should be changed (see p347).

If the maintenance for her daughters was voluntary and Zoe had recently applied to the CSA for as assessment for them, but also for maintenance for Sam (4), the departure officer may not make a decision until these assessments were made.

b) Some months later the CSA issues assessments of £4.80 from Wayne and £30.35 from Terence (see example 12.5). In addition, by this time Zoe is working and a review of Bob's assessment has resulted in an increased liability to £40.39 (see example 12.7).

	£
Total personal allowances for the children	57.00
less maintenance due	35.15
Allowances outstanding	21.85

		£
Zoe's earnings of £90 are compared with		
Personal allowances	Zoe	47.90
	Ricky (half)*	8.23
Family premium (half)*		5.28
Other children's allowances outstanding		21.85
Housing costs		nil
Total		83.26

As her earnings are higher than this, Zoe can therefore afford to support the children herself and Bob's departure application fails.

* it has already been ascertained that Zoe can afford to support half of the joint child, Ricky – see example 9.6b

Travel-to-work costs

This ground deals with those parents whose travel costs are not adequately covered by the allowance in the formula (see p196). As the broad-brush allowance works on straight-line distances, those who have to travel, for example, around estuaries or mountains and in rural areas may benefit, as may those whose second class rail travel is more than 10 pence per mile.

Example 15.2

Steve (see example 9.5) has an allowance of £65 included in his exempt income for travel to work. However Steve's season ticket to London is £5,100 a year or £98 a week. Even with the first £15 disregarded (see p324) this is greater that the allowance. The departure officer has decided that it is reasonable to accept the travel costs as a special expense since Steve lives in Leicestershire in order to be near his two children, and he has not been able to find an equivalent job nearer to home. The special expense of £83 replaces the broad-brush allowance of £65. See example 15.4 for the recalculation of the assessment.

Costs of a long-term illness or disability

This applies to the reasonable costs due to a long-term illness or disability of the applicant or a dependant. Long-term illness will include terminal illnesses and illnesses which are likely to last more than 52 weeks. Disability will be defined as on p37. The types of costs which may be covered are to be stated in the regulations and include domestic help, heating, clothing, laundry and particular dietary requirements.

It is not expected that any costs relating to the qualifying child will be covered, as instead an application can be made to court for additional maintenance (see p37). In addition, only dependants in the family as defined on p50 are considered; hence any support given to an elderly relative, whether living under the same roof or not, is irrelevant.

It is expected that parents will first have applied for any relevant benefits – eg, disability living allowance (DLA) – and, where this is not the case, the parent will be advised to apply to the benefit before the departure application is determined. Any reasonable expenses for services over and above those available free of charge from a voluntary organisation or local authority should be taken into account. Any financial help towards these costs from any source, including DLA and any disability premiums, will be deducted.

Debts from the relationship

An application for departure can be made where one parent continues to pay debts incurred before a couple separated which were for the benefit of either both parents or a child who was living with them at that time. This will only apply where that parent making the payments no longer has the benefit of the purchases – for example, the payments for the former family car: departure may be successful where only the parent with care now has the use of the car, but not if the absent parent retains it. A debt incurred solely for the benefit of the other parent can be covered where the applicant is responsible for all of the debt.Where a couple did not live together, only debts incurred before the child was born will be eligible.

Credit card debts are excluded and overdrafts will be also excluded, unless a regular rate of repayment had been negotiated. In all cases any increase in repayments caused by rescheduling the debt will only be covered where there is a good reason for not having kept up with the original repayments – eg, a period of unemployment. On the other hand, if the parent has negotiated a lower rate of repayment in an effort to maintain the commitment, this would be accepted where there has been a substantial drop in income.

The first £15 is disregarded (see p324).

Pre-1993 financial commitments

In addition to debts of the relationship, other financial commitments made before 5 April 1993 may be a ground for departure if either a parent cannot withdraw from them or it would be unreasonable to expect her/him to withdraw. This case only applies where a court order or other maintenance agreement was in force between the parents at the time.[7] However, the commitments covered include those made after the breakdown of a relationship and those entirely for an absent parent's benefit. In addition, a financial commitment would include the payment of school fees or support for an elderly relative in a nursing home. Whether it is reasonable for him/her to withdraw from that commitment would depend on the circumstances of the case – eg, the age of the child at the private school.

The amount of increase in child maintenance can affect the amount allowed in the departure direction. The DSS has given the example of a single man who was paying £10 a week child maintenance under a court order and entered into a credit agreement before April 1993 to buy a car, a television, and a hi-fi system; it is accepted that it would be unreasonable to expect the absent parent to withdraw from the agreement. The repayments are £46.15 a week and the current CSA assessment is £35 a week. A departure direction might be given at £25 a week (the difference between the court order and the current liability) for the remainder of the repayment period.

Over-generous provision

Departure is possible where:[8]

- a parent's lifestyle is inconsistent with the level of his/her income;
- a parent's assets which do not produce an income are capable of doing so;
- a parent has diverted his/her income;[9]
- the housing costs included in the formula are unreasonably high;
- there are other people living in the home who could contribute towards the housing costs;
- travel-to-work costs taken into account in the formula are unreasonably high; or
- travel-to-work costs should be disregarded completely.

Example 15.3

An absent parent has a large well-furnished house in a stockbroker belt with several cars in the drive and a lifestyle which suggests a certain amount of wealth. He is a director of his own company and pays an average salary to himself and the same to his new partner. His declared income is only a few pounds above the mortgage and hence he is liable for a nil assessment. He is not subject to the excessive housing cost rule (see p191) nor to the minimum payment (see p167) as the couple have a child. The person with care could seek a departure on three grounds:

- the absent parent's lifestyle is incompatible with his declared income;
- the absent parent's new partner should contribute half of the housing costs; *and*
- the housing costs are unreasonably high.

If the new partner does not in fact contribute very much to the business, it would also be worth considering whether his income has been unreasonably diverted to her.

Extravagant lifestyle

Where a parent's lifestyle is inconsistent with his/her declared income, this can be a ground for departure. This will not apply where that parent is on income support (IS) or where s/he is supporting the lifestyle from capital. The whole lifestyle of the parent will be considered – eg, one or two expensive foreign holidays alone will not usually suggest a lifestyle inconsistent with income. It does not apply to situations where the parent's partner is supporting him/her; however, in these situations, it may be appropriate for departure to be applied for on the grounds of a partner's contribution to housing costs (see p331).

The issue of evidence and proof is a difficult one. The CSA will not simply accept allegations but neither will detailed investigations be embarked on. Instead, the evidence provided by the two parties will be weighed up. For example, if a parent with care gives a detailed statement substantiated as far as possible – eg, with registration numbers of cars – and the absent parent fails to respond, the application is likely to succeed; on the other hand, if the parent with care makes only a general allegation with one specific example which is then disproved by the absent parent, the application will most probably fail. Because of the complexity and sensitivity of these cases, they are likely to be referred to an independent tribunal (see p338), certainly in the early days of the full scheme, although not during the pilot.

If the departure is successful, then a notional income will be specified (see p346).

Use of assets

This applies where a parent has an asset worth more than £10,000 which does not produce as much income as it is capable of doing. For example, a second home which is not being rented would come within this. Once it has been decided that such an asset exists, it will be valued and a notional income set, using the judgment debt rate of interest – currently 8 per cent.

This ground will not apply where the parent with the asset is on IS or where s/he is retaining the asset for a purpose which the Secretary of State considers reasonable.

Diversion of income

An application for departure can be made where a parent has diverted his/her assets to someone or somewhere else – for example, where a self-employed parent pays his/her partner an inflated salary or has passed over capital to her/him, or where a parent is putting an unreasonably large amount into a superannuation scheme. It is not clear at this stage why the notional income and capital rules (see p217) should not suffice in many of these cases; indeed, parents in this situation before December should instead seek a review relying on notional income/capital.

Unreasonable housing costs

Where the parent is exempt from the excessive housing costs rule in the formula (see p191), the other party can apply for departure on the basis that the costs are unreasonably high. If the departure is successful, the costs cannot be reduced below the greater of £80 a week or half net income.

Partner's contribution towards housing costs

Although the 1995 Act refers simply to there being other people living in the home who could contribute towards the housing costs (which could include non-dependants – see p253), in the regulations this ground is limited to the situation where a partner can contribute to the housing costs. One of the key factors in deciding whether a partner can contribute will be her/his income and the contribution expected will vary from nil to 100 per cent according to the circumstances of the case. If the partner's income is not declared, a decision will be made on the basis of the information provided. Indeed, this ground can apply to a Category B interim maintenance assessment (see p297).

In addition, it might be reasonable to consider the origin of the housing costs – for example, if the home was purchased jointly by the couple, initially half could be considered as the absent parent's responsibility and often more dependent on their respective incomes; whereas, if the home in fact belongs to the second wife, pre-dates the marriage, she was previously paying the full costs herself and she can still afford to do so, there might be a case for arguing the large part – or even all – of the costs are attributable to her.

Unreasonable travel-to-work allowance

Departure applies both to the case where the travel-to-work allowance included in the formula (see p196) is unreasonably high compared to the costs – eg, the cost of a car is shared with a colleague or on a cheaper than average rail line – and where travel-to-work costs should be disregarded completely – eg, a parent is well off and can easily afford the costs, or he has voluntarily moved further away from his work.

Property or capital transfers

Departure on the grounds of a property settlement applies only where a court order or other written agreement was in force before 5 April 1993 between the absent parent and either the person with care or the child(ren).[10] Where the amount of child maintenance payable under the pre-CSA agreement was reduced or is nil as a result of the property transfer, departure is possible if the property transfer is not properly reflected in the CSA assessment (see p192). In addition, where the amount of child maintenance had not been reduced as part of the pre-1993 agreement, but an allowance for the property settlement has been included in the CSA assessment, departure can be sought on the grounds that any reduction is inappropriate. In practice, it may be very difficult to determine whether or not the property settlement had depressed the child maintenance payments.

In order to decide whether the broad-brush property allowance fairly reflects the amount of child maintenance foregone, the CSA will need as much information as possible about the court decision. The aim is to try and unravel the intention of the court order/agreement – ie, what proportion of the transfer was in lieu of child maintenance? Once this has been ascertained, the equivalent value in weekly child maintenance is obtained by spreading the capital over the years in which the child(ren) would remain dependent from the date of the agreement; this calculation is laid down in a schedule to the regulations. The equivalent weekly value of transfers of less than £5,000 is nil.

The end results of these applications will be difficult to predict (see example 15.7). The assessment may be increased or reduced, irrespective of which party applies for the departure. Therefore it is advisable to seek the help of the solicitor concerned with the case at the time of the transfer who should consult the new regulations.

3. APPLYING FOR DEPARTURE

Once an assessment has been made using the standard formula, a person with care, an absent parent or a child applicant in Scotland may apply to the CSA for a departure direction.[11] This applies to any assessment – whether made on initial application or after a review – but not all categories of interim maintenance assessment (see p334). In addition, a further departure can be sought from an assessment which results from a departure.[12] Information about departure will be provided with the assessment.

The application must be made in writing, stating which of the grounds described above applies.[13] It is essential to include the grounds, as otherwise the application can be rejected out of hand. The applicant should also state whether the circumstances have applied in the same way throughout the period of the assessment or that there has been a relevant change of circumstances since the current assessment was made; a relevant change of circumstances is a change which relates to the type of departure applied for. The CSA will provide an application form for departure; it is intended that different forms will apply to the different grounds in order to avoid having to issue everyone with an enormous form. A client may want to telephone the CSA to ask for the appropriate form in order to make the necessary written application within 28 days (see below).

For assessments made before the system of departure was set up, applications will have to be made before a deadline, which is not yet set.[14] Otherwise, there is no time limit on applying for departure, but a delay can effect the extent of the backdating of any direction. For assessments notified after the full implementation of departure, any direction awarded will be backdated to the beginning of that assessment (or to any subsequent relevant change of circumstances) if the application is made within 28 days of being notified of the assessment.

If the applicant can show that the delay in making an application was unavoidable, again the departure direction will be backdated to the beginning of the assessment or the relevant change. It may be that independent advice needs to be sought about departure, and this could constitute 'unavoidable' delay. However, it is advisable to send a preliminary letter notifying the intention to apply for departure, and, if possible, stating the ground, to which assessment it applies, and whether there has been any relevant change of circumstance recently. Otherwise, if the application is not made within 28 days, any direction will take effect from the date of the application for departure.

It is as yet unknown how long it will take the CSA to deal with departure applications, but it will no doubt take at least a number of weeks, if not a couple of months. During this time the absent parent should if possible pay the current assessment, even though an overpayment (see p393) or arrears (see p397) may result. However, if this level of liability is causing a problem, a regular payments condition may be imposed (see p335).

There is no provision to allow applications for departure before an assessment has been made – for example, on the maintenance application form or maintenance enquiry form. Therefore, even if circumstances relevant to departure are mentioned on the initial form, these will not be taken into account when making the first assessment, and a formal request for departure will have to be made once the notification of the assessment is received.

An application for departure can be made, even if the assessment is also being reviewed (see Chapter 16).[15] Indeed, if the application is accepted (see below), the outstanding review(s) will be dealt with by a 'fast track' procedure. Departure will be carried out by a different officer from the one carrying out the review.

Departure cannot be applied for when a Category A or C interim maintenance assessment (IMA) is in force (see p296). Only the person with care can apply for departure from a Category D IMA. Either party can apply for departure from a Category B IMA, except on the ground of supporting step-children in the absent parent's family.

4. CONSIDERATION OF DEPARTURE

The decisions on departure applications are to be made by CSA staff on behalf of the Secretary of State, and not by child support officers. There will be specific officers in the field (see p21) who deal with departure applications. They will probably be known as departure officers. Not every field office will include these staff, but they will be able to direct the applicant to the office in the area where departures are considered.

If two departure applications are made – for example, one on the grounds of costs of disability and another concerning the costs of contact with the child(ren) – they will be considered together.[16]

The applicant can withdraw an application for departure.[17] S/he may want to do so after seeing the other party's information.

Preliminary consideration

An application can be rejected by the Secretary of State where there are no grounds for departure or where the resulting difference in the assessment would be minimal.[18] Minimal is defined as less than a change of £1 a week. Such a rejection could apply to those liable to pay:

- a minimum assessment of £4.80 (see p167), as departure cannot reduce an assessment below this;
- the maximum under the formula (see p234), as departure cannot increase an assessment above this; *and*
- an additional element (see p229), as the calculation used after a departure direction acts to reduce the effect of including a special expense at higher incomes until there comes a point when no benefit is gained (see p340).

The officer considering departure can refer the assessment for a change of circumstances or second-tier review (see pp353 and 355), even though a request for one has not been made.[19] No notice of such reviews have to be given to the parties.[20] The review and the departure processes will be carried out in parallel; however, such reviews will be fast-tracked in an attempt to ensure that the correct assessment is in place before the departure direction is implemented. If an assessment is reviewed and a fresh assessment notified to the parties, the Secretary of State may decide that the application for departure lapses.[21] However, the applicant has 14 days to notify the CSA that s/he wants the departure application to continue.

If the application is rejected after preliminary consideration, there is a right of appeal (see p348).[22]

The regular payments condition

Where an absent parent applies for departure, he will usually be expected to make regular payments of child maintenance while departure is being considered. If he is not already doing this, the Secretary of State may impose an amount which must be paid in order for the application to proceed.[23] The amount may be either the current assessment or less and will be set by the debt management section (see p388), not the departure officer. It is intended that a lower rate will apply only where an absent parent has applied for special expenses to be taken into account, and the Secretary of State may set the amount on the assumption that the departure application will be successful in order to avoid overpayments. Should the departure application fail after a regular payments condition lower than the current assessment had been set, arrears will have accrued and will have to be paid.

Both parties will be informed of the regular payments condition. If the absent parent fails to make the required payment, the departure application may lapse. Where the absent parent has been paying the person with care direct, if payments are not being made regularly this would have to be reported to the CSA.

The regular payments condition will not apply during the pilot scheme. Once the full scheme is up and running, absent parents who are having problems paying the full assessment – for example, because of special expenses – may want to request a regular payments condition set at a lower rate. On the other hand, persons with care who are not receiving regular payments, on being informed of an application for departure by the absent parent, could contact the debt management section and request that a regular payments condition be set.

Providing information

The other party – ie, the parent with care if it is the absent parent who has made the departure application – will not be notified of the departure application until after it has been accepted on preliminary consideration.

Both parties can submit any relevant information or arguments to the departure officer. It is best if these can be made in writing, as not only will the departure officer making the decision have the full information but it will then appear in any subsequent appeal papers. However, either party can request an interview at a field office (see p21). The Secretary of State must take into account any representations made by the person with care, the absent parent or a child applicant in Scotland.[24] Any representations made may be sent to the other party for comments.

The Secretary of State can request information in connection with a departure application and, if it is not provided within 14 days, the decision can be made without the information.[25] Therefore, it is to the parent's advantage to respond as fully and as quickly as possible. If some evidence cannot be obtained within that time, send an interim reply and ask for additional time.

The departure officer will have access to information already held by the CSA. However, at least during the pilot, there will be no additional information requirements placed on the parties or additional powers given to the Secretary of State (see Chapter 6). Although the CSA can also use inspectors to obtain additional information (see p153), it is unlikely that this will happen. When collecting information for assessments, there is a certain amount of information which the parties must supply and without which the child support officer cannot proceed, and therefore there has to be some form of penalty; however, under the departure process, the provision of information by the parties is voluntary and the only sanction is the risk of the application being refused or a departure direction being awarded against the parent.

Factors to be taken into account

The Secretary of State has to take into account that the parent is responsible for maintaining his children where he can afford to do so and for maintaining all of his children equally.[26] No account can be taken of the fact that the person with care is in receipt of benefit, the level of which is affected by the amount of child maintenance received.[27] In other words, it is no use arguing that the children receiving the maintenance do not benefit because their mother is on income support.

Just and equitable

Satisfying one of the specified grounds is not sufficient to guarantee departure. Even though consideration will already have been given to how much of the expenses it is reasonable to allow for, a departure direction can only be given where it is 'just and equitable' to do so.[28] All the circumstances of both parties have to be considered – in particular, the financial circumstances of the absent parent and the person with care. This suggests that a departure application by an absent parent on the grounds of special expenses would therefore be more likely to succeed where the person with care is in a well-paid job than where she is on income support. However, a government minister has stated that departure will not routinely be refused solely on the ground that the absent parent's income is higher than the person with care's.[29] On the other hand, if the absent parent is substantially better off, even after taking into account the special expenses, the direction is likely to be refused. Presumably, when looking at financial circumstances, the situation of the whole family is taken into account, including any partner's income.

Factors which must and must not be taken into account when deciding whether a departure direction would be just and equitable are contained in the regulations.[30] The Secretary of State *must* take into account:

- whether a direction would be likely to cause either party stopping paid employment;
- where the absent parent is the applicant, any court order or other agreement for child maintenance before the CSA assessment;
- whether the applicant could have made financial arrangements to cover the special expense; *and*
- whether the applicant has other expenses which are not everyday requirements and this money could be used to pay the special expense.

A minister gave the example of a case where an absent parent would otherwise qualify for a special expenses departure on the ground of a reasonable debt but, because he spends a significant amount of money on a racehorse, the departure would be refused on the grounds that it is not just and equitable to reduce the support to the child when the absent parent has money for an expensive hobby.[31]

The Secretary of State must *not* take into account:

- the circumstances of the child's conception;
- the reasons for the breakdown of the relationship;
- the fact that either party is now involved in a new relationship;
- any contact arrangements;
- the failure of the absent parent to pay the CSA assessment or any previous arrangement; *nor*
- any representations made by a third party – ie, not the person with care, the absent parent or a child in Scotland applicant.

Welfare of the child

The welfare of any child likely to be affected by the departure direction has to be taken into account (see p52).[32] Any information on this issue should be submitted to the CSA as it is unlikely that it will be requested.

Departures standards unit

A central unit is to be set up to advise and monitor officers making departure decisions on behalf of the Secretary of State. Although internal to the CSA, this unit will perform a similar function to the Central Adjudication Service headed by the Chief Child Support Officer (see p16). The aim is to ensure as much as possible that discretion is exercised consistently. In addition, the unit will liaise with the Independent Tribunal Service (see p367) over any appeal submissions concerning departure (see below).

Referral to a tribunal

After completing the preliminary consideration, the departure officer may refer the departure application to a child support appeal tribunal for determination instead of making a decision him/herself (see p367).[33] The Government has given assurances that only a small minority of cases will be dealt with in this way and those that are will be particularly novel or complex cases requiring consideration under the guidance of a legally qualified chair. However, these are more likely to occur in the early days of the scheme, although not at all during the pilot. As there is no appeal from a tribunal on the facts, it is very important that both parties make all the representations they want to before or at the tribunal hearing (see p377).

5. THE DEPARTURE DECISION

It will no doubt take the Secretary of State a number of weeks to make the decision, particularly if there has been a delay in obtaining evidence (eg, of a pre-April 1993 property settlement) or a number of stages of information being asked first of one party and then of the other (eg, in disputes about an absent parent's lifestyle). However, review of the pilot scheme aims to streamline the process as far as is possible.

The applicant and the other party will be informed of the decision on the application and the reasons for the decision.[34] Although the Act allows a time to be prescribed within which the notification must be sent, apparently no time limit is to be specified. If the reasons given are inadequate for understanding the decision, ask for a more detailed explanation.

Refusal of the application

A departure direction cannot be given where the effect of that departure on the assessment would be minimal.[35] Although it was initially suggested that this minimum level of change might be set at £10 a week (unless the absent parent is on the protected income level),[36] in fact a change of at least £1 will result in a departure direction.

See p348 for reviews and appeals.

A departure direction

A direction does not reset the maintenance assessment or give a figure by which to reduce or increase the liability. Instead, a direction requires a child support officer (CSO) to reassess the child maintenance and specifies how this calculation should be carried out.[37] The CSO must comply with the direction as soon as possible.[38]

Alternative calculations will be used, taking into account the departure direction.[39] Although the Act allows for a maximum amount by which the new assessment can differ from the standard formula assessment,[40] this is not included in the regulations. Instead, the calculation is devised in such a way that those on higher incomes receive a lower benefit (see below). There will be special rules to cover assessments which are being phased in (see p300).

Departures cannot bring an assessment above the formula maximum (see p234) or below the minimum of £4.80 a week (see p167). An absent parent cannot be left below the protected income level (see Chapter 12) after a departure direction, although the level of protection itself can be amended.[41] The majority of departure directions which affect protected income act to increase it by adding an allowance for a special expense; however, the level of protection can be reduced by reducing the level of housing costs thought to be excessive and reducing or removing a travel-to-work allowance.

Effect of a special expenses allowance

The allowance for special expenses granted to an absent parent will be included in exempt income and protected income to the extent allowed by the departure direction.

The 50 per cent deduction rate is applied to all an absent parent's assessable income when carrying out an assessment, including a special expense for him, instead of reducing the rate to 15, 20 or 25 per cent once the maintenance requirement is met (see p230). In other words, after such a departure direction, the absent parent always pays 50 per cent of his assessable income (unless this would result in his paying more than the previous assessment – see figure 15.1 and example 15.5). There is no additional element calculation to perform, even where the parent with care has assessable income. This removes the role of the maintenance requirement.

If the special expense has been awarded to a parent with care who has assessable income, then the allowance is added into her exempt income and the proposed maintenance calculated as usual under the formula.

Example 15.4: Special expenses – debts and travel costs

Steve has been assessed to pay £65.55 a week to Debbie as maintenance for his three children, Paul (17), Grace (15) and Lewis (10). In December 1996, Steve applies for departure on the grounds of travel-to-work costs, debts of the relationship and pre-April 1993 commitments. He does not apply on the ground of the property settlement (see example 9.5) as he wants to seek advice from his solicitor as to whether it would be to his advantage.

Steve is awarded special expenses of £83 travel-to-work costs (see example 15.2) He divorced in 1991 and has already cleared a couple of the outstanding debts since then, but there remain one debt of the relationship and another commitment which also pre-dates the divorce. The total repayments amount to £34.60 a week; there is no £15 disregard as this has already been applied to the travel costs. As Debbie is employed, it is decided that it is just and equitable to give the departure direction for these debts.

Debbie has net earnings of £210 and assessable income of £39.37; when calculating the formula assessment, this was taken into account when determining whether the parents could meet the maintenance requirement of £104.65. However, after the departure, this no longer applies as Steve simply pays 50 per cent of his own assessable income (as long as this is below the current assessment).

Steve's exempt income:	£
Personal allowance	47.90
Mortgage (in full – see example 9.5)	96.00
Property settlement allowance	40.00
Travel-to-work costs	83.00
Debt repayments	34.60
Total	301.50

Steve's net income for child support purposes: £380 a week earnings
Steve's assessable income = £380 − £301.50 = £78.50
Proposed maintenance = 50% x £78.50 = £39.25

Protected income:		£
Personal allowance	Couple	75.20
Mortgage (interest only)		78.46
Council tax		15.00
Travel-to-work costs		83.00
Debt repayments		34.60
Standard margin		30.00
Basic protected income		316.26

Total family income: Steve's new wife Lisa has net earnings of £270 and therefore total family income = £380 + £270 = £650. This is so far above the basic protected income – even with the special expenses allowance – that there is no need to continue with the protected income calculation. Steve can afford the proposed maintenance of £39.25.

The departure direction has therefore reduced the assessment from £65.55 to £39.25 a week. Furthermore, this is backdated several weeks to the date the departure scheme came into effect, creating an overpayment of over £200. Also, the ongoing reduction causes Debbie problems as her income is only just above the family credit level and she is concerned about not being able to pay her mortgage: she seeks advice – see example 15.8.

As a result of the 50 per cent taper applying right up the income range, there comes a point where an absent parent's income is too high to benefit from departure. However, the departure direction cannot actually increase the assessment; once the alternative calculation produces a higher figure than the current assessment, it is ignored and the formula assessment remains.

Figure 15.1: **REDUCTION IN MAINTENANCE ASSESSMENTS DUE TO SPECIAL EXPENSES ALLOWANCE**

A. Single absent parent with £50 housing costs; parent with care has two children

Gross earnings	£20 expense	£40 expense	£60 expense
under £150*	no effect	no effect	no effect
£200	£17.00	£17.21	£17.21
£250	£17.00	£34.00	£44.83
£300	£10.00	£23.16	£40.16
£350	£7.80	£17.80	£27.80
£400	no effect	£8.53	£18.53
£450	no effect	no effect	£8.48
£500	no effect	no effect	no effect

B. Absent parent with £50 housing costs, a new partner and two step-children; parent with care has two children

Gross earnings	£20 expense	£40 expense	£60 expense
under £250*	no effect	no effect	no effect
£300	£9.73	£9.73	£9.73
£350	£17.00	£34.00	£34.77
£400	£17.00	£34.00	£51.00
£450	£10.47	£27.47	£44.47
£500	no effect	£3.10	£20.10
£550	no effect	no effect	no effect

* these absent parents do not gain as they are already paying the minimum

These are only illustrative figures; do not use them as a guide to the exact effect in any particular case as there can be many variables. The alternative calculation must be carried out.

Example 15.5: The better off and special expenses

a) Jeremy has been assessed to pay £203.78 a week for his four children (see figure 11.3). He applies for a departure on two grounds – first, contact costs and second, a financial commitment in the form of school fees for the children. The children stay with Jeremy every other weekend; he collects and returns the children in his car. This is in fact cheaper than four return train fares; the petrol used is £38 a weekend. As this is £19 a week, once the £15 disregard is made, there only remains a special expense of £4 a week.

All four children are in private education; however the commitments for Henry (8) and Isobel (4) were made after 1993. The Secretary of State could decide that it would not be unreasonable to move Georgina (12) to another school whereas Francis (14) has already begun his GCSE courses. A departure direction could therefore be given to last the next 18 months for £80 a week.

Jeremy's exempt income is therefore increased by £4 + £80 = £84 a week

His assessable income is now £516 (instead of £600)

The proposed maintenance after the departure would be: 50% x £516 = £258. As this is higher than the current maintenance assessment of £203.78, no departure direction would be given. Indeed Jeremy's application could be refused at the preliminary consideration.

b) If instead Jeremy had net income of £500 a week and assessable income of £300 a week, the current assessment would be:

Basic element = maintenance requirement = £107.55 (see example 11.3)
Basic assessable income = £2 x £107.55 = £215.10
Additional assessable income = £300 – £215.10 = £84.90
Additional element = £84.90 x 25% = £21.23
Proposed maintenance = £107.55 + £21.23 = £128.78
Protected income has no effect and therefore the assessment = £128.78

Once Jeremy is awarded special expenses of £84, his assessable income is £300 – £84 = £216

Proposed maintenance = 50% x 216 = £108 which is less than the previous assessment of £128.78

The protected income still needs checking again as the special expenses are included in the basic protected income:

	£
Personal allowance	47.90
Mortgage (interest only)	123.08
Council tax	21.00
Travel-to-contact costs	4.00
Pre-1993 commitments	80.00
Standard margin	30.00
Basic protected income	305.98

His total family income = net earnings = £500
Excess income = £500 – 305.98 = £194.02; 15% x £194.02 = £29.10
Total protected income = £305.98 + £29.10 = £335.08

Jeremy can therefore afford to pay the £108 assessment without his disposable income falling below £335.08 a week.

Jeremy's housing costs in exempt income are £152.10 a week. Although Evie might want to argue that these housing costs are excessive and seek departure on these grounds, she would not be successful as housing costs can only be limited to half a parent's net earnings and in this case half of £500 a week = £250 a week.

c) If Evie had assessable income of £70, the assessment before the departure would be £118.60. Once the £84 special expenses are awarded, Jeremy's assessable income would be £216 and the again the assessment is 50% x £216 = £108. In other words, Jeremy either gains an advantage from Evie having income, or from the departure, but he cannot gain from both at the same time.

The departure addition for step-children is only added to exempt income, and not into protected income as the full allowances for step-children are already contained in basic protected income (see p253).

Example 15.6: Step-children

Bob has been awarded a departure on the grounds of costs of step-children, a special expense of £37: see example 15.1a

The £37 is therefore included in Bob's exempt income, giving him an exempt income of £153.90 (instead of £116.90 – see example 9.6a). His net income is £217.79.

Assessable income = £217.79 – £153.90 = £63.89
Proposed maintenance = £63.89 x 50% = £31.95

Although this is less than the previous proposed maintenance of £50.45 (see example 11.1c), it is more than the current assessment which had been reduced by the protected income step to £30.24. Therefore the departure direction has no effect at the moment, but it might do should Bob's earnings increase. On the other hand, should Zoe's income increase, the allowance for the step-children in exempt income would be reduced (see example 15.1b).

Departure directions for a property settlement

Where a departure direction is granted because of a property or capital settlement (see p232), any allowance in the exempt income (see p192) is removed. Instead the amount allowed under the departure direction is deducted from a proposed maintenance figure calculated using no property settlement allowance.

Example 15.7: Assessment including a direction concerning a property settlement

Hamish and Kirsty divorced in 1987, when their only child Angus was four years old (now 12). The house, then worth £31,000, was transferred to Kirsty with a mortgage of about £9,000. From April 1995, Kirsty's assessment was reduced when Hamish was given an allowance of £40 in his exempt income. Kirsty has remarried, has a baby and has no net income of her own. Hamish is single.

a) The assessment is currently:

Maintenance requirement: £59.78

Hamish's exempt income:	£
Personal allowance	47.90
Housing costs	45.08
Property settlement allowance	40.00
Total	132.98

Hamish's net income = £205 a week net earnings
Assessable income = £205 – £132.98 = £72.02
Proposed maintenance = £72.02 x 50% = £36.01 (less than the maintenance requirement)
Protected income shows that he can afford this.

The purpose of the capital transfer was unspecified and Kirsty believes that it was primarily in lieu of spousal maintenance foregone and to provide a home for Angus. Hamish also had to pay £15 a week under a court order as maintenance for Angus and, given that Angus was to be dependent for at least another 12 years, a transfer of part of £22,000 does not amount to as much as the £20 a week child maintenance in advance as suggested by the £40 exempt income allowance.

The Secretary of State decides that the property transfer in lieu of child maintenance was £7,300 and its weekly equivalent value over 14 years is £19.05.
Hamish's exempt income = £ 47.90 + £45.08 = £92.98
Hamish's net income = £205 a week net earnings
Assessable income = £205 – £92.98 = £112.02
Proposed maintenance = (£112.02 x 50%) = £56.01
The amount under the departure direction is then deducted:
£56.01 – £19.05 = £36.96
Protected income shows that he can afford this.
The departure would make a difference of less than £1 a week and is therefore refused.

b) If Hamish's net income had instead been £305, but exempt income the same, the current assessment would be:

Assessable income = £305 – £132.98 = £172.02

£172.02 x 50% = £86.01 (more than the maintenance requirement of £59.78)

Therefore proposed maintenance =

£59.78 + 15% (£172.02 – £119.56) = £67.65

Protected income shows that he can afford this.

With a property transfer direction of £19.05 a week, the alternative calculation is then:

Assessable income = £305 – £92.98 = £212.02

Proposed maintenance = £59.78 + 15% (£212.02 – £119.56) = £73.65

The amount under the departure direction is deducted:

£73.65 – £19.05 = £54.60

The departure has in fact ended up reducing the assessment by £13.05.

Departure to compensate for the formula's generosity

Directions awarded on these grounds will have slightly different effects:

- a parent's lifestyle inconsistent with the level of his/her declared income – a notional income will be specified which is added to net income (see p203) and total family income (see p250);
- a parent's assets which do not produce an income are capable of doing so – a notional income from those assets will be specified;
- a parent has diverted income – again an income will be specified;
- the housing costs included in the formula are unreasonably high – a lower figure will be substituted in exempt income (see p185) and possibly also protected income (see p253); these can be reduced to half net income (of £80 if greater) and to half total family income (or £80 if greater) respectively;
- there are other people living in the home who could contribute towards the housing costs – the partner's contribution to housing costs will be deducted from the housing costs in exempt income, but not in protected income; and
- travel-to-work costs are unreasonably high or should be disregarded completely – the allowance in both exempt income and protected income will be reduced accordingly or removed.

Example 15.8: Housing costs relating to the partner

As seen in example 15.4, Steve applied successfully for a departure which reduced his assessment from £65.55 to £39.25 a week. Debbie, his ex-wife, then applies for a departure on the grounds that Steve's second wife Lisa can afford to contribute towards the couple's housing costs.

Lisa has net earnings of £270 compared with Steve's net earnings of £380. However, once Steve's travelling expenses of £83 a week are taken from his earnings, both partners have roughly the same amount to contribute towards the joint mortgage. Therefore the Secretary of State decided that Lisa can afford to contribute half the mortgage payments.

Therefore Steve's exempt income is now:	£
Personal allowance	47.90
Mortgage (half of £96)	48.00
Property settlement allowance	40.00
Travel-to-work costs	83.00
Debt repayments	34.60
Total	253.50

Steve's assessable income = £380 – £253.50 = £126.50
Proposed maintenance = 50% x Steve's assessable income = £63.25
The protected income calculation remains the same as in example 15.4 and therefore Steve can afford £63.25 (which is still below the original formula assessment)

Note: the 50 per cent calculation is used because of the special expenses departure; if only the housing costs departure had been awarded, then the proposed maintenance would have been calculated in the usual way described in Chapter 11.

The duration of a direction

The direction will take effect from the date of the application for departure, unless the application was made within 28 days of the notification of the assessment, in which case it would be backdated to the beginning of the current assessment or to the change. See p333 for details. However, no assessment, including a departure, can be backdated before the beginning of the full scheme.

The departure direction may last for a specified period or until the occurrence of a specified event.[42] For example, a departure direction to take into account a joint debt would cease when the repayments were due to stop. A direction may include the instruction to make a fresh assessment on a later change of circumstances,[43] for example, if repayments of a joint debt were to be reduced at a known date.

The departure direction can apply to a future assessment made on review – eg, a periodical review (see p353). Directions can be cancelled at a later date.[44] Most directions will continue to have effect until an application is made for the direction to be cancelled; if relevant, it can be replaced with a direction which takes into account the new set of circumstances.

Reviewing the decision

There are no procedures for reviewing the Secretary of State's decision on departure. A departure direction can be cancelled if it was given in error.[45] Although there is power in the Act for departure applications to be reconsidered in the light of new evidence after the decision is made,[46] this does not yet appear in the regulations.

Appealing the decision

Even though the decisions on departure are made by the Secretary of State, they can be appealed.[47] This is virtually unprecedented for Secretary of State decisions. Unlike most appeals against CSO decisions, decisions on departure can be appealed direct to a child support appeal tribunal (see p367). Either the person with care or the absent parent can appeal a decision on departure; this includes refusal on preliminary consideration. The appeal should usually be made within 28 days of notification of the decision (see p370). Appeals will not be part of the pilot

The tribunal procedures will be the same as for those against CSO decisions, except that tribunals hearing referrals and appeals against departure decisions can be composed only of a legally qualified chair.[48] The reason given for this is to reduce delay. Chairs with expertise in family law will be used, for example, where property transfers are involved. Ministers have suggested that appeals against rejection after preliminary consideration might be most appropriate to be heard by one person, but how frequently one-member tribunals are used will be a matter for the Independent Tribunal Service. Where an appeal is being heard in conjunction with an appeal against a child support officer's decision on a second-tier review, a three-person tribunal would have to be involved.

Consideration is also being given to the use of appeal decisions made on the basis of the papers without a hearing.

Reviews and appeals

This chapter covers:

I. CHANGING CHILD SUPPORT AGENCY DECISIONS

This chapter sets out the ways in which a decision of a child support officer (CSO) can be altered and challenged. There are also decisions which are made by Child Support Agency (CSA) staff on behalf of the Secretary of State and these are looked at briefly below.

It is important to know whether a decision was made by a CSO or made on behalf of the Secretary of State, because the way to change it may depend on who made it. Where a written decision is issued it will usually be clear from that notice. If it is not clear, you should ask the CSA as soon as possible, and consider taking independent advice.

Apart from reviews, assessments can be cancelled or cease to have effect (see pp307–15). For reviews of the benefit penalty (reduced benefit directions) see p120. For reviews of deductions of maintenance from income support see p170. For reviews of departure directions see p348.

Correcting mistakes in CSO decisions

Where there is a simple mistake in the decision – for example, a slip of the pen or some figures have been added up wrongly, the CSO can correct that mistake.[1] CSOs are advised that this can only be done where the decision the CSO intended to make is clear and the mistake was made when the decision was being recorded.[2] A decision can be corrected with or without a request at any time. A corrected decision must be sent as soon as possible to those to whom the original decision was sent.[3] Where a decision is corrected, the time limits for seeking a review of that decision run from the date the corrected decision is issued.[4]

Challenging CSO decisions

There are many reasons why a person may want to challenge a CSO decision – for example, the decision is based on the wrong facts or law, or the person cannot see how the decision was made. The only way to have a CSO decision considered independently of the CSA is by an appeal to a **child support appeal tribunal** (CSAT) (see p367). An appeal can only be made after a **second-tier review** is carried out (see p358). An exception is that a review of a reduced benefit direction can be appealed straight to a CSAT without a second-tier review (see p122).

Therefore, except where the only reason for challenging the decision is that there has been a change of circumstances since it was made, it is usually best to ask for a second-tier review. Where it is too late to do this, a request can be made for a **review instigated by a CSO** (see p364). Where the reason for challenging the decision is a change since it was made, a **change of circumstances review** can be requested (see p355). Instead of these options, it is sometimes better to ask for the decision to be **set aside** (see p352).

Any decision on review (except on a second-tier review) can be challenged by asking for a second-tier review. A CSAT decision can be challenged by appealing to a **child support commissioner** (see p382).

The CSO can carry out more than one type of review of the same case at the same time, except that a CSO cannot instigate a review while a different type of review is being carried out. For example, even though the CSO is carrying out a second-tier review, s/he can also carry out a change of circumstances review if a party requests one. However, many parents have experienced delays because the CSA refuses to do this. If this happens, a complaint should be made (see p28).

Second-tier reviews are carried out by a special section in the Child Support Agency Centre (CSAC), known confusingly as the review section. All other reviews are dealt with by the business team. To avoid confusion, when contacting the CSA about a review, always begin by explaining the type of review involved and the date it was requested.

If an absent parent thinks the review may reduce the amount of his assessment, he may wish to try to negotiate lower payments, though this is usually difficult. For more details see p401.

Most parentage disputes cannot be considered by a CSAT, but may be dealt with by a court (see p38).

Challenging decisions about benefit entitlement

Some CSO decisions depend upon a decision of the Benefits Agency. In particular, a person in receipt of income support (IS) is treated as having no income[5] and an absent parent on IS has to pay no more than £4.80 maintenance (see p168). So, where the parent with care is on IS, the assessment will be on the basis that she has no income. An absent parent who believes that the parent with care should not be on IS, for example, because she is working full-time, must challenge the Benefits Agency decision to pay IS. This can be done by raising it with the CSA. The CSA reports to the Benefits Agency, which investigates. The Benefits Agency reports the result to the CSA but not to the person who made the allegation. If the Benefits Agency refuses to stop IS, the CSO (and CSAT) must treat her as having no income, regardless of the evidence.[6] An absent parent in that situation cannot appeal to a social security appeal tribunal (SSAT) against the Benefit Agency decision.[7] However, if the person with care appeals to an SSAT because, for example, her IS award is ended, the absent parent can ask to take part in that appeal.[8]

Challenging other CSA decisions

Many decisions made by CSA staff are made on behalf of the Secretary of State, especially in the areas of information gathering, collection and enforcement. The only way to have a decision of the Secretary of State considered independently of the CSA is by judicial review (see below). If you are thinking about doing this, you should get legal advice as soon as possible, even if you are also trying to get the CSA to change its mind.

If you are unhappy with a decision of the Secretary of State, you should provide as much relevant information as possible and ask the officer to reconsider. If the officer refuses to change the decision, then a complaint can be made (see p28).

There may be other occasions which do not involve a decision, but where the behaviour of CSA staff is unsatisfactory – eg, intimidating or unnecessarily intrusive questioning, or unwarranted demands for evidence and documentation. In these cases also, a complaint can be made.

Deduction from earnings orders can be appealed to a court (see p413).

Judicial review

A person affected by a decision or action of a public body or one of its officers can ask the High Court to carry out a judicial review of the decision or action. The court can set aside the decision and also order the decision-maker to consider it again in a lawful way. Judicial review may be sought of a Secretary of State's decision or a decision of a CSAT chairperson or a child support commissioner – for example, to refuse to grant leave to appeal. However, it cannot usually be brought where there is a right of appeal to a CSAT or commissioner. Legal aid is available for judicial review cases and legal representation should be sought without delay.

Case law identifies the following circumstances in which judicial review may succeed:[9]

- illegality – where the decision-maker goes against the law regulating her/his decision-making power – eg, s/he deals with a case outside her/his jurisdiction; *or*
- irrationality – where a decision is 'so outrageous in its defiance of logic or of accepted moral standards that no sensible person who had applied his mind to the question could have arrived at it'; *or*
- procedural impropriety.

2. SETTING ASIDE DECISIONS

A CSO can set aside a CSO decision if it is in the interests of justice.[10] This should only be done where there has been a procedural mistake – for example, where a document was not sent or received when it should have been. When a decision has been set aside, it no longer exists. A CSO is then free to make another decision as if the first one had not been made.

A CSO cannot set aside a Category A or D interim maintenance assessment (IMA)[11] or a decision to make or review a reduced benefit direction.[12]

A decision can only be set aside where an application giving reasons is made in writing within 28 days of the notification of the decision.[13] The 28 days run from the date the notification was actually received.[14]

The CSO must notify the person with care, absent parent and Scottish child applicant that an application to set aside the decision has been made.[15] There will be 14 days for the parties to comment before a decision is made. Once it is, the CSO must notify the relevant people as soon as possible, giving reasons for the decision.[16] The notification must not breach confidentiality (see p156).[17]

3. PERIODICAL REVIEWS

This type of review is a section 16 review.

When is a review carried out

Periodical reviews now take place every two years. Assessments with effective dates before 19 April 1996 were reviewed after 52 weeks.[18] A CSO will review an assessment 104 weeks after its effective date.[19] The date of the review is not affected by a fresh assessment made on a section 17, 18 or 19 review.[20]

The exception is where, before 22 January 1996, the CSO decided to carry out a section 17 review and the reason for that review was *not* the changes in the formula on 7 February 1994 or 18 April 1995.[21] In that case, the 104 weeks runs from the fresh assessment made under the review.[22]

In some cases where a section 17 review has been requested, a CSO can carry out a section 16 review instead and the effective date is set by the rules for a section 17 review (see p356).

The CSO can decide not to carry out a review if a fresh assessment would cease to have effect within 28 days of its effective date.[23]

Procedure

Before carrying out the review, the CSO must give 14 days' notice to the parent with care, absent parent and Scottish child applicant.[24] This is done automatically by the CSA computer four weeks before the date the review is due.[25] A review pack containing a CSA 5 form and a covering letter CSA 28 is sent to each of those people. No packs are issued where:[26]

- the absent parent is on IS;
- the only child named in the assessment will turn 19 within 128 days of the date the review is due, so no periodical review will be carried out (see above);
- a pack for a review of an assessment involving one of the parties was issued in the 13 weeks before the date the periodical review is due.

Where the parent with care only is on IS, the pack is sent only to the absent parent while the parent with care is notified of the intention to review by letter CSA 105.

The review pack is similar to the maintenance application and enquiry forms (see pp61 and 133). The persons to whom the pack is sent are given 14 days to respond and the covering letter must warn of the possible consequences of not providing the information requested (see below).[27] The 14 days runs from two working days (including Saturday) after the pack was posted.[28] The rules about what information the CSO can request apply to the review pack (see pp125–9).

Outcome of review

The CSO calculates the proposed assessment as if the person who applied for the original assessment had applied again.[29] When applying the formula, the relevant week is the seven days ending the day before the review pack was issued.[30] If the CSO has enough information to make a fresh assessment, s/he must do so, unless s/he decides to cancel the assessment.[31]

Cancelling

The CSO can cancel where:[32]
- the usual rules apply (see p307);
- the person with care fails to provide enough information for a review to be carried out; or
- the person with care applied for maintenance under section 6 (see p54) and is no longer on IS/family credit/disability working allowance and/or no longer required to give authorisation.

The power to cancel because information is not provided, or because the person with care no longer falls under section 6, was introduced from 22 January 1996 under the 1995 Act. Before cancelling an assessment, the CSO must, if possible, give written notice to the person with care, absent parent and Scottish child applicant of intention to cancel the assessment, and allow 14 days from the date the notice is sent before cancelling.[33]

Where an assessment is cancelled because information is not provided, a benefit penalty may be considered (see p112).

Making an interim maintenance assessment

Where the CSO does not have enough information to carry out a review, s/he can make an IMA. CSOs are instructed to consider this only where the IMA would be more than any full assessment then in force.[34] Before making an IMA, notice of the CSO's intention to do so must be given (see p296). For details of making IMAs, see p296.

Effective date of fresh assessment

The effective date of any fresh assessment or IMA will be set by the 104/52 weeks rules above.[35] The exceptions to this are where that would give a Category A or D IMA an effective date earlier than 16 February 1995, in which case the effective date is 16 February 1995,[36] and where an IMA replaces an IMA of the same category (see p313).[37]

Notification

If the CSO makes a fresh assessment, notification is given as if it were the first assessment (see p299). If the CSO cancels the assessment (except a Category A or D IMA) or decides it has ceased to have effect, notification is also given in the usual way (see pp309 and 311). Any decision can be challenged by a second-tier review (see p358).

4. CHANGE OF CIRCUMSTANCES REVIEWS

This type of review is a section 17 review.

Unlike in social security cases, there is no duty to tell the CSA of all changes of circumstance (see p155). However, a parent with care, absent parent or Scottish child applicant can request a review of a full assessment or a Category B or C IMA which is in force.[38] This must be done on the ground of a change of circumstances after the assessment was made which means there would be a significant change (see p356) in the amount of the assessment if a review were carried out. This includes where after the review there would be no assessment or a nil assessment.

The CSO can refuse to conduct a review (see p357).

If a CSO has refused to make an assessment and circumstances later change, a fresh application can be made. A Category A or D IMA cannot be reviewed under section 17,[39] but a request to cancel can be made instead (see p307).

Procedure

The review application must be made in writing giving details of the change(s) of circumstance.[40] This should be as detailed as possible to increase the chances of the review being carried out.

Where there is an assessment in force and the parent with care applies under section 6 for maintenance for another child of the absent parent, the authorisation she gives is treated as a request for a change of circumstances review.[41] If the child is by a different absent parent, any assessment would be a second, separate case (see p245).

A CSO has a separate power to conduct a review without a request being made if s/he has information about a change of circumstance which satisfies her/him that a fresh assessment would be made (see

Reviews instigated by a CSO – p364). The CSO can also pass information to the Benefits Agency if s/he believes that a change of circumstance is relevant to benefit entitlement (see p159).

When an application for a review is received, the CSO first decides whether, if a review were carried out, there is likely to be a **significant change** in the amount of the assessment (see below). This is done by carrying out a notional assessment, called a **tolerance check**.[42]

If the predicted change is significant, notice of intention to review is given. If the predicted change is not significant, the application is refused. If the application was received eight weeks or less before the date a periodical review is due (see p353), a periodical review is carried out instead.[43]

If the CSO decides to carry out a review, s/he must give 14 days' notice to the parent with care, absent parent and Scottish child applicant before doing so.[44] Before 22 January 1996, a review pack would also have been issued requesting the other person(s) to give full information (see *Handbook*, 1995/96 edition, p344). This is no longer done, though a CSO may decide to ask for information in a particular case. Any information provided, voluntarily or on request, must be taken into account.[45] Where you are notified that the other person has applied for a change of circumstances review, you should let the CSO know about any change of circumstance which may help you.

Change of circumstances

A change of circumstance is any change which may alter the amount of the assessment or lead to the assessment being cancelled. This includes a change in one of the parties' personal circumstances – for example, a fall in wages – and also a change in the Acts of Parliament or in regulations, but not a different interpretation of the law.[46] So, the increase in IS rates each April is a change, though it will not usually be significant on its own.

Significant change

A significant change is assumed where the absent parent is on IS, is liable to pay the minimum payment or is exempt from the minimum payment (see pp167–9).[47] Where a qualifying child has joined or left the household of the person with care since the last assessment, the change is significant if the amount of the assessment would change by £1 or more.[48]

Otherwise, a change is significant only if the amount of the assessment would change by £10 or more a week.[49] However, where a fresh assessment would leave the absent parent on the protected income level (including where it would be capped at 30 per cent of his net income – see p249), the change is significant only if:[50]

- the increase in the assessment is £5 or more a week; *or*
- the reduction in the assessment is £1 or more a week.

The £5/£1 rule does not apply to absent parents who are initially on the protected level but would, if a fresh assessment were made, be lifted off protected income level. In this case, a change is significant only if it is £10 or more.

If an absent parent has assessments in force for more than one parent with care, and *his* circumstances change, whether a change is significant is considered on the total of the assessments. But, if the change of circumstances relates to one of the persons with care, the significant change rules above apply only to *her* individual assessment.[51]

Where an assessment is being phased in, different rules apply (see p300).

Outcome of review

When calculating the proposed assessment, the relevant week (see p205) is the seven days ending with the day before the review application was received.[52] If the CSO has enough information to make a fresh assessment and there would be a significant change s/he will do so, unless s/he decides to cancel the assessment. The rules for cancelling are the same as for a periodical review (see p354). Because the CSO does not normally require the person with care to provide information, s/he is not likely to cancel an assessment on the grounds that such information is not provided.

Where the CSO does not have enough information to carry out a review, s/he can make an IMA. The rules for this are the same as for a periodical review (see p354).

Refusal to review

A section 17 review can be refused at two stages. First, if the tolerance check does not predict a significant change in the amount of the assessment, a review will be refused. Second, if, after carrying out the review, there would not be a significant change, a review will be refused.

Effective date of fresh assessment

The effective date of any fresh assessment or IMA will be the first day of the maintenance period (see p306) in which the review application was received.[53] If the review results from the death of a child named in the assessment, the effective date is the first day of the maintenance period in which the child died.[54] Where a periodical review is carried out instead of a change of circumstances review, the effective date is also set by these rules.[55]

Notification

If the CSO makes a fresh assessment, notification is given as if it were the first assessment (see p299). If the CSO cancels the assessment (except a Category A or D IMA) or decides it has ceased to have effect, notification is also given in the usual way (see pp309 and 311).

If the CSO refuses to carry out a review because the tolerance check shows there will be no significant change, only the applicant is notified of that decision.[56] If a review is carried out but refused, the parent with care, absent parent and Scottish child applicant must be notified.[57] In either case, the notification must be in writing with reasons and explain how to seek a review.[58]

Whether to request a review

Before requesting a review, you should try to work out whether a revised assessment would be higher or lower. The CSA does not normally ask the other person to provide full information before carrying out a review, therefore you only need tell the CSA about the changes in your favour. But the other person is told that you have applied for an assessment and may let the CSA know about any changes. This may cancel out the effect of the changes which led you to ask for the review. This means it is best to consider all the changes which have occurred since the last assessment, including any changes in the other person's circumstances which you know about.

An application for review does not have to be made by the person whose circumstances change – eg, if a person with care knows that an absent parent has begun working overtime, she can request a review. If you believe the other person's circumstances have changed, you can apply for a review and ask the CSA to investigate. The CSA does not have to, but any changes the CSO knows about or finds out about must be taken into account when s/he decides whether to review.

5. SECOND-TIER REVIEWS

This type of review is a section 18 review.

With the exception of a decision to issue a reduced benefit direction (see p112), CSO decisions cannot be appealed direct to the CSAT.

Instead, there is an internal review procedure – a second-tier review – as a first stage of challenging a CSO decision on the grounds of error of either fact or law. A second-tier review must be carried out by a CSO who played no part in the original decision[59] and is carried out by a special review section in the CSAC (see p350).

The following decisions can be reviewed:

- a refusal to make an assessment;[60]
- an assessment which is in force;[61]
- a refusal to review on a change of circumstances;[62]
- a decision that an assessment has or has not ceased to have effect;[63]
- a cancellation of an assessment,[64] including a Category A or D IMA;[65]
- a refusal to cancel an assessment;[66]
- an adjustment of an assessment;[67]
- a cancellation of an adjustment of an assessment.[68]

'Assessment' includes a Category B or C IMA.[69] An assessment in force includes any fresh assessment made on a review. It also includes an assessment which is no longer in force, as long as the review application was made within the time limits (see p360).[70] Where the assessment ceases to be in force after the application is made, a review can continue.[71]

Parentage disputes are not dealt with by second-tier reviews (see p38). If a request for a review includes among other reasons that a person is not a parent of a child, the Secretary of State treats the request as two applications, one to dispute parentage and the other dealing with the other issues raised.[72] Because a CSO cannot make an assessment on review where there has been a denial of parentage,[73] that dispute must be resolved, if need be by a court, before a review can be carried out.

Applying for a second-tier review

The absent parent, person with care or Scottish child applicant can request a review of a maintenance assessment, an adjustment, a cancellation or a refusal to cancel an assessment.[74] Where the CSO has refused to make an assessment or to carry out a review on a change of circumstances, an application for a second-tier review can only be made by the person whose application led to that refusal.[75] Only an absent parent can apply for a review of a refusal to cancel a Category A or D IMA.[76]

The application must be in writing and must give the reasons for requesting a review.[77] Any letter requesting a review which does not mention a change of circumstance is taken to be a request for a second-tier review,[78] as is a letter of appeal where a second-tier review has not already been carried out. The applicant should list all the issues s/he wishes the CSO to reconsider. If the case goes to appeal, the letters concerning review will be given to the CSAT and sent to the other parties (see p372).

Time limits

There is no time limit for requesting a review of a current assessment. However, the sooner the request is made the better, as the fresh assessment is only backdated to the date of the decision under review if it is made within 28 days of that decision or if there is an unavoidable delay (see below). Careful consideration should be given to the date of the request for the review, as this can affect the amount of the assessment (see p205).

All other second-tier reviews must be requested within 28 days of the notification of the CSO decision challenged.[79] The 28 days run from two working days, including Saturday, after the notification was sent out.[80] If an assessment has recently been made and then ceased to be in force, a review of the assessment itself can be requested within 28 days of the notification of that assessment.[81]

Applications for review will be considered outside the time limit if the Secretary of State is satisfied that there was unavoidable delay in applying.[82] As this is a Secretary of State decision, the *Child Support Adjudication Guide* offers no suggestions as to what may constitute 'unavoidable delay'. If a refusal of a late application is unreasonable, judicial review may be possible (see p351).

There is no statutory time limit for conducting the review imposed on the CSO. If there is a delay in reviewing, a complaint can be made (see p28).

Where a CSO refuses to make an assessment and, instead of applying for a second-tier review of that refusal, the applicant applies to a court for a maintenance order and the court decides it has no jurisdiction to make an order, the date of notification of the court decision is treated as the date of the CSO's notification of the refusal to make an assessment.[83]

Refusal to conduct a review

The CSO can refuse to conduct a second-tier review if, in her/his opinion, there are no reasonable grounds for supposing that the decision in question was:[84]

- made in ignorance of a material fact; *or*
- based on a mistake as to a material fact; *or*
- wrong in law (see below).

If there are no such grounds, it appears that the CSO still has a discretion to carry out a review. This discretion may be used particularly where the decision challenged depends on a discretionary decision of a CSO.

You may be unable to decide whether an assessment should be reviewed because the CSA has not given you the details of the other person's circumstances which it used to make the decision. In this situation, it is best to request a review setting out the facts as you understand them, even if these are based on rumour or guesswork. If a review is refused or is unsatisfactory, you can appeal to a CSAT, which can order the details to be produced (see p374).

Wrong in law

There is an error of law if:[85]

- the CSO misinterpreted or overlooked part or all of an Act of Parliament, a regulation or relevant case law;
- there is no evidence to support the decision;
- the facts are such that no reasonable person, given the law, could have come to such a conclusion;
- there is a breach of natural justice, ie, the procedure adopted led to unfairness (see also setting aside a CSO decision on p352) or the CSO made a biased decision;
- the CSO has not given enough reasons for the decision;
- when exercising a discretion the CSO took into account something irrelevant or ignored something relevant.[86]

A decision is wrong in law if it breaches European Community law. European Community law does not include the European Convention on Human Rights, which does not take precedence over British law in the British courts.[87] Commissioners have decided that Article 119 of the European Community Treaty and Council Directives 75/117 and 79/7 on equal treatment of men and women do not apply to the child support scheme.[88]

A decision is also wrong in law if the regulation it is made under is not made lawfully. Such a regulation is said to be *ultra vires* (outside the powers). In theory, a CSO can decide that a regulation is *ultra vires*, but is very unlikely to do so. A CSAT can also decide that a regulation is *ultra vires*,[89] and social security appeal tribunals have done so in benefit cases in the past. CSOs are instructed to seek urgent advice where any regulation is challenged as *ultra vires*.[90]

Apart from European law and *ultra vires*, there can be no review of or appeal against the application of the formula itself as laid down in law, so a request made on this ground alone can be refused.

Procedure

Before carrying out a review the CSO must give 14 days' notice to the parent with care, absent parent and Scottish child applicant.[91] This includes:[92]

- the applicant's reasons for requesting a review;
- where there is an assessment in force, a copy of the notification of that assessment (see p299);
- a request for comments;
- usually a review pack, as for a periodical review, except that no warning needs to given about the possible consequences of failure to provide information (see p363).

The rules about information which the CSO can request apply (see pp125–9). The rules about disclosure apply to the information given in the notice (see p156).[93]

Comments can be made in writing or in person.[94] A request to make comments in person will lead to an interview being arranged.[95] If, within 14 days of the sending of the notice, no comments have been made by a person and that person has not asked for an interview, or has failed without a good reason to keep an appointment for such an interview, the CSO can carry out the review without that person's comments.[96] Where a person has a good reason for not keeping an appointment, the CSO must arrange a further opportunity to make representations.[97]

Where two applications for review are accepted, a single review is conducted taking into account all the representations made.[98] If a second application for a second-tier review is received when a CSO is already carrying out a review, the CSO must notify the second applicant of this and take her/his representations into account.[99]

Outcome of review

The CSO can change the decision s/he has been asked to review. If s/he has enough information to make a fresh assessment and decides that one should be made – for example, where the amount of the assessment would be different from the one in force – s/he will make a fresh assessment.

Any fresh assessment(s) must be calculated taking into account all the facts known to the CSO, including any change of circumstance since the decision under review was made.[100] When an assessment was in force when the application was made, the relevant week (see p205) is that of the assessment under review.[101] The exception is where the decision reviewed is a refusal to carry out a change of circumstances review, when the relevant week is seven days ending with the day before the application for the change of circumstances review.[102]

A CSO can decide to cancel an assessment instead of making a fresh one. This may happen where the parent with care refuses to provide information requested. The rules for cancelling are the same as for a periodical review – for full details see p354. The only difference from these rules is that an assessment which was not validly made can be cancelled from its effective date.[103]

Where the CSO does not have enough information to carry out a review, s/he can make an IMA. The rules for this are the same as for a periodical review (see p354).

Effective date of fresh assessment

If a fresh assessment is issued after a second-tier review, its effective date depends on the type of decision that has been reviewed.

Decision under review	Effective date
Refusal of application	Date that original assessment would have been made.[104]
Current assessment or assessment which ceases to be in force after the review application was made	If the review is requested within 28 days (or longer if there is an unavoidable delay) whatever date the CSO decides, but it should normally be the effective date of the earlier assessment.[105] Otherwise, the first day of the maintenance period in which the request for review is received.[106]
Refusal to review after change of circumstance	As for a change of circumstances review (see p357).[107]
Cancellation of full assessment	Date cancelled assessment ceased to have effect.[108]
Cancellation of IMA	Date cancelled IMA ceased to have effect or 22 January 1996, whichever is later.[109]
Refusal to review after application for an allowance in recognition of a pre-April 1993 capital/property settlement due to a delay in providing evidence	If the Secretary of State believes there was good cause for the delay in providing the evidence, the date which would have applied to the original application. Otherwise, the first day of the maintenance period in which the evidence is supplied.[110]
Refusal to review after April 1995 changes for another reason	If the review is requested within 28 days of notification of the refusal (or longer if there is unavoidable delay), 18 April 1995.[111] Otherwise the first day of the maintenance period in which the application for second-tier review is received.[112]

If the original assessment was given in ignorance of or based on a mistake of fact due to a CSA operational or administrative error, the fresh assessment is backdated to the date of the original assessment.[113] If the effective date of the original assessment (see p303) is incorrect, the fresh assessment will have the effective date the original assessment should have had.[114]

If the incorrect assessment was caused by a misrepresentation of fact or failure to disclose a fact to the CSA by an absent parent or person with care, the fresh assessment has the effective date the original assessment had or would have had.[115] If a series of assessments is incorrect as a result of misrepresentation or failure to disclose, then all the assessments should be replaced. See CPAG's *National Welfare Benefits Handbook* for a discussion of the social security case law on misrepresentation and failure to disclose, but remember that under the child support provisions the parties are *not* under a general obligation to disclose all changes of circumstance (see p155).

Notification

If the CSO makes a fresh assessment, notification is given as if it were the first assessment (see p299). If the CSO cancels the assessment (except a Category A or D IMA) or decides it has ceased to have effect, notification is also given in the usual way (see pp309 and 311).

If the CSO refuses to carry out a review because there are no reasonable grounds (see p360),[116] or where the decision under review was a refusal to make an assessment, only the applicant is notified of the decision.[117] If a review is carried out but no fresh assessment is made, the parent with care, absent parent and Scottish child applicant must be notified.[118]

In all cases the notification must be in writing with reasons and explain how to seek a review, if appropriate, and how to appeal to a CSAT (see p367).[119]

6. REVIEWS INSTIGATED BY A CHILD SUPPORT OFFICER

This type of review is a section 19 review.

The first sort of section 19 review is like a second-tier review (see p358). A CSO can review a CSO decision without a request for a review if s/he is satisfied that the decision is wrong because it was:[120]

- made in ignorance of a material fact; *or*
- based on a mistake as to a material fact; *or*
- wrong in law (see p361).

The types of decision which can be reviewed were extended from 22 January 1996. A CSO can now review any of the following decisions:[121]

- a refusal to make an assessment;
- a refusal to review an assessment because of a change of circumstance;
- an assessment (whether or not in force);
- a cancellation of an assessment;
- a refusal to cancel an assessment;
- an adjustment of the amount of an assessment or a cancellation of an adjustment (see p394).[122]

The only exceptions to these rules are that a CSO cannot review a refusal to make or to cancel a Category A or D IMA.[123]

A CSO can now instigate a review where an appeal has been brought and the CSO agrees with the grounds of appeal (see p376).

The second type of section 19 review is like a change of circumstances review (see p355). If a CSO suspects that a change of circumstances review would be carried out if a person were to apply for one, a review of an assessment can be carried out without an application being made.[124] The significant test rule applies to such a review as if a change of circumstances review were being carried out (see p355).[125] A CSO cannot use this power to review a Category A or D IMA.[126]

The power to begin a section 19 review is discretionary and therefore the welfare of any child involved must be taken into account (see p52).

The CSA learns of some changes automatically from the DSS computer. CSOs are instructed to carry out a review where:[127]

- a third party reports that
  - the absent parent has come off IS, or
  - there is a new qualifying child; *or*
- the amount of family credit changes on review and a significant change in the amount of the assessment is likely.

It is unclear whether CSOs usually undertake a review when they are aware of some other significant change.

The CSO does not have to give anyone notice of intention to carry out a review and review packs are not usually issued.[128] However, where the CSA receives information which may lead to a review, further enquiries may be made. This may lead to a person finding out that the CSO is considering carrying out a review.

Outcome of review

Once the CSO has decided there are grounds for a review, s/he can:[129]

- set aside a cancellation of an assessment;
- make an assessment, including a fresh assessment or IMA;[130] *or*

- cancel the assessment; *or*
- leave the decision under review unchanged.

If a CSO wants to cancel an assessment – for example, where the parent with care refuses to provide information requested, then the rules for cancelling are the same as for a periodical review (see p354).

Where the CSO does not have enough information to carry out a review, s/he can make an IMA. The rules for this are the same as for a periodical review (see p354).

Effective date of fresh assessment

The effective date of any fresh assessment made following the death of a qualifying child is the first day of the maintenance period (see p306) in which the child died.[131] Where the original assessment was given in ignorance of or based on a mistake of fact due to a CSA operational or administrative error or a misrepresentation or failure to disclose by an absent parent or person with care, the effective date is set by the same rules as for a second-tier review in those cases (see p364).

Otherwise, the effective date of any fresh assessment made under a section 19 review, which is like a second-tier review, depends on the reason for the original review, ie:

- refusal to make an assessment – the effective date that original assessment would have had (see p303);[132]
- refusal to carry out a change of circumstances review – the effective date if that review had been carried out (see p357);[133]
- full assessment or Category B or C IMA – whatever date the CSO decides;[134]
- Category A or D IMA – where the effective date of that IMA is correct, the same effective date; where it is wrong, the effective date it should have had, unless those rules would give an effective date earlier than 16 February 1995, when the effective date will be 16 February 1995.[135]

The effective date of any fresh assessment made under a section 19 review, which is like a change of circumstances review, is the first day of the maintenance period in which the CSO first suspected that a fresh assessment might be required if a review were begun.[136]

Notification

If the CSO makes a fresh assessment, notification is given as if it were the first assessment (see p209). If the CSO cancels the assessment (except a Category A or D IMA) or decides it has ceased to have effect, notification is also given in the usual way (see pp309 and 311). The notification must be in writing with reasons and explain how to seek a review.

7. CHILD SUPPORT APPEAL TRIBUNALS

A person who is unhappy with a second-tier review decision or refusal to review can appeal to a child support appeal tribunal (CSAT), part of the Independent Tribunal Service. An appeal from a CSAT can be made on a question of law to a child support commissioner (see p382).

Appealing a decision

An appeal to a CSAT can only be made against the following CSO decisions:

- a reduced benefit direction;[137]
- a review decision on a reduced benefit direction;[138]
- a refusal to conduct a second-tier review;[139]
- a second-tier review decision;[140]
- a review decision on a CSO decision on contributions to child maintenance deducted from IS.[141]

An appeal will also be possible from any decision of the Secretary of State on an application for a departure direction,[142] but at the time of writing the provisions for making departure directions are not yet in force. See Chapter 15 for more details.

If an appeal is made against another type of decision, then the CSAT, or its chairperson, should decide it has no jurisdiction (see p375).

Who can appeal

Anyone aggrieved by one of these decisions may appeal (in the case of a making or review of a reduced benefit direction, only the parent with care can appeal).[143] This is regardless of who asked for the second-tier review or any earlier review. Because the CSO made the decision under appeal, s/he will not be aggrieved by it and so cannot appeal.

Once an appeal is made, the parties are the absent parent, person with care, Scottish child applicant and CSO;[144] but see p123 when a reduced benefit direction is appealed. Any other person may apply to a CSAT chairperson to become a party.[145] This may happen where another person may be affected by the outcome of the appeal. For example, a different parent with care of a child of the same absent parent may be affected if the CSAT decides to increase the assessment appealed. The chairperson will grant this application if the person is 'interested in the proceedings'. Because a party can call a witness (see p378), a person will only need to ask to be made a party if s/he believes that neither the absent parent nor person with care represents her/his interests. For example, the absent parent's partner will not usually need to become a party. Because of confidentiality the chairperson is very unlikely to allow a person who is a stranger to all the parties to be a party. Where a person is made a party and another party objects, the chairperson can be asked to change her/his mind, but there is no appeal.

Regardless of who appealed, all parties have the same rights, except that only the appellant can ask to withdraw the appeal (see p375).

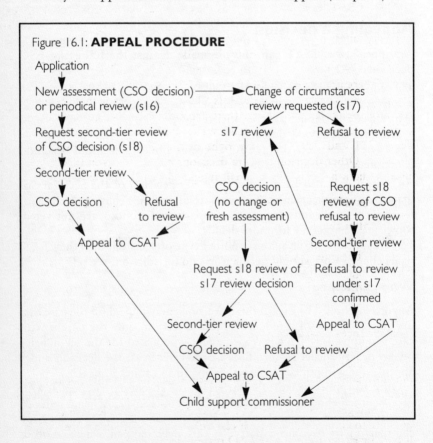

Figure 16.1: **APPEAL PROCEDURE**

What can the CSAT do

The CSAT will look afresh at the case and can consider any evidence and arguments, including those rejected or overlooked by the CSA and those which have not been used before. The CSAT is 'inquisitorial', which means it can raise legal arguments and factual questions on its own initiative.[146] The CSAT is, however, bound by the Acts and regulations, unless these are themselves unlawful (see p361). The CSAT cannot use discretion to override the regulations. The CSAT is also bound by case law (see p385). If the CSAT reaches a different conclusion to the CSO, it will allow the appeal.

Where the appeal is against a refusal to carry out a second-tier review of a decision, including a CSO review of a deduction from IS, the CSAT must decide whether such a review can be carried out. When considering this, the CSAT looks at the facts as they were when the CSO refused to carry out a review, even if the CSO did not know those facts.[147] Two commissioners have decided that, if there were no 'reasonable grounds' (see p360), then the CSAT must dismiss the appeal.[148] The argument that the CSO has a discretion to carry out a second-tier review even where there are no 'reasonable grounds' (see pp360–1) was not used in those cases. We believe that the Acts allow a CSAT to use that discretion to allow an appeal even where there are no 'reasonable grounds'.

For the tribunal's powers if it allows an appeal, and to gather evidence see pp381 and 384. The only right of appeal is from a final CSAT decision. Other decisions – eg, a decision of a chairperson that there is no jurisdiction – can only be challenged by judicial review (see p351).

Changes of circumstance

Where, after the decision being appealed is made, circumstances change or a fresh assessment is made, the CSAT may decide to take this into account, but only if one of the parties to the appeal asks it to do so.[149] This change was introduced on 4 September 1995 by the 1995 Act.

It will often be in all the parties' interests for the CSAT to use this power. Cases can take a long time to come to hearing (see p372) and, if the CSAT does not consider the current position, a change of circumstances review may then be necessary, with a possible further second-tier review and appeal. However, where the change of circumstance would lead to an unfavourable change in the assessment but no change of circumstances review would be possible because the change is not significant (see p356), it is best not to ask. The other disadvantage is that, if the CSAT decision is unfavourable, it may not be possible to change it, because it can only be appealed on a point of law. It may be easier to change a CSO review decision.

Even if one party does not want the CSAT to consider a change or new assessment, the CSAT can still do so if another party, including the CSO, asks it to. It is not yet clear whether CSOs will routinely ask

CSATs to use this power. The CSAT does not have to agree to a request but must take into account all the parties' comments when considering whether to.

Parentage disputes

If the second-tier review or refusal to review was made on the basis that a person was a parent of a child and a ground of appeal is that this basis was wrong, the appeal is made to a court instead of the CSAT (see p38).[150] A Northern Ireland commissioner has decided that, if this ground is raised after the letter of appeal is sent, the CSAT appeal can continue and the challenge on parentage can be made by seeking a review.[151] This overlooks the possibility that the grounds of appeal could be changed after the letter is sent or that a further appeal could be brought against the same decision on parentage grounds. In those cases, it may be that the CSAT would not have jurisdiction and the appeal should be heard by a court.

Why bring an appeal

The CSO decision may be unsatisfactory for different reasons. The CSO may have accepted evidence from the absent parent about his income which the parent with care disputes. The decision may be wrong in law because the CSO has misunderstood or overlooked a regulation. It may also be wrong in law because the CSO has failed properly to exercise a discretion. For details of 'wrong in law', see p361.

But an appeal does not have to be brought only for these reasons. It may not be clear how the decision was reached or what was taken into account. A party may also consider that the CSA did not fully investigate. Bringing an appeal may help because the CSA must provide all the information it has (see p372). The tribunal may be able to get copies of documents which the CSA refused to ask for. Each party will also have an opportunity to explain their case in person, or through a representative, to an independent body.

Because the appeal process may be lengthy and time-consuming, a party should always consider whether it is worth appealing. It may help to take advice when doing this. If a party brings an appeal, but later decides that the CSO decision is right, perhaps because s/he has now seen the evidence the CSA refused to release before, s/he can ask to withdraw the appeal (see p375).

When to appeal

An appeal must be made to the Central Office of CSATs (CSATCO) within 28 days of the decision appealed being notified, ignoring the day notification is given.[152] Notification is treated as made two working days (including Saturday) after posting by the CSA.[153] The letter of appeal is treated as being sent on the day it is actually received by CSATCO.[154]

The CSAT chairperson may extend the time for appealing so that the appeal can be considered, before or after time has run out. S/he will do this only if there are special reasons.[155] This may include late receipt by the appellant of notification of the decision, illness or postal strikes. From 28 February 1996 the meaning of 'special reasons' has been changed for social security appeals.[156] Child support appeals are *not* affected. For full details on special reasons see CPAG's *Rights Guide to Non-Means-Tested Benefits* 1995/96 edition. When appealing late, give as many details as possible, but do not delay appealing to do this. If a full explanation cannot be given immediately, ask for time to explain. If the appeal is late and no reasons are given, the appellant will be asked why the appeal was late.[157] If the chairperson refuses to extend time, there is no right to have this decision reconsidered,[158] though a chairperson may be able to do so.[159] There is no appeal from a refusal to extend time, but an application can be made for it to be set aside (see p382).[160]

How to appeal

Appeals must be in writing and signed either by the appellant or her/his qualified lawyer.[161] Other representatives can only sign a letter where it appears to the CSAT chairperson that the person is unable to sign her/himself. The letter of appeal must be sent to:[162]

> Central Office of the Child Support Appeal Tribunals (CSATCO)
> Anchorage Two, Anchorage Quay, Salford Quays,
> Manchester M5 2YN
> Tel: 0345 626311 (Mon to Thurs 8.30am – 5pm and Fri 8.30am – 4.30pm) Fax: 0161 877 7889

The letter does not have to be in a particular form but must identify the decision being appealed against and set out the grounds of appeal.[163] If the letter does not do both these things, the chairperson may direct the appellant to give further details.[164]

CSA staff are instructed that any appeal letter wrongly sent to the CSA must be forwarded to CSATCO within 24 hours of receipt,[165] but CSOs are advised not to do this if no second-tier review has been carried out.[166]

Preparing a case

Whether you are the appellant, the other party – 'the respondent' – or advising someone, the following are some of the points you should consider when an appeal is brought.

The CSAT may be the first chance for an independent assessment of your case. It may also be the last chance, because there can only be an appeal to a commissioner on a point of law. Whether you are the appellant or the other party – 'the respondent' – try to ensure that the CSAT knows the facts and arguments about your case.

Papers provided by the CSA

The CSO prepares a 'submission' which is a written statement of the facts and law involved in the case. This is usually based on a standard format.[167] In the submission, the CSO will often accept that the second-tier review was wrong. In 1994/95 about half of CSO decisions were wrong.[168] When this is done, the CSO will state what the correct decision should have been.[169] This is not a review and has no legal effect (see p376). It simply explains the decision the CSO is asking the CSAT to make.

The CSO should attach to the submission copies of all evidence received by the CSA, including correspondence and documents.[170] Parts of these will be blanked out because of the confidentiality rules (see p156).[171] If a document is difficult to read, a re-typed version can be provided.[172]

There may be papers on the CSA file which are irrelevant to the appeal – for example, an earlier request for exemption because of a risk of harm when the appeal is about the amount of the assessment. If you do not want the other party to see these, write and ask the CSO not to include these papers. Also, the CSAT chairperson can be asked to direct the CSO not to include them.

The submission is prepared by the CSA's central appeals unit (CAU) in Lytham St Anne's. The CAU asks the CSAC for the case documents when it is ready to write the submission and aims to keep them for only four weeks.[173] The CSA has a target of 18 days for preparing the submission, but in fact it usually takes many months. In November 1995 the average time from the appeal letter to tribunal hearing was 41 weeks.[174] Most of that delay is by the CAU. The submission is sent to the CSATCO where it is photocopied and sent to all the parties.

Considering the facts and law

When you get the submission you should read it, even though it may be very long. It may make the reasons for the decision clearer, though often parts of it will still be confusing. The CSO may now accept some of the arguments previously rejected or ignored. You should try to see what facts or legal issues are still disputed.

Use this book to check the law, or you may wish to use *Child Support: The Legislation* (see Appendix 7). If the CSO quotes a commissioner's decision or you want to use one, you can get a copy (see Caselaw, p385). CSATCO do not have copies of unreported decisions. You may wish to quote the *Child Support Adjudication Guide* (see Appendix 8) if it supports your arguments, but it is not legally binding.

You should also check the documents which the CSO has attached to the submission. The CSO may have left out something you have sent which is relevant, or something the other party has sent which is mentioned in the submission. In that case, it is best to contact the CSA and ask them to send the missing papers to the CSAT.

If there is delay in producing a submission, you may not want to wait any longer. The CSAT does not have to wait for the submission, so you can write to the chairperson and ask her/him to direct that the appeal be heard. This may mean that you do not have all the evidence the CSA has. You could try to get this by also asking the chairperson to direct the CSO to provide copies of all the papers (see p374). Because that may be seen as 'jumping the queue', you should explain why you need those papers and why your case should be heard urgently.

Further evidence

You may have evidence about your circumstances which the CSA does not have. You may also have evidence about the other party's circumstances which the CSA does not have. You may have been sent this by the other party, or been told it by someone who knows her/him. You may have got it through another court or tribunal case – for example, a claim for spousal maintenance. Ask yourself whether the CSAT may need any of this.

You can put further relevant evidence before the tribunal at any stage. It is best to do this soon after the submission is sent out. This means the papers can be copied to the other parties. If you produce evidence or unreported commissioners' decisions at the hearing or send it in shortly before, this may cause an adjournment (see p380).

You can tell the CSAT about the facts and law at the hearing. You can also 'give evidence' – that is, say what you have seen and heard. For example: 'I look after the child from Friday night to Monday night' may be the best evidence of those facts. You may want to consider now whether there should be any other witnesses at the hearing (see p378). It may help if you send a letter setting out what you think is in dispute and what you say the correct answers are. This is particularly important if the points you make are not in the grounds of appeal or if you have changed your mind about something. It does not have to be in any particular form.

The CSAT's powers to obtain information and evidence

You may want the other person to provide further information or documents. It is best to prepare a list of the documents and/or further information you think the tribunal should have. This should be as precise as possible. For example, you may believe the absent parent has received a pay increase and has turned down an offer of overtime. You have written to the CSA but they refuse to investigate. You may want to ask for: pay-slips from February to May 1996 (inclusive); and ask 'Have you been offered overtime at any time since 1 June 1996?' and 'What was your response to any such offer?' If you know the person's address and s/he is happy for you to write to her/him, you could do that by letter. You may want to point out, especially to an employer, that if s/he fails to comply, the chairperson can direct her/him to provide the information or documents or to attend as a witness with the documents.

If that is not possible, or if s/he does not provide everything you ask for, the CSAT chairperson can make a direction.[175] This is done by writing to CSATCO and asking the chairperson to direct the person to 'produce the documents' in the list and to 'provide further particulars' – that is, the answers to the questions in the list. The letter to CSATCO should explain the steps you have taken to get this information and why it is relevant to the case.

The chairperson can direct any party to provide evidence or information. A person who is not a party – for example, an employer – cannot be directed to provide evidence, but it may be possible to direct her/him to provide further particulars. Such a person can also be ordered to attend as a witness and produce documents. It may be useful if this is done before the full hearing, so that each party will have a chance to consider those documents and/or evidence. For details of summoning witnesses, see p378.

The chairperson will usually decide about directions without a hearing, but one may be held. The chairperson may also make a direction when no one has requested it, where s/he has read the papers and considers the document or information is necessary. If the chairperson makes a direction, a copy will be sent to all the parties.

There is no legal requirement to comply with the direction. However, if a person fails to comply without a good explanation, the CSAT may decide that s/he has something to hide. This may lead it to reject that person's evidence. If the person is the appellant, the appeal can be struck out (see p376). A party can ask the High Court in England and Wales to order a person to comply with a direction,[176] but we do not know of any case where that has been done. If the High Court did this, a person could be fined or sent to prison for failing to comply. The Court of

Session in Scotland cannot do this.

There is no appeal from a direction or a refusal to make one, but the chairperson can be asked to reconsider her/his decision.

Ending an appeal without a full hearing

There are four ways an appeal can end without a full hearing. If a party dies, the appeal does not end. The CSA can appoint a person to continue in the place of the person who has died.[177] The CSA decides whom to appoint and probate is not necessary.

No jurisdiction

An appeal may be brought which the CSAT has no jurisdiction to hear. This will arise when the decision appealed does not give a right to appeal. For the decisions which can be appealed, see p367. If the CSA notices that this is the case, CSATCO will be notified.[178] The CSAT will also not have jurisdiction where a ground of the appeal is disputed parentage (see p370). The chairperson may declare that the CSAT does not have jurisdiction.[179] This ends the appeal. There is no appeal from this decision, but the chairperson can be asked to withdraw the declaration. If the position is not clear – for example, there is a legal dispute about jurisdiction – the chairperson should allow a full hearing to take place, because then there is a right of appeal to a commissioner.

Withdrawing appeals

The appellant can ask to withdraw the appeal at any time.[180] If this is done at a hearing, the chairperson will ask the other parties there to comment. If one party is not there, the chairperson may refuse to make a decision until that party has had a chance to comment. If the appellant wishes to withdraw at any other time, s/he must do so by writing to CSATCO. Unless all the parties consent in writing, they will be asked for their comments. After giving them a reasonable chance to comment, the chairperson will make the decision. The CSO is instructed not to consent unless s/he is sure that neither the absent parent nor parent with care will be disadvantaged by the withdrawal.[181] CSOs are instructed to inform CSATCO why consent has been refused. In all cases, it is the chairperson's decision whether to allow the appellant to withdraw the appeal.

A withdrawn appeal cannot be reinstated, but any of the parties (except the CSO) can appeal the same CSO decision again, though an extension of time from the chairperson is likely to be needed (see p371).[182]

Striking out appeals

An appeal can be struck out (ie, dismissed without consideration) if the appellant fails to:[183]

- 'prosecute' the apeal – ie, pursue it properly;
- comply with any chairperson's direction; *or*
- reply to any CSAT query about her/his availability for a hearing.

This is to prevent an abuse of the CSAT by the appellant. Any failure of any other party to the appeal cannot lead to striking out. Before striking out, the appellant must be warned what is being considered and given a reasonable opportunity to explain why that should not happen.[184] There is no appeal against a decision to strike out, but if any party asks for the appeal to be reinstated within one year of the decision to strike out, the chairperson can do so.[185] Any party can ask the chairperson to strike out an appeal at any time, but the chairperson can also strike out when no application has been made.[186]

Review pending appeal

Even though an appeal is 'pending' – ie, it has been brought but not disposed of – reviews may be carried out.

Where the CSO carries out a section 19 review (see p364) after an appeal is brought, and the CSO considers that the decision s/he has made is the same decision the CSAT would make if every ground of appeal had succeeded, the appeal 'lapses', ie, ends; otherwise the review has no effect.[187] This power was introduced on 18 December 1995 by the 1995 Act. At the time of writing it is not known when CSOs will do this.

This will save the time and effort of an unnecessry hearing where the parties agree the second-tier review was wrong.

It is not clear if the CSO can consider only whether the decision satisfies the appellant's grounds, or if s/he must also consider whether the other party's grounds for criticising the decision appealed are satisfied. If this is not the case, it would be wrong for a CSO to carry out a section 19 review, since this would only lead to a further second-tier review and appeal by the other person. The CSO may also not fully understand either party's grounds of appeal. For these reasons, it is our view that a CSO should only carry out a section 19 review in this situation where no other party to the appeal objects.

If you are unhappy with a CSO decision that an appeal has lapsed, you may ask for a CSAT hearing to decide whether the appeal has lapsed or not. In our view, the final decision on this is for the CSAT to make.

A periodical review will normally be carried out at the usual time (see p353) and a change of circumstances review will be carried out if requested (see p355).[188] Where there has been a change of circumstances, or where the CSO is carrying out or has carried out a review before the CSAT hearing, the CSAT can be asked to deal with the review and/or change (see p369). CSOs are instructed not to carry out further second-tier reviews while an appeal is pending.[189]

Hearings

The CSAT must hold an oral hearing of every appeal, unless the appeal has ended without a full hearing (see p375).[190] The CSAT or its chairperson can also hold an oral hearing of any application – for example, an application for a direction. CSATCO must give the parties notice of the time and place of the hearing of at least 10 days ending on the day before the hearing.[191] If a hearing is set and your case is not ready or you or a witness cannot attend, you can ask for the hearing to be postponed.[192] Do this by writing to CSATCO, explaining in detail why you want a postponement and why, if it is the case, you previously said you were ready to go ahead and could attend on the date set. The CSATCO letter giving the hearing date misleads the parties by stating that a request must be made within three days of the letter and that the reasons must be exceptional. This is wrong: the chairperson can postpone the hearing if s/he thinks fit. Good reasons for a postponement include that the appellant cannot get representation. However, if there have been previous postponements or the request is made very late, a refusal is likely. If this happens, the tribunal hearing the case can be asked to adjourn (see p380).

Members of the tribunal

The tribunal consists of three members: a legally qualified chairperson and two lay members.[193] The chairperson must be legally qualified for at least five years and the other members must, in the opinion of the President of the CSATs, have knowledge or experience in the area and be representative of people living or working in the area.[194] The tribunal members must not all be of the same sex, unless the chairperson rules that it is not reasonably practicable to keep to this.[195] All three members must be present for an appeal hearing, though a chairperson may sit alone to consider an application or an appeal about a departure direction (see p348).

Attending the hearing

Every party has the right to be present.[196] The hearing can go ahead in the absence of one, several or all of the parties.[197] The CSA local office usually sends a field officer to present the case. S/he is called a **presenting officer**. This may be a CSA officer who has been involved in the case, for example, who interviewed the parties. A commissioner has decided that this is bad practice.[198] You may want to ask the CSA in advance to send someone who has not been involved. A party may be represented by a lawyer or lay person, whether the party attends the hearing in person or not.[199] Legal aid is not available for representation at CSAT hearings, although it is possible to obtain preliminary advice on the Green Form scheme (Pink Form in Scotland).

Because the other party may be at the hearing, you may want only to send written representations or ask someone to attend on your behalf. CSATCO intends every hearing venue to have separate waiting rooms for the absent parent, parent with care and presenting officer. Where another party or witness may become violent, CSATCO should be told as soon as possible and asked what steps will be taken.

The hearing is usually held in the area of the appellant. Therefore, in some cases, the other party has to travel substantial distances. Expenses, including travel expenses, subsistence and some compensation for loss of earnings, will be paid to those who attend a CSAT as a party, witness or lay representative.[200] The CSAT clerk will pay travelling and subsistence expenses on the day unless these are large. Travel expenses can be paid in advance.

Witnesses

Any person can come voluntarily to a hearing to give evidence. Sometimes a person may not want to come. The chairperson can summon or, in Scotland, cite witnesses to the hearing and require them to answer any relevant questions or produce documents as long as s/he gives 10 days' notice.[201] Before issuing a summons, the chairperson must take into account the need to protect intimate personal or financial circumstances, commercial sensitivity, confidential information and national security.[202] However, since almost all child support cases involve intimate circumstances and confidentiality, those alone ought not to prevent a summons being issued.

A witness cannot be required to give evidence which a court could not compel her/him to give at a trial of an action.[203] An 'action' is a civil case, not a criminal case, so this rule only clearly applies to diplomats and to the Queen! Those people cannot be summoned as witnesses.[204] It does not appear to prevent questions to a person about criminal offences which s/he or her/his spouse are said to have committed or about their convictions, because those rules only apply to criminal trials.[205] CSA staff may be witnesses, for example, if there is a dispute about what was said at an interview.

If you want to obtain information or documents from someone and the chairperson will not issue a direction, or you want them to attend personally, you can apply for a summons. Do this by writing to CSATCO explaining what information or documents you want, why this will help the CSAT to decide the case and why this is the only way of getting the information or documents. This is particularly important where the witness is a CSA staff member, because the chairperson may be reluctant to summons them. If you only want documents, you may want to ask the chairperson to summons the person to produce the documents at a hearing arranged only for that purpose. The documents can then be copied for the parties. This will avoid arranging a full hearing which may be adjourned because of the documents. The witness may decide to post the documents to CSATCO instead. If you want the witness to attend a hearing to give evidence, the tribunal is likely to arrange a full hearing.

There is no legal requirement to comply with a summons or citation, but the CSAT may treat a failure to comply in the same way as it would a failure to comply with a direction (see p374). The High Court has the same powers as it does for a direction (see p374).

A person named in a summons or citation can ask the chairperson in writing to vary it or set it aside.[206] There is no appeal against a summons or citation or a refusal to issue one.

Conduct of the hearing

The hearing will be in private unless the chairperson decides that all, or part of it, should be in public.[207] Even when held in private, anyone who is training to be a tribunal member, a clerk or a CSO is entitled to attend, as well as the President of the Independent Tribunal Service (which runs CSATCO), any full-time chairperson and a member of the Council on Tribunals, but may not take part in the hearing.[208] If all the parties and the chairperson agree, any other person can also attend.

CSATs are modelled on social security tribunals and use the same chairpersons, lay members and staff. The CSAT is concerned to emphasise its informality. The CSAT members usually sit along one side of a table with the chairperson between the lay members. The CSAT clerk will show the parties into the room and the presenting officer will usually sit between them along the opposite side of the table. The chairperson will usually introduce everyone and explain the CSAT's role. If you are unsure about anyone's role – for example, whether the absent parent's wife is representing him, accompanying him or here as a witness – ask the chairperson. While someone may be both representative and witness, each person can only have one representative or friend present, unless all parties consent.

Every party has the right to address the tribunal, to give evidence, to call witnesses and to put questions to any other party, the presenting officer or witnesses.[209] The order in which the parties present their cases is up to the chairperson. The chairperson may begin by asking the presenting officer to present the CSO's case. The presenting officer is not there to argue for the CSO, but to help the CSAT.[210] S/he will usually say very little at this stage. It is rare for her/him to call any witnesses. What the presenting officer says about the case is not evidence, unless s/he decides to be a witness.

The chairperson will then ask the appellant or her/his representative to present her/his case. You should speak to the chairperson but make sure the lay members follow what you are saying. Outline briefly the points you want to make: remember, the CSAT should have read the papers before the hearing. You should then give evidence about any facts you know about personally. You may have to answer questions from the CSAT members, the presenting officer or another party or representative. If you have any witnesses, ask them questions and try to ensure that your questions are dealt with before everyone else's. When you have put forward the evidence, ask the chairperson if you should talk about the legal points. S/he may want to hear the other party's evidence first. When making your legal points, refer the tribunal to the relevant parts of the law or case law. You can ask anyone else's witnesses questions.

The CSAT may, and usually does, require a witness, including a party, to take an oath or affirm.[211] The tribunal may allow an interpreter to act for one of the parties or witnesses and may ask her/him to take an oath or affirm that s/he will carry out the functions correctly.[212] It is CSAT policy to arrange the interpreter if requested in good time.

At any point, the tribunal members can decide to adjourn a hearing whether or not one of the parties asks them to.[213] If the same tribunal cannot continue with the case after the adjournment without causing a significant delay, then the case must be heard by a tribunal consisting of three different people.[214]

Hearings have been averaging one to two hours in length and therefore only two cases tend to be listed for each session.

Decisions

After all the evidence and submissions, the CSAT members consider the appeal. They do this with no one else present.[215] The decision is taken unanimously or by a majority,[216] and it is almost always announced to the parties once it is made. It is best to save any comments until you have seen the full reasons in the written decision.

If the CSAT decides the decision appealed was wrong, it will allow the appeal. When it allows an appeal, the CSAT must send the case back to the CSA for a CSO to deal with.[217] The CSAT may also give directions to the CSO.[218] These should resolve all the issues considered by the CSAT, but the CSAT will not usually calculate any fresh assessment. So, in a case where income was the only disputed fact, the CSAT could direct the CSO to make a fresh assessment from a certain date on the same basis as the decision appealed, except that the absent parent's net income is £234 a week.

The CSAT's written decision, including any findings of fact, reasons any directions and the reasons for dissent if not unanimous,[219] will be sent to all parties as soon as possible.[220] This usually takes about four weeks. The decision will be implemented by a CSO at the CAU who should inform the CSAC and may consider an appeal to a commissioner (see p382).[221]

If a CSO, after receiving the CSAT decision, is unclear about how s/he should deal with the case, s/he may apply to the CSAT for further directions.[222] When the CSAT clerk receives an application for such a direction, all the parties to the case must be notified and given the opportunity to make representations.[223] The CSAT may not change its decision, but only clarify it.

Accidental errors in the decision can be corrected by a CSAT and written notice of the alteration must be given to the parties.[224]

You should check that any subsequent CSO decision and assessment follows the CSAT's directions. If it does not, you should first check that the CSA agrees with you about what the decision means. If you disagree and the CSO will not apply for a further direction, you should consider whether the CSAT decision is clear. If it is, you should consider judicial review of the CSO (see p351). If it is not clear, you can ask for a correction if there is an accidental error. You should also consider an appeal to a commissioner (see p382).

If any party is dissatisfied with the CSAT decision, s/he can appeal on a point of law to a child support commissioner (see p382).

Setting aside decisions

A CSAT decision can be set aside if:[225]

- a document was not received at the appropriate time by one of the parties, a representative or the CSAT;
- a party or a representative was not present at the hearing;
- there was some other procedural irregularity or mishap.

An application to set aside a CSAT decision must be made in writing to the CSAT clerk within three months of the date of the notification of the decision, or of a later correction of that decision, although this can be extended if there are special reasons (see p371).[226] Each of the parties is notified of the application and allowed to comment, before a decision is made.[227]

If a decision is set aside, then another CSAT hearing must be arranged and the case must be re-heard in full.

An application to set aside a CSAT decision can be withdrawn by a written request before a decision on the application is made.[228]

A refusal to extend time for appealing to a CSAT or for applying to set aside a CSAT decision can itself also be set aside.[229] The procedure is the same as for setting aside a CSAT decision.

8. CHILD SUPPORT COMMISSIONERS

Any party, including a CSO, can appeal from a decision of a CSAT to a commissioner on a point of law.[230] When departure is introduced (see p322), the Secretary of State will be able to appeal if the CSAT's decision is about a defective direction.[231] There is an error of law if:[232]

- the CSAT misinterpreted or overlooked any part of the legislation or case law;
- the CSAT made findings of fact for which there was no evidence;
- the CSAT decision does not give a proper statement of facts or reasons;
- the CSAT's decision is inconsistent with the facts it found;
- there is a breach of natural justice in the way in which the appeal was carried out – eg, a request for a postponement was refused even though one of the parties could not attend the hearing, the tribunal refused to allow a relevant witness to be called or to allow a particular line of questioning.

An appeal cannot be made only on the ground that there is further evidence to show the CSAT was wrong or circumstances have changed. These should be dealt with by CSO review.

A commissioner is a very experienced lawyer. Almost all commissioners work full time dealing mostly with social security appeals.

If there is an error of law, the commissioner will set aside the CSAT's decision. S/he will then:[233]

- if appropriate, make further findings of fact, but will not usually do this where relevant facts are disputed; *and/or*
- give the decision the tribunal should have given, which may be to the same effect as the decision appealed; *or*
- refer the case to a CSO or a CSAT giving directions for its determination.

Where the appeal to the commissioner was by the Secretary of State and the CSAT decision was about a departure direction, the commissioner cannot refer the case to a CSO.[234]

How to appeal

Obtaining leave to appeal is the first stage of appealing to a commissioner. An application for leave to appeal must be made in writing to the CSAT chairperson at CSATCO (see p371) within three months of the notification of the CSAT decision.[235]

Notification of the chairperson's decision is sent to all the parties.[236] If s/he gives leave to appeal, a notice of appeal must be sent to the commissioner's office within 42 days of that notification.[237] If the chairperson refuses leave to appeal, an application for leave to appeal can be made to the commissioner within 42 days of the notification refusing leave. Where an application for the CSAT decision to be set aside was made or the decision was corrected,[238] the time limit runs from the date of the decision on the application or the correction, instead of the date of the original decision.[239]

If no application is made to the chairperson within time or the notice of appeal or application for leave is not sent in time to the commissioner, the commissioner can extend time if there are special reasons (see p371) for doing so.[240] The chairperson cannot extend time: any application must be made to the commissioner.

An application for leave or notice of appeal must state the grounds of appeal.[241] Where it is late, detailed reasons should be given for extending time. CSATCO can provide a form for applications and appeals, but this does not have to be used. A copy of any application to the commissioner for leave will be sent to the other parties.[242]

The addresses of the commissioner's offices (OSSC) are:

England and Wales
Harp House
83 Farringdon Street
London EC4A 4DH
Tel: 0171 353 5145
Fax: 0171 936 2171

Scotland
23 Melville Street
Edinburgh
EH3 7PW
Tel: 0131 225 2201
Fax: 0131 220 6782

The commissioner usually considers applications for leave without a hearing, especially when s/he decides to grant leave. If leave is refused, no reasons have to be given, and a short written decision is sent to the parties.

An application for leave can be withdrawn at any time before a decision on it is made, by writing to the office it was sent to.[243] An appeal may be withdrawn by the appellant, but only with the commissioner's permission.[244] A commissioner is unlikely to allow an appeal to be withdrawn if another party supports the appeal. An application for leave made to a commissioner or an appeal which has been withdrawn can be reinstated with the commissioner's permission.[245]

The written procedure

Unlike the CSAT, on a commissioner's appeal the parties are expected to explain their cases mostly in writing. If leave is granted, the papers before the CSAT are sent to all the parties. These are in a particular order and are numbered, and should be checked to see that all the documents are included and whether there are any new ones.

If it is not the CSO's appeal, the CSO will be asked to comment in writing within 30 days of the papers being issued. The CSO may support the appeal, but it is her/his reasons for doing so which matter. This is because a CSO may support an appeal because the CSAT did not make all necessary findings of fact and give adequate reasons. However, s/he may propose that the commissioner give a decision to the same effect or even to worse effect as far as one or both of the other parties are concerned.

The other parties will then be given 30 days to comment. The appellant will then be given 30 days to comment on everyone else's observations. Each party gets at least one chance to comment.

Before commenting, consider whether it would be best to have the case go back to another CSAT or be decided by the commissioner. However, where there is a dispute of fact which has to be resolved, the commissioner is likely to send the case back to a CSAT.

Oral hearings

If one party's case is not fully supported by the CSO or there is a point of law which s/he thinks the commissioner might decide against her/him, s/he should request an oral hearing.[246] The CSO or another party can also request a hearing. The commissioner almost always grants a request for an oral hearing. The CSO is almost always legally represented and other parties should consider getting expert representation.

Oral hearings are usually heard in London or Edinburgh but are also heard in Cardiff. Plenty of notice is given and travel expenses are paid. The hearings are usually in public but, unless the other party brings observers, it is very unlikely that anyone else will be there.[247] The hearing is more formal than a CSAT. While evidence can be given, in practice it is rare. The commissioner can postpone or adjourn a hearing and will usually do so if it will help a parent get representation.[248]

Decisions

A written decision is sent to all the parties.[249] The decision must not contain the surname of the child concerned in the appeal or any other information which may lead to the child being identified.

A commissioner's decision can be set aside for the same reasons as for a CSAT decision (see p381). An application must be made within 30 days of the notification.[250]

Caselaw

Commissioners' decisions are legally binding on CSOs and CSATs. Decisions have a reference number which shows the country they were made in and the year the application or appeal was brought (not the year the decision was made in). CCS 3/94 is from England or Wales; CSCS 3/94 is from Scotland and CSC 3/94 is from Northern Ireland. Each of those appeals was the third child support appeal to be brought in that country in that year. The commissioner who gives a decision may 'star' it if s/he thinks it decides a useful point. The decision is marked with a star and given a 'starred' number. Some starred decisions are reported and are then given a new number: R(CS) 1/95. Reporting takes more than a year. Use the original number (not the starred one) for an unreported decision. Use the 'R number' for a reported decision. Some decisions are taken by a tribunal of three commissioners.

English and Scottish decisions are binding in Great Britain. Where there are conflicting decisions a reported decision carries more weight,[251] but starring does not matter. Where there is no British decision on the point, a Northern Irish decision will be very persuasive. Where there is no child support commissioner's decision, a social security commissioner's decision on the same point – for example, an identically worded regulation – will be persuasive.

Social security decisions follow the same numbering system as child support. So income support decisions will be numbered: CIS 4/91, CSIS 4/91 or R(IS) 4/91.

From 1995 all commissioners' decisions in social security and child support cases have been numbered under a combined system. Whereas before there could be CIS 4/94 and CCS 4/94, from 1995 each number will be allocated to only one decision. This does not affect numbering of reported cases.

Commissioners are bound by judgments of the House of Lords, High Court and Court of Appeal or, in Scotland, Court of Session. A commissioner is not bound by a decision of another commissioner or her/his own previous decisions, though commissioners usually follow long-

standing decisions. A commissioner will follow a tribunal of commissioners unless there are good reasons for not doing so.

Unreported decisions are available from the appropriate commissioners' office (see p383), price £1. Reported decisions are published by
HMSO (see Appendix 8).

Further appeal

Appeals on a point of law can be made from a commissioner's decision
to the Court of Appeal or, in Scotland, the Court of Session.[252]
Applications for leave to appeal must be made first to the commissioner
within three months of notification of her/his decision.[253] Legal advice
must be sought at this stage.

CHAPTER SEVENTEEN

Collection and enforcement

This chapter covers:
1. Payment of child maintenance (p388)
2. Collection of other payments (p395)
3. Arrears (p397)
4. Deduction from earnings orders (p406)
5. Enforcement (p415)

Despite government assurances about the openness of Child Support Agency (CSA) operations, the CSA *Collection and Enforcement Manual* is not yet publicly available. Therefore, there are some unreferenced statements in this chapter based on information gained from conversations with advisers, CSA officials and clients.

The CSA can arrange the collection and enforcement of child maintenance payments, both child support maintenance assessed by the CSA[1] and certain other maintenance payments (see p395).[2] Each regional CSA centre (CSAC) has an accounts section, the staff in which set up an account for each assessment where the collection service applies, and a debt management section. Each CSAC also has a litigation section (formerly called the enforcement section), which is responsible for pursuing court action. Most of the decisions discussed in this chapter are made by CSA staff working in these sections.

Fees for CSA services are not charged where the fee would otherwise be payable on or between 18 April 1995 and 5 April 1997.[3] An assessment fee is payable on the day the assessment is made, and each anniversary of that date. A collection fee is payable on the day the collection account is opened. For details of liability to pay fees, see p398 of the 1995/96 edition of this *Handbook*. For fees for DNA tests, see p397. For collection of fees, see p396.

Decisions about collection and enforcement are taken by CSA staff acting on behalf of the Secretary of State. Within the limits of the regulations, these decisions are discretionary. In almost all areas this discretion is wide, so there is scope for negotiation with CSA staff. Where there are instructions or practices for dealing with a type of case in a certain way, the CSA should be told about these if they are helpful.

If they are not, the CSA can be reminded that they are not binding, and it is up to the individual officer dealing with the case. Because the decisions are discretionary, the welfare of any child likely to be affected must be taken into account by the CSA (see p52).

The assessment itself cannot be altered except by review or appeal, so arguments that the absent parent cannot afford the assessment under the formula will not lead to a reduction in current liability. The only time that the CSA may agree to suspend collection of some of the liability is while a review or appeal is pending, the result of which is likely to lead to a reduction in the assessment.

There is no appeal to a child support appeal tribunal (CSAT) from a decision by the Secretary of State on collection and enforcement. A deduction from earnings order can be appealed to a magistrates' court (see p413) and judicial review may be possible for other decisions (see p351). A child support officer (CSO) decision on an adjustment can be reviewed and appealed (see p359). For complaints, see p28.

I. PAYMENT OF CHILD MAINTENANCE

The CSA has a wide discretion to decide:
- the method by which the absent parent pays child maintenance;[4]
- the person to whom it is paid;[5]
- where payment is made through the CSA or someone else, the method by which payment is made to the person with care;[6]
- the timing of payments;[7] *and*
- the amount of payments towards arrears.[8]

The CSA's power to do this is not affected by whether the person with care is on income support (IS), family credit (FC), disability working allowance (DWA), or none of those.[9] However, where the applicant was not on one of those benefits at the time of the child support application, the CSA can only arrange payment on the request of a party (see below).

Before making these decisions about payments, the CSA must, as far as is possible, give the absent parent and the person with care a chance to make representations and must take any representations into account.[10]

When will the CSA arrange payment

In every case, the CSA must notify the absent parent in writing of the amounts and dates of payments, to whom he must make payment and how he must pay.[11] This notice is sent as soon as possible after the assessment is made and again after any change in the details in the notice.[12]

When the CSA decides that payments are to be made to or via the CSA, the CSA refers to this arrangement as **the collection service**. By November 1995, the collection service had been used for about 60 per cent of assessments.[13] The CSA normally provides the collection service if an applicant requests it but the CSA does not have to do so. CPAG is interested to hear of cases where requests have been refused.

In the case of a section 6 applicant – that is, a parent with care on IS/FC/DWA when she applied for child maintenance (see p54) – the CSA can decide how child maintenance will be paid against the wishes of the parent with care.[14] However, while the CSA almost always specifies the method of payment, in many cases the CSA does not use the collection service.

In the case of section 4 and 7 applicants (see p55) – ie, applicant parents with care who were not on IS/FC/DWA at the time, other persons with care, absent parent applicants and Scottish child applicants – a party must ask the CSA to provide the collection service.[15]

The maintenance application form (MAF) and the maintenance enquiry form (MEF) ask each party whether they want to use the collection service. Guidance to CSA staff does not distinguish clearly between the collection service and payments being made via the CSA. You should always state your wishes and explain your reasons as fully as possible.

If neither party requests the collection service and the CSA does not impose it on a section 6 applicant, the parties are left to make their own arrangements. If you change your mind later you should let the CSA know. This can be done over the telephone,[16] but should be followed up in writing. When the CSA was first set up, the CSA refused to enforce payments due before the collection service was requested, but it should now collect arrears already due when the request is made, though this still does not always happen.[17]

Why use the collection service

The collection service removes the need for direct contact between the absent parent and person with care. The CSA's record of payments from the absent parent and to the person with care is independent of the parties, so disputes about whether payments were made may be avoided. Where the person with care is on IS, using the collection service should mean that IS payments to her will not vary, even if the absent parent does not pay the CSA (see p316). Where the person with care is not on IS, the collection service is supposed to ensure regular payments. While it should mean that the CSA enforces quickly when necessary, this has not happened in practice.

The main disadvantage of the collection service is that it is being badly operated by the CSA. Many collection accounts are in arrears and many persons with care and some absent parents are unhappy with the level of service (see p23). During 1994/95 the CSA failed to meet its targets for collection.[18] In December 1995 collection was at only 72 per cent of target.[19]

Parents with care do not receive regular details of the state of the account. This means that those on IS do not know how changes – eg, taking a job – would affect their finances. See p391 for details.

For CPAG to continue lobbying for a system of guaranteed payments by the CSA, we need examples of where the current system is still failing, especially FC claimants.

Who is paid

The CSA can require the absent parent to make payments of child maintenance:[20]

- direct to the person with care;
- direct to a Scottish child applicant;
- to or through the CSA; *or*
- to or through another person directed by the Secretary of State.

About half of all maintenance paid is paid by the absent parent direct to the person with care and half is collected by the CSA.[21]

Although some absent parents and, indeed, some persons with care, may want to have payments made to a third party – eg, to cover mortgage capital repayments or endowment premiums, nursery school fees, telephone bills – it is highly unlikely that the Secretary of State will consider such arrangements to be child maintenance payments.

Where payments are made via the Secretary of State, only maintenance actually paid to the CSA can be passed on: the CSA cannot pay the person with care before the absent parent pays the CSA. About half of all maintenance collected by the CSA is passed on to the person with care, while the other half is kept to offset payment of IS.[22]

Absent parents on income support

Where an absent parent on IS is required to contribute towards child maintenance (see p168), the Benefits Agency makes the £4.80 (or £2.40 – see p170) deduction from IS and passes it on to the CSA. The CSA in turn hands it on to the person with care[23] (on a quarterly basis if the person with care is not receiving IS.)[24]

Persons with care on income support

The Secretary of State may decide to require payments for ongoing liability via the CSA from the outset, especially if the absent parent has not been making regular payments of child maintenance due under a previous agreement or if there is some other evidence to suggest that the absent parent will not be a reliable payer. Where the person with care is not a *parent* with care, a request by her to the CSA will be necessary.

Arrears will always be collected and retained by the CSA where the person with care is (or was during the relevant period) in receipt of IS (see p317).

Where payments are made via the CSA, the person with care receives one order book or girocheque from the Benefits Agency which includes both IS and child maintenance. If the absent parent does not make a payment to the CSA, the person with care's order is still cashable, but it now represents only IS.[25] In this way IS claimants are guaranteed a weekly income regardless of whether child maintenance is actually paid by the absent parent. For more details, see p316.

A disadvantage of this system is that the person with care is not kept regularly informed about the state of her maintenance account, information which can be important when making a decision about leaving IS and seeking work. However, she can request a payment statement.[26] This request must be made in writing.

Persons with care leaving income support

There are persons with care who, as a result of the payment of child maintenance, are not on IS because their income including child maintenance is now too high. Efficient CSA collection and enforcement is particularly important, given that failure to receive the maintenance will leave such a person below the IS level. If child maintenance is not paid, a fresh claim should be made for IS. If the Benefits Agency delays the processing of that IS claim, please let CPAG know, as we have been lobbying for better procedures.

Any child maintenance payments which are made will be assumed to be current liability and passed on to the person with care. However, payments of arrears due for periods when the person with care was on IS may be retained, at least in part, by the CSA (see p317).

Persons with care on family credit or disability working allowance

If the Secretary of State decides to collect child maintenance payments from the absent parent, the payments will be made to the person with care separately from any FC/DWA order from the Benefits Agency. For the effects of the payment of child maintenance on FC/DWA, see p318.

Method of payment

Payment by the absent parent can be made by standing order, direct debit, automated credit transfer, cheque, postal order or cash.[27] Payments to the person with care can be made by any of those methods and also, if from the CSA, by order book or girocheque.[28] Where payment is not made direct, CSA policy is for the person with care to be paid by automated credit transfer wherever possible; and if not, by girocheque.[29] CSA policy is for the absent parent to pay by the following methods, in order of CSA preference:[30]

- direct to the person with care;
- direct debit to the CSA;
- deduction from earnings orders (DEOs) to the CSA (see p406).

The CSA can direct an absent parent to take all reasonable steps to open a bank or building society account.[31] However, there is no penalty if he fails to do so.

When deciding which method(s) to use, the CSA will follow CSA preference, but takes into account:[32]

- the absent parent's payday;
- whether either party is in receipt of IS;
- any previous payment history;
- whether the person with care has a bank account;
- whether other people have access to the person with care's post.

The CSA must always take into account any representations of the parties.[33]

CSA staff are reminded that the CSA can accept payment by cheque, bankers draft, postal order, cash and foreign currency (notes only).[34] Absent parents who wish to pay by these methods should insist on doing so. So long as payments are made when due, no DEO should be made.

Timing of payments

The CSA decides the day and frequency of payments.[35] The MAF and MEF ask for the person's preference as to weekly, monthly or other intervals. When deciding the day and the interval for payment by the absent parent, the CSA must take into account:[36]

- any representations of the parties, in particular the preference of the absent parent[37]
- the day on which and the interval at which the absent parent receives his income;

- any other relevant circumstances of the absent parent; *and*
- time for cheques to clear and for payments to be transferred to the person with care.

Unless undue hardship would be caused to the absent parent or the person with care, the frequency of payments to the person with care will be the same as the frequency set for the absent parent's payments.[38]

Unless payments are to be by direct debit or standing order, the absent parent is asked to make each payment three to four days before the due date in order to ensure that payments are received on time.[39] However, as the due date is usually set as the absent parent's payday,[40] this may not be easy for the absent parent to manage. In any case, the CSA builds in clearance times from the due date when setting dates for payments to persons with care:[41]

Direct debit	eight banking days
Standing order	two banking days
Cheque	eight banking days
Bank head office collection account	six banking days
Transcash	six banking days
Cash/postal orders	immediate

There have been delays in the CSA passing payments on to the person with care. Sometimes this has been caused by delays in deciding whether the payment is due to be retained by the CSA in lieu of IS paid (see p317). The CSA had a target for 1995/96 of 90 per cent of payments to be passed to persons with care within ten working days of receipt from an absent parent.[42] This target is now being met (see p24).

The CSA cannot pay the person with care before the absent parent makes his payment.

Overpayments

An overpayment can arise either because the absent parent pays more than the regular payment due or because the amount of the assessment for a past period has been reduced on review. Where either of these happens, the CSA has a discretion about allocating the overpayment.[43] It will normally be set against the following, in this order:[44]

- the initial amount due to the Secretary of State when the original assessment was made;
- the initial amount due to the person with care;
- any arrears accrued after the original assessment was made, the oldest debt first;
- any interest due to the person with care;
- any fees;

- any interest due to the Secretary of State.

The practice of giving the Secretary of State priority over the person with care may be unlawful – contact CPAG for more details.

Where there is still a surplus and the overpayment arose because of a review, the child support officer (CSO) will normally make an adjustment to any ongoing liability (see below). Where there is no ongoing liability, the CSA will reimburse the absent parent and may recover that reimbursement from the person with care (see p395).[45] Refunds are paid by girocheque.[46]

Where the surplus arose because of an overpayment by the absent parent, the CSA contacts the absent parent and asks him whether the overpayment should be passed on to the person with care when it is due under the assessment, as a lump sum payment against future liability, or as a gift.[47] A lump sum payment can only be made if the person with care agrees. The absent parent can also ask for the overpayment to be repaid to him.

The CSA will also refund overpayments made because of CSA error, for example, where a person was told to pay more than the assessment required.[48]

Adjustments

If an overpayment remains after offsetting against any arrears from a previous assessment, the CSO can adjust the amount payable under the current assessment in order to recoup the overpayment.[49] When making this discretionary decision, the CSO must consider, in particular:

- the circumstances of the absent parent and person with care;
- the welfare of any children (see p52);
- the amount of the overpayment in relation to the amount of the current assessment; *and*
- the period over which it would be reasonable to recoup the overpayment.

The amount payable cannot be reduced below £4.80 a week.[50]

Where an adjusted assessment is reviewed, the adjustment continues to apply to the fresh assessment, unless a CSO considers that this would be inappropriate,[51] in which case s/he can either alter the amount of the adjustment or cancel it.[52]

The absent parent, person with care and any Scottish child applicant must be notified of an adjustment or cancellation of an adjustment.[53] The CSO decision to make or cancel an adjustment can be reviewed by a CSO on a second-tier review (see p358) or on a review instigated by a CSO (see p364).[54] The normal rules about procedure and notification apply to these reviews.[55]

Recovery of overpayments from the person with care

Where the CSA reimburses an absent parent because his liability was reduced on review, any maintenance overpaid to the person with care can be recovered from her.[56] This is a discretionary decision of the Secretary of State which can only be made from 22 January 1996.[57] The welfare of any children likely to be affected by reimbursement must be taken into account (see p52). The CSA cannot recover the overpayment where:[58]

- the person with care was on IS/FC/DWA at any time during the period she was overpaid; *or*
- she was on IS/FC/DWA on any of the dates reimbursement to the absent parent was made; *or*
- the overpayment was made under an interim maintenance assessment (IMA) and arose because the amount due under the IMA was not changed to the amount of a subsequent full assessment (see p311).

Where the overpayment was made at a time when the parent with care was not entitled to it under a valid assessment, she cannot be required to repay.

2. COLLECTION OF OTHER PAYMENTS

The CSA can collect and enforce other forms of maintenance in addition to child support maintenance.[59] The power to collect periodical payments made for the benefit of a child where there is no child support maintenance payable has not yet come into effect.[60] However, the Government intends to allow persons with care not in receipt of benefit who are barred from obtaining a CSA assessment (see p32) to use the CSA collection service.[61] There is no indication of when this change will occur, but it is unlikely to be during 1996/97. A fee will be charged.

The CSA has a discretion to collect other maintenance. The CSA started collecting other maintenance from April 1994 for section 6 applicants and, where the court order was made after April 1993, for section 4 and 7 applicants.[62] The CSA can only collect other maintenance that falls due after the CSA gives the absent parent written notice that the other maintenance will be collected.[63] At the time of writing the CSA will collect spousal maintenance from April 1996 in cases where the collection service is already provided.

The following payments (see p37) can be collected by the CSA if they are due under a court order:[64]

- additional child maintenance in excess of the maximum payable

under the child support formula;
- maintenance for a child's education or training;
- maintenance paid to meet the expenses of a child with disabilities;
- maintenance paid for a step-child – ie, a child living with the person with care who used to live with the absent parent and was accepted by him as a member of his family;
- spousal maintenance for a person with care of a child for whom child support maintenance is being collected.

The methods of collecting and enforcing other types of maintenance by the CSA are the same as those used for child support maintenance.[65] Where an absent parent is paying more than one type of maintenance, and pays less than the total amount required, he should say how the amounts are to be allocated. The CSA will allocate as requested, except that, where arrears of child support maintenance are specified, current child support maintenance will be paid before arrears. If he does not stipulate, the CSA will allocate[66] according to the following order of priority:[67]

- current child support maintenance liability;
- other current child maintenance;
- current spousal maintenance;
- arrears of child support maintenance;
- arrears of other child maintenance;
- arrears of spousal maintenance;
- interest on child support maintenance (see p404), which is not retained by the Secretary of State;
- fees;
- interest on child support maintenance retained by the Secretary of State.

Some arrears of child support maintenance are retained by the Secretary of State and others are due to the person with care: see p393 for the order of priority when allocating payments.

Collection of CSA fees and court costs

Although fees are not being charged for CSA services in 1995–97 (see p387), any outstanding fees from previous years are still collected.

CSA fees became due 14 days after the date an invoice was given or sent out to the liable person.[68] If sent by post to the person's last known address, the invoice is treated as having been sent on the second working day after posting, including Saturdays.[69] A reminder is sent if payment is not received 16 days from the date the invoice was issued.[70] If a reply is not received, the litigation team writes to the client stating that court action will be taken if neither payment nor a payment agreement is made within seven days.[71]

Payment of fees can be made by cheque, cash or postal order, either direct to the child support agency centre (CSAC) or using a paying-in slip at a bank or post office.[72] If a payment is made by an absent parent who does not indicate what the payment covers, the CSA will assign the amount to child maintenance instead of fees (see p396). The fees account is separate from the child maintenance account.

Usually payment of fees is expected in full immediately, but if the person charged cannot afford to pay a fees bill, s/he should offer to pay in instalments. The bill can be paid over several months. The CSA wants fees paid in the shortest time possible but, although payment was previously required before the end of the assessment year,[73] the CSA may now accept payments over the following two years.

Court costs and DNA test fees

Where the CSA brings a court case to decide if a person is a parent and the court decides that he is, the court can order him to pay the CSA's costs in bringing the case, including the cost of any DNA tests which have been carried out (see p38). An absent parent may also have to pay DNA test fees to the CSA where the court has not ordered him to pay them, but only in certain circumstances (see p148).

The CSA officer who presented the case at the magistrates/sheriff court notifies the CSA accounts section of the amount of costs ordered.[74] The CSA will first write to the absent parent. Payment is by paying-in slip for a specially created account.[75] If payment is not received within four days, the case is referred to the litigation team with which the parent can try to negotiate.

Enforcement of fees and costs

Fees and costs can only be enforced through court action for debt. This means that the rules in the Acts do not apply. In Scotland, this is the sheriff court and, in England and Wales, the county court. If the case is contested, a hearing will be arranged in the court with jurisdiction for the area in which the parent lives. A money judgment can be enforced by the usual debt enforcement procedures – eg, distress, poinding and warrant sale, attachment of earnings.

3. ARREARS

This section assumes that the collection service is being used. If a section 4 applicant has not requested the collection service and a payment is missed, she should consider requesting the collection service at this stage (see p368).

Initial arrears

There are almost always initial arrears accrued when the first assessment is made. The exception is where a court order has been in force, since the order remains in force until two days after the assessment is made, at which time the assessment comes into force instead (see p304).

Waiving collection of initial arrears

Although there is no power to write off child maintenance arrears, the CSA can decide to suspend collection of payments. This is a discretionary decision. The CSA will normally suspend collection of arrears more than six months old where:[76]

- the absent parent requests it; *and*
- three months' arrears are due to CSA delay; *and*
- the CSA does not already have evidence that the absent parent has enough savings to pay the arrears in full; *and*
- he agrees to meet his ongoing liability and pay the last six months' arrears, either immediately or by agreed instalments.

Many absent parents with arrears are not told about the policy of deferring arrears by the CSA. Any absent parent who may benefit from this policy should insist on a written explanation of why arrears cannot be deferred. For details of negotiating an arrears agreement, see p401.

While the absent parent complies, the old arrears will not be enforced, but if the absent parent defaults, they can be enforced (see p403). If the absent parent stops being liable to pay child maintenance or the arrears are more than six years old, the CSA intends not to ever collect the arrears.[77]

Compensation to person with care

Where the CSA decides to suspend recovery of arrears, the person with care may lose money. A person with care who objects to a CSA decision on recovery may be able to bring a judicial review (see p351) or may be able to sue the absent parent or CSA (see p404).

The CSA will, however, pay compensation to the person with care from its own funds. This is a discretionary decision, but will normally be done only where the absent parent has paid current child maintenance and kept to agreed arrears repayments for 52 weeks.[78] Any compensatory payment to the person with care will be calculated as follows:[79]

- for any period she was not on IS/FC/DWA – all the arrears;
- for any period she was on FC/DWA – half the arrears;
- for any period where she was on IS but would not have been if maintenance had been paid when due – the amount by which

maintenance would have exceeded IS.

No payment will be made for any period when the person with care would have stayed on IS had child maintenance been paid when due.[80]

Before a payment is made, the person with care must agree that the CSA can enforce the debt against the absent parent if it decides to and that any money collected from the absent parent for that period will be kept by the CSA.[81] The person with care will be asked to sign a form to agree this.[82]

CPAG is lobbying for improvements in the CSA's policy and is interested to hear about persons with care who lose out because they are on FC/DWA or because of the CSA's policy of delaying compensation.

Offsetting payments made before the first assessment

Any child maintenance paid by the absent parent to the person with care after the effective date should be offset against arrears of child maintenance.[83] This does not always happen immediately, often because the CSA is not aware that payments have been made. The absent parent should keep a record and send a copy to the CSA on receiving the assessment notification. Unless the person with care disputes the payments (in which case the absent parent is asked to provide documentary evidence – eg, receipts and bank statements[84]) the amount paid is deducted from the amount owed.

Payments in kind – eg, presents or clothes for the children – will not be offset against arrears. Payments to third parties on behalf of the person with care – eg, towards the mortgage, nursery school fees, leisure activities for the children – may be offset. The absent parent will have to persuade the CSA that the payments were child maintenance.

If there has been an overpayment, the assessment may be adjusted (see p394).

Negotiating payment of initial arrears

The CSA requests payment of the initial amount as a lump sum. However, if – as is usually the case – an absent parent is unable to pay this amount all at once, he should contact the CSAC arrears management section and offer to pay in instalments. This must be on top of ongoing liability. The CSA will not expect the absent parent to pay more than one-third of net income to cover both ongoing child maintenance and arrears. For details of negotiating an arrears agreement, see p401.

The method of payment of the initial arrears will be the same as for ongoing maintenance. When the person with care is on IS, the Secretary of State seeks payment via the CSA. The method of payment can be changed temporarily to payment via the CSA while the initial amount is being paid in instalments, reverting to payment direct to the person with care for the ongoing liability once the final instalment is paid.[85]

See p393 for how payments are allocated.

Starting arrears action

The CSA begins chasing arrears when:[86]

- a payment from the absent parent to the CSA is not received within two days of its due date;
- the person with care notifies the CSA that a payment has not been received by the due date;
- the person with care requests an increase in IS because child main-tenance has not been paid; *or when*
- the absent parent tells the CSAC that he is having difficulty making the payments due.

Persons with care who are being paid direct by the absent parent should keep records of payments received.

An arrears management officer will try to telephone the absent parent to find out why the payment has not been made.[87] Staff are warned about confidentiality and told not to leave messages on answerphones or with third parties. They should introduce themselves as CSA staff only when talking to the absent parent. Arrears management and litigation staff often work early and late shifts in order to be able to contact absent parents at home.

Delays in the collection service

Arrears action has not begun as quickly as the CSA intended. Persons with care who want quicker collection and enforcement have sometimes found it difficult to identify the right person to contact within the CSA. The accounts section should be contacted for initial information about the state of the account. Otherwise the arrears management team should be contacted, unless court action has begun, in which case the litigation team is involved (see p387). A person with care affected by delay in collection may want to write to, as well as telephone, the arrears management section to explain that the lack of arrears action is affecting the welfare of the child(ren).

If CSA delays mean that arrears are unlikely to be recovered, the person with care should claim compensation (see p30).

Arrears notice

Where the absent parent has missed one or more child maintenance payments, the CSA must send him an arrears notice which itemises the amounts owed. The notice also explains the regulations about arrears and interest, and requests payment of all outstanding arrears.[88] Generally the arrears notice is sent eight days after the due date of the missed payment.[89]

The absent parent should check that the amount owed is correct, and should tell the CSAC of any payments which have been made but are not mentioned.

The absent parent can contact the CSAC to negotiate payment by instalments (see below). If the assessment is an interim maintenance assessment (IMA), the absent parent should consider providing the outstanding information as the ongoing assessment is likely to be lower: this is especially true of a Category A IMA (see p297).

Once an arrears notice has been served, another does not have to be sent if arrears remain uncleared *unless* the absent parent has paid all arranged payments for a 12-week period.[90]

Negotiating an arrears agreement

The absent parent can enter an agreement with the CSA to pay all arrears.[91] Where there are more than six months' arrears, the CSA may defer collection of arrears more than six months old (see p398).

The CSA will not normally agree to defer payment of current liability, though this may happen where there is a review or appeal pending (see p388).

If the absent parent refuses to negotiate or negotiations break down, a deduction from earnings order or other methods of enforcement will be considered (see pp406 and 415).

Where an agreement is made, it will be confirmed in writing and a schedule of dates and amounts of payments will be sent to the absent parent.[92] A copy will normally be sent also to the person with care.

There are no regulations limiting the amounts of payments or how quickly the arrears must be cleared. Although CSA staff always begin by requesting full payment of the outstanding arrears, they are instructed to use the following guidelines as a starting point for negotiating repayments:[93]

- if the liability results from a full maintenance assessment, one-third of ongoing liability;
- if the liability results from an IMA, one-fifth on ongoing liability;
- arrears repayments should not take the absent parent's disposable income (see p256) below the protected income level minus £4.80;
- if the absent parent is on protected income the rate of repayment requested will be £4.80 a week;
- the arrears repayments together with the current assessment must not

take more than one-third of the absent parent's net income (see p203).[94]

Repayments may extend over a number of years. Although this may help absent parents who are in financial hardship, it is very late payment from the person with care's point of view: she may want to make representations to the CSA.

In some cases the arrears management staff may be willing to increase the length of time for repayment, and an absent parent who cannot afford the instalments requested should make an alternative offer. Remember to take account of any increases which may be due under the phasing-in of assessments (see p300). The absent parent can prepare a statement of his income and outgoings, although this may show that he is unable to pay even the weekly liability, let alone the arrears. Child maintenance is considered a priority debt – ie, of more importance than consumer credit. If an absent parent has other priority (eg, housing, fuel) or other large debts, he should seek independent money advice. Existing agreements with other creditors may have to be renegotiated to take into account the CSA assessment.

The CSA can use other methods of enforcement, such as a deduction from earnings order (DEO). Therefore, CSA staff are unlikely to agree to an absent parent making low payments over a very long period (unless he is on protected income or covered by the one-third net income rule – see above). It is in his interests to come to an agreement if he wishes to avoid further enforcement action. If he has children living with him, the welfare of those children has to be taken into account by the CSA (see p52).

Much of the negotiation is conducted over the telephone. An absent parent may request an appointment at the field office if he wishes to discuss the payment of the arrears face-to-face with CSA staff. Arrears management staff will suggest an interview if the absent parent is blind, illiterate or has difficulty understanding written English.[95] Where an interpreter is required, this should be requested from the CSA.

Review or appeal pending

The CSA can suspend collection of arrears if a review or appeal is pending. Where the assessment is likely to be reduced, the CSA may agree to suspend collection of some of the ongoing payments.

An absent parent who requests a review/appeal and is having problems paying the current assessment should make an offer to the CSAC – if possible in writing – for weekly payments. There may be accumulated arrears if the review/appeal is unsuccessful. On the other hand, if full payments are maintained and the assessment is subsequently reduced, the new assessment can be adjusted to recover the overpayment (see p394).

Payment of arrears

There is no requirement that arrears must be paid by the same method as continuing child maintenance payments. For example, arrears could be collected via the CSA, while ongoing payments are made to the person with care. For the allocation of payments by the CSA, see p393.

The Secretary of State will always arrange for absent parents to make payments of arrears to the CSA where the person with care is on IS or IS is paid for her.[96] The CSA retains any payments of arrears where the IS claimant would have received less IS had the child maintenance payments been made when due.[97] Before 22 January 1996 this could only be done where the person with care was the claimant.[98]

When the absent parent defaults

If the absent parent fails to keep to an arrears agreement involving arrears which have been deferred indefinitely (see p298), the CSA's approach depends upon when that default occurred. If the default was within 52 weeks of the agreement, the entire deferred debt will be recharged to the account unless the default was outside the absent parent's control – eg error by the bank – or due to exceptional circumstances.[99] These circumstances include the death of an immediate member of the family or the unexpected hospitalisation of the absent parent.

Because the deferred arrears may be large, a minor default by an absent parent with this type of agreement could have drastic consequences for him. If you have this type of agreement and believe you may be unable to make a payment, you should contact the CSA as soon as possible to explain your situation.

Where the absent parent has kept to the agreement for 52 weeks, CSA policy is to recharge the deferred debt to his account only if he deliberately refuses to comply with the agreement.[100]

In all cases an absent parent who wants to co-operate should try to renegotiate an agreement in good time before a change in his circumstances (eg, redundancy). Where the absent parent has paid regularly and the change means the CSA's negotiation guidelines (see p401) would produce a more favourable result, the CSA ought to accept a proposal based on those guidelines.

Unenforceable interim maintenance assessments

Where a CSO instigates a review of a Category A IMA and one of the reasons for that review is that the effective date of that IMA was wrong, any Category A IMA which is made on that review cannot have an effective date earlier than 16 February 1995 (see p366). The CSA believes that the reviewed IMA still has legal existence for any period before 16 February 1995 in respect of which it was made.[101] However, because the reviewed IMA was defective, the CSA cannot enforce the amount due under it or any interest which has accrued on that amount, though any payments made by the absent parent of the amount due or interest are not refundable to him.

CSA staff are instructed to:[102]

- notify the absent parent and person with care in writing;
- accept voluntary payments from the absent parent up to the amount which would have been due under the IMA had it been correct;
- reduce the amount of arrears under the reviewed IMA by any payments the absent parent has already made or makes voluntarily;
- compensate the person with care if the rules on p398 apply; *and*
- pass to the person with care any payments due to her after deducting any compensation already paid to her for the same period.

Enforcement by the person with care

Where the CSA goes against the wishes of the person with care by deferring arrears or making an arrears agreement which is unacceptable to her, she can ask the CSA to reconsider. A judicial review may also be possible (see p351), especially where the welfare of her children is affected. It is not clear whether she also has the right to bring her own court action against the absent parent to recover child maintenance due from him; anyone considering doing this should seek legal advice. Where the person with care has lost out because of CSA delay, the CSA may pay compensation, or it may be possible to sue the CSA for negligence. CPAG would like to hear of any cases where these approaches have been tried.

Interest

Interest cannot be charged on arrears of child maintenance due after 17 April 1995.[103] However, the power to enforce interest on arrears due for an earlier period remains. Indeed, interest can continue to accrue on arrears outstanding at 17 April 1995 and new demands for interest may still be issued – eg, where an absent parent defaults on an arrears agreement concerning amounts due before 17 April 1995. The 1995 Act provides for a simpler penalty, an 'additional amount'.[104] This is not yet in force, but the Government intends to introduce it in April 1997.[105]

Interest cannot be charged unless an arrears notice has been issued and then only on arrears due for a period more than a fortnight before the date of the arrears notice.[106] However, once a notice has been issued, interest is then charged on further arrears which had accumulated up to 17 April 1995.[107] Interest is charged daily at a rate 1 per cent over the base rate.[108]

Interest is *not* payable where:

- the absent parent did not know and could not have been expected to realise that there were arrears;[109] *or*
- the arrears arose from an increased assessment on review or appeal and relate to the period before the absent parent was notified of the fresh assessment;[110] *or*
- the arrears arose only as a result of a CSA administrative or operational error;[111] *or*
- the absent parent paid all outstanding arrears of child maintenance within 28 days of the due date.[112]

If an arrears agreement was entered into within 28 days of the due date, there is no interest on the arrears covered by the agreement as long as the absent parent makes the agreed payments.[113] If the agreement was entered into more than 28 days after the due date, then interest is payable on the amounts due for the period before the agreement was made.[114]

If the absent parent defaults on the agreement, then interest becomes due on the whole amount outstanding up to 17 April 1995.[115] Failing to pay ongoing maintenance on the due date counts as default.[116] However, a second arrears agreement can be made for all the outstanding arrears.[117]

Absent parent paying interest

Payment of any interest is expected in the same way as any payment of child maintenance and is due within 14 days of being demanded.[118] However, the demand is not sent until the arrears have been cleared. No interest is chargeable on any arrears of interest.[119] Otherwise, the enforcement procedures described in this chapter apply in exactly the same way to interest payments.[120]

Who gets the interest

The CSA keeps any payments of interest where the person with care is a section 6 applicant, is still on IS or IS is paid for her to her partner.[121] The interest is paid to the person with care where she would have been taken off IS had the absent parent paid the maintenance on the due date.[122] Interest paid to the person with care is paid in the same way as maintenance – ie, either direct or via the CSA.

4. DEDUCTION FROM EARNINGS ORDERS

The Secretary of State may make a deduction from earnings order (DEO), that is, an order to the absent parent's employer to make deductions from earnings and pay them to the CSA.[123] DEOs are used in a large minority of cases. In January 1996 there were just under 40,000 DEOs in force where there is ongoing liability.[124]

If payment is not to be made directly to the person with care or by direct debit when the collection service is first used, CSA staff are instructed to make a DEO if possible (see p392).[125] A DEO will also be made if possible where the account is in arrears and the absent parent does not respond to enquiries,[126] or refuses to make an arrears agreement[127] or persistently defaults on an agreement (often defined as three defaults in six months). Persons with care complain that the CSA is slow to make DEOs. A DEO will be made if the absent parent requests it.[128]

The best way for an absent parent to avoid a DEO is to negotiate an arrears agreement (see p401) and keep to it wherever possible. However, making ongoing payments may be enough to prevent a DEO being made. Though an absent parent may object to a DEO, if it is unlikely that regular payments will be made using a different method, the preference of the absent parent will probably be ignored.

The decision to make a DEO is a discretionary one and therefore the welfare of any children must be considered by the Secretary of State. In a High Court decision in December 1994, Mr Justice Thorpe said, 'I am not convinced that the Agency is at liberty to decide whether or not to issue a deduction of earnings order without giving considerable weight to the welfare principle.'[129] If warned of a DEO, the absent parent should tell the CSAC, preferably in writing, how any child(ren) would be affected by a DEO. CPAG would be interested to hear of any cases where the welfare of children is not taken into account. Any challenge should be by judicial review (see p351) rather than appeal to a court (see p413).[130]

A DEO can be made while the absent parent is awaiting a review or appeal. However, before making a DEO in these circumstances, arrears management staff are instructed to consider the grounds of review or appeal and may ask review staff about the likelihood and timing of any change in the assessment. An absent parent may want to make representations about the level and method of payments (see p392).

A DEO cannot be made where the employer is based outside the United Kingdom,[131] but a DEO can be made in Great Britain against an employer in Northern Ireland and vice versa.[132]

A DEO cannot be made if the absent parent is in the armed forces.

Instead, the armed forces can be required by the Secretary of State to make deductions for child maintenance under legislation concerning armed forces.[133] This legislation, however, does set limits to the amounts which can be deducted.

If the full amount requested by the CSA cannot be deducted from earnings, the Secretary of State will use other methods to collect and enforce the remainder.

How does a DEO work

A DEO is an instruction to the employer of an absent parent to make deductions from his earnings.[134] A copy of the DEO must be served on the employer and the absent parent.[135] The employer has to comply with the order and, seven days after receiving the DEO, can be prosecuted for not complying with it.[136] Failure to take all reasonable steps to comply with a DEO is an offence punishable by a fine of up to £500.[137]

The DEO must state:[138]

- the name and address of the absent parent;
- the name of the employer;
- where the CSA knows, the absent parent's place of work, the nature of his work, works number and national insurance number;
- the normal deduction rate(s) (see p409) and the date on which each takes effect;
- the protected earnings rate;
- the address to which the deductions are to be sent.

A DEO should normally set payments for 52 weeks only and a revised DEO will be issued 21 days before the end of that period.[139]

There is a help-line providing further information for employers, with calls charged at local rate: 0345 134134. The CSA has also produced a leaflet, *Advice for Employers*.

Date of payment

The employer must pay the Secretary of State monthly by the 19th of the month following the month in which the deduction is made.[140] This means that there will always be a delay before the person with care receives the first payment from the CSA. As the employer makes monthly payments, the person with care will receive monthly payments, even if the absent parent is having weekly deductions. These monthly payments may not always be the same amount (see p410).

The payment by the employer may be by credit transfer, cheque or any other method to which the CSA agrees.[141] The DEO reference number must be given so that the CSA can identify the person with care.

Providing information

In each of the following cases, any notice which is sent from the CSA will be treated as though it was sent two working days after it was posted, including Saturdays.[142]

Failure to take all reasonable steps to comply with any of the following requirements to provide information to the Secretary of State is an offence punishable by a fine of up to £500.[143]

The absent parent

The absent parent must provide the name and address of his employer, the amount of earnings and anticipated earnings, place of work, nature of work and any works number, within seven days of being asked to do so in writing by the CSA.[144] Once a DEO is in force, an absent parent must inform the Secretary of State within seven days of leaving employment or becoming employed or re-employed.[145]

The employer

An employer must inform the Secretary of State in writing within 10 days of being served with a DEO if s/he does not, in fact, employ the absent parent.[146] If an absent parent who is subject to a DEO leaves his job, the employer must notify the CSA within 10 days of his leaving.[147] If an employer finds out that a DEO is in force against an employee – eg, on becoming an absent parent's employer – s/he must notify the CSA within seven days of becoming aware of this information.[148]

For each deduction the employer makes from the absent parent's earnings, s/he must inform him in writing of the amount of the deduction no later than the date of the deduction or, if not practicable, by the following payday.[149] Child support law imposes no penalty for an employer's failure to do this, but employment protection law also requires the employer to give the absent parent a written statement of deductions on or before the payday.[150] Where the deduction will always be the same amount, this can be done by a standing statement given at least annually.[151] If the employer does not do this, the absent parent may complain to an industrial tribunal, which can order the employer to pay the absent parent a fine up to the total amount of the unnotified deductions.[152] This would not affect payments made to the CSA.

For other duties about the provision of information, see p128.

What are earnings

Earnings include wages, salary, fees, bonus, commission, overtime pay, occupational pension or statutory sick pay, or any other payments made under an employment contract or a regular payment made in compensation for loss of wages.[153] Earnings does not include a payment by a foreign government or the government of Northern Ireland.[154] Net earnings means, in this context, the amount remaining after tax, national insurance and contributions towards a pension scheme have been deducted.[155]

How much will be deducted

The DEO states a **normal deduction rate** and a **protected earnings rate**.[156] These rates should usually correspond to the pay periods of the absent parent – ie, at a weekly rate for weekly paid employees and a monthly rate for monthly paid employees.[157] More than one normal deduction rate can be set, each applying to a different period.[158]

Normal deduction rate

The normal deduction rate is the amount that will be deducted each payday as long as net earnings are not brought below the protected earnings rate. The normal deduction rate can include not only current maintenance liability but also an amount for any arrears and interest due. There are no special rules for DEOs as to how quickly the CSA should seek to clear the arrears and interest. This will normally be negotiated and CSA guidance sets limits for payments towards arrears (see p401). However, no arrears or interest can be included in the normal deduction rate if that would have brought the absent parent's disposable income, on the date the current assessment was made, below the protected income level (not the protected earnings rate) less the minimum payment (£4.80 at 1996/97 rates).[159] This does not apply where the current assessment is an IMA (see p296). See Chapter 12 for protected income level and disposable income.

Protected earnings rate

The protected earnings rate is the level below which earnings must not be reduced by the deductions. It is normally set at the exempt income level (see Chapter 9).[160]

Where an IMA is being collected via a DEO, the protected earnings rate is either:[161]

- if the CSA knows something of the absent parent's circumstances:
  - the IS single (£47.90) or couple (£75.20) personal allowance;
  - the IS personal allowance for any children living with them (where the child's age is not known, £16.45 is used);
  - any relevant IS premiums (see Appendix 2); *plus*

– £30; *or*
- otherwise, the IS adult personal allowance (£47.90) plus £30.

Where there is no assessment in force, the protected earnings rate is the exempt income level for the last assessment. If the absent parent satisfies a CSO that his circumstances have since changed, the protected earnings rate will be the exempt income level he would have if his assessment were reviewed.[162] The CSO's decision on this is not subject to review in the usual way. Where the last assessment was a Category A or C IMA, the protected earnings rate continues to be calculated as for IMAs above.

Administering a DEO

The employer can deduct a charge for administrative costs each time a deduction is made under the DEO.[163] This means that employees paid weekly can be charged more for administrative costs. The additional amount must not exceed £1 per deduction and can be made even where this would bring earnings below the protected earnings rate.

Each payday the employer should make a deduction from net earnings at the normal deduction rate plus any administration charge, unless deducting the normal deduction rate would reduce net earnings below the protected earnings rate. If this would be the case, the amount of the deduction is the excess of net earnings over the protected earnings rate, with any administration charge deducted in addition.[164]

Where the employer fails to make a deduction or the deduction is less than the normal deduction rate, arrears accrue and are deducted at the next payday in addition to the normal deduction, applying the same rules for protected earnings.[165]

If on any payday net earnings are below the protected earnings rate, then no deduction or charge can be made. When this occurs, the difference between net earnings and protected earnings is carried over and treated as additional protected earnings on the next payday.[166]

Such variations in deductions mean that the person with care will receive irregular payments. This should not affect persons with care on IS paid via the CSA as their benefit will be paid gross (see p316).

Priority of orders

Where two or more DEOs have been issued, the employer should deal with the earliest first.[167] A DEO takes priority over an attachment of earnings order for a judgment or administration debt (non-priority debts), and any arrestment of earnings under Scottish law.[168] In England and Wales, when a DEO is served on an employee who is already subject to an attachment of earnings order for a priority debt (eg, for council tax or a fine), the order of priority for taking deductions is again date order.[169]

Any deductions under a lower priority order would be taken from the net earnings remaining after deductions under the first order have been made.[170]

Example 17.1: Deductions from earnings order

An absent parent is due to pay child maintenance of £20.50 a week. His exempt income is £89 a week and net earnings are £150 a week. He is paid weekly. Arrears of £328 accrued by the time the assessment was made and a further £210 subsequently accrued as the absent parent paid only £10 a week, which he felt he could afford. The Secretary of State has decided that these arrears should be paid off at the rate of £10 per week. The DEO issued at the end of June, therefore, shows a normal deduction rate of £30.50 and a protected earnings level of £89. His employer can deduct £1 administrative costs in weeks that a deduction is made.

Payday	Net pay £	Protected earnings	Child support due	Deduction £	Pay £
7/7/95	150.00	89.00	30.50	31.50	118.50
14/7/95	160.00	89.00	30.50	31.50	128.50
21/7/95	120.00	89.00	30.50	31.50	88.50
28/7/95	110.00	89.00	30.50	22.00	88.00
4/8/95	110.00	89.00	40.00	22.00	88.00
11/8/95	120.00	89.00	49.50	32.00	88.00
18/8/95	150.00	89.00	49.00	50.00	100.00
25/8/95	130.00	89.00	30.50	31.50	98.50
1/9/95	75.00	89.00	30.50	nil	75.00
8/9/95	120.00	103.00	61.00	18.00	102.00
15/9/95	120.00	89.00	74.50	32.00	88.00
22/9/95	150.00	89.00	74.00	62.00	88.00
29/9/95	130.00	89.00	43.50	42.00	88.00
6/10/95	130.00	89.00	33.00	34.00	96.00

In the week 28/7/95, net earnings do not exceed protected earnings by the amount due (£30.50). Therefore, a smaller deduction is made, leaving the absent parent with his protected pay less the £1 administration charge.

The shortfall of £9.50 is carried forward, but the next week again he is unable to pay even the full current amount and further arrears accrue. His net earnings the following week (11/8/95) cover the normal deduction but are insufficient to pay off any of the arrears other than 50p. The arrears are therefore carried over again and this time fully paid off the following week.

In the week of 1/9/95, net earnings are less than protected pay. No deduction is made and both the shortfall in deductions (£30.50) and the shortfall in protected earnings (£14) are carried forward. The following week, because of the increased protected earnings, the absent parent cannot pay the full normal deduction and further arrears accrue which take four weeks to clear.

Payment to the person with care

The employer has to pass the month's payments to the CSA by the 19th of the following month. When this has reached the CSA's account, action should be taken to pass the payment to the person with care within 10 days – unless it is due to be retained because the person with care is on IS (see p316). Where the person with care has left IS, the current liability will be due to her, but some or all of the arrears may be retained in lieu of IS paid for an earlier period.

Month	Payment to CSA by the 19th of the month	Current liability paid (£20.50 a week due)	Arrears paid (assigned to oldest debt)
July	–	nil	nil
August	£112.50	£82.00	£30.50
September	£131.50	£82.00	£49.50
October	£140.00	£102.50	£37.50

This means that while some arrears have been paid off, further arrears of £82 have accrued for July despite the fact that the DEO had been made.

Variation and review of DEOs

A DEO must be reviewed if there is a change in the amount of the assessment or where any arrears and interest included has been paid off.[171] This does not apply where a normal deduction rate which takes into account the change has already been specified. A DEO can be varied on such a review.[172] The employer must comply with the change within seven days of a copy of the new DEO being served on her/him.[173] The usual penalties for non-compliance apply (see p408).

The Secretary of State can cancel the DEO if:[174]

- no further payments are due under it;
- the DEO is ineffective or there appears to be a more effective way of collecting the payments;
- the DEO is defective (see p413) or does not comply with some other procedural provision in the legislation;
- the Secretary of State did not have, or has ceased to have, jurisdiction to make a DEO; *or*
- a DEO being used to enforce an IMA is no longer appropriate given

the compliance of the absent parent or his attempts to co-operate with the CSA.

The CSA must send written notice that the DEO has been cancelled to the absent parent and employer.[175] A refusal to cancel can only be challenged by judicial review (see p351) or appeal to a court (see below).

A DEO lapses when an absent parent leaves the employment.[176] The CSA can revive it if he finds a new job with the same or a different employer.[177] If it is revived, copies of the notice must be served on the absent parent and new employer.[178] Any shortfall under the DEO prior to the revival cannot be carried over to the revived DEO.[179]

Appeals

An absent parent can appeal against a DEO to the local magistrates' court in England and Wales or sheriff court in Scotland.[180] The appeal must be made within 28 days.[181] An appeal can only be made on the grounds that the order is defective (see below) or that the payments made to the absent parent are not earnings (see p408).[182] Where the complaint is that the CSA has not exercised its discretion to make a DEO properly, only judicial review should be used (see p351).[183] An appeal cannot be made on the ground that the amount of the assessment is wrong.

A DEO is defective if it is impracticable for the employer to comply with it because it does not include the correct information required.[184] Many DEOs have included incorrect information (such as errors in names, addresses and dates) but an appeal will not succeed on this basis if the employer can still comply with the DEO. Although some appeals have been upheld because the DEO was unsigned, there is no requirement in the regulations for a signature.

In Scotland, the form of the application is laid out in the child support rules.[185] In England and Wales, a complaint is made against the Secretary of State for Social Security. As there is no specific form given, we suggest that the Scottish wording is followed as an example (see figure 17.1), although it would be helpful to include 'This complaint is made under section 53(5) of the Child Support Act 1991 and regulation 22 of the Child Support (Collection and Enforcement) Regulations 1992'.

Once the complaint or application is made, the CSA is notified by the court and will check the DEO. Usually the DEO will be varied and reissued by the CSA if it contains the wrong amounts and the employer will be contacted to check the earnings. If the case does get as far as a court hearing, the magistrate/sheriff may quash the DEO or specify which, if any, payments constitute earnings.[186] The court cannot question the maintenance assessment itself.[187]

Even if the court quashes the DEO, it cannot order the CSA to repay deductions to the absent parent.[188] Because of this, where deductions are being made from payments which are not earnings or on the basis of the wrong normal deduction rate or protected earnings rate, it may be better to challenge the DEO by judicial review. Otherwise, the assessment should be challenged by CSO review and/or appeal to a CSAT (see Chapter 16).

Figure 17.1: **APPLICATION FOR APPEAL AGAINST A DEO IN SCOTLAND**

APPEAL AGAINST A DEDUCTION FROM EARNINGS ORDER

by

[A.B.]

(insert full name and address of appellant)

Appellant

against

SECRETARY OF STATE FOR SOCIAL SECURITY

(insert address)†

Respondent

1. The appellant is (insert full name and address of appellant).

2. The respondent is the Secretary of State for Social Security.

3. The appellant is a liable person within the meaning of section 31 of the Child Support Act 1991.

4. On (insert date) a deduction from earnings order was made against the appellant by the Secretary of State for Social Security. The making of the deduction from earnings order was intimated to the appellant on (insert date).

5. *(a) The appellant states that the deduction from earnings order is defective on the ground(s) that (state reason),
      or

   *(b) The appellant disputes that the following payments, which were taken into account by the Secretary of State for Social Security in making the deduction from earnings order, are earnings on the ground(s) that (give details of payments and nature of dispute)
   and accordingly appeals to the sheriff.

6.   The appellant asks the court to award expenses to him.

Date (insert date)   signed (signature of appellant)

*(delete as appropriate)

†(the address of the CSA on the DEO should be used)

---

5. ENFORCEMENT

A case is passed to the litigation team by the accounts section if:[189]

- maintenance arrears of over £25 have accrued; *and*
- an arrears agreement has been broken, or has not been reached; *and*
- a DEO cannot be implemented.

To take enforcement action, the CSA must obtain a liability order. The CSA cannot get an injunction to prevent the absent parent from disposing of assets or removing them out of the jurisdiction until a liability order is made.[190] When making any discretionary decision about enforcement, the Secretary of State must consider the welfare of any children likely to be affected (see p52).

The CSA will not enforce where the absent parent is under 18 years old.[191] Enforcement action cannot be begun if the debt is more than six years old.

Obtaining a liability order

If a DEO is inappropriate – eg, because the absent parent is not employed – or one has been made but proved ineffective, the Secretary of State may apply to the magistrates' court in England and Wales, or sheriff court in Scotland, for a liability order.[192] A liability order allows the CSA to take further enforcement measures.

If the court decides that the payments are due but have not been made, it has to make the order.[193] The court cannot question the maintenance assessment itself,[194] but we understand that courts do adjourn where a review of or appeal against an assessment is pending. In 1995, about 100 liability orders were made each month.[195] The great majority of these were against self-employed absent parents.[196]

Orders made in England and Wales can be enforced in Scotland or Northern Ireland and vice versa.[197]

England and Wales

The Secretary of State must give the absent parent seven days' notice of the intention to seek a liability order.[198] The notice must state the amount of maintenance outstanding, including any interest. If the absent parent pays part of the amount due, the application can still go ahead without any need for a new notice. The application must be made to the court having jurisdiction for the area in which the absent parent lives and within six years of the date the amount became due.[199]

The form of the court order in England and Wales is set out in the regulations and has to specify the amounts outstanding of child support maintenance, interest and other forms of maintenance.[200]

Scotland

When the Secretary of State applies to the sheriff court for a liability order, notice is served on the liable person by court officials.[201] The absent parent has 21 days to object to the liability order being made. This should be done in writing by returning the notice stating the grounds of the objection and enclosing evidence. If objections are received, a hearing is held. An extract of the liability order may be issued 14 days after the order is actually made. All the forms used in this procedure are included in the child support rules.[202]

Any party to the application for a liability order may be represented by an advocate, a solicitor or any other person the sheriff believes to be suitable.[203] An authorised lay representative does not have the full rights of a legal representative, but may be entitled to expenses. The same rule applies to appeals against a DEO.

Figure 17.2: **LIABILITY ORDER PRESCRIBED FORM**

Section 33 of the Child Support Act 1991 and regulation 29(1) of the Child Support (Collection and Enforcement) Regulations 1992

.............................Magistrates' Court

Date:

Defendant:

Address:

On the complaint of the Secretary of State for Social Security that the sums specified below are due from the defendant under the Child Support Act 1991 and Part IV of the Child Support (Collection and Enforcement) Regulations 1992 and are outstanding, it is adjudged that the defendant is liable to pay the aggregate amount specified below.

Sum payable and outstanding

___ child support maintenance

___ interest

___ other periodical payments collected by virtue of section 30 of the Child Support Act 1991

Aggregate amount in respect of which the liability order is made:

Justice of the Peace

[*or* by order of the Court

Clerk of the Court]

Enforcing a liability order in England and Wales

The CSA can use distress or take action in the county court.

Distress

Where a liability order has been made, the amount specified on the order can be enforced in England and Wales by distress and sale of goods.[204] The bailiff levying distress must carry written authority and hand to the absent parent, or leave at the address where distress is to be levied, a copy of the relevant regulations and a memorandum setting out the amount to be levied.[205] If payment is made in full, the levy of the goods or the subsequent sale will not take place.[206]

Certain items cannot be seized. These are:[207]

- tools, books, vehicles and other items necessary for work; *and*
- clothing, bedding, furniture, household equipment and provisions necessary to meet the basic domestic needs of the absent parent and any member of his family who lives with him; *and*
- any money, promissory notes, bond or other securities for money belonging to the absent parent.

Charges can be made at each of the stages involved in distress proceedings[208] – eg, a £10 charge for sending a letter, a charge for making a visit to the property (the maximum for this charge is £12.50 if the amount owed is less than £100, or if the amount is more than £100, £12.50 plus 4 per cent of the next £400 due, 2.5 per cent of the next £1,500, 1 per cent of the next £8,000 and 0.25 per cent of anything more).

The CSA uses Rayner Ferrar and Co of Ickenham, Middlesex, as bailiffs and has negotiated a code of practice with them (see Appendix 5). The company has to provide monthly reports on each case to the CSA. There have been some complaints about this company and CPAG would wish to hear of any others.

Any person aggrieved by the levy, or by an attempt to levy distress, can appeal to the magistrates' court by making a complaint to the court.[209] If the court is satisfied that the levy was irregular, it may order the goods to be returned if they have been seized, and order compensation in respect of any goods sold.

County court action

Once a liability order has been made, the CSA can arrange for the county court to record the order as if it were a judgment debt.[210] This record is publicly available and will damage the liable person's credit rating. The CSA can also use the county court to recover any amount which remains unpaid.[211] This means applying for a charging order or using garnishee proceedings.

A **charging order** is an order placed on property – eg, a house – owned by the liable person so that, should that property be sold, the proceeds of the sale up to the value on the liability order will be passed to the CSA. The CSA could apply to the courts for an order of sale.

A **garnishee order** names a person who owes the liable person money – eg, his bank account or a trade creditor – and requires that person to release funds to the CSA up to the value specified on the liability order.

Enforcing a liability order in Scotland

In Scotland, a liability order can be enforced by poinding and sale.[212] The form of the demand for payment sent by the sheriff court is given in the child support rules.[213] It states the sum owed, including court charges, and specifies that further action will be taken if payment is not made within 14 days (28 days if the liable person is outside the UK). Otherwise, there are no procedures specific to child maintenance. The procedures are the same as for any other debt enforced under Part II of the Debtors (Scotland) Act 1987.

The liability order may also be enforced by inhibition of sale of houses and arrestment of bank accounts.[214]

Imprisonment

In Scotland, where an amount payable under a liability order is outstanding, committal to prison is possible under the Civil Imprisonment (Scotland) Act 1882.[215]

In England and Wales, if either distress or county court proceedings have failed to recover the full amount due, the Secretary of State can apply to the magistrates' court for a warrant committing the liable person to prison.[216] The hearing must take place in the presence of the absent parent. The court can summon the absent parent to appear in court and, if he does not, issue a warrant for his arrest.

The court must enquire into the person's means and whether there has been 'wilful refusal or culpable neglect' on the absent parent's part. The power to commit an absent parent to prison is discretionary and may only be used in cases where the court believes that the absent parent wilfully refused or culpably neglected to pay the child maintenance. An absent parent should seek advice in preparing a statement of his income and outgoings. A warrant cannot be issued against an absent parent who is under 18.[217]

The court may also fix a term of imprisonment and postpone it until such time and on such conditions as it thinks fit. A warrant of commitment will then be issued which includes the full amount outstanding including interest, court costs and any other charges as well as the child maintenance owed.[218] If the amount is paid in full, the absent person will not be imprisoned.

The maximum period of imprisonment is six weeks.[219] If, after the warrant has been issued, part payment is made, then the period of imprisonment will be reduced by the same proportion as that by which the debt has been reduced.[220]

The court cannot write off the arrears, but the CSA has indicated that it would be unlikely to continue to pursue those arrears once a prison sentence had been served. Current liability would, of course, continue.

Child Support Agency addresses

Chief Executive

Ann Chant
Chief Executive
Child Support Agency
Millbank Tower
21-24 Millbank
London SW1 4QU
(CSA HQ will be moving to the
Dudley CSAC in April 1996)

Directors

Tony Ward, Director of
Operations, is based at
headquarters (see above)

Dennis Coombs, Central
Operations Director, is based at
Hastings CSAC (see below)

John McKay, CSAC Operations
Director, is based at Falkirk CSAC
(see below)

Steve Bocking, Field Operations
Director, is based at Northampton
field office

Minister with responsibility for child support

Andrew Mitchell MP
Under Secretary of State for
Social Security
DSS
Richmond House
79 Whitehall
London SW1A 2NS

Child Support Agency Centres (CSACs)

See over for telephone numbers

Hastings
Ashdown House
Sedlescombe Road North
Hastings
East Sussex TN34 1AS
Manager: Alan Hofmann

Plymouth
Clearbrook House
Towerfield Drive
Bickleigh Down Business Park
Plymouth
Devon PL6 7TN
Manager: Jean Brown

Dudley
Pedmore House
The Waterfront
Level Street
Brierley Hill
Dudley
West Midlands DY5 1XA
Manager: Norman Egan

Birkenhead
Great Western House
Woodside Ferry Approach
Birkenhead
Merseyside L41 6RG
Manager: David Carbery

Belfast (GB)
Great Northern Tower
17 Great Victoria Street
Belfast, Northern Ireland BT2 7AD
Manager: John Johnston

Falkirk
Parklands
Callendar Business Park
Callendar Road
Falkirk FK1 1XT
Manager: Andy Bowman

Local rate telephone lines

National enquiry line	0345 133133
Employers' help line	0345 134134
Child Support literature line	0345 830830

Hastings CSAC	0345 134000
Plymouth CSAC	0345 137000
Dudley CSAC	0345 131000
Birkenhead CSAC	0345 138000
Belfast (GB) CSAC	0345 132000
Falkirk CSAC	0345 136000

Divisional Offices

London and the Downs
Divisional Manager:
Joan Garcia, 40 East Street,
Epsom, Surrey KT19 1HL
Tel: 01372 749904
Fax: 01372 748430
Offices covered:
Barnet, Hendon, Edgware, Harlesden,
Cricklewood, Brixton, Lewisham,
Greenwich Park, Hither Green, Oval,
Brighton, Hove, Lewes, Eastbourne,
Hastings, Euston, Paddington,
Finsbury Park, Highgate, Harrow,
Uxbridge, Ealing, Acton, Notting Hill,
Tunbridge Wells, Southall, Croydon,
Sutton, Wimbledon, Mitcham,
Woolwich, Bexley, Dartford, Bromley

South East
Divisional Manager:
Patricia Anderson, Room 224N,
30 Main Street, Romford, Essex
RM1 3HH
Tel: 01708 774002
Fax: 01708 737083
Offices covered:
Barking, Plaistow, Canning Town,
Stratford, Romford, Dover, Folkestone,
Canterbury, Thanet, Stoke Newington,
Hoxton, City, Hackney, Shoreditch,
Poplar, Stepney, Leytonstone,
Sittingbourne, Maidstone, Chatham,
Gravesend, Southend, Colchester,
Chelmsford, Clacton, Basildon,
Braintree, Grays, Harlow, Ilford,
Edmonton, Wood Green, Walthamstow,
Tottenham, Hornchurch, Ashford

South West
Divisional Manager:
Rory Hearn, Clearbrook House,
Towerfield Drive, Bickleigh Down
Business Park, Plymouth PL6 7TN
Tel: 01752 726701
Fax: 01752 726195
Offices covered:
Gloucester, Cheltenham, Launceston,
Penzance, St Austell, Truro, Bristol East,
Plymouth Durley, Plymouth Crownhill,
Torbay, Exeter, Barnstaple, Newton
Abbot, Yeovil, Bournemouth, Taunton,
Fareham, Southampton, Portsmouth,
Poole, Havant, Isle of Wight, Weymouth

Central Southern
Divisional Manager:
Anne Ferries, Room 309, St Paul's
House, 1 Mashfield Road,
Chippenham SN15 1LA
Tel: 01249 428045
Fax: 01249 428050
Offices covered:
Bloomsbury, Kennington Park,
Southwark, Westminster, Fulham,

Dulwich, Crystal Palace, Kensington, Worthing, Chichester, Bognor Regis, Crawley, Wandsworth, Battersea, Balham, Streatham, Hounslow, Kingston-upon-Thames, New Malden, Twickenham, Guildford, Redhill, Woking, Swindon, Basingstoke, Aldershot, Winchester, Andover, Chippenham, Salisbury, Reading, Bracknell, Newbury, Slough

Central North
Divisional Manager:
Gillian Turner, Quay House, Brierley Hill, Dudley DY5 1XA
Tel: 01384 488090
Fax: 01384 488540

Offices covered:
Burton-on-Trent, Derby Becket Street, Derby London Road, Ilkeston, Cannock, Lichfield, Stockport, Hanley, Longton, Shrewsbury, Warrington, Telford, Wolverhampton, Manchester–Wythenshawe, Macclesfield, Manchester–Rusholme, Widnes, Wilmslow, Manchester–Bishopsgate, Manchester–Cheetham, Sale, Chester, Manchester–Longsight

West Midlands and Chilterns
Divisional Manager:
John Mills, c/o Pedmore House, Brierley Hill, Dudley
Tel: 01384 488070
Fax: 01384 488540

Offices covered:
Perry Barr, Edington, Washwood Heath, Northfield, Ravenhurst, South Yardley, Aylesbury, West Bromwich, Bedford, Luton, Milton Keynes, Coventry, Leamington Spa, Nuneaton, Rugby, Banbury, Hereford, Redditch, Worcester, Halesowen, Dudley North, Kidderminster, Oxford, High Wycombe, Walsall, Edgbaston

Anglia and East Midlands
Divisional Manager:
Howard Grant, Room 315, Olympic House, Olympic Way, Wembley HA9 0DL
Tel: 0181 795 8708
Fax: 0181 795 8868

Offices covered:
Northampton, Wellingborough, Nottingham David Lane, Nottingham Milton, Cambridge, Peterborough, Sutton-in-Ashfield, Worksop, Chesterfield, Hertford, St Albans, Stevenage, Watford, Hemel Hempstead, Leicester–Yeoman Street, Leicester–Wellington Street, Loughborough, Lincoln–Orchard Street, Newlands, Grantham, Skegness, Boston, Chantry, Great Yarmouth, King's Lynn, Bury St Edmunds, Ipswich, Lowestoft, Diss

North West
Divisional Manager:
Ken McLean, Room 219, St Mark House, Woodside Ferry Approach, Birkenhead, Merseyside L41 6RG
Tel: 0151 649 2780
Fax: 0151 649 2784

Offices covered:
Lancaster, Kendal, Barrow-in-Furness, Burnley, Carlisle, Whitehaven, Workington, Penrith, Bolton, Salford, Toxteth, Garston, Bootle, Southport, Crosby, Kirby, Preston, Blackpool North, Blackpool South, Wigan, Leigh, Breckfield, Norris Green, Huyton, St Helens, Skelmersdale, Ashton, Failsworth, Hyde, Oldham, Blackburn, Bury, Accrington, Manchester City, Salford, Liverpool City, Birkenhead North

Wales and Merseyside
Divisional Manager:
John McCann, c/o Great Western House, Woodside Ferry Approach, Birkenhead, Merseyside L41 6DA
Tel: 0151 649 2775
Fax: 0151 649 2779
Offices covered:
Rhyl, Colwyn Bay, Newtown, Wrexham, Swansea, Llanelli, Haverfordwest, Ammanford, Newport, Cwmbran, Caerphilly, Blackwood, Barry, Cardiff East, Cardiff West, Caernarfon, Dolgellau, Holyhead, Aberystwyth, Pontypridd, Merthyr, Ebbw Vale, Aberdare, Neath, Bridgend
Customer service outlets: Cardiff Central, Porth, Tonypandy, Port Talbot

Yorkshire and Humberside
Divisional Manager:
Nelson Hewitson, c/o 49 High Street, Hull HU1 1QJ
Tel: 01482 584816
Fax: 01482 584874
Offices covered:
Doncaster West, Rotherham, Barnsley West, Wath-on-Dearne, Bradford East, Halifax, Keighley, Dewsbury, Huddersfield, Bridlington, Scarborough, Pontefract, Grimsby, Hull, Scunthorpe, Sheffield

Eastern (Edinburgh to Leeds)
Divisional Manager:
Sam Lavery, Parklands, Callendar Business Park, Callendar Road, Falkirk FK1 1XT
Tel: 0345 136130
Fax: 0345 136627
Offices covered:
Ashington, Bathgate, Berwick, Bishop Auckland, Blyth, Chester-Le-Street, Darlington, Durham, Edinburgh, Edinburgh East, Edinburgh North, Edinburgh South, Eston, Galashiels, Gateshead, Harrogate, Hartlepool, Jarrow, Leeds East, Leeds North, Leeds West, Livingston, Middlesbrough, Newcastle East, Newcastle St James, Newcastle West, Northallerton, North Shields, Peterlee, Redcar, Seaham, Stanley, South Shields, Stockton, Sunderland North, Sunderland South, Wallsend, York

Scotland (excluding Lothian and the Borders)
Divisional Manager:
Eileen Lewis, 67 Minerva Street, Cranstonhill, Glasgow G3 8LD
Tel: 0141 204 2722
Fax: 0141 204 4356
Offices covered:
Wick, Elgin, Inverness, Stirling, Oban, Falkirk, Greenock, Clydebank, Dumbarton, Campbeltown, Paisley, East Kilbride, Laurieston, Irvine, Glasgow South West, Motherwell, Bellshill, Coatbridge, Ayr, Dumfries, Stranraer, Glasgow City, Anniesland, Cumbernauld, Springburn, Dundee, Dunfermline, Cowdenbeath, Aberdeen, Peterhead, Lerwick, Perth, Dundee, Arbroath, Shettlestone

Income support premiums – conditions of entitlement

For more details of premiums and how they affect means-tested benefits, see CPAG's *National Welfare Benefits Handbook*.

Premiums are added to income support (IS) personal allowances and are intended to help with the extra expenses caused by age, disability or the cost of children. The premiums are used in the child support formula, irrespective of whether the parent is in receipt of IS, although not all apply at each stage.

Family premium	£10.55
Lone parent premium (IS)	£5.20
Disabled child premium	£20.40
Carer premium (per carer)	£13.00
Disability premium	
single	£20.40
couple	£29.15
Severe disability premium	
single	£36.40
couple (both qualify)	£72.80
Pensioner premium	
(i) if aged 60-74	
single	£19.15
couple	£28.90
(ii) if aged 75-79	
single	£21.30
couple	£31.90
Higher pensioner premium	
single	£25.90
couple	£37.05

Family premium

A person is entitled to this if her/his family includes a child, even if s/he is not the child's parent and that child has capital over £3,000. A family includes a child where the claimant or partner receives child benefit for a child living in the same household. However, only one family premium is payable regardless of the number of children a person has. Where a child who is in the care of or being looked after by a local authority, or who is in custody, comes home for part of a week, a proportion of the premium is payable, according to the number of days the child is at home.

Disabled child premium

A person is entitled to a disabled child premium for each child who gets disability living allowance (DLA) or who is blind. A child is treated as blind if s/he is registered as blind and for the first 28 weeks after s/he has been taken off the register on regaining her/his sight. For how to qualify for DLA, see CPAG's *Rights Guide to Non-Means-Tested Benefits*.

If DLA has stopped because the child is in hospital, this premium continues. But if the child ceases to be treated as a member of your family, the premium stops after 12 weeks. See CPAG's *National Welfare Benefits Handbook* for more details.

If a child has over £3,000 capital, there is no entitlement to this premium.

Carer premium

A person qualifies for this if s/he or her/his partner is getting invalid care allowance (ICA), or would get it but for the overlapping benefit rules (ie, because s/he is receiving another benefit paid at a higher rate). For example, a woman getting ICA who at 60 is awarded retirement pension at a higher rate than ICA, continues to qualify for the premium. To take advantage of the overlapping rule, s/he must have claimed (or re-claimed) ICA since September 1990, and the person being cared for continues to get the higher or middle-rate care component of DLA, or attendance allowance (AA).

A double premium is awarded where both the person concerned and her/his partner satisfy the conditions for it.

See CPAG's *National Welfare Benefits Handbook* for more details on the premium and CPAG's *Rights Guide to Non-Means-Tested Benefits* for the conditions of entitlement for ICA.

Lone parent premium

A person is entitled to this if s/he is a lone parent. S/he can continue to get it for as long as a child is treated as her/his dependant, which in some cases can be until the child reaches the age of 19. A person does not have to be the *parent* of the child, but s/he must be receiving child benefit for the child and they must be members of the same household.

A person may qualify for a lone parent premium even if s/he has a partner who does not count as a member of her/his household – eg, if her/his partner is living abroad and is not able to come to this country because of the immigration rules. A lone parent premium is paid even if a person does not get a personal allowance for any child because the child has capital over £3,000. Only one lone parent premium is payable regardless of the number of children a person has.

If a child is in local authority care or in custody for part of a week, this premium can be apportioned as for family premium (see above).

The Government has indicated that from April 1997 this premium will be incorporated into the family premium so that its value could be eroded with time – see the next edition of this *Handbook*.

Disability premium

A person can get a disability premium if s/he is under 60 and one of the following applies to her/him (note that in the exempt income step of the child support formula, the age rule does not apply):

- A person is getting a qualifying benefit. These are AA (or an equivalent benefit paid to meet attendance needs because of an injury at work or a war injury), DLA, disability working allowance (DWA), mobility supplement, incapacity benefit paid at the long-term rate or when terminally ill, or severe disablement allowance (SDA). A person or her/his partner must be getting the benefit for her/himself, not on behalf of someone else (eg, as a parent or an appointee). In some situations, entitlement to the premium continues after the person stops receiving the qualifying benefit – see CPAG's *National Welfare Benefits Handbook*. See CPAG's *Rights Guide to Non-Means-Tested Benefits* for who can claim these benefits.
- A person is registered as blind with a local authority (England and Wales) or regional or Islands council (Scotland); if sight is regained, s/he will still qualify for 28 weeks after s/he is taken off the register.
- A person has an NHS invalid trike or private car allowance because of disability.
- A person is 'incapable of work' (or exempt from the 'all-work test') and either entitled to statutory sick pay or has been incapable for at least:
  - 196 days if certified as 'terminally ill' (ie, it can reasonably be expected that s/he will die within six months due to a progressive disease);
  - 364 days in all other cases, provided s/he has claimed incapacity benefit (it is not necessary to send in medical certificates).

Breaks in incapacity/entitlement of up to 56 days are included in these periods. For more on 'incapacity for work', see CPAG's *Rights Guide to Non-Means-Tested Benefits*.

At the protected income stage of the child support calculation, couples will get the disability premium at the couple rate provided either of them qualifies under one of the first three of the above rules. But they will only get the premium under the last condition if the person who qualifies is the parent being assessed for child maintenance.

Pensioner premium

The pensioner premium is paid at two rates according to age:

- the lower rate is paid if a person is aged 60–74 inclusive;
- the enhanced rate is paid if a person is 75–79 inclusive.

Each of these can be paid at a couple rate if one partner fulfils the age condition. If a person or her/his partner is sick or disabled, check to see if the higher pensioner premium described below applies.

Higher pensioner premium

A person can get this if one of the following applies:

- a person or her/his partner is 80 or over; *or*
- a person was getting a disability premium as part of her/his IS, HB or CTB at some time during the eight weeks before s/he was 60 and has continued to get that benefit since the age of 60 (breaks of up to eight weeks are ignored). Couples can qualify under this rule regardless of which partner meets the condition; *or*
- a person or her/his partner is aged 60–79 *and* either of them receives a qualifying benefit (as for the disability premium), is registered blind, or has an NHS trike or private car allowance. If a person stops getting incapacity benefit or SDA to change to retirement pension, the higher pensioner premium still applies if there is a continuous entitlement (apart from breaks of eight weeks or less) to IS, HB or CTB.

Severe disability premium

This gives additional help to severely disabled people who need care. The conditions for receipt are:

- a person is receiving AA (or the equivalent war pension or industrial injury benefit), or the higher or middle-rate care component of DLA (or extra-statutory payments to compensate for not receiving any of these). If s/he is part of a couple, they must both be getting one of these benefits or the partner who does not get AA/DLA must be registered or treated as blind; *and*
- no non-dependant aged 18 or over is living with her/him (see below). S/he only counts as living with a person if s/he shares accommodation apart from a bathroom, lavatory or a communal area such as a hall, passageway or a room in common use in sheltered accommodation. If s/he is separately liable to make payments for the accommodation to the landlord, s/he does not count as living with the person concerned, even if s/he does share facilities – eg, a kitchen; *and*
- no one is getting ICA for looking after her/him.

A couple where both are severely disabled only get the single rate if someone is getting ICA in respect of one of them or one of them qualifies only because they are registered or treated as blind.

Non-dependants aged 18 or over

The following people living with a person do not count:

- a person's partner (but s/he must be getting AA/DLA or be blind – see above);
- any child living with her/him (this includes a child who is not treated as part of her/his household);
- anyone staying in a person's home who normally lives elsewhere;
- a person (or, for IS only, her/his partner) employed by a charitable or voluntary body as a resident carer for a person or her/his partner if s/he pays for that service (even if the charge is only nominal);
- a person receiving AA or the higher or middle-rate care component of DLA;
- a person who is registered blind or treated as blind;
- a person, or her/his partner, who jointly occupies her/his home and is either a co-owner with the person or her/his partner, or jointly liable with them to make payments to a landlord in respect of occupying it;
- a person, or any member of her/his household, who is liable to pay on a commercial basis for occupying the dwelling (eg, tenant or licensee), unless s/he is a close relative;
- a person, or any member of her/his household, to whom a person or her/his partner is liable to make such payments on a commercial basis, unless s/he is a close relative.

Close relative means parent, parent-in-law, son, son-in-law, daughter, daughter-in-law, step-parent, step-son, step-daughter, brother, sister, or partners of any of these. It does not include a grandparent, aunt or uncle.

If someone (other than those listed above) comes to live with a person in order to look after her/him or her/his partner, her/his severe disability premium will only remain in payment for the first 12 weeks.

Severe disability premium and carer premium

If someone gets ICA for looking after a person, that excludes her/him from the severe disability premium. If her/his carer is not getting ICA, s/he may get the severe disability premium. But if her/his carer stops or refrains from claiming ICA, the notional income rules could apply.

If a person's carer has claimed ICA but it is not being paid because of the overlapping benefit rules, s/he can get a carer premium *and* the person concerned will be entitled to the severe disability premium. ICA is not in this case 'in payment' to her/his carer.

For more detail of these rules, see CPAG's *National Welfare Benefits Handbook*.

Steps of the formula

Where parent with care is on income support

Step 1:   The maintenance requirement

Step 2:   Exempt income of absent parent

Step 3:   Assessable income of absent parent

Step 4:   **Proposed maintenance**
  Step 4a   50% deduction rate
  Step 4b   Refer back to maintenance requirement (step 1) – if the proposed maintenance in step 4a is equal to or smaller than the maintenance requirement, continue to step 5 using the figure proposed in step 4a
  Step 4c   Additional element calculation – to give the proposed maintenance in cases where the maintenance requirement is met
  Step 4d   Check the figure proposed in step 4c is not over the maximum payment

Step 5:   **Protected income**
Can the absent parent afford the proposed maintenance?
  Step 5a   30% cap – if proposed maintenance is more than 30% net income, it is reduced to 30% net income
  Step 5b   Basic protected income
  Step 5c   Total family income
  Step 5d   Total protected income
  Step 5e   Disposable income = total family income minus proposed maintenance (see p257 for alternative method)
  Step 5f   If disposable income is more than total protected income, the parent can afford the **proposed maintenance**
           If disposable income is below total protected income, **maintenance payable = total family income minus total protected income**

Minimum payment
If the maintenance figure is below £4.80, the maintenance payable becomes either £4.80 or nil (see p167)

Where neither parent is on income support

Step 1:   The maintenance requirement

Step 2:   Exempt income
Step 2a   Exempt income of absent parent
Step 2b   Exempt income of parent with care

Step 3:   Assessable income
Step 3a   Assessable income of absent parent
Step 3b   Assessable income of parent with care

Step 4:   Proposed maintenance
Step 4a   Add together the assessable incomes of both parents to give joint assessable income
Step 4b   50% of joint assessable income
Step 4c   Refer back to maintenance requirement (step 1) – if the figure in Step 4b is equal to or less than the maintenance requirement, proposed maintenance is 50% of absent parent's own assessable income; go to step 5
Step 4d   Additional element calculation – to give the proposed maintenance in cases when the maintenance requirement is met
Step 4e   Check the figure proposed in step 4d is not over the maximum payment

Step 5:   Protected income
Can the absent parent afford the proposed maintenance?
Step 5a   30% cap – if proposed maintenance is more than 30% of the absent parent's net income, it is reduced to 30% net income
Step 5b   Basic protected income
Step 5c   Total family income
Step 5d   Total protected income
Step 5e   Disposable income = total family income minus proposed maintenance (see p257 for alternative method)
Step 5f   If disposable income is more than total protected income, the parent can afford the **proposed maintenance**
If disposable income is below total protected income, **maintenance payable = total family income minus total protected income**

Minimum payment
If the maintenance figure is below £4.80, the maintenance payable becomes either £4.80 or nil (see p167)

Child support formula

You do not have to do a calculation if the absent parent is on income support (IS) (see p168).

The calculation is based on IS rates; the 1996/97 amounts are given at each stage. The IS personal allowances for dependent children are:

aged under 11	£16.45	aged 11–15	£24.10
aged 16–17	£28.85	aged 18	£37.90

Calculation sheet no 1 (see Chapter 8)

STEP 1: MAINTENANCE REQUIREMENT

If the absent parent has to pay more than one person with care for different children, this step has to be carried out separately for each person with care.

Personal allowances

Adult:*£47.90 if at least one of the children is under 11 years old
    or £35.93 if at least one of the children is 11–13 years old
    or £23.95 if at least one of the children is 14–15 years old   _____

Children of the absent parent living with the person with care

Name _____   _____

Name _____   _____

Name _____   _____

Name _____   _____

Premiums

Family* (£10.55)   _____

Lone parent* (£5.20) if the person with care is a lone parent   _____

Sub total

minus child benefit   — _____

MAINTENANCE REQUIREMENT   Box A

*These amounts will be reduced if the person with care looks after children who have different absent parents (see p177)

Calculation sheet no 2 (see Chapter 9)

STEP 2: EXEMPT INCOME OF ABSENT PARENT

If the parent has care of children for part of the week only, see Chapter 13.

Personal allowances

Parent   £47.90

Children living with parent* (only count the parent's own child)

Name _____   _____

Name _____   _____

Name _____   _____

Premiums (if eligible)

Family* (£10.55)   _____

Disabled child premium* (£20.40)   _____

Disability premium (£20.40) or lone parent premium (£5.20)   _____

Carer premium (£13.00)   _____

Severe disability premium (£36.40)

Housing costs (see p185)   _____

Allowance for pre-April 1993 property settlement (see p192)   _____

Allowance towards travel-to-work costs (see p196)   _____

EXEMPT INCOME   [   ] Box B

*These amounts may be halved if the child's other parent is the absent parent's partner and she can afford to help maintain the joint child (see p198)

Calculation sheet no 2 (continued)

STEP 2: EXEMPT INCOME OF PARENT WITH CARE

Do not do this step if the parent with care is on income support.
If the parent has care of any child for part of the week only, see Chapter 13.

Personal allowances

Parent   £47.90

Children living with parent* (only count the parent's own child)

Name _____   _____

Name _____   _____

Name _____   _____

Name _____   _____

Name _____   _____

Premiums (if eligible)

Family   £10.55

Disabled child premium* (£20.40)   _____

Disability premium (£20.40) or lone parent premium (£5.20)   _____

Carer premium (£13.00)   _____

Severe disability premium (£36.40)   _____

Housing costs (see p185)   _____

Allowance towards travel-to-work costs (see p196)   _____

EXEMPT INCOME   [   ] Box C

*These amounts may be halved for any joint children of the parent and her partner, if the partner can afford to help maintain the joint child (see p198)

Note: an allowance for a pre-April 1993 property settlement is included only where the parent with care was the absent parent at the time of the settlement (see p192).

Calculation sheet no 3 (see Chapter 10)

STEP 3: ASSESSABLE INCOME

Do not include income of any partner.

Absent parent		**Parent with care** (Do not do this if the parent with care is on income support – her assessable income is nil.)	
Net earnings (see p203)	_____	Net earnings (see p203)	_____
Income from benefits (see p210 for disregards)	_____	Income from benefits (see p210 for disregards)	_____
Income from capital (see p214)	_____	Income from capital (see p214)	_____
Other income (see p211)	_____	Other income (see p211)	_____
Children's income (see p216)	_____	Children's income (see p216)	_____

Net income ☐ Box D

Net income ☐ Box E

minus exempt income —
(from Box B) _____

minus exempt income —
(from Box C) _____

ABSENT PARENT'S ASSESSABLE INCOME ☐ Box F

PARENT WITH CARE'S ASSESSABLE INCOME ☐ Box G

If the absent parent has to pay maintenance to more than one person with care, the assessable income carried forward to step 4 is apportioned between the persons with care (see p239).

If the parent with care is claiming maintenance from more than one absent parent, the assessable income carried forward to step 4 is apportioned between the absent parents' calculations (see p247).

Calculation sheet no 4 (see Chapter 11)

STEP 4: PROPOSED MAINTENANCE

This is the amount which the absent parent will pay unless it is reduced by the protected income calculation (step 5).

If the absent parent has to pay maintenance to more than one person with care for different children, this step has to be carried out separately for each person with care using a proportion of assessable income (see p239).

If the absent parent looks after the child(ren) for part of the time, see Chapter 13.

To decide whether the 50% calculation applies:

Maintenance requirement   Box A

Absent parent's assessable income   Box F

Parent with care's assessable income   Box G

(if both parents are absent, include the other
absent parent's assessable income in Box G –
see p236)

Joint assessable income: add Box F and Box G   Box H

50% Box H equals   Box I

If Box I is smaller than (or equal to) Box A, do the 50% calculation

If Box I is larger than Box A, do the additional element calculation

50% calculation:

Proposed maintenance equals 50% Box F   Box J(i)

Now go to step 5 (unless proposed maintenance is £4.80 or less, in which case see p167).

Calculation sheet no 4 (continued)

Additional element calculation for proposed maintenance:

Basic element = ☐ x ☐ Box F = ☐

Box A ☐ Box H Box K

Box H

Basic assessable income = ☐ x 2 = ☐

Box K Box L

Additional assessable income = ☐ − ☐ = ☐

Box F Box L Box M

Additional element = ☐ x ☐%* = ☐

Box M Box N

* use 15% if there is one qualifying child, 20% if there are two, or 25% if there are three or more.

Proposed maintenance = ☐ + ☐ = ☐

Box K Box N Box J(ii)

Check this figure is below maximum (see p234) ☐

Box J(iii)

The proposed maintenance is the smaller of the figures in Box J(ii) and Box J(iii)

Now go to step 5.

Calculation sheet no 5 (see Chapter 12)

STEP 5: PROTECTED INCOME OF ABSENT PARENT

5a: Thirty per cent cap

Proposed maintenance from step 4 ⬚ Box J(i), J(ii) or J(iii)

30% absent parent's net income ⬚ x 30% = ⬚ Box O
Box D

Put whichever of Box J or Box O is lower into Box P ⬚
Box P

5b: Basic protected income

If the absent parent has care of a child for part of the time, see Chapter 13.

Personal allowances

Single (£47.90) or couple (£75.20) _____

Children (all in the family)

Name _____ _____

Name _____ _____

Name _____ _____

Name _____ _____

Premiums

Family (£10.55) _____

Disabled child premium (£20.40) _____

Disability premium (£20.40/£29.15) *or* lone parent premium (£5.20) _____

Carer premium (£13.00 per carer) _____

Severe disability premium (£36.40/£72.80) _____

Any applicable pensioner premium _____

Housing costs (see p253) _____

Council tax (minus any CTB) _____

Travel-to-work costs (see p254) _____

Standard margin £30.00

BASIC PROTECTED INCOME ⬚ Box Q

Calculation sheet no 5 (continued)

5c: Total family income

Absent parent's net income (Box D)* _____

Partner's net income _____

Child benefit _____

TOTAL FAMILY INCOME [   ] Box R

* Note that the rules about children's income are different and therefore an adjustment may need to be made – see pp216 and 251.

5d: Total protected income

Excess family income = [   ] — [   ] = [   ]

Box R   Box Q   Box S

Additional protected income = 15% of [   ] = [   ] Box T

Box S

+

plus basic protected income (Box Q) _____

TOTAL PROTECTED INCOME [   ] Box V

5e: Income above total protected level (see p255)

Total family income (Box R) _____

minus total protected income (Box V) — _____

[   ] Box W

5f: Maintenance payable

The maintenance payable is the smaller of Box P and Box W.

If the figure is less than £4.80, the absent parent pays the minimum payment of £4.80 a week (unless he is exempt – see p167).

Code of practice for bailiffs

[Note: *The National Association of Citizens' Advice Bureaux has produced a critique of this code and is seeking improvements. It would be useful to hear of any cases where the code has proved inadequate.*]

General

1. The bailiff will levy distress in a humane, firm but fair manner in line with the Child Support Agency's requirements.

2. The bailiff will comply with any instruction given by or on behalf of the Child Support Agency's Representative, other than those that the bailiff considers will prejudice the rights of debtor under relevant legislation or this code.

Contact with the debtor

3. The bailiff shall undertake visits to enforce Liability Orders or effect Distraint between 07:00 to 21:00 unless the exceptional circumstances of a case dictate the need to visit outside those hours, for example a debtor working irregular hours.

4. In all cases the bailiff will introduce himself, with identification, which will include a photograph, to the debtor and give reasons for his visit.

5. The bailiff will be dressed smartly, be courteous and polite in all circumstances.

6. The bailiffs will carry with them on all enforcement visits the written authority of the Agency giving instructions to the bailiff to act on behalf of the Agency in respect of enforcement proceedings.

7. The name of the bailiff who attended the debtor's premises must be shown on any documents left with or posted to the debtor.

8. Bailiffs must not seek access to domestic premises when there is no person over the age of 18 on the premises.

9. Bailiffs must not, as a means of intimidation, discuss with liable persons other means of enforcement (eg, imprisonment).

10. If the liable person or partner is not available the purpose of the bailiff's visit must not be discussed with any other person.

11. Bailiffs seeking information about the whereabouts or movements of a liable person should do so using the utmost discretion and without specifying the nature of their business.

12. Every effort will be made to discuss the arrears with the debtor and to arrange for reasonable payment to be made weekly, monthly or otherwise where required.

Payment arrangements

13. All payment arrangements entered into will be, where possible, in the form of a Walking Possession Agreements whereby goods are itemised on an inventory as security in case payments are not made. All goods of the debtor must be fully detailed on the inventory and all reasonable steps taken to ensure the goods belong to the debtor.

14. The Child Support Agency requires that receipts shall be given to the debtor for all payments. The form of receipting should give:
    - the name of the person making the payment;
    - the name of the debtor (where this is different);
    - The Child Support Agency's case reference number shown on the authority to enforce;
    - the amount of the payment;
    - the date and time of receipt.

15. Having issued a receipt, the bailiff must advise the debtor to keep all receipts in a safe place in case they are required to verify any payment.

Distraint

16. No distress can be levied unless the debtor is present on the premises in person at the time of distress.

17. Distress should only be levied by carrying out the following steps:
    1. gain physical access to the premises without the use of force;
    2. identify specific items of property which are not required to be exempted as belonging to the debtor;
    3. list those items in duplicate including an estimate of the sale value of each item. Provide the debtor with a copy and allow him time to read the document in full;
    4. obtain the signature of the debtor to a copy of the Walking Possession agreement.

18. In the event of goods being distrained upon the bailiff must adhere to the current law appertaining to distress proceedings as to what goods may or may not be seized. However, bailiffs must not distrain upon the following goods:
    a) Such tools, books, vehicles and other items of equipment as are necessary to the debtor for use personally by him in his employment, business or vocation.

b) Such clothing, bedding, furniture, household equipment and provisions as are necessary to satisfy the '**Basic Domestic Needs**' of the debtor and his family with whom he resides.

'**Basic Domestic Needs**' is defined as follows:

a   Clothes reasonably required for the debtor and family.
b   Medical aids/equipment, eg, first aid boxes.
c   Educational/training articles reasonably required for the debtor and family. This does not include home computers.
d   Toys of a child.
e   Articles for the care and upbringing of a child, eg, prams, pushchairs.
f   Articles for the care of someone physically or mentally disabled, eg, wheelchair or other aid.
g   Articles used for cleaning, mending or pressing clothes.
h   Articles used for cleaning the dwelling.
i   Bed and bedding required by the members of the household.
j   Household linen.
k   A table (unless a breakfast bar or the like is available) and a chair for each member of the family.
l   Food.
m   Lights or light fittings except where free standing.
n   Heating appliances, except where free-standing, unless they provide the only form of heating in the dwelling or specific areas, eg, bedroom. Where they are required specifically for a child, elderly or infirm person they should not be removed.
o   Curtains
p   Floor coverings, where the bare floor (ie, exposed floorboards or a concrete base) would be left.
q   Cooking utensils, refrigerators, a cooker (excluding microwaves which are not the only form of cooking) or washing machines (where there is a child under 11 or if there is incontinence in the family), cleaning equipment including vacuum cleaners, articles for the safety of people in the dwelling, eg, staircases.
r   Any articles required for the safety of the persons living in the dwelling.
s   Tools used within the household reasonably required for domestic repair.

Excepting those items listed above, any goods in respect of which a Hire Purchase Agreement remains outstanding may be removed provided there is evidence the repayment arrangement has been maintained and is up to date.

18.   Nothing can be distrained that is not properly listed on the Walking Possession agreement.

19. No distress can be levied constructively, for example by posting a Walking Possession agreement through a letter box and having it signed and returned by post.

Removal and sale of goods

20. The bailiff will ensure that all debtor's goods taken into the bailiff's possession are handled with due care and attention and properly secured for the purposes of transporting them. The bailiff shall also ensure that the goods are adequately insured and safely stored pending sale.

21. The bailiff must inform the debtor of the date, time and location of the auction at the same the arrangement for the sale are publicised.

22. Following the sale the bailiff must inform the debtor of the name of the buyer and the price for which each item was sold.

Complaints

23. The bailiffs will record all complaints made by the debtor or anyone else against them in respect of Child Support Agency cases. The record will be kept up-to-date at all times and kept separate from usual files.

24. A senior manager of the bailiff company should have a specific duty to investigate and respond to complaints in line with clearly laid down procedures in use throughout the company.

25. Following investigation the bailiff company should report all complaints to the Child Support Agency, giving full details of the complaint and the outcome of the bailiff company's investigation.

Getting independent advice

It is often difficult for unsupported individuals to get a positive response from the Child Support Agency (CSA). They may be more successful if they have taken advice about their rights or have an adviser assisting them. The following agencies may be able to help:

- Citizens' Advice Bureaux (CABx) and other local advice centres provide information and may be able to represent people.
- Law centres can often help in a similar way to CABx/advice centres.
- Solicitors can give free legal advice under the Green Form scheme (Pink Form in Scotland). This does not cover the cost of representation at an appeal tribunal hearing but can cover the cost of preparing written submissions and obtaining evidence such as medical reports. If you are considering a judicial review (see p351), you should seek legal advice.
- Local authority welfare rights workers provide an advice and representation service for benefit claimants in many areas.
- Lone parent organisations may offer help and advice about child support. For details of your local group contact: Gingerbread – 0171 240 0953; Single Parent Action Network – 0117 051 4231; National Council for One Parent Families – 0171 267 1361; Scottish Council for Single Parents – 0131 556 3899.
- There are a large number of local groups campaigning against the scheme. For details of your local group, contact:
  - the Network Against the Child Support Act (NACSA): England – Mike Pimblott 01703 324323 (between 7 and 9pm) or Thelma Green 01908 368915; Scotland – Alistair Ferrie 01877 386245; Wales – Sally Kay 01446 751790; Northern Ireland – Bill Hammer 01232 658662; *or*
  - the Scottish Child Support Act Campaign Group (SCSACG): Marion Davis 0141 333 1450; *or*
  - the Northern Ireland Child Support Order Lobby Group: c/o Gingerbread Northern Ireland 01232 231417; *or*
  - the National Alliance of Caring Parents (NACP): John Coxhead 01430 873734; *or*
  - the Campaign Against the Child Support Act (CACSA), which is co-ordinated by the Wages for Housework Campaign and Payday men's network: 0171 837 7509, 0117 9426 608 and 0161 344 0758.

- Many trade unions are providing advice to members on child support.
- Joint Council for the Welfare of Immigrants advises people from abroad: 0171 251 8706.
- Local organisations for particular groups may offer help – eg, unemployed centres, claimants' unions, centres for people with disabilities.

However, since not all agencies have a good working knowledge of the child support rules, it may be advisable to shop around.

If details of these agencies are not in the telephone book, the local library should have more information.

Representation at appeal tribunals

Some parents have been finding it difficult to obtain representation at appeal hearings. Although many parents, especially with the help of Chapter 16, will be perfectly able to present their own cases, it can be invaluable to obtain objective independent advice which draws on the legislation. An advice centre which has a copy of the legislation (see Appendix 7) and experience of representing at other tribunals – eg, social security appeal tribunals – should be able to provide a representative for a child support appeal tribunal (CSAT). If the adviser wants support on the case, suggest that s/he sends CPAG a copy of the tribunal papers, as soon as they are available, for our comments. Advisers can also join the Child Support Practitioners' Group (see p13).

Child Poverty Action Group

Unfortunately, CPAG is a small organisation and is unable to deal with enquiries directly from members of the public. Please do find local advice as we are unable to respond adequately to individuals' enquiries.

Advisers can phone our advice line which is open from 2pm to 4pm on Monday to Thursday – 0171 253 6569. This is a special phone line for advice enquiries; please do not ring the main CPAG number.

Alternatively, ask an adviser to write to us at Citizens' Rights Office, CPAG, 4th Floor, 1-5 Bath Street, London EC1V 9PY. We can take up a limited number of complex cases, including appeals to the child support commissioners or courts, if referred by an adviser. CPAG also runs training courses on child support.

We are continuing to monitor the implementation of the legislation and to lobby for changes, both at an operational level and a policy level. We would therefore be pleased to receive notes of any case which demonstrates a difficulty, anomaly, delay or where hardship has been caused by the child support scheme.

Books and reports

Many of the books listed here will be in a main public library.

I. LEGISLATION

Available from CPAG Ltd, 4th Floor, 1-5 Bath Street, London EC1V 9PY. Prices include p&p.

Child Support: The Legislation by E Jacobs and G Douglas (Sweet & Maxwell, 2nd edn, Dec 1995, £32.50). Contains the primary and secondary legislation with a detailed commentary.
A supplement to this edition will be available in late 1996 for £9.50.

CPAG's Income-Related Benefits: The Legislation by J Mesher and P Wood (Sweet & Maxwell, 1995/96 edn, £42.25 with updating supplement). Contains the most useful legislation with a detailed commentary.
The 1996/97 edition will be available in August 1996 and a supplement containing jobseeker's allowance published in December 1996; these are available as a set from CPAG for a pre-publication price of £47.00.

CPAG's Housing Benefit and Council Tax Benefit Legislation by L Findlay, R Poynter and M Ward (CPAG Ltd, 8th edn, Feb 1996, £39.95). Contains the main legislation with a detailed commentary. The 1996/97 edition will be available in autumn 1996 and a supplement in December 1996; the pre-publication price for the set is £38.00.

Legislation can also be purchased from HMSO – see Appendix 8. See p385 for obtaining copies of Child Support Commissioners' decisions.

2. PERIODICALS

Available from CPAG Ltd, 4th Floor, 1-5 Bath Street, London EC1V 9PY. Prices include p&p.

The *Welfare Rights Bulletin* is published every two months by CPAG. It covers developments in social security and child support law and updates this *Handbook* as well as CPAG's *National Welfare Benefits Handbook* and CPAG's *Rights Guide to Non-Means-Tested Benefits* (see below). The

Bulletin includes summaries of all significant Child Support Commissioner decisions and judicial review cases concerning child support.

The annual subscription is £17.70 but it is sent automatically to CPAG Rights and Comprehensive members. Telephone 0171 253 3406 for membership details.

3. CHILD SUPPORT AGENCY PUBLICATIONS

For guidance issued to CSA staff, see Appendix 8.

CSA leaflets and most other CSA publications can be obtained from the CSA literature line: 0345 830830. The leaflet *For parents who live apart* is available in braille and on audio cassette, and in 13 languages.

CSA Business Plan, DSS, April 1993
CSA Charter, DSS, April 1993
CSA Framework document, DSS, April 1993
CSA The First Two Years, Annual Report 1993/94 (CSA 2066), and
　　Business Plan 1994/95, CSA, July 1994
CSA Business Plan 1995/96 (CSA 2091), CSA, March 1995
CSA Annual Report 1994/95 and Accounts 1994/95 (CSA596), July 1995
CSA Monthly Statistics are placed in the House of Commons library and
　　can be obtained via an MP.

4. OTHER PUBLICATIONS – CHILD SUPPORT

Enquiries concerning HMSO publications can be made on 0171 873 0011 and orders can be placed on 0171 873 9090 and fax 0171 873 8463.

White Paper, *Children Come First*, Volume 1, HMSO, October 1990
White Paper, *Children Come First*, Volume 2, HMSO, October 1990
White Paper, *Improving Child Support*, Cm 2745, HMSO, January 1995
House of Commons Social Security Committee, *The Operation of the
　　Child Support Act*, First Report – Session 1993/94, HC 690, HMSO,
　　1 December 1993
Reply by the Government to the First Report from the Social Security
　　Committee on the operation of the Child Support Act, Cm 2469,
　　HMSO, February 1994
House of Commons Social Security Committee, *The Operation of the
　　Child Support Act: Proposals for Change*, Fifth Report – Session
　　1993/94, HC 470, HMSO, 26 October 1994
Reply by the Government to the Fifth Report from the Committee on
　　Social Security Session 1993/94, Cm 2743, HMSO, January 1995
Memorandum to the Social Security Select Committee by the Chief
　　Executive of the CSA, HC 303, HMSO, 15 March 1995

House of Commons Social Security Committee, *The Performance and Operation of the Child Support Agency*, Second Report – Session 1995/96, HC 50, HMSO, 24 January 1996

Parliamentary Commissioner for Administration, Third Report – Session 1994/95, *Investigation of Complaints against the Child Support Agency*, HC 135, HMSO, 18 January 1995

House of Commons Select Committee on the Parliamentary Commissioner for Administration, Third Report, *The Child Support Agency*, HC 199, HMSO, 15 March 1995

Reply by the Government to the Third Report of the Select Committee on the Parliamentary Commissioner for Administration 1994/95, Cm 2865, HMSO, May 1995

House of Commons Select Committee on the Parliamentary Commissioner for Administration, First Special Report – Session 1995/96, HC 88, HMSO, 6 December 1995

Parliamentary Commissioner for Administration, Third Report – Session 1995/96, *Investigation of Complaints against the Child Support Agency*, HC 20, HMSO, 6 March 1996

House of Commons Committee of Public Accounts, *Child Support Agency*, First Report – Session 1995/96, HC 31, HMSO, 20 November 1995

Annual Report of the Chief Child Support Officer, Central Adjudication Services, 1994/95, HMSO, October 1995

DSS Research Report No. 39, *Child Support Agency National Client Satisfaction Survey 1994*, HMSO, July 1995 (the 1993 survey is research report No. 29)

Putting the Treasury First: the truth about child support, A Garnham and E Knights, CPAG Ltd, £7.95, May 1994

5. OTHER PUBLICATIONS – GENERAL

Available from CPAG Ltd, 4th Floor, 1-5 Bath Street, London EC1V 9PY. Prices include p&p.

National Welfare Benefits Handbook, April 1996, £8.95 (£3 for claimants)

Rights Guide to Non-Means-Tested Benefits, April 1996, £7.95 (£2.80 for claimants)

Jobseeker's Allowance Handbook, October 1996, £5.95

Guide to Housing Benefit and Council Tax Benefit, July 1996, £12.95

Debt Advice Handbook, December 1995, £9.95

Disability Rights Handbook, April 1996, £9.95

Rights Guide for Homeowners, October 1996, £8.95

Fuel Rights Handbook, March 1996, £8.95

Council Tax Handbook, late 1996, £9.95

Abbreviations used in the notes

AC	Appeal Cases
All ER	All England Reports
App	Appendix
Art	Article
CCR	County Court Rules
CCS	Child Support Commissioner decision from England and Wales
CCSO	Chief Child Support Officer
Ch	Chapter
Cm	Command paper
CSC	Child Support Commissioner decision from Northern Ireland
CSCS	Child Support Commissioner decision from Scotland
col	column
FLR	Family Law Reports
HC	House of Commons
HL	House of Lords
O	Order
para	paragraph
PQ	Parliamentary Question
PCA	Parliamentary Commissioner for Administration
QBD	Queen's Bench Division
Reg	Regulation
s	section
SJ	*Solicitors' Journal*
ss	sections
Sch	Schedule
Vol	Volume
WLR	Weekly Law Reports

(DC), (CA), (HL) and (ECJ) indicate decisions of the Divisional Court, Court of Appeal, House of Lords and European Court of Justice respectively.

(R) indicates a reported commissioners' decision (see p385).

Abbreviations relating to CSA guidance are covered at the end of this appendix.

I. THE LEGISLATION

Acts and regulations may be ordered from HMSO Books, PO Box 276, London SW8 5DT (tel: 0171 873 9090; fax: 0171 873 8463). Enquiries to PC51D, HMSO Books, 51 Nine Elms Lane, London SW8 5DR (tel: 0171 873 0011).

A volume of annotated child support legislation by Douglas and Jacobs can be purchased from CPAG Ltd (see Appendix 7).

Acts of Parliament

AA 1976	Adoption Act 1976
A(S)A 1978	Adoption (Scotland) Act 1978
CA 1989	Children Act 1989
CSA 1991	Child Support Act 1991
CSA 1995	Child Support Act 1995
DPMCA 1978	Domestic Proceedings and Magistrates' Courts Act 1978
FL(S)A 1958	Family Law (Scotland) Act 1958
FLRA 1969	Family Law Reform Act 1969
LR(PC)(S)A 1986	Law Reform (Parent and Child)(Scotland) Act 1986
MCA 1973	Matrimonial Causes Act 1973
MO(RE)A 1992	Maintenance Orders (Reciprocal Enforcement) Act 1992
SSCBA 1992	Social Security Contributions and Benefits Act 1992
SSAA 1992	Social Security Administration Act 1992

Statutory instruments (SI)

Each set of Regulations or Order of the Secretary of State or Lord Chancellor has an SI number and a year. Ask for them by giving their date and number.

AS(CSA)(AOCSCR)	The Act of Sederunt (Child Support Act 1991) (Amendment of Ordinary Cause and Summary Cause Rules) 1993 No. 919
AS(CSR)	The Act of Sederunt (Child Support Rules) 1993 No. 920
C(AHE)O	The Children (Admissibility of Hearsay Evidence) Order 1993 No. 621
C(AP)(A)O	The Children (Allocation of Proceedings) (Amendment) Order 1993 No. 624 (L.7)
C(AP)O	The Children (Allocation of Proceedings) Order 1991 No. 1677
CB&SS(FAR) Regs	The Child Benefit and Social Security (Fixing and Adjustment of Rates) Regulations 1976 No. 1267
CM(WA)O	The Child Maintenance (Written

	Agreements) Order 1993, No. 620 (L.4)
CS(AIAMA) Regs	The Child Support (Arrears, Interest and Adjustment of Maintenance Assessments) Regulations 1992 No. 1816
CS(APL)(S)O	The Child Support (Amendments to Primary Legislation)(Scotland) Order 1993 No. 660 (S.98)
CS(C&E) Regs	The Child Support (Collection and Enforcement) Regulations 1992 No. 1989
CS(CEOFM) Regs	The Child Support (Collection and Enforcement of Other Forms of Maintenance) Regulations 1992 No. 2643
CS(CRFCDWA) Regs	The Child Support (Compensation for Recipients of Family Credit and Disability Working Allowance) Regulations 1995 No. 3263
CS(IED) Regs	The Child Support (Information, Evidence and Disclosure) Regulations 1992 No. 1812
CS(MA) Regs	The Child Support (Miscellaneous Amendments) Regulations 1995 No. 123
CS(MA)2 Regs	The Child Support (Miscellaneous Amendments)(No. 2) Regulations 1995 No. 3261
CS(MAJ) Regs	The Child Support (Maintenance Arrangements and Jurisdiction) Regulations 1992 No. 2645
CS(MAP) Regs	The Child Support (Maintenance Assessment Procedure) Regulations 1992 No. 1813
CS(MASC) Regs	The Child Support (Maintenance Assessments and Special Cases) Regulations 1992 No. 1815
CS(MASC)SS(C&P)A Regs	The Child Support (Maintenance Assessments and Special Cases) and Social Security (Claims and Payments) Amendment Regulations 1996 No. 481
CS(MATP) Regs	The Child Support (Miscellaneous Amendments and Transitional Provisions) Regulations 1994 No. 227
CS(Misc) Regs	The Child Support (Miscellaneous Amendment) Regulations 1993 No. 913
CS(NI)O	The Child Support (Northern Ireland) Order 1991
CS(NIRA) Regs	The Child Support (Northern Ireland Reciprocal Arrangements) Regulations 1993 No. 584

CSA(CA)O	The Child Support Act 1991 (Consequential Amendments) Order 1993, No. 785
CSA(Comm 3)O	The Child Support Act 1991 (Commencement No. 3 and Transitional Provisions) Order 1992 No. 2644
CSA1995(Comm1)O	The Child Support Act 1995 (Commencement No. 1) Order 1995 No. 2302 (C.46)
CSA1995(Comm2)O	The Child Support Act 1995 (Commencement No. 2) Order 1995 No. 3262 (C.76)
CSA(JC)O	The Child Support Appeals (Jurisdiction of Courts) Order 1993 No. 961 (L.12)
CSAT(P) Regs	The Child Support Appeal Tribunals (Procedure) Regulations 1992 No. 2641
CSC(P) Regs	The Child Support Commissioners (Procedure) Regulations 1992 No. 2640
CSC(P)(A) Regs	The Child Support Commissioners (Procedure) (Amendment) Regulations 1996 No. 243
CSDD(AA) Regs	The Child Support Departure Direction (Anticipatory Application) Regulation 1996 No. 635
CSF Regs	The Child Support Fees Regulations 1992 No. 3094
CSIS(A) Regs	The Child Support and Income Support (Amendment) Regulations 1995 No. 1045
CTB Regs	The Council Tax Benefit (General) Regulations 1992 No. 1814
DWA Regs	The Disability Working Allowance (General) Regulations 1991 No. 2887
FC Regs	The Family Credit (General) Regulations 1987 No. 1973
FP(A)R	The Family Proceeding (Amendment) Rules 1992 No. 295 (L.1)
FPC(CSA)R	The Family Proceedings Courts (Child Support Act 1991) Rules 1993 No. 627 (L.8)
FPR	The Family Proceedings Rules 1991 No. 1247
HB Regs	The Housing Benefit (General) Regulations 1987 No. 1971
IS Regs	The Income Support (General) Regulations 1987 No. 1967
IS (LR) Regs	The Income Support (Liable Relatives) Regulations 1990 No. 1777

MO(B)O	The Maintenance Orders (Backdating) Order 1993 No. 623 (L.6)
SS(A) Regs	The Social Security (Adjudication) Regulations 1995 No. 1801
SS(A)CSA Regs	The Social Security (Adjudication) and Child Support Amendment Regulations 1996 No. 182
SS(C&P) Regs	The Social Security (Claims and Payments) Regulations 1987 No. 1968
SS(PAOR) Regs	The Social Security (Payments on Account, Overpayments and Recovery) Regulations 1988 No. 664

2. CSA GUIDANCE

CSAG	Child Support Adjudication Guide, Central Adjudication Services, HMSO
CSM	Child Support Manual, Child Support Agency, consists of a number of volumes which were up-dated until 1996
CSM(MA)	Child Support Manual (Maintenance Assessment: Volumes 1 and 2), 1993
CSM(MA4)	Child Support Manual (Maintenance Assessment: Volume 3 – Release 4), April 1995
CSM(RL)	Child Support Manual (Revised legislation), February 1994
CSM(OA)	Child Support Manual (Operational Accounting: Volume 1), 1993
CSM(OA4)	Child Support Manual (Operational Accounting: Volume 2 – Release 4, 4.5 and 5), April 1995
CSM(APP)	Child Support Manual (Appendices)
FOG	Field Operations Guide, Child Support Agency, 1996
old FOG	Field Operations Guide, Child Support Agency, 1993 – now superseded by the 1996 FOG. However, some references to the old FOG remain in the notes as they refer to issues which are to be incorporated into the forthcoming CSG, not the new FOG.

The Child Support Manual is shortly to be replaced by the Child Support Guide, consisting of nine volumes and several supplementary guides on specific issues:

CSG	Child Support Guide volumes 1–9
CSEFIG	Child Support Effective Full Maintenance Assessments and Interim Maintenance Assessments Guide
CSPG	Child Support Paternity Guide
CSQCG	Child Support Quality Checking Guide
CSRCG	Child Support Requirement to Co-operate Guide
CSTG	Child Support Tracing Guide

Where known, the volume and chapter number which will contain information currently in a CSM reference is given in square brackets.

The CSG and FOG are not published by HMSO but are public documents and can be viewed at the field office (see p21). Advisers doing a lot of child support work can ask the Child Support Agency to be added to the mailing list and receive their own copies.

Notes

The legislation referred to is as contained in the 1995 edition of Jacobs and Douglas (see Appendix 7); only amendments made since that volume went to press are specified. There is a list of abbreviations in Appendix 8. Details of any reports referred to can be found in Appendix 7.

Chapter 1: Introduction to the child support scheme
(pp1-13)

1. CS(MATP) Regs
2. CSIS(A) Regs
3. CSA 1995 (Comm2)O; CS(MA)2 Regs
4. s1(1) CSA 1991
5. s1(2) and (3) CSA 1991
6. s3 CSA 1991
7. s2 CSA 1991
8. s6 CSA 1991
9. s6(2) CSA 1991
10. s46 CSA 1991
11. s11 and Sch 1 CSA 1991
12. ss1–9 CSA 1995
13. ss29-41 CSA 1991
14. CS(NI)O
15. *Children Come First*, 1990

Chapter 2: The Child Support Agency
(pp16-39)

1. s13(3), (4) and (5) CSA 1991
2. s56 CSA 1991; CS(NI)O; CS(NIRA) Regs
3. s23 CSA 1991
4. s13(1) and (2) CSA 1991
5. s2 CSA 1991
6. s20 CSA 1991
7. Para 1041 CSAG
8. s2 CSA 1991
9. ss48 and 49 CSA 1991
10. s40(13) and (14) CSA 1991
11. s15 CSA 1991

12. HC Social Security Committee, *The Operation of the Child Support Act*, 1 December 1993, p5; HC Committee of Public Accounts, *CSA*, 20 November 1995, p11
13. Para 18021 CSM(MA)
14. HC *Hansard*, 26 October 1995, col 805
15. Business Plan 1995/96, CSA, March 1995, p13
16. HC *Hansard*, 1 February 1996, col 905; CSA monthly statistics; CSA Customer Satisfaction Surveys
17. *CSA the first two years*, Annual Report 1993/94, and Business Plan 1994/95, CSA, July 1994, p8
18. Annual Report 1994/95, CSA, July 1995, p10
19. HC Social Security Committee, *The Operation of the Child Support Act*, 1 December 1993, pp25-6
20. CSA Business Plan 1995/96, March 1995, p13; HC, *Hansard*, 23 November 1995, col 232
21. HC *Hansard*, 13 June 1995, col 492; HC, *Hansard*, 23 November 1995, col 232
22. *See* note 17, p12
23. CSA monthly statistics
24. HC *Hansard*, 8 March 1995, col 221
25. HC Social Security Committee, 2nd report, 24 January 1996, p10
26. Reg 3(3A) CSF Regs
27. *CSA Charter*, DSS, April 1993;

Annual Report 1994/95, CSA, July 1995, p14

28. HC Select Committee on the PCA, 1st Special Report, 6 December 1995, para 11

29. CSA Business Plans, April 1993 and March 1995

30. Annual Report 1994/95, CSA, July 1995, p12

31. CSA Business Plan 1995/96, March 1995

32. PCA, Investigation of complaints against the CSA, 18 January 1995, para 1

33. HC Select Committee on the PCA, 3rd Report, 15 March 1995, para 30

34. *See* note 33, paras 31-34, and note 28, para 12

35. HC *Hansard*, 1 February 1996, col 945

36. s8(3) CSA 1991

37. ss4(10) and 7(10) CSA 1991; s18(8) CSA 1995

38. s18(5) CSA 1995

39. ss8(3A) and 9(6) CSA 1991

40. *E v C (Fam D)*, *Times Law Report*, 24 December 1995

41. s8(4) CSA 1991; *B v M* (Child Support: Revocation of Order) [1994] 1 FLR 342

42. MO(RE)A 1992

43. MO(B)O; s29(7) MCA 1973; s5(7) DPMCA 1978; Sch 1 para 3(7) CA 1978

44. Rules 8.1 and 10.24 FPR as amended by FP(A)R; FPC(CSA)R

45. ss8(1) and (3) CSA 1991

46. s8(2) CSA 1991

47. s8(3) and (4) CSA 1991

48. s8(11) CSA 1991; reg 2 CS(MAJ) Regs

49. s18(9) CSA 1995

50. Paras 1(2) and 5(2) Schedule to CSA(Comm 3)O

51. Reg 8(2) CS(MAJ) Regs

52. s45 CSA 1991

53. s9(2) CSA 1991

54. s9(3) CSA 1991

55. s9(6) CSA 1991

56. s9(5) CSA 1991

57. s9(4) CSA 1991

58. s8(5) CSA 1991; CM(WA)O

59. ss10(1) and (2) CSA 1991

60. Reg 3(2)(a) and (5) CS(MAJ) Regs

61. Reg 3(2)(b) CS(MAJ) Regs

62. Reg 3(6) CS(MAJ) Regs

63. Reg 3(3) CS(MAJ) Regs

64. Reg 4 CS(MAJ) Regs

65. Reg 4(3) CS(MAJ) Regs

66. MO(B)O; s29(5) and (6) MCA 1973; s5(5) and (6) DPMCA 1978; Sch 1 para 3(5) and (6) CA 1989

67. Reg 8(1) CS(MAJ) Regs

68. Reg 3(4) CS(MAJ) Regs

69. Reg 5(1) CS(MAJ) Regs

70. Reg 5(1) CS(MAJ) Regs

71. Reg 6 CS(MAJ) Regs

72. Reg 5(4) CS(MAJ) Regs

73. Order 1 Rule 3 CCR 1981

74. s8 CSA 1991

75. MCA 1973, or, in Scotland, the FL(S)A 1958 meaning of 'child of the family'

76. s8(6) CSA 1991

77. s8(7) CSA 1991

78. s8(8) and (9) CSA 1991

79. s8(10) CSA 1991

80. *Mawson v Mawson* [1994] 2 FLR 985

81. *Crozier v Crozier* [1994] 2 All ER 362

82. *See* note 66

83. s26 CSA 1991

84. s27 CSA 1991

85. s26(1) CSA 1991

86. s28 CSA 1991; s7 LR(PC)(S)A 1986

87. s20 FLRA 1969

88. Rule 152 AS(CSA)(AOCSCR)

89. Paras 11040, 11173 and 11200 CSM(MA)

90. CSA monthly statistics; HC *Hansard*, 2 February 1996, col 993

91. CSA(JC)O; Art 3(1)(s) and (t) C(AP)O as amended by C(AP)(A)O

92. CSC/1/1994; CSC/3/1994

93. *Crozier v Crozier* [1994] 2 All ER 362

Chapter 3: Who is covered by the scheme
(pp40-53)

1. s1(1) CSA 1991
2. s54 CSA 1991
3. s39 AA 1976; Part IV A(S)A 1978; Case A s26(2) CSA 1991
4. s30 Human Fertilisation and Embryology Act; Case B s26(2) CSA 1991
5. s26 CSA 1991
6. s56 Family Law Act 1986
7. s5(1) LR(PC)(S)A 1986
8. The proceedings are listed in s12 Civil Evidence Act 1968
9. s54 CSA 1991 meaning of 'parent'; meaning of 'adopted' in Part IV AA 1976, or in Scotland, Part IV A(S)A 1978
10. s3(4) CA 1989; C(S)A 1995
11. s8 CSA 1991; MCA 1973 or, in Scotland, FL(S)A 1958, meaning of 'child of the family'
12. s3(1) CSA 1991
13. s55(1) CSA 1991
14. s55(2) CSA 1991; ss11 and 12 MCA 1973
15. Sch 1 para 2 CS(MAP) Regs
16. s55(1)(b) CSA 1991
17. Sch 1 para 3 CS(MAP) Regs
18. Sch 1 para 5(3) CS(MAP) Regs
19. Sch 1 para 5(1) CS(MAP) Regs
20. Sch 1 para 5(2) CS(MAP) Regs
21. Sch 1 para 5(6) and (7) CS(MAP) Regs
22. Sch 1 para 5(5) CS(MAP) Regs
23. Sch 1 para 4(1) CS(MAP) Regs
24. Sch 1 para 4(2) CS(MAP) Regs
25. s55(1)(c) CSA 1991; Sch 1 para 1 CS(MAP) Regs
26. Sch 1 para 1(1)(b) CS(MAP) Regs
27. Sch 1 para 1(3)(b) CS(MAP) Regs
28. Sch 1 para 1(2) CS(MAP) Regs
29. s3(3) CSA 1991
30. s3(3)(c) CSA 1991; reg 51 CS(MAP) Regs
31. s23(5) CA 1989
32. s21 Social Work (Scotland) Act 1968
33. s3(5) CSA 1991
34. Reg 1(2) CS(MASC) Regs as amended by reg 40(2) CS(MA)2 Regs
35. Reg 1(2) CS(MASC) Regs as amended by reg 40(2) CS(MA)2 Regs; para 6022 CSAG; paras 7400-14 CSM(MA4)
36. Para 1577 CSAG
37. Reg 27A CS(MASC) Regs
38. Reg 27 CS(MASC) Regs
39. R(IS) 11/91
40. Reg 1(2) CS(MASC) Regs
41. Paras 5120-21 CSAG
42. s54 CSA 1991
43. s6(1) CSA 1991
44. s6(2) CSA 1991
45. s3 CSA 1991
46. Reg 20 CS(MASC) Regs
47. s1(3) CSA 1991
48. *Santos v Santos* [1972] 2 WLR 889
49. CSB 463/86
50. R(SB) 4/83
51. R(SB) 35/85
52. R(SB) 8/85
53. Letter to CPAG from DSS, 8 December 1992
54. Para 1568 CSAG
55. Para 1569 CSAG
56. Para 1570 CSAG
57. Para 1572 CSAG
58. s44(1) CSA 1991
59. s44(2) CSA 1991
60. Sch 1 Interpretation Act 1978
61. CCS/7395/1995 (starred 8/96)
62. *Kapur v Kapur* [1984] FLR 920
63. *Shah v Barnet LBC* [1983] 2 WLR 16, [1983] 1 All ER 226 per Lord Scarman p235
64. Para 1709 CSAG
65. *Lewis v Lewis* [1956] 1 WLR 200, [1956] 1 All ER 375
66. *Re J (A Minor) (Abduction: Custody Rights)* [1990] 3 WLR 492, [1990] 2 All ER 961
67. *Shah v Barnet LBC; Re Mackenzie* [1940] 4 All ER 310
68. *Shah v Barnet LBC*
69. CCS/7395/1995 (starred 8/96)
70. [1949] All ER 34; see also *Lewis v Lewis*

71. *See* note 66
72. *See* note 66
73. *Re M (Minors: Residence Order; Jurisdiction)* [1993] 1 FLR 495
74. *Re A (Minors: Abduction; Acquiescence)* [1992] 2 FLR 14
75. *Re M (A Minor) (Abduction: Child's Objections)* [1994] 2 FLR 126
76. Para 1717 CSAG
77. Para 1720 CSAG
78. Paras 1711-19 CSAG
79. Para 1753 CSAG
80. Sch 1 para 16(5) CSA 1991; reg 7 CS(MAJ) Regs; para 1751 CSAG
81. Para 1724 CSAG
82. Para 1725 CSAG
83. Para 1710 CSAG
84. Reg 1(2) CS(MASC) Regs
85. CFC 7/92
86. s2 CSA 1991
87. CCS/1037/1995 para 11 (starred 10/96)
88. CCS/1037/1995 para 13 (starred 10/96)
89. Heading to s2 CSA 1991
90. *R v Secretary of State for Social Security ex parte Biggin* [1995] 1 FLR 851
91. Para 1382 CSAG (for CSOs)
92. Secretary of State, *Guidance on the Welfare of the Child*, 1995
93. *Wednesbury Corporation v Ministry of Housing and Local Government* (No.2) [1966] 2 QB 275; [1965] 3 WLR 956; [1965] 3 All ER 571

Chapter 4: Applications
(pp54-80)
1. ss 4 and 6 CSA 1991
2. Reg 51 CS(MAP) Regs; reg 1 CS(MASC) Regs meaning of 'person'
3. s7(1) CSA 1991
4. s6(1) CSA 1991
5. s4(10)(b) CSA 1991
6. s9(4) CSA 1991
7. s5(1) CSA 1991
8. s9(3) CSA 1991
9. ss4(10) and 7(10) CSA 1991

10. Reg 9 CS(MAJ) Regs as inserted by reg 14 CS(MA) 2 Regs
11. CCS/11/1994 (starred 5/96)
12. s8(11) CSA 1991; reg 2 CS(MAJ) Regs
13. s8(3A) CSA 1991
14. *B v M* (Child Support: Revocation of Order) [1994] 1 FLR 342
15. CCS/11/1994 (starred 5/96)
16. s11(1A) CSA 1991
17. *Improving child support*, 1995, para 4.3
18. Reg 2 CS(MAP) Regs
19. Para 3010 old FOG
20. s4(10(b) CSA 1991
21. DSS Press Release, 1 November 1993; *Improving child support*, 1995, para 6.3
22. s6(5) CSA 1991
23. Para 2062 CSAG
24. Paras 1400 and 10715 CSM(MA) [CSG Vol 1 Ch 1-3]
25. Reg 1(7) CS(MAP) Regs
26. Reg 2(4) CS(MAP) Regs
27. Reg 2(5) CS(MAP) Regs
28. Reg 5 CS(MAP) Regs
29. s11 CSA 1991
30. HC Social Security Committee, 2nd report, 24 January 1996, p4
31. s11 CSA 1991; reg 12(1) CS(MAP) Regs as amended by reg 19 CS(MA)2 Regs; CCS/100/1995 (starred 12/95)
32. CCS/11/1994 (starred 5/96); CCS/14/1994 (starred 3/96); CCS/17/1994 (starred 6/95)
33. Reg 2(6) and (7) CS(MAP) Regs
34. s6(7) CSA 1991
35. ss4(4), 6(9) and 7(5) CSA 1991
36. s7(5) CSA 1991
37. s46 CSA 1991
38. Reg 53(1) CS(MAP) Regs
39. Reg 53(2) CS(MAP) Regs
40. Para 2023 CSAG
41. Para 2025 CSAG
42. ss4(5) and 7(6) and Sch 1 para 16(2) CSA 1991
43. ss4(6) and 7(7) CSA 1991
44. Sch 1 para 16(2) CSA 1991; CCS/013/1994 (starred 2/96)

45. s7(6) CSA 1991
46. s6(11) CSA 1991
CSM references in notes 47–63 will be found in CSRCG Ch 11
47. s2 CSA 1991; paras 10650-58 CSM(MA)
48. Para 10602 CSM(MA)
49. s6(11) CSA 1991
50. s6(12) CSA 1991
51. Sch 1 para 16(3) CSA 1991
52. s6(2)(b) and (11) CSA 1991
53. Para 10840 CSM(MA)
54. Para 10841 CSM(MA)
55. Para 10842 CSM(MA)
56. Para 10630 CSM(MA)
57. Para 10640 CSM(MA)
58. Paras 10666-7 CSM(MA)
59. Paras 10668 and 10845 CSM(MA)
60. Paras 9020 and 9310 CSM(MA)
61. Para 10846 CSM(MA)
62. s6(12) CSA 1991; para 10843 CSM(MA)
63. s2 CSA 1991; para 10847 CSM(MA)
64. CCS/17/1994 (starred 6/95)
65. Para 9400 CSM(MA) [CSG Vol 8]
66. s11(1A) CSA 1991
67. s11(1C) CSA 1991
68. s11(1B) CSA 1991
69. CCS/7062/1995 (starred 1/96)
70. *See* note 69; CCS/499/1995 (starred 7/96)
71. Reg 7 CS(MAP) Regs
72. s5(2) CSA 1991
73. Sch 2 paras 1, 2 and 3 CS(MAP) Regs
74. s4(9) CSA 1991
75. Sch 1 para 6 CS(NIRA) Regs
76. s5(2) CSA 1991; reg 4 and Sch 2 CS(MAP) Regs
77. Reg 4(3) CS(MAP) Regs
78. Reg 4(2) CS(MAP) Regs
79. Sch 2 para 1(1) CS(MAP) Regs
80. Sch 2 para 1(2) CS(MAP) Regs
81. Sch 2 para 2 CS(MAP) Regs
82. Sch 2 para 3(11) CS(MAP) Regs
83. Sch 2 para 3(12)(a) and (b) CS(MAP) Regs; para 2034 CSAG
84. Sch 2 para 3(12)(c) CS(MAP) Regs

85. Sch 2 para 3(13) CS(MAP) Regs
86. Sch 2 para 3(14) CS(MAP) Regs; para 2030-1 CSAG
87. Sch 2 para 3(1) CS(MAP) Regs; para 2033 CSAG
88. Sch 2 para 3(2) CS(MAP) Regs
89. Sch 2 para 3(3) CS(MAP) Regs
90. Sch 2 para 3(4) CS(MAP) Regs
91. Sch 2 para 3(5) CS(MAP) Regs
92. Sch 2 para 3(6) CS(MAP) Regs
93. Sch 2 para 3(7) CS(MAP) Regs
94. Sch 2 para 3(8) CS(MAP) Regs
95. Sch 2 para 3(9) CS(MAP) Regs
96. Reg 20 CS(MASC) Regs
97. Sch 2 para 3(9)(a) CS(MAP) Regs
98. Sch 2 para 3(10) CS(MAP) Regs
99. Sch 2 para 3(11) and (12) CS(MAP) Regs
100. Sch 2 para 4 CS(MAP) Regs; para 2037 CSAG
101. Sch 2 para 5 CS(MAP) Regs
102. Sch 2 para 6(1) CS(MAP) Regs
103. Sch 2 para 6(2) CS(MAP) Regs; para 2040 CSAG
104. Sch 2 para 6(3) CS(MAP) Regs

Chapter 5: The requirement to co-operate
(pp81-123)

1. s6(1) CSA 1991; reg 34 CS(MAP) Regs
2. s46 CSA 1991
3. s6(8) CSA 1991
4. s6(14) CSA 1991
5. s6(1) CSA 1991
6. HC Social Security Committee, 2nd report, 24 January 1996, pp16/17
7. Paras 10002, 10711 and 10778 CSM(MA) [CSRCG App 1]
8. s6(2) CSA 1991
9. s6(3) CSA 1991
10. Forms CSA12 and CSA13
11. s6(2) CSA 1991
12. Para 3611 old FOG; para 10223 CSM(MA) [CSRCG Ch 9]
13. s6(5) CSA 1991
14. s6(3) CSA 1991
15. s6(1) CSA 1991; Michael Jack MP, *Hansard*, 11 February 1992, col 452;

letter to CPAG from CSA dated 28 July 1993

16. s6(9) CSA 1991
17. s6(9) CSA 1991
18. s46(1)(b) and (5) CSA 1991
19. Para 1208 CSAG
20. s6(9) CSA 1991
21. Para 1206 CSAG
22. Paras 473 and 485 part 4 FOG
23. s6(2) CSA 1991
24. s46(3) CSA 1991
25. s6(2) CSA 1991; paras 2551-2 CSAG
26. CCS/1037/1995 (starred 10/96)
27. *Shorter Oxford English Dictionary; The Concise Oxford Dictionary*
28. CSA Training module C10, 1993
29. s46(3) CSA 1991
30. Para 10113 CSM(MA); paras 3640-1 old FOG [CSRCG Ch 9]
31. Para 10510 CSM(MA) [CSRCG Ch 9]
32. R(SB) 33/85
33. Alistair Burt MP, *Hansard*, 22 June 1992; DSS press release (92/191), 24 November 1992
34. Para 2553 CSAG; para 3630 old FOG; para 10760 CSM(MA) [CSRCG Ch 4]
35. Memo to the HC Social Security Committee from the CSA, 15 March 1995
36. Paras 10021-2 CSM(MA); paras 3650-1 old FOG [CSRCG Ch 4]
37. Paras 1203-4 CSAG
38. CSA monthly statistics
39. HC *Hansard*, 26 October 1995, col 804
40. Para 10715 CSM(MA)
41. Reg 1(6) CS(MAP) Regs
42. Reg 1(8) CS(MAP) Regs
43. Reg 1(6)(a) and (7) CS(MAP) Regs
44. Paras 3650-1 old FOG; para 10021 CSM(MA) [CSRCG Ch 4]
45. Para 10022 CSM(MA) [CSRCG Ch 4]
46. Para 190 part 3 FOG; para 3131 old FOG; para 14380 CSM(MA) [CSRCG Ch 4]

47. Para 10718 CSM(MA); para 3052 old FOG
48. Paras 3670 and 3060-4 old FOG
49. Reg 3(2) CS(IED) Regs
50. Paras 200-399 part 4 FOG; para 10760 CSM(MA)
51. Para 210 part 4 FOG
52. Para 10750 CSM(MA)
53. Para 10171 CSM(MA)
54. Para 10717 CSM(MA)
55. Para 3333 old FOG
56. Reg 3(2) CS(IED) Regs
57. Paras 10730-1 CSM(MA) [CSRCG Ch 4]
58. Para 473 part 4 FOG
59. Para 200 part 5 FOG
60. Para 220 part 5 FOG
61. Para 221 part 5 FOG
62. Para 230 part 5 FOG
63. Para 250 part 5 FOG
64. Para 260 part 5 FOG
65. Paras 230 and 240 part 5 FOG
66. s6(1) CSA 1991
67. Reg 2(2) CS(IED) Regs as amended by reg 7 CS(MA)2 Regs
68. Paras 130, 160, 180 and 200 part 3 FOG
69. Paras 230-50 part 3 FOG
70. Para 220 part 3 FOG
71. Reg 35(1) and (2) CS(MAP) Regs
72. Para 3712 old FOG [CSRCG Chs 5 & 7]
73. Reg 35(2) CS(MAP) Regs
74. Paras 3730-1 old FOG; CSA Training module C10, p69, 1993 [CSRCG Chs 5 & 7]
75. Para 3720 old FOG [CSRCG Chs 5 & 7]
76. Para 3611 old FOG; para 10223 CSM(MA) [CSRCG Chs 5 & 7]
77. Para 3732 old FOG [CSRCG Chs 5 & 7]
78. s46(2) CSA 1991; reg 35(3) CS(MAP) Regs
79. s46(2) and (3) CSA 1991
80. s46(10) CSA 1991
81. s46(3) CSA 1991
82. s46(4) CSA 1991
83. s46(5) CSA 1991

84. Reg 35A CS(MAP) Regs as inserted by reg 37 CS(MA)2 Regs
85. s46(4) CSA 1991
86. Para 2561 CSAG
87. s46(9) CSA 1991; reg 36 CS(MAP) Regs
88. Reg 36(8) and (9) CS(MAP) Regs
89. s46(2) CSA 1991
90. s46(5) CSA 1991
91. s2 CSA 1991
92. CCS/1037/1995 (starred 10/96)
93. Reg 42(2A) and (2B) CS(MAP) Regs
94. Reg 36 CS(MAP) Regs; Sch 2 col (2) para 1(1)(e) IS Regs
95. Reg 50 CS(MAP) Regs
96. Reg 36(7) CS(MAP) Regs
97. Reg 37 CS(MAP) Regs; paras 2601-2 CSAG
98. Reg 39 CS(MAP) Regs
99. Reg 36(8) CS(MAP) Regs
100. Reg 36(9) CS(MAP) Regs
101. Reg 36(8) CS(MAP) Regs
102. Reg 36(9) CS(MAP) Regs
103. Reg 47 CS(MAP) Regs
104. Reg 47(1) and (2) CS(MAP) Regs
105. Reg 47(3) CS(MAP) Regs
106. Reg 47(4) CS(MAP) Regs
107. Reg 47(6) and (7) CS(MAP) Regs; para 2768 and App 9 part 2 CSAG
108. Reg 36(4) CS(MAP) Regs
109. Reg 2(1) IS Regs
110. Reg 36(6) CS(MAP) Regs; App 10 part 2 CSAG
111. Reg 40A CS(MAP) Res as inserted by reg 38 CS(MA)2 Regs
112. Regs 40A(3) and 49A CS(MAP) Regs as inserted by regs 38 and 39 CS(MA)2 Regs
113. Reg 36(5) CS(MAP) Regs
114. Reg 26(2) SS(C&P) Regs
115. ss128(3) and 129(6) SSCBA 1992
116. Reg 51A FC Regs; reg 56A DWA Regs
117. Reg 36(4) CS(MAP) Regs
118. Reg 16(3)(b) SS(C&P) Regs
119. Reg 36(4) CS(MAP) Regs
120. Reg 36(5B) CS(MAP) Regs
121. Reg 36(5E) CS(MAP) Regs
122. Reg 36(5D) CS(MAP) Regs
123. Reg 38(1) and (3) CS(MAP) Regs
124. Reg 38(6) CS(MAP) Regs
125. Reg 38(5) CS(MAP) Regs
126. Reg 38(2) CS(MAP) Regs
127. Reg 38(7) CS(MAP) Regs; Apps 6 and 8 part 2 CSAG
128. Reg 48(1) CS(MAP) Regs
129. Reg 48(3) CS(MAP) Regs
130. Reg 48(2) CS(MAP) Regs
131. Reg 40(1) and (1A) CS(MAP) Regs
132. Reg 40(1) and (1A) CS(MAP) Regs
133. Reg 40(2) CS(MAP) Regs
134. Reg 40(3)(c) CS(MAP) Regs; Sch 7 para 10B(3) IS Regs
135. Reg 41(2) CS(MAP) Regs
136. Reg 41(3) CS(MAP) Regs
137. Reg 44 CS(MAP) Regs
138. s4(10) CSA 1991
139. Reg 43 CS(MAP) Regs
140. Reg 45(2) CS(MAP) Regs
141. Reg 45(3) CS(MAP) Regs
142. Reg 46 CS(MAP) Regs
143. Reg 46 CS(MAP) Regs
144. Reg 42 CS(MAP) Regs
145. Reg 42(2A) CS(MAP) Regs
146. Reg 42(2B) CS(MAP) Regs
147. Reg 42(3) CS(MAP) Regs
148. Reg 42(8) CS(MAP) Regs
149. Reg 42(11) CS(MAP) Regs
150. Reg 42(4) CS(MAP) Regs
151. Reg 42(5) CS(MAP) Regs
152. Reg 42(6) CS(MAP) Regs
153. Reg 49 CS(MAP) Regs
154. Reg 49(1) CS(MAP) Regs
155. Reg 49(2) CS(MAP) Regs
156. Reg 38(5) and (6) CS(MAP) Regs
157. s46(7) and (8) CSA 1991
158. Reg 42(9) and (10) CS(MAP) Regs
159. s20(2) CSA 1991
160. Para 2564 CSAG
161. s20(4) CSA 1991

Chapter 6: Information
(pp 124-160)
1. s14 and Sch 2 CSA 1991
2. Paras 1041-2 CSAG
3. Reg 6(1) CS(MAP) Regs
4. Reg 2(5) CS(MAP) Regs
5. Reg 5(2) CS(IED) Regs as amended

by reg 10 CS(MA)2 Regs; reg 17(4) CS(MAP) Regs

6. Reg 5(1) CS(IED) Regs as amended by reg 10 CS(MA)2 Regs

7. Reg 3A CS(IED) Regs as amended by reg 9 CS(MA)2 Regs

8. Reg 2 CS(IED) Regs as amended by reg 7 CS(MA)2 Regs

9. Reg 3(1) CS(IED) Regs as amended by reg 8 CS(MA)2 Regs

10. Reg 3(2) CS(IED) Regs

11. Reg 2(1) CS(IED) Regs as amended by reg 7(2) CS(MA)2 Regs

12. *Purdew v Seress-Smith, The Times,* 9 September 1992

13. Regs 1(2) (definition of 'relevant person') and 2(2)(a) CS(IED) Regs

14. Reg 2(2)(b) CS(IED) Regs as amended by reg 7(3) CS(MA)2 Regs and reg 3(1)(b) and (d) CS(IED) Regs

15. Reg 2(2)(c) CS(IED) Regs as amended by reg 7(4) CS(MA)2 Regs

16. Reg 3(1)(d)–(f), (h) and (j) CS(IED) Regs

17. Reg 2(2)(ba) CS(IED) Regs

18. Reg 2(2)(cc) and (cd) CS(IED) Regs as amended by reg 7(4) CS(MA) 2 Regs

19. Reg 2(3) CS(IED) Regs

20. Order 1 rule 3 CCR 1981

21. Reg 2(2)(e) CS(IED) Regs

22. Regs 2(2)(e) and 3(1)(g), (h) and (k) CS(IED) Regs

23. s14(2) and (2A) CSA 1991

24. Regs 2(2)(d) and 3(1)(a) CS(IED) Regs

25. Sch 2 para 2 CSA 1991

26. Sch 2 para 2(2) CSA 1991

27. Reg 4 CS(IED) Regs

28. Sch 2 para 1 CSA 1991

29. Income and Corporation Taxes Act

30. s2 Theft Act 1968

31. s105 SSAA

Notes 32–67: CSM and old FOG refs will be found in CSTG

32. Paras 14010 and 14200 CSM(MA)

33. Para 11003 CSM(MA)

34. CSTG

35. Para 14001 CSM(MA)

36. CSA monthly statistics April–December 1995

37. HC *Hansard*, 2 February 1996, col 988

38. Para 14110 CSM(MA)

39. Para 14216 CSM(MA)

40. Para 14242 CSM(MA)

41. Para 14245 CSM(MA)

42. Para 14250 CSM(MA)

43. Para 14260 CSM(MA)

44. Para 14280 CSM(MA)

45. Para 14281 CSM(MA)

46. Para 14291 CSM(MA)

47. Paras 14410-5 and 14523 CSM(MA)

48. Para 14330 CSM(MA)

49. Para 14390 CSM(MA)

50. Para 14320 CSM(MA)

51. Para 14361 CSM(MA)

52. Para 14363 CSM(MA)

53. Para 14367 CSM(MA)

54. Paras 14371-2 CSM(MA)

55. Paras 3353 old FOG

56. Para 14350 CSM(MA)

57. Para 14351 CSM(MA)

58. Para 14352 CSM(MA)

59. Para 14356 CSM(MA)

60. Para 14526 CSM(MA)

61. Para 14380 CSM(MA)

62. Para14356 CSM(MA)

63. Paras 3020-3033 old FOG

64. Paras 3333 old FOG

65. Para 14112-16 CSM(MA)

66. Para 14504 CSM(MA)

67. Para 14526 CSM(MA)

68. Regs 5(1) and 1(2) CS(MAP) Regs, meaning of 'relevant person'

69. Regs 5(2) and 6(1) CS(MAP) Regs

70. Reg 5(3) CS(MAP) Regs

71. Para 11010 CSM(MA)

72. Para 11012 CSM(MA)

73. Para 11014 CSM(MA)

74. Para 11016 CSM(MA)

75. Para 11015 CSM(MA)

76. Reg 53(2) CS(MAP) Regs

77. Reg 53(1) CS(MAP) Regs; para 2023 CSAG

78. Reg 53(1) CS(MAP) Regs; para 2025 CSAG

79. Reg 6(1) CS(MAP) Regs
80. Reg 6(2)and (3) CS(MAP) Regs
81. Reg 1(7) CS(MAP) Regs
Notes 82–151: CSM and old FOG refs will be found in CSPG
82. Paras 11002-3 CSM(MA)
83. Para 9510 CSM(MA)
84. ss27 and 28 CSA 1991
85. Para 11153 CSM(MA); para 561 part 4 FOG
86. Paras 11110-19 CSM(MA)
87. Para 11120 CSM(MA)
88. Paras 11132 and 11140 CSM(MA); para 460 part 4 FOG
89. Paras 11140 CSM(MA)
90. Para 600 part 4 FOG
91. Para 11164 CSM(MA)
92. Paras 483, 490 and 630-4 part 4 FOG
93. Paras 484-5 part 4 FOG
94. Para 11172 CSM(MA)
95. Para 11179 CSM(MA)
96. Para 11181 CSM(MA)
97. Paras 454 and 730 part 4 FOG
98. Para 11186 CSM(MA)
99. Para 11188 CSM(MA)
100. Para 11192 CSM(MA)
101. Para 11191 CSM(MA)
102. Paras 11179, 11193 and 9400 CSM(MA)
103. Para 11200 CSM(MA)
104. Paras 11201-2 CSM(MA)
105. Para 11203 CSM(MA)
106. Para 11206 CSM(MA)
107. Para 11207 CSM(MA)
108. Para 11212 CSM(MA)
109. Para 11213 CSM(MA)
110. Para 11324 CSM(MA)
111. Paras 511-3 part 4 FOG
112. Para 210 part 3 FOG
113. Para 512 part 4 FOG
114. Para 531 part 4 FOG
115. Paras 540-7 part 4 FOG
116. Para 510 part 4 FOG
117. Para 210 part 4 FOG
118. Para 561 part 4 FOG
119. Para 518 part 4 FOG
120. Para 591 part 4 FOG
121. Para 592 part 4 FOG
122. Para 597 part 4 FOG

123. Paras 10779 and 11030 CSM(MA); para 581 part 4 FOG
124. Para 11030 CSM(MA)
125. Para 580 part 4 FOG
126. Para 11031 CSM(MA)
127. Para 3291 old FOG
128. Para 570 part 4 FOG
129. Para 571 part 4 FOG
130. Para 460 part 4 FOG
131. Paras 461 and 482 part 4 FOG
132. Paras 600-1 part 4 FOG
133. Para 517 part 4 FOG
134. Para 483 part 4 FOG; training module C11 (CSAC 11HO), handout 2, 1993
135. Para 484 part 4 FOG
136. Para 11402 CSM(MA)
137. Paras 11400-1 CSM(MA)
138. Paras 11410-15 CSM(MA)
139. Para 11421 CSM(MA)
140. HC *Hansard*, 2 February 1996, col 991
141. Letter from CSA to CPAG 27 March 1995
142. s27A CSA 1991
143. Paras 11520 and 11523 CSM(MA)
144. Para 11561 CSM(MA)
145. Para 11522 CSM(MA)
146. Para 11600 CSM(MA)
147. Para 11570 CSM(MA)
148. Para 11560 CSM(MA)
149. Para 11600 CSM(MA)
150. Para 11583 CSM(MA)
151. Para 11613 CSM(MA)
Notes 152–182: CSM and old FOG refs will be found in CSG Vol 2 and CSTG
152. Para 3121 CSM(MA)
153. Para 3123 CSM(MA)
154. Para 3180 CSM(MA)
155. Letter to CPAG from DSS 5 March 1993
156. Para 1208 CSAG
157. Paras 1209 and 1212 CSAG
158. Paras 1203-5 CSAG
159. Para 1206 CSAG
160. Para 1225 CSAG
161. Para 1209 CSAG
162. Para 1223 CSAG; para 2301 CSM(MA)

163. Para 2100 CSM(MA)
164. Para 2322 CMS(MA)
165. Paras 2012-13 and 2066 old FOG
166. Para 1207 CSAG
167. Para 1220 CSAG
168. Para 2012 old FOG; para 2417 CSM(MA)
169. Paras 2105-6 CSM(MA)
170. Para 2127 CSM(MA)
171. Paras 2140-2 CSM(MA)
172. Para 5(2) Sch 1 CS(MASC) Regs
173. Para 5(2A) Sch 1 CS(MASC) Regs
174. Para 5(3) Sch 1 CS(MASC) Regs; paras 2245-6 CSM(MA)
175. Paras 2620 and 2624 CSM(MA)
176. Para 2423 CSM(MA)
177. Para 2162 CSM(MA)
178. Para 2160 CSM(MA)
179. Para 2168 CSM(MA)
180. Para 2800 CSM(MA)
181. Para 2205 CSM(MA); App 1 CSM(APP)
182. s15(1) CSA 1991
183. HC *Hansard*, 2 February 1996, col 990
184. s15(3) CSA 1991
185. s15(2) CSA 1991
186. s15(8) CSA 1991
187. Paras 520-2 part 5 FOG
188. Sch 1 para 8 CS(NIRA) Regs
189. s15(4) CSA 1991
190. s15(5) CSA 1991
191. s15(6) CSA 1991
192. s57 CSA 1991; reg 7 CS(IED) Regs
193. s15(6) CSA 1991
194. s15(9) CSA 1991
195. s15(9) CSA 1991
196. s15(7) CSA 1991
197. Paras 510-11 part 5 FOG
198. Reg 6 CS(IED) Regs
199. Reg 9A(1) CS(IED) Regs as amended by reg 11(3) CS(MA)2 Regs
200. Reg 9A(2) CS(IED) Regs
201. Reg 9A(3) CS(IED) Regs
202. Reg 9A(4) CS(IED) Regs
203. Reg 9 CS(IED) Regs
204. Reg 8 CS(IED) Regs
205. Regs 10 and 10A CS(IED) Regs as amended by reg 12 CS(MA)2 Regs

206. Para 1215 CSAG
207. Para 1216 CSAG
208. Para 1217 CSAG
209. Para 1218 CSAG
210. s14(2A) CSA 1991
211. Reg 10 CS(IED) Regs as amended by reg 12 CS(MA)2 Regs
212. Sch 1 para 7 CS(NIRA) Regs
213. s50 CSA 1991; reg 11 CS(IED) Regs
214. s50 CSA 1991
215. s50(3) CSA 1991
216. *The Times*, 7 December 1994
217. s50(4) CSA 1991

Chapter 7: The formula in outline
(pp162-172)

1. Regs 3(2), 9(5) and 11(5) CS(MASC) Regs
2. Reg 33(1) CS(MAP) Regs; reg 2(1) CS(MASC) Regs
3. Reg 2(2) CS(MASC) Regs
4. s24 CSA 1995
5. CS(CRFC&DWA) Regs
6. Sch 1 para 7 CSA 1991
7. Reg 13 CS(MASC) Regs as amended by reg 2 CS(MASC)SS(C&P)A Regs
8. Reg 22(4) CS(MASC) Regs
9. Reg 26 and Sch 4 CS(MASC) Regs
10. Reg 7(3) CS(MASC) Regs
11. s43 CSA 1991
12. Sch 1 para 5(4) CSA 1991; Sch 9 para 7A(1) SS(C&P) Regs
13. Reg 28 CS(MASC) Regs
14. Reg 28(2) CS(MASC) Regs; Sch 9 para 7A(3) SS(C&P) Regs as amended by reg 5 CS(MASC)SS(C&P)A Regs
15. Reg 28(3) and (4) CS(MASC) Regs
16. s43(2)(a) CSA 1991
17. s43(2)(b) CSA 1991
18. Sch 9 para 7A(2) SS(C&P) Regs
19. Sch 9 para 7A(1) SS(C&P) Regs
20. Sch 9 paras 1 and 2(1)(f) SS(C&P) Regs
21. Sch 9 para 2(2) SS(C&P) Regs
22. Sch 9 para 8 SS(C&P) Regs
23. Sch 9 para 9 SS(C&P) Regs
24. Sch 9 para 7A(4) SS(C&P) Regs as

inserted by reg 5
CS(MASC)SS(C&P)A Regs
25. Sch 5 para 9 CS(MASC) Regs
26. Sch 5 CS(MASC) Regs
27. Sch 5 para 3A CS(MASC) Regs
28. Sch 5 para 2(a) CS(MASC) Regs
29. Sch 5 para 2(b) CS(MASC) Regs
30. Sch 5 para 6 CS(MASC) Regs
31. Sch 5 para 8 CS(MASC) Regs
32. Sch 5 para 4(b) CS(MASC) Regs
33. Sch 5 para 4(2) and (4) CS(MASC) Regs
34. Sch 5 para 4(3) CS(MASC) Regs
35. Sch 5 para 7A(b) CS(MASC) Regs
36. Sch 5 para 7A(a) CS(MASC) Regs
37. Para 5411 CSM(MA4)
38. Part III CS(MASC) Regs

Chapter 8: The maintenance requirement
(pp173-181)
1. Sch 1 para 1(1) CSA 1991
2. Reg 8(2) CS(MAP) Regs
3. Sch 1 para 1 CSA 1991; reg 3 CS(MASC) Regs
4. Reg 3(2) and 4 CS(MASC) Regs
5. Sch 1 para 1(2) CSA 1991
6. Reg 4 CS(MASC) Regs
7. *Children Come First*, vol 1/8; DSS Press Release, 22 December 1993
8. *Children Come First*, vol 1/9
9. s8(8) and (9) CSA 1991
10. Reg 19(2)(c) CS(MASC) Regs
11. Reg 23 CS(MASC) Regs
12. Reg 23(3) CS(MASC) Regs
13. Reg 23(1) CS(MASC) Regs
14. Reg 23(2A) CS(MASC) Regs
15. Reg 23(3) CS(MASC) Regs
16. Reg 2 CB&SS(FAR) Regs
17. s143(1)(b) SSCBA 1992
18. Sch 10 para 2 SSCBA 1992

Chapter 9: Exempt income
(pp182-201)
1. *Children Come First*, vol 1/10
2. Sch 1 para 5(4) CSA 1991
3. Reg 19(2)(a) CS(MASC) Regs
4. Reg 10 CS(MASC) Regs
5. Reg 9(5) CS(MASC) Regs

6. Sch 1 para 5 CSA 1991; regs 9 and 10 CS(MASC) Regs
7. Reg 15(4)-(9) CS(MASC) Regs as amended by reg 48 CSIS(A) Regs; reg 64 CSIS(A) Regs
8. Sch 3 para 4(1) CS(MASC) Regs
9. Sch 3 para 4(2)(a) CS(MASC) Regs; para 5165 CSAG
10. Reg 15(3) CS(MASC) Regs
11. Para 5526 CSAG
12. Sch 3 para 4(2)(b) CS(MASC) Regs
13. Reg 15(4) CS(MASC) Regs as amended by reg 44 CS(MA)2 Regs
14. CSCS/2/1994 (starred 3/95); CSCS/5/1995
15. Regs 14 and 15(1) CS(MASC) Regs
16. Sch 3 para 1 CS(MASC) Regs; CCS/12/1994 (starred 11/95)
17. Sch 3 paras 1, 2 and 3 CS(MASC) Regs; CCS/12/1994 (starred 11/95)
18. Reg 15(2) CS(MASC) Regs
19. Regs 9(1)(h) and 11(1)(i) CS(MASC) Regs as amended by regs 42 and 43 CS(MA)2 Regs
20. Reg 1(2) CS(MASC) Regs
21. CCS/4/1994 (starred 13/95)
22. Sch 3 para 5 CS(MASC) Regs; para 5501 CSAG
23. Sch 3 para 3 CS(MASC) Regs
24. Sch 3 para 3(4) CS(MASC) Regs
25. Para 5359 CSAG
26. CSCS/1/1994 (starred 119/94); para 5410 CSAG
27. Sch 3 para 3(5A) and (5B) CS(MASC) Regs
28. Sch 3 para 3(5B) CS(MASC) Regs
29. Sch 3 para 3(5) and (5A) CS(MASC) Regs
30. Sch 3 para 3(6) CS(MASC) Regs
31. Sch 3 para 3(2A) CS(MASC) Regs as inserted by reg 47(2) CS(MA)2 Regs
32. Sch 3 para 6 CS(MASC) Regs as amended by reg 47(3) CS(MA)2 Regs
33. Sch 3 para 6(d) CS(MASC) Regs as inserted by reg 47(3)(iv) CS(MA)2 Regs
34. Reg 16 CS(MASC) Regs
35. Reg 18(2) CS(MASC) Regs
36. Reg 18(1) CS(MASC) Regs

37. Reg 9(1)(bb) and Sch 3A CS(MASC) Regs
38. Reg 10(a) CS(MASC) Regs
39. Sch 3A paras 1, 8 and 9 CS(MASC) Regs
40. Sch 3A para 1(1) CS(MASC) Regs
41. Para 3155 CSAG
42. Para 3162 CSAG
43. Para 3183 CSAG
44. Sch 3A paras 1(1) and 11 CS(MASC) Regs
45. Para 3165 CSAG
46. Sch 3A para 2(2) CS(MASC) Regs
47. Para 1010 CSM(MA4)
48. Para 1084 CSM(MA4)
49. Reg 31A(5) CS(MAP) Regs as amended by reg 34 CS(MA)2 Regs
50. Sch 3A para 2(1) CS(MASC) Regs; para 3161 CSAG
51. Para 3168 CSAG; paras 1065-70 CSM(MA4)
52. Sch 3A para 4(1) CS(MASC) Regs
53. Sch 3A para 4(2) CS(MASC) Regs
54. Sch 3A para 5 CS(MASC) Regs
55. Sch 3A paras 4-6 CS(MASC) Regs
56. Sch 3A para 7 CS(MASC) Regs
57. Sch 3A para 1 CS(MASC) Regs
58. Sch 3A para 8A CS(MASC) Regs as inserted by reg 48 CS(MA)2 Regs
59. Sch 3A para 8 CS(MASC) Regs
60. Sch 3A para 9 CS(MASC) Regs
61. Sch 3A para 10 CS(MASC) Regs
62. Reg 9(1)(i) and Sch 3B CS(MASC) Regs
63. Sch 3B para 2 CS(MASC) Regs
64. Sch 3B para 1 CS(MASC) Regs
65. Sch 3B paras 21-23 CS(MASC) Regs
66. Sch 3B paras 3-6 CS(MASC) Regs; para 3077 CSAG
67. Sch 3B paras 7, 14 and 20 CS(MASC) Regs
68. Letter from DSS to CPAG, 28 April 1995
69. Sch 3B paras 8-20 CS(MASC) Regs as amended by reg 49 CS(MA)2 Regs
70. Sch 3B paras 8(2) and 15(2) CS(MASC) Regs
71. Sch 3B paras 9-13 and 16-19

CS(MASC) Regs as amended by reg 49 CS(MA)2 Regs
72. Reg 9(2) CS(MASC) Regs
73. Reg 9(2)(c) CS(MASC) Regs
74. Reg 9(1)(f) and (g) CS(MASC) Regs
75. Reg 9(2)(c)(iv) CS(MASC) Regs

Chapter 10: Assessable income (pp202-222)

1. Sch 1 para 5(1) and (2) CSA 1991
2. Regs 8 and 10 CS(MASC) Regs
3. Sch 1 para 5(4) CSA 1991
4. Reg 7(1) CS(MASC) Regs
5. Sch 1 CS(MASC) Regs
6. Sch 2 CS(MASC) Regs
7. Reg 9(2)(c) CS(MASC) Regs
8. Reg 11(2) CS(MASC) Regs as amended by reg 43(5) CS(MA)2 Regs
9. Reg 7(5) CS(MASC) Regs
10. Reg 7(4) CS(MASC) Regs
11. Sch 1 para 9(a) CSA 1991; reg 7(1)(d) CS(MASC) Regs
12. Sch 1 para 1(1) CS(MASC) Regs
13. Sch 2 para 48B CS(MASC) Regs
14. Paras 4107-22 CSAG
15. Sch 1 para 1(2) CS(MASC) Regs
16. Sch 2 para 6 CS(MASC) Regs
17. Para 4102 CSAG
18. CCS/4/1994 (starred 13/95)
19. Reg 1(2) CS(MASC) Regs
20. Sch 1 para 2(1) CS(MASC) Regs
21. Para 4070 CSAG
22. Para 4071 CSAG
23. Sch 1 para 2(3) CS(MASC) Regs
24. Sch 1 para 2(4) CS(MASC) Regs; CCS/556/1995 (starred 14/95)
25. Para 4076 CSAG
26. Sch 1 para 2(2) CS(MASC) Regs
27. Sch 1 para 1(3) CS(MASC) Regs
28. CSCS/5/1994 (starred 9/95)
29. Para 4051 CSAG
30. Reg 1(2A) CS(MASC) Regs as amended by reg 40(3) CS(MA)2 Regs
31. Sch 1 para 3(1) and (2)(a) CS(MASC) Regs
32. Sch 1 para 3(2)(b) CS(MASC) Regs; paras 4437-9 CSAG

33. Sch 1 para 4 CS(MASC) Regs
34. Sch 1 para 3(3) CS(MASC) Regs
35. Sch 1 para 3(5) and (8) CS(MASC) Regs
36. Sch 1 para 3(6) and (8) CS(MASC) Regs; paras 4380-9 CSAG
37. Para 4266 CSAG
38. Para 4270 CSAG
39. Paras 4322-51 CSAG
40. Sch 1 para 3(4) CS(MASC) Regs
41. Sch 1 para 3(7) CS(MASC) Regs; paras 4410-8 CSAG
42. Sch 1 para 5(2) CS(MASC) Regs
43. Sch 1 para 5(2A) CS(MASC) Regs
44. Paras 4236-40 CSAG
45. Sch 1 para 5(1) CS(MASC) Regs
46. Paras 4211-12 CSAG
47. Sch 1 para 5(2) CS(MASC) Regs; paras 4280-91 CSAG
48. Sch 1 para 5(3) CS(MASC) Regs
49. Paras 4221-3 CSAG
50. Sch 1 para 6 CS(MASC) Regs
51. Sch 1 para 6(3) CS(MASC) Regs
52. Sch 1 para 7(1) CS(MASC) Regs
53. Sch 1 para 7(2) CS(MASC) Regs
54. Sch 1 para 7(3) CS(MASC) Regs
55. Sch 1 para 7(4) CS(MASC) Regs
56. Sch 1 para 7(5) CS(MASC) Regs
57. Sch 2 para 16 CS(MASC) Regs
58. Reg 11(2)(a)(i) CS(MASC) Regs
59. Sch 2 para 7 CS(MASC) Regs
60. Sch 2 para 7 CS(MASC) Regs
61. Sch 2 para 8 CS(MASC) Regs
62. Sch 2 para 9 CS(MASC) Regs
63. Sch 2 para 11 CS(MASC) Regs
64. Sch 2 para 48A CS(MASC) Regs
65. Sch 2 para 10 CS(MASC) Regs
66. Sch 2 paras 8 and 12-15 CS(MASC) Regs
67. Sch 2 para 40 CS(MASC) Regs
68. Sch 2 para 18 CS(MASC) Regs
69. Sch 1 para 16 CS(MASC) Regs
70. Sch 1 para 15 CS(MASC) Regs
71. Sch 1 para 9 CS(MASC) Regs
72. Sch 2 para 35 CS(MASC) Regs
73. Sch 2 para 24 CS(MASC) Regs
74. Sch 2 para 22 CS(MASC) Regs
75. Sch 2 para 23 CS(MASC) Regs
76. Reg 1(2) CS(MASC) Regs; paras
4961-9 CSAG
77. Regs 7(3)(b) and 26(1)(b)(v) CS(MASC) Regs
78. Sch 1 paras 11 and 12 CS(MASC) Regs
79. Reg 1(2) CS(MASC) Regs; para 4974 CSAG
80. Sch 1 para 16(3) CS(MASC) Regs
81. Sch 1 para 16(4) CS(MASC) Regs
82. Sch 2 para 20 CS(MASC) Regs as amended by reg 3 CS(MASC)SS(C&P)A Regs
83. Sch 2 para 36 CS(MASC) Regs
84. Regs 7(3)(a) and 26(1)(b)(v) CS(MASC) Regs
85. Sch 2 para 21 CS(MASC) Regs
86. Sch 1 paras 14 and 16(2) CS(MASC) Regs
87. Sch 2 para 28 CS(MASC) Regs
88. Reg 11(2) CS(MASC) Regs
89. Sch 1 para 15 and Sch 2 para 44 CS(MASC) Regs
90. Sch 2 para 29 CS(MASC) Regs
91. Sch 2 para 31 CS(MASC) Regs
92. Sch 2 para 26 CS(MASC) Regs
93. Sch 2 para 25 CS(MASC) Regs
94. Para 4615 CSAG
95. Sch 1 para 16(5) and (6) CS(MASC) Regs
96. Reg 7(4) CS(MASC) Regs
97. Sch 2 para 45 CS(MASC) Regs
98. Paras 4617-20 CSAG
99. Regs 7(3) and 26(1)(b) CS(MASC) Regs
100. Sch 2 para 19 CS(MASC) Regs
101. R(SB) 53/83; CCS/15/1994 (starred 10/95)
102. Sch 1 para 31 CS(MASC) Regs
103. Sch 2 paras 19 and 20 CS(MASC) Regs as amended by reg 3 CS(MASC)SS(C&P)A Regs
104. Reg 4 CS(MASC)SS(C&P)A Regs
105. Sch 2 para 46 CS(MASC) Regs
106. Sch 2 para 17 CS(MASC) Regs
107. Sch 2 para 33 CS(MASC) Regs
108. Sch 2 para 42 CS(MASC) Regs
109. Sch 2 para 32 CS(MASC) Regs
110. Sch 2 para 36 CS(MASC) Regs
111. Sch 2 para 27 CS(MASC) Regs as

amended by reg 46 CS(MA)2 Regs
112. Sch 2 para 48 CS(MASC) Regs
113. Sch 2 para 34 CS(MASC) Regs
114. Sch 2 para 30 CS(MASC) Regs
115. Sch 2 para 5 CS(MASC) Regs
116. Sch 2 para 38 CS(MASC) Regs
117. Sch 2 para 47 CS(MASC) Regs
118. Sch 2 para 39 CS(MASC) Regs
119. Sch 2 para 37 CS(MASC) Regs
120. Sch 2 para 2 CS(MASC) Regs
121. Sch 2 para 3 CS(MASC) Regs
122. Sch 2 para 4 CS(MASC) Regs
123. Sch 2 para 41 CS(MASC) Regs
124. Sch 1 Part IV CS(MASC) Regs
125. Reg 9(2)(c) CS(MASC) Regs
126. Sch 1 paras 7 and 22 CS(MASC) Regs
127. Letter from DSS to CPAG, 23 February 1993
128. Sch 2 para 28 CS(MASC) Regs
129. Sch 1 para 23 CS(MASC) Regs
130. Sch 1 para 23 CS(MASC) Regs
131. Sch 1 para 24 CS(MASC) Regs
132. Sch 1 para 21 CS(MASC) Regs
133. Sch 1 para 19 CS(MASC) Regs
134. Sch 1 para 20 CS(MASC) Regs
135. Reg 7(1)(e) and Sch 1 Part V CS(MASC) Regs
136. Sch 1 para 32 CS(MASC) Regs
137. Sch 1 para 26 CS(MASC) Regs; paras 4831-39 CSAG
138. Para 4836 CSAG
139. Sch 1 para 27 CS(MASC) Regs
140. Para 4903 CSAG
141. Sch 1 para 30 CS(MASC) Regs; paras 4910-11 CSAG
142. Sch 1 para 28 CS(MASC) Regs
143. Paras 4827 and 4901 CSAG
144. Sch 1 para 29 CS(MASC) Regs
145. Paras 4808 and 4888 CSAG
146. R(SB) 38/85
147. Para 4891 CSAG
148. R(SB) 38/85
149. Paras 4812-13 and 4892-4 CSAG
150. Sch 1 para 31 CS(MASC) Regs
151. Reg 26(b)(v) CS(MASC) Regs
152. Sch 1 para 5(3) CSA 1991

Chapter 11: Proposed maintenance
(pp223-248)

1. Sch 1 para 2(1) CSA 1991
2. Sch 1 para 2(2) CSA 1991
3. Sch 1 para 2(3) CSA 1991
4. Sch 1 para 2 CSA 1991; reg 5 CS(MASC) Regs
5. Sch 1 para 4 CSA 1991; reg 6 CS(MASC) Regs
6. Sch 1 para 2(2) CSA 1991
7. Sch 1 para 4(1) CSA 1991; reg 6(1) CS(MASC) Regs
8. Sch 1 para 3 CSA 1991
9. Sch 1 para 3 CSA 1991
10. Sch 1 para 4(2) CSA 1991
11. Sch 1 para 4(3) CSA 1991
12. Reg 6(2) CS(MASC) Regs
13. Reg 19(2) CS(MASC) Regs
14. Reg 19(3) CS(MASC) Regs
15. Reg 19(4) CS(MASC) Regs
16. Reg 22(5) CS(MASC) Regs
17. Reg 22(1) CS(MASC) Regs as amended by reg 45 CS(MA)2 Regs
18. Reg 22(2) CS(MASC) Regs
19. Reg 22(3) CS(MASC) Regs
20. Reg 22(4) CS(MASC) Regs
21. Reg 22(1)(a) CS(MASC) Regs as amended by reg 45(2) CS(MA)2 Regs
22. Reg 22(1)(b) and (2A) CS(MASC) Regs as amended by reg 45 CS(MA)2 Regs
23. Reg 22(2) CS(MASC) Regs
24. Reg 23(4) CS(MASC) Regs

Chapter 12: Protected income
(pp249-265)

1. Sch 1 para 6 CSA 1991
2. Regs 11(6) and 12 CS(MASC) Regs
3. Regs 11(1)-(5) CS(MASC) Regs as amended by reg 43 CS(MA)2 Regs
4. Regs 11(1)(l) and 12(1)(a) CS(MASC) Regs
5. Reg 11(2) CS(MASC) Regs as amended by reg 43(5) CS(MA)2 Regs
6. Reg 11(2)(a)(ii) CS(MASC) Regs
7. Reg 11(2)(a)(v) CS(MASC) Regs as inserted by reg 43(5) CS(MA)2 Regs

8. Reg 12(2) CS(MASC) Regs
9. Reg 12(3) CS(MASC) Regs
10. Reg 11(1)(a-kk) CS(MASC) Regs
11. Reg 11(1)(b) CS(MASC) Regs
12. Sch 3 para 3(1) CS(MASC) Regs
13. Reg 11(1)(b) CS(MASC) Regs
14. Reg 18(1)(b) CS(MASC) Regs
15. Reg 1 CS(MASC) Regs; reg 3 IS Regs; reg 3 HB Regs
16. Reg 63(1) and (2) HB Regs
17. Reg 63(9) HB Regs
18. Reg 11(1)(j) CS(MASC) Regs
19. Sch 1 para 5(4) CS(NIRA) Regs
20. Reg 11(1)(kk) CS(MASC) Regs
21. Reg 11(1)(l) CS(MASC) Regs
22. Reg 12(2) CS(MASC) Regs
23. Reg 12(3) CS(MASC) Regs
24. Reg 22(3) CS(MASC) Regs

Chapter 13: Shared care
(pp266-289)

1. Regs 20(1)(a) and 24(1)(a) CS(MASC) Regs
2. Reg 1(2) CS(MASC) Regs as amended by reg 40(2)(a) CS(MA)2 Regs
3. Reg 1(2) CS(MASC) Regs as amended by reg 40(2)(a) CS(MA)2 Regs; CCS/6/1994 (starred 7/95)
4. Para 6022 CSAG
5. s5(1) CSA 1991
6. s5(2) CSA 1991
7. Reg 20(2) and (3) CS(MASC) Regs
8. s1 CSA 1991
9. Reg 20(2)(a) CS(MASC) Regs
10. Reg 20(2)(b)(i) CS(MASC) Regs
11. s147(3) and Sch 10 SSCBA 1992
12. Reg 20(2)(b)(ii) CS(MASC) Regs
13. Reg 20(4) CS(MASC) Regs; letter from DSS to CPAG, 23 February 1993
14. Reg 9(4) CS(MASC) Regs
15. Reg 9(3) CS(MASC) Regs
16. Reg 9(1)(f) and (2)(c)(iv) CS(MASC) Regs
17. Reg 20(3) and (4) CS(MASC) Regs
18. Reg 20(5) CS(MASC) Regs
19. Reg 20(6) CS(MASC) Regs
20. Reg 20(6) CS(MASC) Regs

21. Reg 11(3) and (4) CS(MASC) Regs
22. Para 3251 CSAG
23. Reg 20 CS(MASC) Regs
24. Reg 20(4)(i) CS(MASC) Regs
25. Reg 20(4)(ii) CS(MASC) Regs
26. Reg 24(1) CS(MASC) Regs
27. Reg 24(2)(a) CS(MASC) Regs
28. Reg 24(2)(b) CS(MASC) Regs
29. Reg 24(2)(c) CS(MASC) Regs
30. Reg 24 CS(MASC) Regs
31. Reg 51 CS(MAP) Regs
32. Reg 25 CS(MASC) Regs
33. Reg 25(3) CS(MASC) Regs; para 6762 CSAG
34. Reg 9(3) and (4) CS(MASC) Regs; para 3202 CSAG

Chapter 14: Assessments
(pp292-321)

1. s11(1) CSA 1991
2. Para 1387 CSAG
3. Para 1388 CSAG
4. HC *Hansard*, 1 February 1996, cols 942-3
5. Para 1387 CSAG
6. Paras 1303, 1703 and 5054 CSM(MA); App 7 CSM(APP)
7. Para 2748 CSM(MA) [CSG Vol 3 Ch 6]
8. Paras 2800-16 CSM(MA) [CSQCG]
9. Sch 1 Art 5(5) CS(NIRA) Regs
10. Sch 1 Art 5(1) CS(NIRA) Regs
11. Sch 1 Art 5(3) CS(NIRA) Regs
12. Sch 1 Art 5(2) and (6) CS(NIRA) Regs
13. Sch 1 Art 5(4) and (7) CS(NIRA) Regs
14. Sch 1 para 15 CSA 1991
15. Reg 7(2) CS(MAP) Regs
16. Sch 1 para 13 CSA 1991
17. Reg 12(1) CS(MAP) Regs as amended by reg 19 CS(MA)2 Regs
18. s12 CSA 1991
19. s12(1)(b) and (c) CSA 1991; CSA 1995 (Comm2)O
20. Para 5202 CSM(MA)
21. HL *Hansard*, vol 527, cols 570-1
22. Paras 6210 and 6410 CSM(MA); para 3857 CSAG

23. s12(4) CSA 1991
24. Reg 8(1) CS(MAP) Regs
25. Para 3858 CSAG; paras 6210 and 6410 CSM(MA) [CSEFIG Ch 6]
26. Reg 8(2) CS(MAP) Regs as amended by reg 16 CS(MA)2 Regs
27. Reg 8(3) CS(MAP) Regs as amended by reg 16 CS(MA)2 Regs
28. Reg 8A(1) CS(MAP) Regs as amended by reg 16 CS(MA)2 Regs
29. Reg 8(3)(b) CS(MAP) Regs as amended by reg 16 CS(MA)2 Regs
30. Reg 8A(3) CS(MAP) Regs as amended by reg 16 CS(MA)2 Regs
31. Reg 8A(4) CS(MAP) Regs as amended by reg 16 CS(MA)2 Regs
32. Reg 8A(5) CS(MAP) Regs as amended by reg 16 CS(MA)2 Regs
33. Reg 8(3)(c) CS(MAP) Regs as amended by reg 16 CS(MA)2 Regs
34. Reg 8(3)(c)(iii) CS(MAP) Regs as amended by reg 16 CS(MA)2 Regs
35. HC Hansard, 2 February 1996, col 990
36. Reg 8A(6) CS(MAP) Regs as amended by reg 16 CS(MA)2 Regs
37. Reg 8A(8) CS(MAP) Regs as amended by reg 16 CS(MA)2 Regs
38. Reg 8A(7) CS(MAP) Regs as amended by reg 16 CS(MA)2 Regs
39. Reg 8(3)(d) CS(MAP) Regs as amended by reg 16 CS(MA)2 Regs
40. Reg 8A(9) CS(MAP) Regs as amended by reg 16 CS(MA)2 Regs
41. Para 3651-2 CSM(MA4) [CSTG Ch 4]
42. Reg 8A(10) CS(MAP) Regs as amended by reg 16 CS(MA)2 Regs
43. Paras 3943 and 4085-91 CSAG
44. Para 3653-4 CSM(MA4) [CSEFIG Ch 10]
45. Reg 10(1) CS(MAP) Regs as amended by reg 18(2) CS(MA)2 Regs
46. Reg 10(2) CS(MAP) Regs as amended by reg 18 CS(MA)2 Regs
47. Sch para 10 CSA(Comm 3)O
48. Reg 10(4) and (5) CS(MAP) Regs
49. Reg 11 CS(AIAMA) Regs
50. Reg 10(2B) CS(MAP) Regs
51. Reg 10(2A) CS(MAP) Regs
52. Sch para 7(1)(a) CSA(Comm 3)O; reg 7(1)(a) CS(MATP) Regs
53. Sch para 7(1)(d) CSA(Comm 3)O; reg 8(2) CS(MATP) Regs
54. Sch para 9 CSA(Comm 3)O; reg 6(2) CS(MATP) Regs
55. Para 30 CSM(RL)
56. Sch para 6 CSA(Comm 3)O
57. Sch para 7(2) CSA(Comm 3)O
58. Sch para 7(1) CSA(Comm 3)O
59. Sch paras 6 'modified amount' and 8 CSA(Comm 3)O
60. Para 31 CSM(RL) [CSG Vol 3 Ch 17]
61. Reg 6(1) CS(MATP) Regs
62. Reg 7(2)(a) CS(MATP) Regs as amended by reg 51 CS(MA)2 Regs
63. Reg 7(1) CS(MATP) Regs
64. Reg 7(2)(b) CS(MATP) Regs
65. Reg 7(2)(c) CS(MATP) Regs as amended by reg 51 CS(MA)2 Regs
66. Reg 8(2)(a) CS(MATP) Regs
67. Reg 6(1) CS(MATP) Regs 'transitional period'
68. Reg 8(2) CS(MATP) Regs
69. Reg 10 CS(MATP) Regs
70. Para 7000 and App 1 Part 7 CSAG
71. Reg 7(2)(b) CS(MATP) Regs
72. Para 435 CSM(RL) [CSG Vol 2 Ch 7]
73. Sch para 8 CSA(Comm 3)O
74. Sch para 12 CSA(Comm 3)O; reg 11 CS(MATP) Regs as amended by reg 52 CS(MA)2 Regs
75. Reg 1(2) CS(MAP) Regs
76. Reg 30(2)(a) CS(MAP) Regs
77. Reg 30(2)(b) CS(MAP) Regs
78. Reg 30(2A) CS(MAP) Regs
79. Reg 30(3) CS(MAP) Regs
80. Paras 1703-4 CSM(MA) [CSG Vol 3 Ch 7]
81. Reg 30(4) CS(MAP) Regs
82. Reg 4(3) CS(MAP) Regs
83. Reg 3(5) CS(MAJ) Regs as amended by reg 13 CS(MA)2 Regs
84. Reg 3(6) CS(MAJ) Regs
85. Reg 3(7) CS(MAJ) Regs
86. Reg 3(8) CS(MAJ) Regs as amended

by reg 13 CS(MA)2 Regs
87. Reg 33(7) MAP Regs as amended by reg 36 CS(MA)2 Regs
88. Reg 3(1) CS(MAP) Regs
89. Reg 3(2) CS(MAP) Regs
90. Reg 3(3) CS(MAP) Regs
91. Reg 33(1) CS(MAP) Regs
92. Reg 33(6) CS(MAP) Regs as amended by reg 36(5) CS(MA)2 Regs
93. Reg 8C(1)(a) CS(MAP) Regs as amended by reg 16 CS(MA)2 Regs
94. Reg 8C(1)(b) and (c) CS(MAP) Regs as amended by reg 16 CS(MA)2 Regs
95. Reg 8C(1)(d) CS(MAP) Regs as amended by reg 16 CS(MA)2 Regs
96. Sch 1 para 16(2) CSA 1991
97. Sch 1 para 16(3) CSA 1991
98. Sch 1 para 16(4) CSA 1991
99. Sch 1 para 16(6) CSA 1991
100. Reg 1(2) CS(MASC) Regs 'unmarried couple'
101. Para 8053 CSAG
102. Para 7901 CSM(MA) [CSG Vol 3]
103. Sch 1 para 16(5) CSA 1991; reg 7(1) CS(MAJ) Regs
104. Reg 32A(1) CS(MAP) Regs
105. Sch 1 para 16(6) CSA 1991; para 8056 CSAG
106. Sch 1 para 16(4) CSA 1991
107. Reg 7(3) CS(MAJ) Regs
108. Reg 32A(2) CS(MAP) Regs
109. Reg 32 CS(MAP) Regs
110. Paras 8014 and 8035 CSAG
111. Sch 1 para 16(2) and (3) CSA 1991
112. Reg 33(5) CS(MAP) Regs
113. Reg 8D(4) CS(MAP) Regs as amended by reg 16 CS(MA)2 Regs
114. Reg 14 CS(MAP) Regs as amended by reg 20 CS(MA)2 Regs
115. Reg 9A(4) and (5) CS(MAP) Regs as amended by reg 17 CS(MA)2 Regs
116. Reg 13 CS(MAP) Regs; reg 9A(4) and (5) CS(MAP) Regs as amended by reg 17 CS(MA)2 Regs;
117. Sch 1 para 16(1) CSA 1991
118. Reg 52(1) CS(MAP) Regs
119. Reg 52(2) and (3) CS(MAP) Regs
120. Paras 3890-6, 3930 and 3945 CSAG
121. Reg 8D(1) CS(MAP) Regs as amended by reg 16 CS(MA)2 Regs
122. Reg 8D(2) CS(MAP) Regs as amended by reg 16 CS(MA)2 Regs
123. Reg 8C(3) and (4) CS(MAP) Regs as amended by reg 16 CS(MA)2 Regs
124. Regs 8C(3) and 8D(6) and (7) CS(MAP) Regs as amended by reg 16 CS(MA)2 Regs
125. Reg 8D(5) CS(MAP) Regs as amended by reg 16 CS(MA)2 Regs
126. Reg 8D(6) CS(MAP) Regs as amended by reg 16 CS(MA)2 Regs
127. Reg 9(15) CS(MAP) Regs as amended by reg 17 CS(MA)2 Regs
128. Reg 9(1) CS(MAP) Regs as amended by reg 17 CS(MA)2 Regs
129. Reg 9(4) CS(MAP) Regs as amended by reg 17 CS(MA)2 Regs
130. Reg 9(2) CS(MAP) Regs as amended by reg 17 CS(MA)2 Regs
131. See note 130
132. Reg 8(7) CS(MAP) Regs before amendment by reg 16 CS(MA)2 Regs
133. Reg 9(3) CS(MAP) Regs as amended by reg 17 CS(MA)2 Regs
134. Reg 9(9)(i) CS(MAP) Regs as amended by reg 17 CS(MA)2 Regs
135. Reg 9(5)(i) CS(MAP) Regs as amended by reg 17 CS(MA)2 Regs
136. Reg 9(5)(ii) and (6) CS(MAP) Regs as amended by reg 17 CS(MA)2 Regs
137. Reg 9(10) and (11) CS(MAP) Regs as amended by reg 17 CS(MA)2 Regs
138. Reg 9(9)(ii) CS(MAP) Regs as amended by reg 17 CS(MA)2 Regs
139. Reg 9(12)(a) CS(MAP) Regs as amended by reg 17 CS(MA)2 Regs
140. Para 3962 CSAG
141. Reg 9(12)(b) CS(MAP) Regs as amended by reg 17 CS(MA)2 Regs
142. Paras 3963-4 CSAG
143. Reg 9(12) CS(MAP) Regs as amended by reg 17 CS(MA)2 Regs
144. Reg 9A(1) CS(MAP) Regs as

amended by reg 17 CS(MA)2 Regs

145. Reg 9A(2) CS(MAP) Regs as
     amended by reg 17 CS(MA)2 Regs
146. Reg 9A(3) CS(MAP) Regs as
     amended by reg 17 CS(MA)2 Regs
147. Reg 9A(4) and (5) CS(MAP) Regs as
     amended by reg 17 CS(MA)2 Regs
148. s10 CSA 1995; *Improving Child
     Support* 1995 paras 5.5 and 7.3
149. Reg 60B IS Regs
150. Reg 60D IS Regs
151. Reg 60B IS Regs
152. Reg 60C(2) and (3) IS Regs
153. Reg 60C(4) Reg
154. Reg 40 IS Regs
155. s136(1) SSCBA 1992; reg 23(1) IS
     Regs
156. s74A SSAA 1992 as inserted by s25
     CSA 1995
157. Regs 5(1)(b) CS(C&E) Regs
158. Letter from DSS to CPAG, 8 March
     1993
159. Reg 8 CS(AIAMA) Regs as amended
     by reg 2 CS(MA)2 Regs
160. See note 159
161. s74(1) SSAA 1992; reg 7(1)(b)
     SS(PAOR) Regs
162. Sch 3 para 14(2) IS Regs
163. Reg 16(2A) FC Regs; reg 18(2A)
     DWA Regs
164. Reg 16(2A)(a) FC Regs; reg
     18(2A)(a) DWA Regs
165. Reg 16(2A)(c) FC Regs; reg
     18(2A)(c) DWA Regs
166. Reg 16(2A)(b) FC Regs; reg
     18(2A)(b) DWA Regs
167. Reg 2(1) FC Regs 'week'; reg 2(1)
     DWA Regs 'week'
168. Reg 16(2A) FC Regs; reg 18(2A)
     DWA Regs
169. Reg 16(2A)(4)(b) FC Regs; reg
     18(2A)(4)(b) DWA Regs
170. Sch 2 para 47 FC Regs; Sch 3 para
     13 DWA Regs
171. ss128(3) and 129(6) SSCBA 1992
172. Sch 4 para 47 HB Regs; Sch 4 para
     46 CTB Regs
173. Reg 35(2) HB Regs; reg 26(2) CTB
     Regs

Chapter 15: Departures
(pp322-348)

1. s28I(2) CSA 1991
2. s28I(4) CSA 1991; HC Social
   Security Committee, 2nd Report, 24
   January 1996, Q63
3. s28I(5) CSA 1991
4. Sch 4B CSA 1991
5. Sch 4B para 2 CSA 1991
6. Sch 4B para 6(5) CSA 1991
7. Sch 4B para 2(5) CSA 1991
8. Sch 4B para 5 CSA 1991
9. Reg 24 CSDD(AA) Regs
10. Sch 4B paras 3 and 4 CSA 1991;
    reg 21(1)(b) CSDD(AA) Regs
11. s28A CSA 1991
12. Sch 4A para 7 CSA 1991
13. s28A(2) CSA 1991
14. s28I(1) CSA 1991
15. s28A(4) CSA 1991
16. Sch 4A para 8 CSA 1991
17. s28D(2)(a) CSA 1991
18. s28B CSA 1991
19. s28B(4) CSA 1991
20. s28B(5) CSA 1991
21. s28B(6) CSA 1991
22. s28H CSA 1991
23. s28C CSA 1991
24. s28E(3) CSA 1991
25. Sch 4A para 4(2) CSA 1991; reg 6
    CSDD(AA) Regs
26. s28E(2) CSA 1991
27. s28E(4) CSA 1991
28. s28F(1)(b) CSA 1991
29. HC *Hansard*, Standing Committee,
    30 March 1995, col 80
30. Reg 30 CSDD(AA) Regs
31. HL *Hansard*, Committee State, 19
    June 1995, vol 565, col 83
32. ss2 and 28F(2)(c) CSA 1991
33. s28D CSA 1991
34. s28F(8) CSA 1991
35. s28F(4) and (5) CSA 1991
36. *See* note 29
37. s28F(6) CSA 1991
38. s28G(1) CSA 1991
39. Sch 4B para 6(3) CSA 1991
40. Sch 4B para 6(4) CSA 1991
41. Sch 4B para 6(6) &(7) CSA 1991

42. s28G(2) CSA 1991
43. Sch 4A para 5 CSA 1991
44. s28G(3) CSA 1991
45. Reg 34 CSDD(AA) Regs
46. Sch 4A para 2(d) CSA 1991
47. s28H CSA 1991
48. Sch 4A para 9 CSA 1991

Chapter 16: Reviews and appeals
(pp349-386)

1. Reg 54(1) CS(MAP) Regs
2. Para 9003 CSAG
3. Reg 54(2) CS(MAP) Regs
4. Reg 56(1) CS(MAP) Regs
5. Sch 1 para 5(4) CSA 1991
6. CCS/7062/1995 (starred 1/96)
7. s23(3) SSAA 1992
8. Reg 1(2) 'party to the proceedings' (e) SS(A) Regs
9. *Council of Civil Service Unions v Minister for the Civil Service* [1984] 1 WLR 1174; [1984] 3 All ER 935
10. Reg 55(1) CS(MAP) Regs
11. Reg 8D(4) CS(MAP) Regs as amended by reg 16 CS(MA)2 Regs
12. Reg 55(7) CS(MAP) Regs
13. Reg 55(1) and (2) CS(MAP) Regs
14. Reg 55(6) CS(MAP) Regs
15. Reg 55(3) CS(MAP) Regs
16. Reg 55(5) CS(MAP) Regs
17. Reg 55(4) CS(MAP) Regs
18. Reg 17(1)(i) CS(MAP) Regs as amended by reg 24(2) CS(MA)2 Regs
19. Reg 17(1) CS(MAP) Regs as amended by reg 24(2) CS(MA)2 Regs
20. Reg 17(2) CS(MAP) Regs as amended by reg 24(3) CS(MA)2 Regs
21. Regs 12(3) and 13 CS(MATP) Regs; reg 63(4) CSIS(A) Regs
22. Reg 17(1)(c) CS(MAP) Regs as amended by reg 24(2) CS(MA)2 Regs
23. Reg 17(3) CS(MAP) Regs
24. Reg 17(4) CS(MAP) Regs
25. Para 7530 CSM(MA) [CSG Vol 8 Ch 2]

26. Para 7531 CSM(MA) [CSG Vol 8 Ch 2]
27. Regs 17(5) CS(MAP) Regs as amended by reg 24(4) CS(MA)2 Regs
28. Reg 1(6) CS(MAP) Regs
29. s16(3) CSA 1991
30. Reg 1(2) 'relevant week' (b) CS(MASC) Regs as amended by reg 40(2) CS(MA)2 Regs
31. s16(4) CSA 1991
32. Sch 1 para 16(4A) CSA 1991
33. Reg 32B CS(MAP) Regs as amended by reg 35 CS(MA)2 Regs
34. Para 7632 CSM(MA) [CSG Vol 8 Ch 2]
35. Regs 31(1) and 8B(1) CS(MAP) Regs as amended by regs 34 and 16 CS(MA)2 Regs respectively
36. Reg 8B(4) CS(MAP) Regs as amended by reg 16 CS(MA)2 Regs
37. Reg 8C(2) CS(MAP) Regs as amended by reg 16 CS(MA)2 Regs
38. s17(1) and (2) CSA 1991
39. Reg 8D(3) CS(MAP) Regs as amended by reg 16 CS(MA)2 Regs
40. Reg 19(2) CS(MAP) Regs as amended by reg 26(2) CS(MA)2 Regs
41. Reg 19(5) CS(MAP) Regs
42. Paras 7400-39 CSM(MA)
43. Reg 18 CS(MAP) Regs as amended by reg 25 CS(MA)2 Regs
44. Reg 19(1) CS(MAP) Regs
45. s17(5) CSA 1991
46. R(A) 4/81; para 9171 CSAG
47. Reg 20(4) CS(MAP) Regs
48. Reg 20(3) CS(MAP) Regs as amended by reg 27(4) CS(MA)2 Regs
49. Reg 20(1) CS(MAP) Regs as amended by reg 27(2) CS(MA)2 Regs
50. Reg 20(2) CS(MAP) Regs as amended by reg 27(3) CS(MA)2 Regs
51. Reg 21 CS(MAP) Regs as amended by reg 28 CS(MA)2 Regs
52. Reg 1(2) 'relevant week' (c) CS(MASC) Regs as amended by reg 40(2) CS(MA)2 Regs
53. Reg 31(3) CS(MAP) Regs as amended by reg 34 CS(MA)2 Regs

54. Reg 31(4) CS(MAP) Regs as amended by reg 34 CS(MA)2 Regs
55. Reg 31(2) CS(MAP) Regs as amended by reg 34 CS(MA)2 Regs
56. Reg 11(1) CS(MAP) Regs
57. Reg 12(1) CS(MAP) Regs as amended by reg 19 CS(MA)2 Regs
58. Reg 11 CS(MAP) Regs; reg 12 CS(MAP) Regs as amended by reg 19 CS(MA)2 Regs
59. s18(7) CSA 1991
60. s18(1)(a) CSA 1991
61. s18(2) CSA 1991
62. s18(1)(b) CSA 1991
63. Reg 52(4) CS(MAP) Regs
64. s18(3) CSA 1991
65. Reg 9(13) CS(MAP) Regs as amended by reg 17 CS(MA)2 Regs
66. s18(4) CSA 1991
67. Reg 12(1) and (2) CS(AIAMA) Regs
68. See note 67
69. s54 'maintenance assessment' CSA 1991; reg 8D(3) CS(MAP) Regs as amended by reg 11 CS(MA)2 Regs
70. Reg 29 CS(MAP) Regs
71. s18(6A) CSA 1991
72. Reg 26A CS(MAP) Regs
73. s27 CSA 1991
74. s18(2)-(4) CSA 1991; reg 12(1) CS(AIAMA) Regs; reg 9(13) CS(MAP) Regs as amended by reg 17 CS(MA)2 Regs
75. s18(1) CSA 1991
76. Reg 9A(6) CS(MAP) Regs as amended by reg 17 CS(MA)2 Regs
77. s18(5) CSA 1991
78. Para 7220 CSM(MA) [CSG Vol 8 Ch 18]
79. Reg 24(1) CS(MAP) Regs
80. Reg 1(6)(b) CS(MAP) Regs
81. Reg 29 CS(MAP) Regs
82. Regs 24(2) and 29(3) CS(MAP) Regs
83. Reg 24(3) CS(MAP) Regs
84. s18(6) CSA 1991
85. R(A) 1/72; R(SB) 11/83
86. *Wednesbury Corporation v Ministry of Housing and Local Government (No 2)* [1965] 3 WLR 956; [1965] 3 All ER 571
87. *Brind v Secretary of State for the Home Department* [1991] 1 All ER 720
88. CSCS/1/1994 (starred 119/94); CCS/2/1994 (starred 3/95); CCS/17/1994 (starred 6/95)
89. *Chief Adjudication Officer v Foster* [1993] AC 754; [1993] 2 WLR 292; [1993] 1 All ER 705
90. Paras 1363-5 CSAG
91. Reg 25(1) CS(MAP) Regs
92. Reg 25(2) CS(MAP) Regs
93. Reg 25(6) CS(MAP) Regs
94. Reg 25(2)(c) CS(MAP) Regs
95. Reg 25(3) CS(MAP) Regs
96. Reg 25(3)-(5) CS(MAP) Regs
97. Reg 25(4) CS(MAP) Regs
98. Reg 26(1) CS(MAP) Regs
99. Reg 26(2) CS(MAP) Regs
100. s18(9) and (10) CSA 1991
101. Reg 1(2) 'relevant week' (e) CS(MASC) Regs as amended by reg 40(2) CS(MA)2 Regs
102. Reg 1(2) 'relevant week' (d) CS(MASC) Regs as amended by reg 40(2) CS(MA)2 Regs
103. s18(10A) CSA 1991
104. Reg 31A(1) CS(MAP) Regs as amended by reg 34 CS(MA)2 Regs
105. Reg 31A(2)(a) CS(MAP) Regs as amended by reg 34 CS(MA)2 Regs; CCS/11/1994 (starred 5/96)
106. Reg 31A(2)(b) and (6) CS(MAP) Regs as amended by reg 34 CS(MA)2 Regs
107. Reg 31A(7) CS(MAP) Regs as amended by reg 34 CS(MA)2 Regs
108. Reg 31A(8) CS(MAP) Regs as amended by reg 34 CS(MA)2 Regs
109. Reg 9(14) CS(MAP) Regs as amended by reg 17 CS(MA)2 Regs
110. Reg 31A(5) CS(MAP) Regs as amended by reg 34 CS(MA)2 Regs
111. Reg 31A(3)(a) CS(MAP) Regs as amended by reg 34 CS(MA)2 Regs
112. Reg 31A(3)(b) CS(MAP) Regs as amended by reg 34 CS(MA)2 Regs
113. Reg 31C(2) CS(MAP) Regs as amended by reg 34 CS(MA)2 Regs

114. Reg 31C(3) CS(MAP) Regs as amended by reg 34 CS(MA)2 Regs
115. Reg 31C(1) CS(MAP) Regs as amended by reg 34 CS(MA)2 Regs
116. Reg 11(1) CS(MAP) Regs
117. Reg 12(1)(iv) CS(MAP) Regs as amended by reg 19 CS(MA)2 Regs
118. Reg 12(1)(iii) CS(MAP) Regs as amended by reg 19 CS(MA)2 Regs
119. Regs 10(4)(c), 11(2)(b) and (c), 13(2)(b) and (c) CS(MAP) Regs; reg 15(2) CS(MAP) Regs as amended by reg 21(3) CS(MA)2 Regs
120. s19(2) CSA 1991
121. s19(1) CSA 1991
122. Reg 12(3) CS(AIAMA) Regs as amended by reg 4 CS(MA)2 Regs
123. Reg 8D(3) CS(MAP) Regs as amended by reg 16 CS(MA)2 Regs
124. s19(6) CSA 1991
125. Reg 23 CS(MAP) Regs
126. Reg 8D(3) CS(MAP) Regs as amended by reg 16 CS(MA)2 Regs
127. Para 7255-6 CSM(MA) [CSG Vol 8 Ch 5]
128. Para 7250 CSM(MA) [CSG Vol 8 Ch 5]
129. s19(3) and (6) CSA 1991
130. s12(1A)(b) and (c) CSA 1991
131. Reg 31B(5) CS(MAP) Regs as amended by reg 34 CS(MA)2 Regs
132. Reg 31B(1) CS(MAP) Regs as amended by reg 34 CS(MA)2 Regs
133. Reg 31B(2) CS(MAP) Regs as amended by reg 34 CS(MA)2 Regs
134. Reg 31B(3) CS(MAP) Regs as amended by reg 34 CS(MA)2 Regs
135. Reg 8B(2)-(4) CS(MAP) Regs as amended by reg 16 CS(MA)2 Regs
136. Reg 31B(4) CS(MAP) Regs as amended by reg 34 CS(MA)2 Regs
137. s46(7) CSA 1991
138. Reg 42(9) CS(MAP) Regs
139. s20(1)(b) CSA 1991
140. s20(1)(a) CSA 1991
141. Sch 5 para 8 CS(MASC) Regs
142. s28H(1) CSA 1991
143. ss20(1) and 46(7) CSA 1991; Sch 5 para 8 CS(MASC) Regs; reg 42(9)

CS(MAP) Regs
144. Reg 1(2) 'party to proceedings' (a) – (d) CSAT(P) Regs
145. Reg 1(2) 'party to proceedings' (e) CSAT(P) Regs
146. CSCS/2/1994 para 20 (starred 3/95); CCS/12/1994 para 46 (starred 11/95)
147. CSCS/2/1994 paras 10, 20 and 23 (starred 3/95); CSCS/3/1994 paras 14-15 (starred 5/95)
148. CSCS/2/1994 paras 10 and 20 (starred 3/95); CCS/511/1994 paras 8-9 (starred 12/96)
149. s20(2A) CSA 1991
150. Arts 3 and 4 CSA(JC)O
151. CSC/1/1994; CSC/3/1994
152. s20(2) CSA 1991; reg 3(3) CSAT(P) Regs
153. Reg 1(6)(b) CS(MAP) Regs
154. Reg 2(1) CSAT(P) Regs
155. Reg 3(6) CSAT(P) Regs
156. Reg 2 SS(A) CSA Regs
157. Reg 3(7) CSAT(P) Regs
158. Reg 3(8) CSAT(P) Regs
159. CIS 93/92
160. Reg 3(8) CSAT(P) Regs
161. Reg 3(1A) CSAT(P) Regs
162. Reg 3(2) CSAT(P) Regs
163. Reg 3(9) and (10) CSAT(P) Regs
164. Reg 3(11) CSAT(P) Regs
165. Paras 12130-2 CSM(MA) [CSG Vol 8 Ch 1]
166. Para 9529 CSAG
167. Para 9602 CSAG
168. HC Committee of Public Accounts, *Child Support Agency*, 20 November 1995, p3
169. Para 9627 CSAG
170. Para 9646 CSAG
171. Reg 17 CSAT(P) Regs
172. Para 9653 CSAG
173. Paras 12102-3 CSM(MA) [CSG Vol 8 Ch 1]
174. HC *Hansard*, 19 December 1995, cols 1119-20
175. Reg 5 CSAT(P) Regs
176. Rules of the Supreme Court, Order 38 rule 19
177. Reg 3A CSAT(P) Regs

178. Para 9529 CSAG
179. Reg 4 CSAT(P) Regs
180. Reg 7(1) CSAT(P) Regs
181. Para 9542 CSAG
182. CIS 68/91 to be reported as R(IS) 5/94
183. Reg 6(1) CSAT(P) Regs
184. Reg 6(2) CSAT(P) Regs
185. Reg 6(3) CSAT(P) Regs
186. Reg 6(1) CSAT(P) Regs
187. s20A CSA 1991
188. Para 9532 CSAG
189. Para 9531 CSAG
190. Reg 11(1) CSAT(P) Regs
191. Reg 11(2) CSAT(P) Regs
192. Reg 8 CSAT(P) Regs
193. Sch 3 para 2(1) CSA 1991
194. Sch 3 paras 3(3) and 5 CSA 1991
195. Sch 3 para 2(2) and (3) CSA 1991
196. Reg 11(3) CSAT(P) Regs
197. Reg 11(6) CSAT(P) Regs
198. CCS/1037/1995 para 16 (starred 10/96)
199. Reg 9 CSAT(P) Regs
200. Sch 3 para 7 CSA 1991
201. Reg 10(1) CSAT(P) Regs
202. Reg 10(3) CSAT(P) Regs
203. Reg 10(2) CSAT(P) Regs
204. Arts 31(2) and 37(1-3) Sch 1 Diplomatic Privileges Act 1964; Art 44(1) Sch 1 Consular Relations Act 1968; paras 9, 14 and 20-23 Sch 1 International Organisations Act 1968
205. s1 Criminal Evidence Act 1898; s80 Police and Criminal Evidence Act 1984
206. Reg 10(4) CSAT(P) Regs
207. Reg 11(7) CSAT(P) Regs
208. Reg 11(8) and (10) CSAT(P) Regs
209. Reg 11(3) and (4) CSAT(P) Regs
210. Para 9601 CSAG
211. Reg 11(5) CSAT(P) Regs
212. Reg 11(5A) CSAT(P) Regs
213. Reg 12(1) CSAT(P) Regs
214. Reg 12(2) CSAT(P) Regs
215. Reg 11(9) CSAT(P) Regs
216. Reg 13(1) CSAT(P) Regs
217. s20(3) CSA 1991
218. s20(4) CSA 1991

219. Reg 13(2) CSAT(P) Regs
220. Reg 13(3) CSAT(P) Regs
221. Para 12173 CSM(MA) [CSG Vol 8 Ch 1]
222. Reg 13(4) CSAT(P) Regs
223. Reg 13(5) CSAT(P) Regs
224. Reg 14 CSAT(P) Regs
225. Reg 15(1) CSAT(P) Regs
226. Regs 3 and 15(2) CSAT(P) Regs
227. Reg 15(3) and (4) CSAT(P) Regs
228. Reg 7(2) CSAT(P) Regs
228. Reg 3(8) CSAT(P) Regs
230. s24 CSA 1991
231. s24(1A) CSA 1991 to be amended by Sch 3 para 7(2) CSA 1995
232. R(SB) 11/83
233. s24(3) CSA 1991
234. s24(3)(c) CSA 1991 to be amended by Sch 3 para 7(3) CSA 1995
235. Regs 2(1)(a) and 3(1) CSC(P) Regs
236. Reg 4(1) CSC(P) Regs
237. Regs 5(1) and 6(1) CSC(P) Regs
238. Reg 2(1)(b) CSC(P) Regs
239. Reg 16(1) CSAT(P) Regs
240. Regs 3(3) and 6(2) CSC(P) Regs
241. Regs 3(1)(b) and 5(1)(c) CSC(P) Regs
242. Reg 3(4) CSC(P) Regs
243. Regs 3(5) and 16(2) CSC(P) Regs
244. Reg 16(2) CSC(P) Regs
245. Reg 16(3) CSC(P) Regs
246. Reg 11(2) CSC(P) Regs
247. Reg 13(4) CSC(P) Regs
248. Reg 15 CSC(P) Regs
249. Reg 18 CSC(P) Regs
250. Reg 20 CSC(P) Regs
251. R(I) 12/75
252. s25 CSA 1991
253. Reg 25 CSC(P) Regs

Chapter 17: Collection and enforcement
(pp387-419)

1. s29(1) CSA 1991
2. s30(1) CSA 1991
3. Reg 3(3A) CSF Regs
4. Reg 3 CS(C&E) Regs
5. Reg 2 CS(C&E) Regs
6. Reg 5 CS(C&E) Regs

7. Reg 4 CS(C&E) Regs
8. Reg 5 CS(AIAMA) Regs
9. s29(1) CSA 1991; reg 2 CS(C&E) Regs
10. Reg 6 CS(C&E) Regs
11. Reg 7(1) CS(C&E) Regs
12. Reg 7(2) CS(C&E) Regs
13. HC *Hansard*, 2 February 1996, col 991
14. s29(1)(a) CSA 1991
15. s29(1)(b) CSA 1991
16. Para 1200 CSM(OA)
17. Letter from CSA to CPAG, 12 April 1995
18. CSA, *Annual Report and Accounts 1994/95*, July 1995
19. Calculated using CSA statistical information April–December 1995
20. s29 CSA 1991; reg 2 CS(C&E) Regs
21. *See* note 19
22. *See* note 19
23. Sch 5 para 9 CS(MASC) Regs
24. Para 5734 CSM(OA) [CSG Vol 3 Chs 1 & 2]
25. Letter from DSS to CPAG, 8 March 1993
26. Para 5000 CSM(OA)
27. Reg 3(1) CS(C&E) Regs
28. Reg 5(1) CS(C&E) Regs
Notes 29–41: CSM refs will be found in CSG Vol 3 Ch 2 and Vol 7 Ch 15
29. Paras 3113 and 3124 CSM(OA)
30. Paras 3121 and 3300 CSM(OA)
31. Reg 3(2) CS(C&E) Regs
32. Para 3111 CSM(OA)
33. Reg 6 CS(C&E) Regs
34. Paras 3123 and 11750 CSM(OA)
35. Reg 4(1) CS(C&E) Regs
36. Reg 4(2) CS(C&E) Regs
37. Reg 6 CS(C&E) Regs
38. Reg 5(3) CS(C&E) Regs
39. Para 4622 CSM(OA)
40. Para 3134 CSM(OA)
41. Paras 4620-1 CSM(OA)
42. CSA Business Plan 1995/96, p13
43. Reg 9 CS(AIAMA) Regs; para 1850 CSM(OA4)
Notes 44–48: CSM refs will be found in CSG Vol 17 Ch 11

44. Para 5321 CSM(OA); reg 10(1)(a) CS(AIAMA) Regs
45. Para 9000 CSM(OA4)
46. Para 9031 CSM(OA4)
47. Paras 5500-47 CSM(OA)
48. Para 4313 CSM(OA)
49. Reg 10(1)(b) CS(AIAMA) Regs
50. Reg 10(4) CS(AIAMA) Regs
51. Reg 10(2) CS(AIAMA) Regs
52. Reg 10(3) CS(AIAMA) Regs
53. Reg 11 CS(AIAMA) Regs
54. Reg 12 CS(AIAMA) Regs as amended by reg 4 CS(MA)2 Regs
55. Reg 13 CS(AIAMA) Regs as amended by reg 5 CS(MA)2 Regs
56. s41B CSA 1991
57. Reg 1(2) CS(MA)2 Regs
58. Reg 10A(1) CS(AIAMA) Regs as amended by reg 3 CS(MA)2 Regs
59. s30 CSA 1991; CS(CEOFM) Regs
60. s30(2) CSA 1991; para 2 CSA(Comm 3)O
61. *Improving Child Support* 1995 para 4.3
62. Para 13032 CSM(OA)
63. Reg 5 CS(CEOFM) Regs
64. Reg 2 CS(CEOFM) Regs
65. Regs 3 and 4 CS(CEOFM) Regs
66. s30(3) CSA 1991
67. Letter to CPAG from the CSA, 15 March 1993
68. Reg 4(7) CSF Regs
69. Reg 4(8) CSF Regs
70. Paras 1080 and 1090 CSM(OA)
71. Paras 1081 and 1090-1101 CSM(OA)
72. Para 1060 CSM(OA)
73. Para 1110 CSM(OA)
74. Para 9211 CSM(OA4) [CSPG Chs 6, 7 & 19]
75. Paras 9221 and 9270-2 CSM(OA4) [CSPG Chs 6, 7 & 19]
76. *Improving Child Support* 1995 para 6.4; paras 2110-16 CSM(MA4); paras 3610-3612 and 3620-1 CSM(OA4) [CSPG Chs 6, 7 & 19]
77. Para 3677 CSM(OA4)
78. Para 9420 CSM(OA4)
79. Paras 9440-3 CSM(OA4)

80. Para 9435 CSM(OA4)
81. Para 9460 CSM(OA4)
82. Para 9461 CSM(OA4)
83. Para 4200-30 CSM(OA)
84. Para 4212 CSM(OA)
85. Para 1017 CSM(OA)
86. Para 7300 CSM(OA)
87. Paras 7550-1 CSM(OA)
88. Reg 2 CS(AIAMA) Regs
89. Para 7501 CSM(OA)
90. Reg 2(4) CS(AIAMA) Regs
91. Reg 5(1) CS(AIAMA) Regs
92. Reg 5(2) CS(AIAMA) Regs
93. Paras 7400-25 CSM(OA)
94. *Improving Child Support* 1995 para 3.1
95. Para 7575 CSM(OA)
96. Letter from DSS to CPAG, 8 March 1993
97. s41(2) and (2A) CSA 1991; reg 8 CS(AIAMA) Regs as amended by reg 2 CS(MA)2 Regs; paras 8700-20 CSM(OA4)
98. Reg 1(2) CS(MA)2 Regs, para 8704 CSM(OAL)
99. Paras 3640-59 CSM(OA4)
100. Paras 3660-1 CSM(OA4)
101. Paras 6600-22 CSM(OA4)
102. Paras 6630-74 CSM(OA4)
103. Reg 4(1) CS(AIAMA) Regs
104. s41A CSA 1991 to be amended by s22 CSA 1995
105. *Improving Child Support*, para 6.20
106. Reg 3(2) CS(AIAMA) Regs
107. Reg 3(3) CS(AIAMA) Regs
108. Reg 6(1) and (3) CS(AIAMA) Regs
109. Reg 4(2)(a) CS(AIAMA) Regs
110. Reg 3(4)-(6) CS(AIAMA) Regs
111. Reg 4(2)(b) CS(AIAMA) Regs
112. Reg 4(3) CS(AIAMA) Regs
113. Reg 5(3) CS(AIAMA) Regs
114. Reg 5(4) CS(AIAMA) Regs
115. Reg 5(6) and (7) CS(AIAMA) Regs
116. Reg 5(7) CS(AIAMA) Regs
117. Reg 5(5) CS(AIAMA) Regs
118. Reg 7(1) CS(AIAMA) Regs
119. Reg 6(2) CS(AIAMA) Regs
120. s41(5) CSA 1991
121. Reg 7(2) CS(AIAMA) Regs
122. reg 7(3) CS(AIAMA) Regs
123. s31 CSA 1991
124. HC *Hansard*, 2 February 1996, col 990

Notes 125–139: CSM refs will be found in CSEFIG Chs 18-21

125. Paras 3112 CSM(OA)
126. Paras 7540-3 CSM(OA)
127. Paras 7558-60 and 7582-4 CSM(OA)
128. Para 3121 CSM(OA)
129. *R v Secretary of State for Social Security ex parte Biggin* [1995] 1 FLR 851 aka *B v Secretary of State for Social Security, The Times*, 30 January 1995.
130. *See* note 129
131. Para 4611 CSM(OA4)
132. Sch 1 para 10 CS(NIRA) Regs
133. CSA(CA)O; Army Act 1955; Air Force Act 1955; Naval Forces Act 1947; Merchant Shipping Act 1970
134. s31(5) CSA 1991
135. s31(6) CSA 1991
136. s31(7) CSA 1991
137. s32(8)–(11) CSA 1991
138. Reg 9 CS(C&E) Regs as amended by reg 6 CS(MA)2 Regs
139. Paras 4000-42 CSM(OA4)
140. Reg 14(1) CS(C&E) Regs
141. Reg 14(2) CS(C&E) Regs
142. Reg 1(3) CS(C&E) Regs
143. s32(8) and (11) CSA 1991; reg 25 CS(C&E) Regs
144. Reg 15(1) CS(C&E) Regs
145. Reg 15(2) CS(C&E) Regs
146. Reg 16(1) CS(C&E) Regs
147. Reg 16(2) CS(C&E) Regs
148. Reg 16(3) CS(C&E) Regs
149. Reg 13 CS(C&E) Regs
150. s8 Employment Protection (Consolidation) Act 1978
151. s9 Employment Protection (Consolidation) Act 1978
152. s5 Wages Act 1986
153. Reg 8(3) and (4) CS(C&E) Regs
154. Reg 8(4)(a) CS(C&E) Regs

155. Reg 8(5) CS(C&E) Regs
156. Reg 9 CS(C&E) Regs as amended by reg 6 CS(MA)2 Regs
157. Regs 10(1) and 11(1) CS(C&E) Regs
158. Reg 9(d) CS(C&E) Regs
159. Reg 10 CS(C&E) Regs
160. Reg 11(2) CS(C&E) Regs
161. Reg 11(3) CS(C&E) Regs
162. Reg 11(4) CS(C&E) Regs
163. Reg 12(6) CS(C&E) Regs
164. Reg 12(2) CS(C&E) Regs
165. Reg 12(4) CS(C&E) Regs
166. Reg 12(5) CS(C&E) Regs
167. Reg 24(1) CS(C&E) Regs
168. Reg 24(2)(a), (3) and (4) CS(C&E) Regs
169. Reg 24(2)(b) CS(C&E) Regs
170. Reg 24(1)(b), (2) and (4) CS(C&E) Regs
171. Reg 17 CS(C&E) Regs
172. Reg 18 CS(C&E) Regs
173. Reg 19 CS(C&E) Regs
174. Reg 20(1) CS(C&E) Regs
175. Reg 20(2) CS(C&E) Regs
176. Reg 21(1) CS(C&E) Regs
177. Reg 21(4) CS(C&E) Regs
178. Reg 21(5) CS(C&E) Regs
179. Reg 21(6) CS(C&E) Regs
180. Reg 22(1) CS(C&E) Regs
181. Reg 22(2) CS(C&E) Regs
182. Reg 22(3) CS(C&E) Regs
183. *See* note 129
184. Reg 8(1) CS(C&E) Regs
185. Rule 5 and form 6 AS(CSR)
186. Reg 22(4) CS(C&E) Regs
187. s32(6) CSA 1991
188. *Secretary of State for Social Security v Shotton and others*, Mr Justice Latham, *Independent*, 30 January 1996, aka *Department of Social Services v Taylor, Secretary of State for Social Security v McKay, Brown and Shotton, The Times*, 8 February 1996
189. Paras 7600-11 CSM(OA)
190. *DSS v Butler* [1995] 4 All ER 193, CA; *The Times*, 11 August 1995
191. Para 5031 CSM(MA)
192. s33 CSA 1991
193. s33(3) CSA 1991
194. s33(4) CSA 1991; *Secretary of State v Shotton*
195. *See* note 19
196. HC *Hansard*, 2 February 1996, col 990
197. Reg 29 CS(C&E) Regs; rule 3 AS(CSR)
198. Reg 27 CS(C&E) Regs
199. Reg 28 CS(C&E) Regs
200. Reg 29(1) and Sch 1 CS(C&E) Regs
201. Rule 2 AS(CSR)
202. Forms 1-4 AS(CSR)
203. Rule 6 AS(CSR)
204. s35 CSA 1991
205. Reg 30(2) CS(C&E) Regs
206. Reg 30(4) and (5) CS(C&E) Regs
207. s35(3) and (4) CSA 1991
208. Reg 32 and Sch 2 CS(C&E) Regs
209. Reg 31 CS(C&E) Regs
210. s33(5) CSA 1991
211. s36 CSA 1991
212. ss38(1)(a) and 58(9) CSA 1991
213. Rule 4 and form 5 AS(CSR)
214. s38(1)(b) CSA 1991
215. s40(12)-(14) CSA 1991
216. s40(1)-(11) CSA 1991
217. s40(5) CSA 1991
218. Sch 3 CS(C&E) Regs
219. s40(7) CSA 1991
220. Reg 34(5) and (6) CS(C&E) Regs

Index

harm or undue distress 97
phasing-in of assessments 31-2, 32,
  300-3
preventing access to CSA 35, 55
variation 33, 34, 35, 56
voluntary payments
net income 214-15
of child support 134
voluntary unemployment
deprivation of income 219
voluntary work
expenses 215
notional income 217

waiving collection of arrears 398
war pensions/benefits 210
exemption from deduction for child
  maintenance 169
exemption from paying child
  maintenance 168
water charges
ineligible housing cost 189-90
weekly amount of housing costs 190
weekly earnings 205-6, 207-8
welfare of child 3, 17, 18, 52-3, 73, 82,
  296, 308, 311, 365, 388, 406
departure 338
refusal to co-operate 110, 111-12
white paper
Improving Child Support 2
withdrawal of applications 10-11, 69
compulsory applications 10-11, 70-4,
  294
voluntary applications 69-70, 142, 294
withdrawing authorisation 10-11, 62, 70-4
benefit claim ends 71-2
challenging decision 74
compulsory applications 70-4
no longer a parent with care 71
risk of harm or undue distress 72-3
voluntary applications 69-70, 74
withholding authorisation 11, 62-3, 84,
  87-8, 101-12, 307, 317-18
notice to comply 108-10
reduced benefit direction 110-11
refusing to return MAF 103
welfare of the child 111-12
*see also: benefit penalty, harm or
  undue distress*

witness
allowances 215
appeals 378-9
parentage disputes 148
written maintenance agreements 31-2, 32,
  33, 35
see also: consent orders

young parents
disclosure of information to police 95
exempt from giving authority 83
harm or undue distress 95
parentage disputes 144-5
young person
exemption from paying child
  maintenance 168
qualifying child defined 3, 41-3
see also: young parents
youth trainees
exemption from paying child
  maintenance 168
net income 212

National Welfare Benefits Handbook 1996/97

26th edition

The new CPAG Handbook is fully revised and updated to give clear, practical guidance on means-tested benefits. There is full coverage of income support, housing benefit, council tax benefit, family credit, the social fund and disability working allowance, as well as information on health and education benefits. However, from October 1996 Handbook coverage of IS for unemployed claimants is replaced by the *Jobseeker's Allowance Handbook*.

New features of this edition include:

- the latest changes to income support including April changes paving the way for jobseeker's allowance and advance info on other aspects of the new benefit, plus changes to IS housing costs
- HB restrictions from January 1996, and for under-25s from October
- changes for lone parents and people in residential care
- the latest developments for persons from abroad including asylum seekers, plus new habitual residence test case law
- funeral payments and other social fund changes.

There are explanations of how benefits are administered, how to claim and how to appeal. Also helpful hints on tactics, and coverage of such issues as overpayment and backdating of benefits. Information is fully indexed and cross-referenced to law, regulations and official guidance, and also to Court and Commissioners' decisions.

The *National Welfare Benefits Handbook* is widely recognised as the authoritative guide to means-tested benefits and how to obtain them.

April 1966   0 946744 80 7   £8.95

Send a cheque/PO for £8.95 (incl p&p) to **CPAG Ltd, 1–5 Bath Street, London EC1V 9PY**

Comments on the *Handbook* and *Guide*

'Excellent guides' – *Daily Mirror*

'Important handbooks for anyone claiming benefits or advising those who do' – *The Independent*

'It has taken a charity, CPAG, to explain in plain English who is entitled to benefit and how to claim it' – *Today*

'Invaluable guides' – *The Observer*

'The most complete guides to social security benefits' – *Sunday Times*

'Rated the best in the benefits business' – *Scotland on Sunday*

'Invaluable for anyone intending to claim any benefit' – *Time Out*

'Two excellent guides ... both are great for finding out your rights' – *Bella*

'The best advice to give lawyers new to welfare rights work is to start with the CPAG benefit handbooks. They set the standard by which work in this field is judged' – *The Public Law Project*

'The best value in publishing ... Anyone who advises those in receipt of benefit will struggle without them' – *Solicitors Journal*

'Have deservedly received glowing comments from both the national press and specialist publications ... packed with useful information and no padding' – *Family Law*

'Working "bibles" for CABx advisers, lawyers, health visitors and welfare rights advisers' – *Consumer Voice*

'These are the books – buy them!' – *The Adviser*

Rights Guide to Non-Means-Tested Benefits 1996/97

19th edition

This companion volume to the National Welfare Benefits Handbook is fully revised and updated to give clear, practical guidance on non-means-tested benefits. It is fully indexed and cross-referenced to social security law, regulations and official guidance, and also to Court and Commissioners' decisions.

This edition includes:

- the latest on benefits for the unemployed, including April changes paving the way for the introduction of the jobseeker's allowance and advance information on other aspects of the new benefit
- the latest on incapacity benefit, particularly appeals and challenging decisions
- new disability living allowance case law
- developments on equal treatment for women and men
- the latest on asylum seekers and other persons from abroad
- maternity pay and benefits
- how the contributions system works
- statutory sick pay, pensions and benefits for widows
- industrial injuries and diseases
- benefits administration and how to appeal

Please note that from October 1996 Rights Guide *information on unemployment benefit is replaced by the* Jobseeker's Allowance Handbook.

The *Rights Guide* is widely recognised as the authoritative guide to non-means-tested benefits and how to claim them.

April 1996   0 946744 81 5   £7.95

Send a cheque/PO for £7.95 (incl p&p) to
CPAG Ltd, 1–5 Bath Street, London EC1V 9PY

Welfare Rights Bulletin

The *Bulletin* is essential reading for welfare rights advisers, lawyers and anyone needing to keep up to date with social security issues. One of its unique roles is to provide a bi-monthly update to the *National Welfare Benefits Handbook* and *Rights Guide*, as well as to CPAG's *Jobseeker's Allowance Handbook* and *Child Support Handbook*.

Contents will include the fullest coverage of:

- the new jobseeker's allowance, changes affecting HB and IS housing costs, incapacity benefit and changes affecting persons from abroad
- new regulations, guidance and procedure, with comment, analysis and practical advice
- Social Security Commissioners' decisions
- reports on benefit law and service delivery issues – eg, Chief Adjudication Officer, Parliamentary and advisory committees, ombudsmen
- news from welfare rights workers – campaigns, issues and tactics

Like the CPAG benefit guides, the *Welfare Rights Bulletin* is the best value in the field – and compulsory reading for any adviser needing the very latest benefits information.

£17.70 for a full year's subscription (6 issues)

ISSN 0263 2098

Jobseeker's Allowance Handbook

Richard Poynter

CHILD POVERTY ACTION GROUP

This practical handbook will be accessible, comprehensive and fully up-to-date as at implementation in October. It can be used as a stand-alone guide, but is also designed to be an integrated part of the 1996/97 benefits handbook package.

It explains the Jobseekers Act and its impact, including: the qualifying system; the new administrative system for claiming; changes to contributory benefit, eg abolition of dependant's addition; the new Jobseekers Agreement; tougher 'actively seeking' and 'availability for work' tests; disqualification from benefit and the new discretionary hardship payments; the 'directions' that can be issued requiring improvements in appearance and behaviour; the new back-to-work bonus.

The **National Welfare Benefits Handbook** and **Rights Guide** will include all the April changes introduced to pave the way for the new benefit – as well as advance information on other aspects of the scheme. From October the **Jobseeker's Allowance Handbook** will supersede both **Benefits Handbook** information on income support for unemployed claimants and **Rights Guide** information on unemployment benefit. From April 1997 coverage will be integrated into the **Benefits Handbook** and **Rights Guide**.

The **Jobseeker's Allowance Handbook** is fully indexed and cross referenced to law, regulations and the benefits handbooks.

250 pages   0 946744 85 8   October 1996   £5.95

**Send a cheque/PO for £5.95 (incl p&p) to
CPAG Ltd, 1–5 Bath Street, London EC1V 9PY**

CPAG COURSES

CPAG courses provide comprehensive rights training and detailed coverage of up-to-the-minute legislative changes. Our tutors are expert in their area of work and draw on the extensive training experience of the Citizens' Rights Office.

CPAG training ranges from Introductory level to courses for advisers with more knowledge of the issues involved. Our current programme includes courses on: Jobseeker's Allowance, Income Support Housing Costs, Lobbying in Europe, Working with the Media, Benefits for Young People, Introduction to the Child Support Scheme, The Child Support Formula, Habitual Residence Test, Disability Benefits, Dealing with Debt, Community Care, Vulnerable Young People, Immigration Law and Social Security, Disability Appeals Tribunals and Medical Appeal Tribunals, Housing Benefit Review Boards, Commissioners' Appeals, Parliamentary Procedure and Lobbying, EC Social Security Law, Training for Trainers and our week-long Welfare Rights Advocacy Courses. **CPAG's Welfare Rights for Franchising Lawyers has been chosen by the Law Society as the approved course for all lawyers needing to qualify for legal aid work.**

Our courses can also be tailored to meet the needs of specific groups, including those not normally concerned with welfare rights. To assess your training needs, we are happy to discuss your requirements for 'in-house' training to meet the internal needs of your organisation. For further information contact Judy Allen at the address given below.

FEES	Lawyers	Statutory organisations	Voluntary organisations
One-day	£170	£120	£80
Two-day	£230	£180	£150
Three-day	£270	£220	£190
Week-long	£360	£290	£220

Most of CPAG's courses are Law Society accredited and carry continuing education points.

For a full programme please contact:
Judy Allen, Training Administrator,
Child Poverty Action Group, 1–5 Bath Street, London EC1V 9PY
Tel 0171 253 3406 • Fax 0171 490 0561